CONTENTS

Foreword by Paul E. Minnis   *ix*

Introduction: Letter to Young Ethnobiologists   *3*

**PART I. REDEFINING ETHNOBIOLOGY: TOWARD A GENERAL
THEORY OF THE INTERACTIONS OF BIODIVERSITY AND
CULTURAL DIVERSITY**   11

1   Ethnobiology Emerging from a Time of Crisis   13

2   Defining New Disciplinary Trajectories: Mixing Political Ecology
    with Ethnobiology   18

3   Ethnoscience, the "Oldest Science": A Needed Complement to
    Academic Science and Citizen Science to Stem the Losses of
    Biodiversity, Indigenous Languages, and Livelihoods   23

4   Autobiology?: The Traditional Ecological, Agricultural, and
    Culinary Knowledge of Us!   36

5   Searching for the Ancestral Diet: Did Mitochondrial Eve and
    Java Man Feast on the Same Foods?   42

6   Microbial Ethnobiology and the Loss of Distinctive Food Cultures   63

7   Ethnophenology and Climate Change   67

PART II. EXEMPLIFYING HOW ETHNOBIOLOGY SERVES AS A PIVOTAL INTERDISCIPLINE IN BIOCULTURAL CONSERVATION   73

8   Safeguarding Species, Languages, and Cultures in a Time of Diversity Loss: From the Colorado Plateau to Global Hotspots   75

9   Agrobiodiversity in an Oasis Archipelago   96

10   Passing on a Sense of Place and Traditional Ecological Knowledge between Generations   144

11   Biocultural and Ecogastronomic Restoration: The Renewing America's Food Traditions Alliance   156

12   Conservation You Can Taste: Heirloom Seed and Heritage Breed Recovery in North America   184

13   Multiple Lines of Evidence for the Origin of Domesticated Chile Pepper, *Capsicum annuum,* in Mexico   197

14   Traditional Ecological Knowledge and Endangered Species: Is Ethnobiology for the Birds?   215

PART III. WRITING ETHNOBIOLOGY FOR BROADER APPEAL AND IMPACT   223

15   Guadalupe Lopez Blanco: Reflections on How a Sea Turtle Hunter Turned His Community Toward Conservation   225

16   Paleozoologist Paul Martin, the Ghosts of Evolution, and the Rewilding of North America   233

17   Parque de la Papa: Vavilov's Dream for Potatoes?   243

18   Why Poetry Needs Ethnobiology: Hawkmoth Songs and Cross-Pollinations   249

19   Aromas Emanating from the Driest of Places   261

20   The Ethnobiology of Survival in Post-Apocalyptic Dystopias   277

Afterword: Ethnobiology in Metamorphosis   288

Contributors   297

Index   303

ETHNOBIOLOGY
FOR THE FUTURE

The Southwest Center Series

JOSEPH C. WILDER, EDITOR

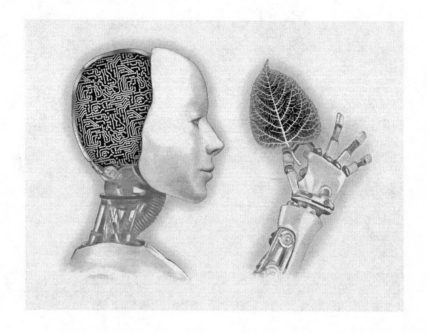

EDITED BY
GARY PAUL NABHAN

FOREWORD BY PAUL E. MINNIS
WITH DRAWINGS BY PAUL MIROCHA

ETHNOBIOLOGY
FOR THE FUTURE

Linking Cultural and Ecological Diversity

THE UNIVERSITY OF
ARIZONA PRESS

TUCSON

The University of Arizona Press
www.uapress.arizona.edu

Printed in the United States of America

21 20 19 18 17 16   6 5 4 3 2 1

ISBN-13: 978-0-8165-3274-2 (paper)

Cover designed by Paul Mirocha

Publication of this book is made possible in part by a grant from the W. K. Kellogg Foundation to
the Southwest Center of the University of Arizona and from the Southwest Center of the University
of Arizona.

Library of Congress Cataloging-in-Publication Data
Names: Nabhan, Gary Paul, editor.
Title: Ethnobiology for the future : linking cultural and ecological diversity / edited by Gary Paul Nabhan.
Other titles: Southwest Center series.
Description: Tucson : The University of Arizona Press, 2016. | Series: The Southwest Center series |
    Includes bibliographical references and index.
Identifiers: LCCN 2015038536 | ISBN 9780816532742 (pbk. : alk. paper)
Subjects: LCSH: Ethnobiology. | Biodiversity. | Cultural pluralism.
Classification: LCC GN476.7 .E747 2016 | DDC 306.4/5—dc23 LC record available at http://lccn.loc
    .gov/2015038536

♾ This paper meets the requirements of ANSI/NISO Z39.48-1992 (Permanence of Paper).

This book is dedicated to my former interns,
students, and "precocious mentors" who have
begun and will change ethnobiology and the
world in ways so wondrous I can barely wait:

Steve Buckley, Culver Cassa, Rafael Routson
de Grenade, Regina Fitzsimmons, Lois Ellen
Frank, Jacquie Gage, Kristin Huisinga,
Lillian Hill, Tony Joe, Colin Khoury, Kraig
Kraft, Alberto Mellado Moreno, Andy Miller,
Roberto Nutlouis, Carolyn O'Meara, Nate
O'Meara, Humberto Romero-Morales, Ashley
Rood, Kanin Routson, Sara St. Antoine, Josh
Tewksbury, Jon Tuxill, James Veteto, DeJa
Walker, Patty West, and Ben Wilder.

FOREWORD

I T WAS AROUND 1976 when I first met Gary Nabhan, if my memory is correct. I was a graduate student working on an archaeological project in the Mimbres Valley of New Mexico, and Gary, who was also a graduate student surveying wild *Phaseolus* beans, came by. Little did I know then I was meeting a remarkable scholar, advocate, and humanist. That soon became quite clear with Gary's first publications. The contributions in this volume demonstrate his intellectual breadth, scholarly depth, and profound concern for all humanity and our planetary home. Even if one doesn't appreciate all his talents—I for one am too much of an unrepentant materialist to appreciate fully his spiritual and poetic sides—one still can't help but be in awe of his range of interests and contributions.

To almost steal the title of a Gregory Bateson book, Gary displays a unique ecology of mind. Ecology is about connections. Sometimes these connections are obscure; sometimes they are essential and critical. Often they are both; rarely are they neither. Gary sees connections, quite often before others. He not only sees connections and studies them scientifically, but he can communicate their value in a wide range of forms, from the often arcane-appearing language of science to an engrossing narrative for everyone. Communication is good, but Gary often goes further as a master of advocacy and action.

The core connections are ecological relationships between plants, other animals, humans and our environmental setting. This is the heart and soul of ethnobiology, and of this volume. The historical origins of ethnobiology often concerned either plants or animals, especially the economic use of the former. But plants and animals are bound together in an intricate dance of connections. Looking at only plants or only animals tends to miss important relationships. Gary's work, and that of his collaborators, has always focused on all the interconnections. As many essays in this volume also demonstrate, ecological relationships are far more complicated than energy and matter. As ecologists have long recognized, "information" is a key relationship; organisms communicate in a variety of ways. Information, however, also involves the observer. For example, the definitions of plants or animals are cultural constructs, not natural truths, which differ among cultures. Indigenous science is a major contribution to all humanity. Therefore, ecological perspectives from many cultures flesh out a fuller understanding of the world around us. And we surely need as full an understanding as possible when facing the future.

Other obvious connections cross borders. The scholars and writers assembled in this book have long worked in the North American borderlands, especially El Norte, an area sandwiched between the more frequently studied U.S. Southwest and central Mexico. The lessons learned in human ecology from the indigenous and mestizo communities, both north and south of the international border, may be invaluable for coping with environmental problems, which include climate change and depleted water availability, among many others. The deserts and plateaus of these areas are too often viewed as harsh and unforgiving, poor locations for secure and sustainable livelihoods. Nabhan's work, along with that of many others, demonstrates that environmental "quality" or "desirability" is more in the eye of the beholder than in the history and lived experiences of inhabitants. Humans are creative and adaptable. The simple evidence is that dozens of groups have lived and thrived for thousands of years throughout the borderlands. Although the borderlands have been the center of Gary's research, he has worked in many other regions, including his ancestral roots in the Near East.

The essays show how we are enriched by understanding the ethnobiology of peoples with whom we have no direct historical or intellectual connections. We can learn from many cultures, all of which have faced difficulties and have developed ingenious solutions. This view has a long intellectual history, as some of this volume's chapters note. One of the chapters, for example, is based on the work of the great (and martyred) plant scientist, Nikolai Vavilov.

Connections often have long histories. The present has a past, which lives on in us, ecologically, culturally, and politically. While we are the sum of our ancestors' histories, the history of the human experiment is so much more. We won't be able to understand all human history by only studying the present and the recent past. We won't know, for example, that the ancient peoples of Eastern North America relied on a suite of local crops long before the Three Sisters—corn, beans and squash—became farming mainstays. These cultigens were lost to time and only rediscovered through painstaking archaeobotanical research.

Superficially, fostering connections between academic disciplines might seem pedestrian compared to the other connections mentioned here. Yet, the boundaries between areas of studies, such as biology, history, or poetry, have too often become rigid walls limiting collaboration, narrowing our field of vision. Gary's work demonstrates the value of transcending disciplinary borders. Nearly twenty-five people, with a wide range of expertise, collaborate in this limited collection of essays. Gary would be the first to say that he wouldn't be Gary without his collaborators.

One of the hallmark characteristics of this volume, as one would expect, is a call to advocate for change. Ethnobiological information has real and pressing value. This has been a Nabhan concern since the beginning of his career, when Gary was a key founder of the Tucson-based NGO, Native Seeds/SEARCH. His advocacy has focused especially on crops, traditional farming, the knowledge of communities long rooted in a region, both indigenous and otherwise, and food security in all settings, both for rural and urban peoples.

One can advocate to simply make the world a better place, a more sustainable and resilient home for humanity in the face of profound challenges. That is more than enough. However, in Gary's work we see his poetic and spiritual sides. Beauty may be, in fact, in the eye of the beholder. If so, then Gary's eyes seem especially well attuned to the beauty and joys of ethnobiological connections. It is clear that Gary believes that to truly build a fair and bright future, we need to rekindle deep emotional and spiritual connections, which are firmly rooted in a comprehensive scientific understanding of ethnobiology. It is as daunting a task as it is necessary. The essays in this volume shine a light on the path ahead.

—*Paul E. Minnis*

ETHNOBIOLOGY
FOR THE FUTURE

INTRODUCTION

Letter to Young Ethnobiologists

I.

YOU MAY NOT have realized it, but I have noticed your inquisitive presence in the front row at some recent gatherings. Once when I was helping a few friends with a field workshop on saving seeds, and recording the oral histories of "cultural memories" associated with them, I heard you ask a thoughtful question about how ethnobiological conservation might play out in and around your home.

So I am writing you this letter and offering you the following essays in the hope that the wonderful insights made by dozens of ethnobiologists—not just my co-authors in this volume—will feed the fires that may already be burning in your mind and in your heart.

Fires? At that recent gathering, I immediately sensed your attentiveness, your vitality, and enthusiasm for the topics up for discussion. During the exchanges around a campfire that night, it warmed my heart to hear you express your desire to make a difference in the world. Because I myself am already over the hill and partially out to pasture, I sense that what you intend to do on behalf of (and in collaboration with) the diverse cultures and species of our planet will likely be far more important and have far more impact than anything that my contemporaries and I have tried to do.

And so, I offer this letter not merely to bless your own emerging contributions to all things ethnobiological, but also to remind you how much the future of this planet and its peoples hinges upon efforts by you, your young friends, and allies. Perhaps this collection will broaden your portfolio of ethnobiological principles and amplify your tool kit for working in the "ethnobiosphere," which surrounds and resounds in us.

Few scholars or activists take issue anymore with the notion that we live in a world of diminishing natural and linguistic diversity. Whether they tend to blame those losses on climate change or unbridled capitalism, they concede that unrelenting homogenization is trumping the once-resplendent heterogeneity all around us. The "blessed unrest" embedded in diversity is far more than just the "spice of life" that keeps our senses alert and delighted; it is literally the stuff of life that makes our world work (and play) in myriad ways.

When I heard your comments at the forum, it was obvious that you are well-read and well-traveled enough to know that we cannot afford to squander the remaining living riches of Planet Earth-and-Ocean. You have already gained a sense of how the perspectives of other cultures, within our own nation and beyond, truly matter with regard to the health of our own species and that of other species as well. Those other perspectives are not frilly window-dressing; they embody an incalculably rich legacy of all those who have struggled to live and express themselves up until this moment in time.

I am amazed by just how many of your cohort have so "precociously" gained such insights, ethics, and sensibilities in response to the loss of biological and cultural diversity occurring at our doorsteps. It appears that you, and many of your friends, already "get that" to a greater extent than most of my generation during our own fleeting time here on this planet. You have apparently taken the risk to get beyond your own comfort zone in order to listen, understand, and support others from different cultures who have come to bear witness and express themselves in this fragile world. By doing so, you have already put one foot in front of the other and set out as a pilgrim on adventures to other landscapes and mindscapes, which have often been neglected or dismissed by mainstream society.

It does not immediately matter whether we agree on what those other "scapes" or spaces should be called, since they may be called one name from deep inside their cores, and another from their outer edges. These spaces of intense interaction among cultures, habitats, and creatures go by many names, as does the study of such interactions. We can call the study of these cultural ecotones *ethnobiology, environmental anthropology, biocultural geography, agrarian ecology, archeobotany, zooarchaeology,* or simply *indigenous studies.* But none of these names perfectly circumscribe our domain of shared concerns. No matter.

As you more deeply enter into such inquiries, you may experience difficulty in deciding what to call yourself, which is to say, you may be stumbling in your efforts to identify your future vocation or profession of choice. Do not get too hung up on aligning with a single discipline or letting an esoteric title define who you are or who you will become. Instead, take the path of least resistance. When your cynical uncle or authoritative family physician asks you what you are studying, just say you are apprenticing yourself to herbalists, artisans, and hunters, or farmers, foragers, and fishers, or storytellers, songsters, and shamans. Keep the skeptics guessing; throw them off-kilter. No one ever correctly guessed what Gandhi or Teresa of Cabora, Hakim Ibn Sina or Vandana Shiva, Winona LaDuke, or Paul Stamets would be when they grew up! These innovators and healers did not necessarily care what discipline others said they should belong to; they just went about doing good work with their *own* discipline, passion, and compassion. For my part, I can assure you that I have given up trying to describe what I do to others anymore, but I am "over" worrying about whether a tag line can define our value to society.

So forgive me if I choose to call you "a young ethnobiologist"; I do so not to recruit, pigeonhole, or constrain you, but simply offer it as shorthand for your interdisciplinary tendencies and your capacity to "think" as if you never noticed "the box." Scholarly disciplines are simply tributaries into the same river of knowledge, where each of us tries to fathom just how human cultures have interacted with the other-than-human world(s), in complex and often quixotic ways. The tributaries may change names as they aggregate, but they still flow into something that is greater than the sum of their parts.

II.

From your questions directed at me and my colleagues, I sense that you wish to be guided onto "the right path." That is, you want to learn the best means for understanding and engaging with the biocultural complexity that nourishes us, astonishes us, disorients us, and occasionally brings us to our knees with awe and humility. That is exactly why my colleagues and I have shaped this collection to ask a few big questions (Section 1), to profile some tools or methodologies that may help us answer them (Section 2), and to ponder how we might best communicate these issues not merely to other scholars, but to society at large (Section 3).

It is true, as J.P.S. Haldane once quipped, "nature is not only more complex than we think, it is also more complex than we *can* think." But when we add the interactions of human consciousness *with* the natural world into the mix, the whole mess seems unbearably complex. And it is not simply that we shape or "construct" nature with our minds, but we also do so with our eyes, hands, feet, and taste buds. Every previous construction with any staying power also reverberates in that chimerical field that we glibly call "nature."

And yet, as some of the following essays attest, humans not only establish and circumscribe their identities through their thoughts and actions, but with their physical, emotional, and spiritual attachments to place, flora, fauna, fungi, and feasts. Most of us intuitively grasp that our very lives—from our physical health to our imaginative depths—would be impoverished if we were denied contact with myriad other species.

Unfortunately, perhaps, for all the lip service some scientists give to maintaining biological, cultural, and linguistic diversity, Western science has rather clumsily advanced its understanding of the interactions of these domains of diversity. Worse yet, certain scientists still feel uncomfortable in committing adequate resources to safeguarding and restoring—not merely documenting— these biocultural interactions.

And so, I must encourage you to be courageous enough to include ethical, moral, and even spiritual dimensions in your future work regarding the fate of biocultural diversity.

There is an urgent need for a general but nuanced theory of how biological and cultural diversity interact in space and time. It might even encompass how human cognition, expression, and selective action shape genes, genomes, demes, species, interspecific relationships, ecological guilds, and landscape-level communities. In shorthand, let's just call it a unifying theory of all things biological and cultural. I probably do not have the philosophical grounding or the quantitative skills to fully elaborate such a theory, rigorous test, or any theorem that emerges out of it. But I have the faith that your generation might have the interest, computing capacity, and societal need to do so.

III.

The following essays are but a blind man's stab at describing the elephant in the room, albeit with a little help from my friends. If I were to suggest a few broad hypotheses for you to refine and test, here are just a few touched on in this book that seem worthy of your protracted attention, even if you ultimately fail to make much headway with them:

- That the diversity of organisms living upon, within, and in contact with our human bodies not only affect our physical and nutritional health, but our psychological health and behavior as well.

- That human constructs, behaviors, and actions encoded in various linguistic and gestural expressions guide the management of domesticated livestock and crops. Consciously or unconsciously, humans also select for the survival, reproductive fitness, and abundance of many so-called "wild" microbes, plants, and animals.

- That the cessation or erosion of various culturally elaborated management practices for soil, water, food, fuel, medicines, and fiber may tangibly diminish habitat heterogeneity and species diversity in a locale or a region.

- That this reduction in biological diversity subtly but tangibly diminishes the richness of human consciousness as expressed through story, song, art, and dreams.

- That stories, songs, and other artistic expressions relating to the other-than-human world have survival value in the sense that they bring us to an awareness that the elements of the world have intrinsic, as well as broadly extrinsic (i.e., not just narrowly economic), value to humankind.

- That human genes, cultural demes, and ecological guilds of foods and medicines have co-evolved over centuries, under the processes of both natural and cultural selection, by means more complex than what Darwin could easily ascertain.

- That it may be possible to compute and predict the consequences of cascading species extinctions AND cascading declines of traditional knowledge and management of those species.

IV.

I apologize if this list of to-dos implies that I simply want you to take on a quest for knowledge about matters that my colleagues and I have not been able to resolve. In fact, I want to encourage you to ask big questions in order to learn the limits of science. Not everything can be easily wrapped up in the simple package that Harvard biologist E.O. Wilson called "consilience." The fortunate aspect of ethnobiology, as opposed to Wilson's sociobiology, is that we are unlikely to conclude that biology and its evolutionary processes can explain everything. In that sense, the profession of ethnobiology is a career track into humility, a trait which all of us must desperately learn to embrace.

Implied in Harshberger's initial coinage of the term *ethnobotany*—and by extension, of the term *ethnobiology*—is that we have become curious about, and humbled by the natural world and cultures *beyond our own*. In contrast to *economic botany*, a sub-discipline that has always carried an imperialistic or extractive shadow with its inquiries, practitioners of ethnobiology seem to understand and accept that "they don't know it all." Perhaps this counter-reaction to our hubris emerged out of the historic tendency among its first field practitioners, as recent immigrants to the Americas. They were caught off guard by the sheer bounty of their adopted home, and humbled by how much skill and reserve First Nations peoples demonstrated in the face of the same bounty. Henry David Thoreau clearly expressed such humility when he saw how the First Nations people of Maine maneuvered their way along the rivers there, with all plants and animals as their familiars.

In short, perhaps the most apt description of a practicing ethnobiologist is of one who abdicates "the throne" of being an expert among the scientific priesthood in deference to others. We often regain the pleasure of using a "beginner's mind" to look at something freshly, rather than having to see it as dogma dictate. We are in a sense "inquirers who wear no clothes," because we gradually learn to admit what we do not know and concede what we cannot control.

And that is ultimately why I cannot straightforwardly guide you down "the best path" for becoming an ethnobiologist, any more than Rainer Maria Rilke could teach his young friend how to write a memorable poem through their correspondence more than a century ago.

An open field awaits you. Listen carefully for its cues; it will guide you where you need to go. I only hope that this slumgullion stew of essays will serve as cairns to help you find your way across a few obscure passages.

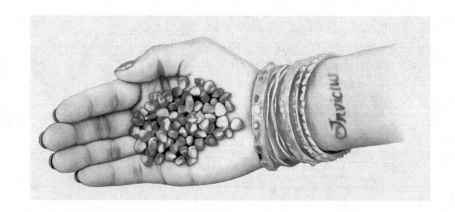

PART I

REDEFINING ETHNOBIOLOGY

Toward a General Theory of the Interactions
of Biodiversity and Cultural Diversity

I N THIS FIRST SECTION, we wish to recast ethnobiology as *the* interdiscipline
with the greatest explanatory power in helping society understand biocultural complexity. We sense that if our contemporary society plans to better
address the social and environmental challenges of the present era, we need to
more fully understand the complex interactions among cultures, their languages
and resource management practices with genes, demes, memes, foods, medicines, habitats, and anthropogenic landscapes. This section offers frameworks
for addressing critical links between cultural and ecological diversity, which may
build a "general theory of everything biocultural," helping us better navigate
through such complex domains.

Several of these essays were first printed in the column I have shared with
many colleagues, "Ethnobiology for a Diverse World," included in issues of the
Journal of Ethnobiology, between 2010 and 2015. Others were more recently written with interdisciplinary teams of colleagues, who were intent on bringing the
natural and cultural sciences together in fresh and fruitful ways.

In each essay, there is one key issue regarding the "ethnobiosphere," which is
presented in a provocative manner. First, how can ethnobiology better function
as an interdiscipline with unique integrative capacity, gracefully accommodating ideas from other *disciplines* that ethnobiologists have often neglected in
the past (e.g., political ecology, climate science, conservation biology, language
revitalization, nutritional therapies designed on the basis of diverse paleo-diets,

etc.). And second, how can joining forces with scholars from other disciplines, and with thought leaders, activists, or traditional elders help us better deal with today's challenges, from climate change to endangered species recovery, to the impending loss of traditional knowledge? The emphasis in most of these essays is theoretical, or at least topical, with just one or a few short synopses of case studies used to illustrate the conceptual underpinnings of each theory.

The very act of co-authoring most of these essays was often an interdisc-iplinary endeavor, and in a few cases, a cross-cultural collaboration as well. Although the perspectives of my co-authors may often remain different from my own, with respect to our training and our cultural biases, we sought out the "creative tensions" and "synergies" between or among our personal and cultural perspectives. We do not wish to sweep under the rug any differences in our opinions, but find common ground wherever we can. In some cases, we hoped to resolve any remaining incongruities, particularly between "Western science" and "indigenous science," which we regard as "the oldest science."

In summary, these mini-essays or "opinion-editorials" offer new directions for ethnobiology to grow and gain a pivotal capacity to address society's most pressing issues. Some of these essays are intended to be "verbal hand grenades," which can wake us up in time to pay greater attention to our own practices at a moment in history when we certainly need a broader perspective if we are to act and deal with these critical issues.

1

ETHNOBIOLOGY EMERGING
FROM A TIME OF CRISIS

GARY PAUL NABHAN, FELICE WYNDHAM,
AND DANA LEPOFSKY

W E WOULD LIKE to take stock of where ethnobiology is going as a field. That's because a recent survey has revealed the rapidly changing demography of ethnobiologists, but also their concern for leveraging the insights and applications of the field to address contemporary ecological and social issues that have reached the magnitude of "crises" (Wyndham et al. 2011). These crises include the ongoing and perhaps accelerating loss of both biological and linguistic diversity (Harmon 2002; Maffi 2001), as well as climate change and the rising economic, social, and health costs resulting from the inequalities between the rich and the poor. These crises and disparities ultimately impoverish us all (Wilkinson and Pickett 2009).

Wyndham, Lepofsky and Tiffany (2011) have asserted that now is the time for ethnobiologists to more actively play a role in addressing these global crises. Ethnobiologists, perhaps more than any other group of researchers, have the moral will, the perspectives, the know-how, and grassroots networks to be potential allies and resources for emerging coalitions of problem-solvers during such times of dramatic ecosystem and social change. They term this

Originally published as "Ethnobiology for a Diverse World: Ethnobiology Emerging from a Time of Crisis," *Journal of Ethnobiology* 31.2 (Fall/Winter 2011): 172–175. Reprinted with permission of the *Journal of Ethnobiology*.

development of the discipline, "Ethnobiology 5." Ethnobiology 5 takes off from Hunn's (2007:4) description of a fourth stage of development in ethnobiology—which has already begun to develop in significant ways—"by and for the [indigenous] community," recognizing that some of these crises can be addressed by acknowledging and restoring the deep traditions of indigenous practices.

An Ethnobiology 5 will utilize the field's unique location at the interstices of many disciplines and culturally mediated scientific traditions to address some of the core problems that we face as a globalized society. Continuing the long tradition of ethnobiological research, Ethnobiology 5 will be truly multicultural as well as multidisciplinary. This means that we must make a commitment to immediately addressing and engaging in debates regarding the underlying ideological, political, and economic assumptions of scientific endeavor. It also means a welcoming of, and mature generosity toward, all points of view, rather than privileging Western science over indigenous science, or vice versa. Furthermore, an Ethnobiology 5 must be bolder, more highly visible, and creative in its communications, relinquishing its comfortable marginality within academia in order to articulate its positions and insights more publicly. Why is it that several best-selling books and internationally acclaimed films documenting ethnobiology's contributions have reached millions of enthusiasts but we have never redirected their "popular interest" toward our profession as conservation biologists have done? Considering the number of people who actually study and work in ethnobiology-related fields, our collective ranks in three professional societies have never surpassed 5,000 members.

Here we discuss two main interacting domains of Ethnobiology 5. The first is the descriptive, empirical, collaborative, and applied processes of assessing culture-environment interactions that can slowly, steadily, and surely effect positive social and ecological change. The second is the analytical, epistemological, and theoretical inquiry taken up by ethnobiologists whose work is in provocative and creative interaction with indigenous theories, epistemologies, and social action.

Some key aspects and principles of Ethnobiology 5's descriptive, empirical research programs include:

- A predilection to do applied science in the service of social and environmental justice.
- A seamless gradient between "professional science" and "citizen science" that embraces rather than merely describes the many indigenous sciences.

- Training of public land managers in landscape ethno-ecology, so that they understand and protect the indigenous practices of the past and present which shape cultural landscapes, as well as adhere to attendant legal, political, and intellectual rights and responsibilities.
- Protection, restoration, and promotion of cultural practices and knowledge systems that increase resilience in the face of ecological and social crises, with particular emphasis on food security, health, and livelihoods.
- Increased public awareness of the structural and political implications of *longue durée*, indigenous ecological innovation and management.

Some key aspects of the analytical and theoretical elements of Ethnobiology 5 include:

- An elucidation of theories regarding interactions among the key factors linking biological, cultural, and linguistic diversity through both genes and demes.
- An attention to and testing of novel ethical approaches to "open source biology and knowledge-sharing" that potentially protect seed sovereignty and traditional ecological knowledge from economic exploitation (Kloppenburg 2010).
- A synthesis of cultural and natural sciences to elaborate the processes of cultural landscape formation and restoration that provides incentives to land stewards and communities, which maintain or restore ethno-ecosystem services in those cultural landscapes.
- The emergence of more ethnobiologists as public intellectuals, who are sought out for their critical socioecological and historically informed insights to advise on and participate in current events, policy development, and activism.

In fact, a "fifth world of ethnobiology," where Western scientific principles, methodologies, and ethics no longer exclusively guide the future development of this field, may occur through a demographic transformation of its practitioners, which is already in process. If we are correctly reading the trends of minorities in science periodically compiled and released by the American Association for the Advancement in Science, by 2020 the majority of students who will enroll in U.S. graduate schools in the biological sciences and natural resource management disciplines (including agricultural research) will be foreign-born (and often of indigenous descent), or labeled as African, Hispanic, or Native American according to the rather crude but official U.S. delineations of these categories.

In essence, there will be fewer graduate students in the United States and Canada of Western European descent than there will be from the diverse cultures not as historically associated with Western scientific traditions. Of course, some "ethnic minority" students who enter North American graduate schools will do so because they have already begun to master the ideologies and methodologies of Western science, but many will certainly bring worldviews, cosmologies, and ethics that may challenge the more restricted paradigms of classical Western science. While such encounters of Western science with indigenous and other scientific traditions will be welcomed by many of us in ethnobiology, they will likely bring about much of the "blessed unrest" that Paul Hawken has welcomed in the grassroots organizations of the social and environmental justice movements (Hawken 2007).

Now is the time to more fully embrace an Ethnobiology 5. If the field of ethnobiology thoroughly engages this more radical trajectory, we predict there will be a flowering of ethnobiology that will attract a broader set of constituencies. That trajectory aims for sustained and critical engagement with the perspectives of indigenous and diaspora peoples who are recognized as co-creators of our ethical frameworks, co-designers of healthy and just food systems, co-actors in landscape conservation and restoration, and co-leaders in a global conversation that addresses the planetary crises in biological and cultural diversity, health, and survival. As we write, a remarkable public conversation is emerging about the critical need for structural system changes in many regions of the world. Ethnobiologists potentially have a great deal to contribute to this conversation. We encourage you to help us co-imagine what those contributions will look like!

REFERENCES CITED

Harmon, David. 2002. *In Light of Our Differences: How Diversity in Nature and Culture Makes Us Human*. Smithsonian Institution Scholarly Press, Washington, DC.

Hawken, Paul. 2007. *Blessed Unrest: How the Largest Movement of the World Came into Being and Why No one Saw It Coming*. Viking, New York.

Hunn, Eugene. 2007. Ethnobiology in Four Phases. *Journal of Ethnobiology* 27:1–10.

Kloppenburg, Jack, Jr. 2010. Seed Sovereignty: The Promise of Open Source Biology. In *Food Sovereignty: Reconnecting Food, Nature and Community*, eds. Annette

Desmarais, Hannah K. Wittman and Netta Wiebe, pp. 152–67. Fernwood Publishing, Black Point, Nova Scotia.

Maffi, L., ed. 2001. *Biocultural Diversity: Linking Language, Knowledge and Environment*. Smithsonian Institution Press, Washington DC.

Wilkinson, R. and K. Pickett. 2009. *The Spirit Level: Why Greater Equality Makes Societies Stronger*. Bloomsbury Press, New York.

Wyndham, Felice S., Dana Lepofsky, and Sara Tiffany. 2011. Taking Stock in Ethnobiology: Where Do We Come From? What Are We? Where Are We Going? *Journal of Ethnobiology* 31: 110–27.

2

DEFINING NEW DISCIPLINARY TRAJECTORIES

Mixing Political Ecology with Ethnobiology

GARY PAUL NABHAN, KIMBERLEE CHAMBERS, DAVID
TECKLIN, ERIC PERRAMOND, AND THOMAS E. SHERIDAN

T HAT WHICH WE assume to be a distinct scholarly discipline today may
not be so tomorrow; boundaries shift, and territories become redefined
in academia just as they do in geopolitics. It would not be surprising to
see within just a few decades the methodological pretexts of ethnobiological
inquiries once again overhauled as they have been several times already. We
anticipate, and in fact, welcome the re-delineation of the boundaries of this
discipline as a result of advances made in political ecology and in other fields.

Although the term "political ecology" was first used in print more than 80
years ago (Thone 1935), it has been more widely used over the last 30 years in
a particularly rigorous manner by cultural ecologists and human geographers.
Since anthropologist Eric R. Wolf published his seminal article entitled "Ownership and Political Ecology," social scientists have used the concept of political ecology to balance their understanding of "the pressures emanating from
the larger society and the exigencies of the local ecosystem" (Wolf 1972:202).
As noted a quarter century ago by applied anthropologist Thomas Sheridan

Originally published as "Ethnobiology for a Diverse World: Defining New Disciplinary Trajectories: Mixing Political Ecology with Ethnobiology," *Journal of Ethnobiology* 31.1 (Spring/
Summer 2011): 1–3. Reprinted with permission of *Journal of Ethnobiology*.

(1988:xvi), this is because it has become increasingly necessary to "wed the approaches of political economy, which focus upon society's place in a region, nation, or 'world sphere,' with those of cultural ecology, which examine adaptations to local environmental and demographic factors."

We are of the opinion that there is also a need to wed insights from political ecology with ethnobiology, which has largely ignored the global and macro-economic pressures on the so-called "traditional" agricultural, fishing, hunting, and foraging cultures with which ethnobiologists have characteristically been engaged. Despite the broad use of both the concepts and methodologies of political ecology in geography, anthropology and history, articles in the *Journal of Ethnobiology* have seldom used this term, and it is even in less currency in *Economic Botany*, the *Journal of Ethnopharmacology*, and the *Journal of Ethnobiology and Ethnomedicine*. Indeed, a survey of scientific citations of the term "political ecology" in these four journals found only a dozen research articles since 1972 that discuss the precepts of political ecology, relative to the 943 research articles about political ecology from all sources noted on the Web of Science over the same period. With a few notable exceptions, such as Anderson et al. (2005), most ethnobiological monographs, books, dissertations, and refereed journal articles have sidestepped the examination of the political, economic, cross-cultural, and media-driven "external" pressures, which have affected not only the natural resources themselves, but the cultural perceptions and their uses.

Early cultural geography was heavily critiqued in the last forty years for treating culture as some monolithic "super-organism," stuck in some idyllic "ethnographic present" that never existed (Duncan 1980). Nevertheless, many ethnobiologists have continued to describe the communities in which they work in some harmonious "ethno-ecological present" that may also be considered to be a highly contested construct today. It takes young ethnobiologists but one reading of a book such as Peluso's and Watts's (2001) *Violent Environments* to be challenged to leave such simplistic paradigms behind, for it is ever more difficult to remain as politically and economically naïve as our field once was. To use Peluso's (1992) argument in a paraphrase of Wendell Berry, eating, foraging, and extracting resources are always political and moral acts.

While our commentary up until now may sound as if we are implying that ethnobiology has become irrelevant or obsolete in addressing larger issues in cultural ecology, nothing could be further from the truth. To be sure, ethnobiologists have generally served the larger domains of cultural ecology, landscape ecology, and conservation biology well by documenting the internal community dynamics and orally transmitted knowledge about the use of local natural resources. They may, in fact, be better than other scholars in describing heterogeneity within communities through a political ecological context (Chambers and Momsen 2007; Perramond 2005). At the same time, the weakness of some scholars of political ecology is that they appear to be ignorant or dismissive toward understanding the internal community dynamics of how members gain access to natural resources, and their processing and distribution networks (Vayda and Walters 1999).

Although there remain a few scholars in anthropology and geography who may assume that *all* ethnographic or ecological fieldwork is inherently imperialistic, most of us recognize that if we are truly concerned about the fate of peoples, their resources and lands, we must have direct interaction with them. The practice of ethnobiology can offer to political ecology, and other less field-oriented disciplines, something that they desperately need: a kind of direct and protracted contact with the diverse faces, voices, values, and behaviors still active on this planet, as well as with the equally diverse and quixotic non-human world. Ethnobiologists tend to practice an integrative form of science, which cares as much (or more) about the peoples it engages with as it cares about the plants, animals, microbes, and habitats. Ethnobiology is inherently an ecological science because its focus is on "relationships" more than on "things." As such, ethnobiology and ethnoecology have immediate relevance to conservation biology as it is practiced in culturally managed landscapes (Berkes 1999; Johnson and Hunn 2010).

Ultimately, we offer these commentaries not merely to encourage ethnobiologists to brush up on one of the many fine texts regarding political ecology (Biersack and Greenberg 2006; Robbins 2004; Zimmerer and Bassett 2003), but to see their fields through this special lens. In addition, we encourage ethnobiologists to think more deeply about what we can offer to other disciplines in terms of novel theories, values, and methodologies, which can emerge directly from our practice. Rather than thinking of ethnobiology as a field that will simply borrow its approaches and skill sets from evolutionary biology, ethnology, comparative linguistics, critical theory, Marxist history, paleoecology, or cultural geography, it is time we offer cutting-edge theoretical paradigms and principles to the other disciplines with which we interact. If we cannot do this, then ethnobiology risks remaining the poor stepchild of ethnology, descriptive archaeology, and natural history. We are confident that it can and will accomplish far more than that, given the inspiring work that young field ethnobiologists, cross-trained among many disciplines, are currently accomplishing. No other field, perhaps, is in such a strategic position to integrate knowledge regarding the interactions between cultural diversity and ecological diversity at a time when both entities are facing unprecedented challenges. If ethnobiologists intend to be of service in sustaining such diversity, we need to set our sights high, and intellectually cast our nets broadly.

REFERENCES CITED

Anderson, Eugene N. with Aurora Dzib Xihum de Cen, Felix Medina Tzuc, and Pastor Valdez Chale. 2005. *Political Ecology in a Yucatec Maya Community*. University of Arizona Press, Tucson.

Berkes, Fikret. 1999. *Sacred Ecology: Traditional Ecological Knowledge and Resource Management*. Taylor and Frances, Philadelphia.

Biersack, Aletta and James B. Greenberg, eds. 2006. *Reimagining Political Ecology*. Duke University Press, Durham.

Chambers, Kimberlee J. and Janet H. Momsen. 2007. From the Kitchen and the Field: Gender and Maize Diversity in Mexico. *Singapore Journal of Tropical Geography on Gender and Agriculture* 28:39–56.

Duncan, J. 1980. The Superorganic in American Cultural Geography. *Annals of the Association of American Geographers* 70:181–98.

Johnson, Leslie Main and Eugene S. Hunn. 2010. *Landscape Ethnoecology: Concepts of Biotic and Physical Space*. Berghahn Books, New York.

Peluso, Nancy Lee. 1992. *Rich Forests, Poor People: Resource Control and Resistance in Java*. University of California Press, Berkeley.

Peluso, Nancy Lee and Michael Watts. 2001. *Violent Environments*. Cornell University Press, Ithaca.

Perramond, Eric P. 2005. The Politics of Ecology: Local Knowledge and Wild Chili Collection in Sonora, Mexico. *Journal of Latin American Geography* 4(1):59–75.

Robbins, Paul. 2004. *Political Ecology: A Critical Introduction*. Wiley/Blackwell, New York.

Sheridan, Thomas E. 1988. *Where the Dove Calls: The Political Economy of a Peasant Corporate Community in Northwestern Mexico*. University of Arizona Press, Tucson.

Thone, Frank. 1935. Nature Rambling: We Fight for Grass. *The Science Newsletter* 27(717) Jan. 5:14.

Vayda, A., and B. Walters. 1999. Against Political Ecology. *Human Ecology* 27(1):167–79.

Wolf, Eric E. 1972. Ownership and Political Ecology. *Anthropological Quarterly* 45(3):201–05.

Zimmerer, Karl S. and Thomas J. Bassett, eds. 2003. *Political Ecology: An Integrative Approach to Geography and Environment-Development Studies*. Guilford Publishing, New York.

3

ETHNOSCIENCE, THE "OLDEST SCIENCE"

A Needed Complement to Academic Science and
Citizen Science to Stem the Losses of Biodiversity,
Indigenous Languages, and Livelihoods

BENJAMIN T. WILDER, CAROLYN O'MEARA,
LAURA MONTI, AND GARY PAUL NABHAN

W ITH ACCELERATING LOSSES of biodiversity, habitats, and native languages, ethnoscience—including the study of traditional ecological knowledge of species and landscapes held by indigenous cultures—has become ever more significant. Globally, 20 percent of described species are likely to face extinction over the next two to three decades (Maffi 2001). Indeed, current extinction rates vastly exceed background rates among vertebrate taxa by 114 times under the most conservative of calculations (Ceballos et al. 2015). Simultaneously, Rogers and Campbell (in press) estimate that one language goes extinct every 3.5 months, and that 3,134 of the 6,901 known living languages are endangered. Linguistic and biological diversity are tightly coupled and face similarly grim futures (Gorenflo et al. 2011).

Collaborative efforts to adequately document local biological classifications and associated traditional knowledge of species distributions and habitats are, in a very real sense, time-sensitive. While indigenous knowledge of the natural world can arguably be honored as "the oldest science," since it predates the formal articulation of Western scientific tenets and organized citizen science by thousands of years, it is in many ways rapidly shifting, if not dramatically

---

A complementary discussion of this topic is in preparation with the journal *Bioscience* as this volume goes to press.

eroding. This is especially true among communities suffering from declining use of their indigenous languages. As such, there is an urgent need to support the communities attempting to revitalize their native tongues and maintain their traditional livelihoods based on natural resources. Fortunately, there are growing efforts among indigenous cultures to direct projects that restore habitats of declining species and resuscitate lost practices and knowledge.

Recently, citizen scientists' efforts to help inventory and monitor the world's declining biodiversity have been given the attention they have long deserved (Miller-Rushing et al. 2012). Laudable efforts are underway to reengage a broader segment of the population in making natural history observations of biodiversity imperiled by climate change, and discussing the moral implications of such changes (Nisbet et al. 2010; Miller-Rushing et al. 2012). Here we wish to direct comparable attention to the value of indigenous knowledge embedded in local taxonomies. Few scientists open to citizen science collaborations have found appropriate means of accommodating observations made by indigenous foragers, fishers, hunters, farmers, and artisans who have a particularly sophisticated grasp of place-based changes in biodiversity through time and space. Accommodating their knowledge should be of keen interest to those scholars working to bridge the environmental sciences with social sciences, arts, and religion to better engage the diverse constituencies in addressing the biological and cultural consequences of climate change (Nisbet et al. 2010). It may help us avoid a truncated approach to knowledge that limits the horizon of discovery and merely pays lip service to averting the loss of biocultural diversity.

INDIGENOUS SCIENCE AS COMPARED TO ACADEMIC AND CITIZEN SCIENCE

As never before, direct comparisons of relatively comprehensive treatments of species, habitats, and landscapes from Western and indigenous perspectives are now possible. The junction of different ways of perceiving and cataloguing biodiversity is a bountiful realm for collaboration and respectful learning across cultures. The nexus of diverse worldviews can be the departure point for future efforts to both document and conserve. However, we must consider that disparate cultures have not necessarily arrived at parallel typologies and classification structures for discerning the lives and habitats around them. Why are there widely heralded cases of one-to-one correspondences of Western and local classifications, but intriguing divergences as well? Can indigenous names and mythology of the geographic origins of certain species serve as the basis of testable hypotheses, just as a scientist's observations have been utilized?

The knowledge base of most indigenous science is ancient yet dynamic. Place-based natural history observations gathered over centuries or millennia are distilled in the lexicon, calendars, place names or maps, and other practices of indigenous resource managers. Indigenous scientific knowledge is in many ways complementary to—not contradictory or redundant with—academic science and citizen science (Table 3.1). In fact, local taxonomies already bridge detailed place-based natural history observations with moral dimensions and artistic, effective communication strategies that some biodiversity and climate scientists are now striving to encompass in their own work (Nisbet et al. 2010).

As linguistic loss accelerates and traditional livelihoods decline, there is a concomitant loss of traditional ecological knowledge of biodiversity and habitats within which it is nested. This compromised knowledge base—as indicated by disuse of lexemes that refer to particular organisms—may hamper the indigenous community itself and humanity at large in gaining a more holistic understanding and management framework for dealing with imperiled species, habitats, and the stresses currently being placed on them (Berkes 2012). Nevertheless, the distributions, habitat needs, and behavior of locally declining or globally endangered species may remain better known by indigenous or local peoples who have long resided in their territories than by Western-trained scientists (Nabhan 2000). We desperately need such place-based knowledge to help guide both species recovery and habitat restoration efforts. These efforts may also be essential in supporting the persistence of resources on which livelihoods for indigenous fishers, foragers, or hunters are based (Berkes 2012).

Fortunately, for decades, individuals in the biological and social sciences have worked with leaders in indigenous communities to document the biocultural diversity still extant in First Nations' lands and waters (Maffi 2001). Until recently, only a small minority of studies were formally guided or directed by traditional tribal elders, with technical support being provided by professional or academic scientists (Gupta et al. 1993). But more than ever before, indigenous leaders are taking full leadership in documenting the diversity in their territory. Foremost among them are the ethno-ornithological and traditional medicinal plant inventories in the Kuna Yala homelands of the Kuna in Panama.

There remain creative tensions to deal with when attempting to integrate information, values, and cosmologies of distinct cultures. Perhaps there has

TABLE 3.1. Comparison of features of Western science, citizen science, and indigenous knowledge/ethnoscience, following Berkes (2012) and Miller-Rushing et al. (2012)

CHARACTERISTICS	WESTERN SCIENCE	CITIZEN SCIENCE	INDIGENOUS KNOWLEDGE/ ETHNOSCIENCE
Goals	Seeking universals and testing theories through experiments, analysis of data, and models	Offering local data to those seeking universals and testing theories	Usually offering data and pattern analysis specific to or bounded by a culturally-defined space and time
Participants	Largely done by academically trained professional technicians, some of them naturalists	Largely done by enlightened/committed "amateur" naturalists, often trained in other professions	Largely done by "proto-professional" naturalists: foragers, hunters, fishers, farmers, and shamans
Communication	Primarily transmitted through written works, graphs, and formal oral presentations	Primarily transmitted through field notes, social media, online databases, and informal oral presentations	Primarily transmitted orally in an indigenous language, also through song, story, maps, and art
Framework	Done by individuals, small teams, or cyber-networks for universal benefit	Done for pleasure by cohorts of volunteer participants in informal networks often guided by professionals	Done in multi-generational communities primarily for the community
Worldview	In most cases, wary of spiritual dimensions and ambivalent on ethical-moral context	Variable in directly addressing spiritual, moral, and ethical dimensions, depending on community	Seamlessly linked to spiritual dimensions and ethical-moral considerations
Methodological concerns	Insists on separation of object-subject	Ambivalent on object-subject dichotomy	Less object-subject dichotomy
Location/Scale	Increasingly done irrespective of place or focused on model systems	Preferably affectionately done as place-based inquiry	Embedded in cultural cosmology specific to place

been a prevailing ideological bias among linguists and biologists toward finding "universal principles" of classification embedded in folk biological taxonomies to which most, if not all known cultures have adhered to. Such apparent commonalities have been enough to convince some scientists that the prevailing one-to-one correspondences of folk and scientific taxonomies indicate that such taxa are "biologically real" entities and not just arbitrary constructs of human minds (Begossi et al. 2008). Such over-simplified use of universal principles risk ignoring the very essence of diversity itself. Instead, we must give particular attention to the anomalies, the unique cultural expressions, and the collisions of dissonant taxonomic structures. Historically, while linguists or taxonomists may have favored certitude over dissonance, we no longer wish to risk doing so at the expense of the very diversity we wish to honor.

PRIORITIZING ACTIONS

As Gewin (2002) has capably described, there are many new emerging collaborations to adapt taxonomic inventories for the Internet age. These innovative approaches often involve broader collaborations and participatory strategies to inventory the world's remaining biodiversity before it is too late. Some of these engage citizen scientists as "parataxonomists" to assist academic scientists with All Taxa Biodiversity Inventories (ATBI), such as those initiated in the Guanacaste Conservation Area of Costa Rica (Janzen 2004), the NaturaLista program spearheaded by the Mexican National Commission for the Knowledge and Use of Biodiversity (CONABIO, http://conabio.inaturalist.org), and in Great Smoky Mountains National Park in the United States. However, we wish to encourage comprehensive collaborative work toward documenting inventories of indigenous and Western knowledge for local biodiversity such as the case study we present below. We also stress that knowledge maintained in rural communities is equally valuable and in need of recognition and collaboration.

Given that the crisis in biocultural diversity is more complex and time-sensitive than what we can gain by merely inventorying species, we argue that before more species and languages (or merely lexical items) are lost, indigenous, rural, citizen, and professional scientists should collaborate to accomplish five tasks:

1. Document in understudied/minority languages not only the local names (simple or compound lexemes) for, but descriptive natural history knowledge about

as many plants and animals as possible, with particular focus on endangered and endemic species;

2. Document more precisely the convergence and congruency between local taxonomies and Western knowledge schemas, as well as which species appear to have culturally influenced distributions and abundances;

3. Attempt to discern the extent to which the very structures of local classification systems in languages now at risk appear to be aberrant or incongruous with the Western (or Linnaean) scientific classification system;

4. Engage indigenous or local communities in biodiversity documentation and stewardship through culturally driven intergenerational learning, using native language-based approaches as well as other ecological knowledge tools and strategies;

5. Empower and support indigenous or local communities that choose to develop their own programs for managing and recovering rare species in their homelands and waters, as a means to maintain or revitalize native languages and customs in order to sustain traditional livelihoods.

CASE STUDY INVOLVING THE COMCAAC OF THE GULF OF CALIFORNIA, MEXICO

Let us consider as a case study the progress made on these five tasks through long-term collaborations between the *Comcaac* (Seri People) of Sonora, Mexico, and a group of linguists, ethnobiologists, anthropologists, geographers, and conservation biologists who have gained momentum and diversity over the last quarter-century. The Comcaac are a seafaring and hunter-gatherer culture. They or their ancestors or predecessors have lived in the arid coastal region of the Sonoran Desert and Gulf of California for millennia (Bowen 2009). There are around 900 speakers of *Cmiique Iitom* (the Seri language) as of 2007 (Lewis et al. 2015), almost all of whom are bilingual in Spanish. *Cmiique Iitom* has been described as vibrant and its status as "vigorous" (Lewis et al. 2015), even while taking into consideration its status as an endangered language (Moser and Marlett 2010). *Cmiique Iitom* is not genealogically related to the neighboring cultures in the family of Uto-Aztecan languages, and it has been classified as a language isolate, meaning that we do not know with any precision its linguistic relatives.

A group of professional scientists from Mexico and the United States has been engaged with Comcaac community leaders and young "para-ecologists" in what began *ad hoc*, but has emerged as an ATBI. It encompasses both land-scapes and seascapes along the Sonoran Desert coast of the Gulf of California of Sonora and among the Midriff Islands. These efforts have documented several sets of taxa in *Cmiique Iitom* and Western or Linnaean scientific terminology to classify the biodiversity of that region.

In recent years, young Seri para-ecologists as well as elders have been co-authors or listed as contributors on several significant studies of biodiversity inventory, habitat conservation, and restoration published in a half-dozen refereed journals and four books from academic presses. Substantive collaborative studies have been completed with contributors who are Comcaac regarding vascular plants, marine invertebrates, fish, reptiles, birds, and mammals regarding species migration, endangered species recovery, habitat restoration, and indigenous (economic) uses.

These multicultural assessments of biodiversity serve as the departure point for a more refined grasp of a region, in this case, the remarkably diverse Gulf of California and the surrounding Sonoran Desert. Many researchers (e.g., Marlett and Moser 1995; O'Meara 2010) have considered the way that the Comcaac conceptualize and talk about their land and seascapes, containing abundant references to plants and animals, as well as other "affordances," or knowledge that conveys the interweave between humans and their environments. Examples include *Moosni Oofija* (lit. 'what the green sea turtles encircle'), which refers to a shoal in the ocean where *Chelonia mydas* individuals of certain age classes aggregate, and *Seenel Iitxo* (lit. 'where there are many butterflies') an aggregation site around scarce springs, seeps, or floral resources. The latter term may have offered human survival value, since it refers to a place where one would find fresh water after rains on the extremely arid San Esteban Island. These names clearly provide a context regarding biological resources located at culturally significant sites.

As such, the collective knowledge of biodiversity among the Comcaac that evolved over millennia is embedded in complex local linguistic expressions and cultural practices, which contributes new and often surprising information to regional conservation efforts, particularly with regard to endemic or endangered species (Nabhan 2003).

These efforts have often led Western taxonomists to populations of plant species previously uncollected in the region (Felger and Moser 1985). They also document observed behaviors and interspecific interactions not initially encountered by academic scientists (Nabhan 2000), such as an undocumented overwintering population of sea turtles previously thought by scientists to migrate away from the region during cold periods (Felger et al. 1976).

Seri place names also encode biological knowledge that has otherwise been lost. The name in *Cmiique Iitom* for Rasa Island, a small yet globally important seabird island in the middle of the Gulf of California is *Tosni Iti Ihiiquet* (lit. 'where the pelicans have their offspring'). However, the island has not had breeding pelicans in the recent past (Anderson et al. 2013). Yet, translation of Italian naturalist Federico Craveri's journals from an 1856 voyage in the Gulf reveals the presence of young pelicans on Rasa Island and corroborates the accuracy of the Seri name (Bowen et al. in press).

Conversely, scholarly research can be incongruous with knowledge held by the Comcaac. Seri mythology and historical records supported a longstanding absence of desert bighorn sheep on Tiburón Island. The recent finding of 1,500-year-old dung of this herbivore on Tiburón demonstrates the presence of this species on the island prior to its unintentional rewilding to the island in 1975 (Wilder et al. 2014). This is a situation where science is finding something traditional knowledge has not preserved. We see opportunities to increasingly use Seri knowledge and mythology to inform scientific hypotheses to be tested through cross-cultural collaboration.

We equally value the contributions of professionally trained botanists and citizen scientists in refining the scientific taxonomy and geography of desert plants and animals in this region, especially when they attempt to correlate it with Seri knowledge. Nabhan (2003), Bowen (2009), and Davy et al. (2011) have refined our biological knowledge of which plant and animal taxa the Seri themselves culturally dispersed among islands and coastal habitats. O'Meara (2010) showed that the landscape domain conceptualized by the Comcaac (based on generic landscape terms) describes unique environmental characteristics. These landscape categorizations could lead to new understanding of distribution patterns of local species guilds.

Still other studies reveal major knowledge gaps, such as the names of mollusks that refer to species currently unidentified by scientists or that have possibly been locally extirpated already (Marlett 2014). Accounts of mythological sea creatures and reptiles also unknown to Western science are embedded within the songs and stories of their ancient navigation journeys throughout the Gulf of California (Monti 2002).

As any other source of knowledge, indigenous ecological knowledge is fluid and dynamic. Emerging medicinal knowledge of the Comcaac has been demonstrated by Narchi et al. (2014) in their documentation of the recent adoption of a marine algae for medicinal purposes. Monti (2002) and her indigenous collaborators have also demonstrated how the Comcaac have adapted traditional knowledge to deal with emerging diseases and climate-driven environmental stresses affecting human health in their region. Climate change, loss of habitat, recently dispersed pathogens, and dietary changes have forced Comcaac herbalists to innovate new uses of medicinal plant species.

Active efforts are being made not merely to archive but also to share this knowledge within indigenous communities. With respect to language conservation and maintenance, Moser and Marlett (2010) have compiled and published a trilingual Seri-Spanish-English dictionary that defines and describes folk taxa documented over the course of a half-century. Their efforts also encompass the publication of numerous monolingual booklets of stories in *Cmiique Iitom* for community use (Marlett 2013). Intensive courses and workshops on native language literacy have been offered in recent years, which support language maintenance and restoration that have involved dozens of younger Seri individuals. Thanks to these efforts, various Seri adults have some reading and writing ability in their own language. Now the younger generation can assure that traditional knowledge held by Seri elders is being documented, retained, and celebrated in their communities.

In short, strengthening intergenerational knowledge transmission processes in indigenous communities may be a necessary investment for engaging the next generation in biodiversity stewardship. The combined efforts of community and academic researchers over decades has led to both traditional knowledge and Western scientific knowledge being readily taught, accepted, and resulting in measureable benefits to species recovery and habitat restoration. Comcaac ecologists and researchers are gaining recognition in their community and throughout the world, as their impressive list of publications and on-the-ground achievements only hints.

Seri individuals who underwent para-ecologist training are now working for Mexico's Commission for Natural Protected Areas (CONANP), and the tribal natural resources program. The quality of their work has been recognized by the Smithsonian Institution's Museum of the American Indian, the National Geographic Society, the Cousteau Society, Conservation International, the Amazon Conservation Team, Slow Food International, and many other international organizations. Many of the participating researchers (academics and Comcaac alike) are now members of the Next Generation Sonoran Desert Researchers

(N-Gen; Wilder et al. 2013), a network of 300+ of the leading scholars in the region—50 percent based in the United States, and 50 percent based in Mexico. Indigenous leaders from different cultures together with academics in the region have convened the Biocultural Network of Sonora—an affiliate of the national Biocultural Network in Mexico—to address some of the most pressing ecological challenges confronting their communities. The next era of collaboration can increasingly support the Comcaac as leaders in science and conservation projects.

It is important to recognize the persistent external pressures not just on the Seri, their language and homelands, but also on those of other indigenous communities in rapid-changing coastal areas. The loss of their traditional livelihoods is strongly linked to economic pressures. Efforts to appropriate indigenous territory and natural resources by outside forces are unabated in many parts of the world. Strategies to conserve and honor traditional ecological knowledge must take into account the rights of indigenous communities for self-governance, intellectual property, prior informed consent, and maintenance of their language and culture, while seeking sustainable economic development options as affirmed in the United Nations Declaration on the Rights of Indigenous Peoples in 2008.

The complex nuances of local classification systems are intricately connected with the biocultural diversity that global actions aim to maintain. By not fully honoring the real and potential value of indigenous science, as society often does, our institutions risk ignoring the opportunity for consilience among the many funds of knowledge collected over the millennia. It is especially dangerous to do so in a time of paired and accelerated loss of biodiversity and traditional knowledge. We strive for a future in which academics, governments, and nonprofits working in civil society will document, honor, and value every bit of cultural information regarding biodiversity, whether or not it initially appears anomalous, incongruent, or not fitting with the prevailing opinion. Much may be at stake if we sweep such "messiness" under the rug.

ACKNOWLEDGMENTS

Many individuals among the Comcaac, fellow researchers, foundations, universities, nonprofit organizations, and federal agencies have been instrumental in making this collective work possible. We particularly thank our many collaborators and students in the two Comcaac communities of Punta Chueca and Desemboque for what they have imparted to us in terms of knowledge and values. Foremost among supporting foundations have been: the Mac-Arthur Foundation, the Overbrook Foundation, the Agnese Lindley Haury Foundation, the Pew Charitable Trusts, the W. K. Kellogg Foundation, the David and Lucille Packard Foundation, the Christensen Fund, the National Science Foundation, Mexican Federal and State Agencies such as Consejo Nacional de Ciencia y Tecnología (CONACYT), Comisión Nacional de Áreas Naturales Protegidas (CONANP), Culturas Populares, Instituto Nacional de Antropología e Historia, complemented by the U.S. Fish and Wildlife Service Sonoran Joint Venture and Wildlife Without Borders, UC MEXUS, Comunidad y Biodiversidad, Prescott College Kino Bay Center for Cultural and Ecological Studies, and the CIAD-Centro de Information y Desarrollo Indígena.

LITERATURE CITED

Anderson, D.W., Henny, C.J., Godínez-Reyes, C., et al. 2013. Size and distribution of the California Brown Pelican metapopulation in a non-ENSO year. *Marine Ornithology* 41: 95–96.

Begossi, A., Chauer, M., Figueiredo. J.L., et al. 2008. Are biological species and higher-ranking categories real? Fish folk taxonomy on Brazil's Atlantic coast and in the Amazon. *Current Anthropology* 49(2): 291–96.

Berkes, F. 2012. Sacred ecology. New York, NY: Routledge.

Bowen, T. 2009. The record of native people on Gulf of California Islands. Arizona State Museum Archaeological Series 201. Tucson, AZ: University of Arizona Press.

Bowen, T., Velarde E., Anderson, D.W., and Marlett, S.A. Federico Craveri and changes in nesting seabirds on Isla Rasa since 1856. *Southwest Naturalist.* In press.

Ceballos, G., Ehrlich, P.R., Barnosky, A.D., et al. 2015. Accelerated modern human–induced species losses: Entering the sixth mass extinction. *Science Advances* 1: e1400253.

Davy, C.M., Mendez de la Cruz, F.R., Latrop, A. et al. 2011. Seri Indian traditional knowledge and molecular biology agree: no express train for island-hopping spiny tailed iguanas in the Sea of Cortes. *Journal of Biogeography* 38(2): 272–84.

Felger, R.S., Cliffton, K., and Regal, P.J. 1976. Winter dormancy in sea turtles: independent discovery and exploitation in the Gulf of California by two local cultures. *Science* 191: 283–85.

Felger, R.S. and Moser, M.B. 1985. People of the desert and sea: ethnobotany of the Seri Indians. Tucson, AZ: University of Arizona Press.

Gorenflo, L.J., Romaine, S., Mittermeier, R.A., et al. 2011 Co-occurrence of linguistic and biological diversity in biodiversity hotspots and high biodiversity wilderness areas. *Proceedings of the National Academy of Sciences USA* 1209(21): 8032–37.

Gewin, V. 2002. Taxonomy: all living things, online. *Nature* 418: 362–63.

Gupta, M.P., Jones, A., Solís, P.N., et al. 1993. Medicinal plants inventory of Kuna Yala: part I. *Journal of Ethnopharmacology* 40: 77–79.

Janzen, D.H. 2004. Setting up tropical biodiversity for conservation through non-damaging use: participation by para-taxonomists. *Journal of Applied Ecology* 41: 181–87.

Lewis, M.P., Simons, G.F., and Fennig, C.D. (eds.). 2015. Ethnologue: languages of the world, eighteenth edition. Dallas, TX: SIL International. Online version: http://www.ethnologue.com. Viewed June 9, 2015.

Maffi, L. 2001. On biocultural diversity: linking language, knowledge and the environment. Washington, DC: Smithsonian Institution Press.

Marlett, C.M. 2014. Shells on a desert shore: mollusks in the Seri world. Tucson, AZ: University of Arizona Press.

Marlett, S.A. 2013. A bibliography for the study of Seri history, language and culture. http://www.und.nodak.edu/instruct/smarlett/Stephen_Marlett/Publications_and_Presentations_files/SeriBibliography.pdf. Viewed July 9, 2015.

Marlett, S.A. and Moser, M.B. 1995. Presentación y análisis preliminar de 550 topónimos seris. In: Gaxiola López, J., and Mendoza Guerrero, E. (eds.). Coloquio de toponimia: los nombres del pueblo del noroeste. Culiacán, Sinaloa: Colegio de Sinaloa.

Miller-Rushing, A., Primack, R., and Bonney, R. 2012. The history of public participation in ecological research. *Frontiers in Ecology and Environment* 10(6): 285–90.

Monti, L. 2002. Seri Indian adaptive strategies in a desert and sea environment: Three case studies. A navigational song map in the Sea of Cortes; the ironwood tree as habitat for medicinal plants; desert plants adapted to treat diabetes. (PhD dissertation). Tucson, AZ: University of Arizona.

Moser, M.B., and Marlett, S.A. 2010. Diccionario seri-español-ingles. Hermosillo, Sonora: Universidad de Sonora, Mexico D.F.: Plaza y Valdes Editores.

Nabhan, G.P. 2000. Interspecific relationships affecting endangered species recognized by O'odham and Comcáac cultures. *Ecological Applications* 10(5): 1288–95.

Nabhan, G.P. 2003. Singing the turtles to sea: Comcáac art and science of reptiles. Berkeley, CA: University of California Press.

Narchi, N.E, Cornier, S., Canu, D.M., et al. 2014. Marine ethnobiology a rather neglected area, which can provide an important contribution to ocean and coastal management. *Ocean and Coastal Management* 89: 117–23.

Nisbet, M.C., Hixon, M.A., Moore, K.D., et al. 2010. Four cultures: new synergies for engaging society on climate change. *Frontiers in Ecology and Environment* 8: 329–31.

O'Meara, C. 2010. Seri landscape classification and spatial reference (PhD dissertation). Buffalo, NY: State University of New York at Buffalo.

Rogers, C. and Campbell, L. Endangered languages. In: Aronoff, M. (ed.). Oxford research encyclopedia of linguistics. Oxford: Oxford University Press. 2015. doi:10.1093/acrefore/9780199384655.013.21.

Wilder, B.T., O'Meara, C., Medel, A., et al. 2013. The need for a next generation of Sonoran Desert researchers. *Conservation Biology* 27: 243–44.

Wilder, B.T., Betancourt, J.L., Epps, C., et al. 2014. Local extinction and unintentional rewilding of bighorn sheep (*Ovis canadensis*) on a desert island. *PLoS ONE* 9(3): e91358.

4

AUTOBIOLOGY?

The Traditional Ecological, Agricultural, and Culinary Knowledge of Us!

GARY PAUL NABHAN

THE PREFIX *ETHNO* ('OTHER') might be considered one of the unfortunate flaws associated with the origins of our (inter-)discipline that has pervasively shaped the history of ethnobiology. Since the late 19th century, when John William Harshberger (1896) first coined the term "ethnobotany," the prevailing strategy of most fieldworkers trained in ethnobiology has been to go and bear witness to *some other culture's* knowledge of plants and animals. We would be remiss to ignore the blatantly colonial or imperialistic tone of some of the earliest ethnobotanical studies. They were explicitly undertaken to either a) learn what of value could be extracted from another culture's natural resource base as export crops, or b) learn how immigrants could take cues from native residents on how to make a living on their shared home ground, even as some of those immigrants usurped water and harvested native plants and wildlife from the homelands of the people that they were studying.

As my fellow Arab American Edward Said (1993:5) once wrote, "We are at a point in our work when we can no longer ignore empires and the imperial context in our studies." Readers of Said's *Orientalism* (1978) will remember his contention that portrayals of Arabs and Persians as "the other"—whether those

Originally published as "Ethnobiology for a Diverse World: Autobiology? The Traditional Ecological, Agricultural and Culinary Knowledge of Us!," *Journal of Ethnobiology* 33.1 (Spring/Summer 2013): 2–6. Reprinted with permission of *Journal of Ethnobiology*.

portrayals represent them as primitives or as exotic sophisticates—historically served as implicit justifications for both European and North American political and colonial ambitions. The same can be said of English-, Spanish-, French- and Portuguese-speaking immigrants to the "New World," who may have either vilified or romanticized indigenous peoples of the Americas as being in some timeless homeostatic balance with the natural world. It both trivializes and simplifies their more nuanced knowledge and their complex interactions— positive and negative—with the biota of the Americas.

One way out of this intellectual trap that many ethnobiologists have discussed and practiced is to devote time to encouraging (and in some cases, assisting) members of a particular cultural community to describe their own traditions from an emic view anchored in local language, belief, behavior, and custom. Perhaps there is no better example of this in twentieth-century ethnobiology than Ian Saen Majnep's (Majnep et al. 1977) collaboration with ethnobiologists Ralph Bulmer and Christopher Healey, *Birds of My Kalam Country*.

And yet, there is another pathway that ethnobiologists can and should take, and that is the investigation of the terms and underlying principles of ethnobiological classification and resource management, which can be found within their own cultures –what we might call "autobiology." Autobiology is what an early editor of the *Journal of Ethnobiology*, Willard Van Asdall, called the "ethnobiology of us." Van Asdall suggested that if only as a heuristic tool, it is well worth teaching students to inquire within their own ethnic, class, gender, or language communities to discern and document what kinds of orally transmitted ecological, agricultural, and culinary knowledge remain in currency. Although this exercise in and of itself does not erase past imperialistic pursuits, nor guarantee that our (inter-)discipline will be free of them in the future, it does offer us much underexplored intellectual as well as pragmatic territory to reveal within our own linguistic and cultural communities.

There are many examples of such autobiological inquiries already, including James Veteto's excellent work on the agrobiodiversity of American English– speaking farming communities in Appalachia (see Veteto 2011). So that the potential of this approach can be made more apparent, I have recently begun to compile an ethnobiological lexicon for regional borderlands where Spanish and English are still used, in the six Mexican and four U.S. border-states that include much of the desert habitats in North America. I have been prompted to do so out of the belated recognition that I have more than 500 relatives of Lebanese descent living in the border states, whose ancestors immigrated to this region through Mexico to the United States, and many of them are at least bilingual (American English, Mexican Spanish) and some trilingual (with Levantine Arabic retained). With 40 years of my own work in all eight border-states, I had accumulated a vocabulary of regional terms that do not appear in either the Oxford English Dictionary nor in the Real Academia Española's lexicon of "official" terms mandated by royal decree.

While involved in borderlands fieldwork with bilingual Spanish, English, Arab, Piman, Navajo, and Hopi ethnobiology students over the last quarter century, I have recorded many terms that have "jumped the border" and are now used in this region on both sides of the international boundary, but not necessarily the same way they might be used in the rest of Mexico or the rest of the United States. Undoubtedly, some of these terms were used in or across this entire arid landscape prior to the current placement of the U.S.-Mexico border after the Treaty of Guadalupe Hidalgo around 1850, and before current economic dominance of American English and Spanish, when Native American nations were the primary populations dwelling in the region. While a significant percentage of terms diffused from indigenous languages into Spanish or English before the present construction of the borderlands emerged, other terms have their ultimate roots in Persian, Arabic, Greek, Roman, Hebrew, and Sanskrit, not just in Spanish and English.

Whatever the case, these "endemic" terms and special regional uses of more widespread terms harbor an extraordinary amount of knowledge about how to feed oneself in the arid and semi-arid landscapes of southwestern North America, and in the waters of the adjacent Gulf of California and Gulf of Mexico. And so, I consulted Spanish and English farmers, ranchers, foragers, hunters, fishers, home cooks, bootleggers, and chefs living in the region. I also verified the Western scientific equivalents of regional folk taxa and expanded the lexical range using linguists' and folklorists' collections of agrarian terms such as those found in the recently completed *Dictionary of American English* (Cassidy 1985; Hall 2012) and *A Dictionary of New Mexico and Southern Colorado Spanish* (Cobos 2003). Finally, I reviewed and updated terms and their linguistic transcriptions in older compilations such as Sobarzo's (1966) *Vocabulario Sonorense*.

Of a 16 percent sample of the 1,800 word borderlands lexicon compiled to date, 75 percent of the terms currently used in the binational region are recognizable to most residents as being Spanish in origin, and 23 percent as English in origin, although their etymologies reflect much more nuanced trajectories of origin and diffusion. The ethnobiology of "us," when defined by words used by Spanish and English speakers in the region, inevitably directs us to broader historic and linguistic considerations. (In other words, we remain indebted to those who came before us in this landscape and in others; we could hardly live here on "pure" Spanish or "pure" English alone.) This three-to-one ratio does not reflect current demographics, but rather demonstrates the greater antiquity of Spanish in this region, and perhaps its greater capacity to absorb terms and concepts borrowed from indigenous languages than American English. About 15 percent of the terms in the sample can be traced back to Native American languages, with Algonkian, Southern Athabaskan, Cahitan, Cahuilla, Costanoan, Guayacura, Opata, Nahuatl, Piman, Tanoan, and Tarahumara terms being directly traceable into Spanish. By far the most terms in the current regional lexicon diffused from contact with and/or multilingualism among the Aztec or Puchtecan traders, Navajo herders and foragers, and O'odham, Opata, Tarahumara, Tewa, and Yaqui farmers. Less than 2 percent are currently traceable to Arabic, Farsi, French, Hebrew, Latin, Greek, Portuguese, and Turkic languages, and nearly all of these diffused into Spanish well before European colonization of the region began around 1540.

One upshot of this autobiological exercise is to remind us that multilingualism and multiculturalism have been the norm, not the exception in most American landscapes. Early historic records suggest that desert nomads such as the Hia C-eḍ O'odham ('Sand Papago' or 'Papagos Areneños') spent much of their yearly cycle in multicultural encampments with the Seri, the Tohono O'odham, the Cucupa, the Mohave, and the Southern Yavapai. The seasonal residents in these encampments spoke three, maybe four indigenous languages, and possibly used some rudimentary Nahuatl and later, Spanish, as a means of trade as well. Perhaps certain kinds of traditional ecological knowledge were exchanged for centuries across languages in such encampments, and were seldom kept within an exclusively strongly monolingual context.

Since the Indian boarding school era in the United States and the introduction of horses and automobiles in Mexico, there has been a resurgence of cross-cultural marriages among young people, which have exposed them to the languages and traditional knowledge of neighboring cultures early enough in their lives for this knowledge to guide some of their behaviors and land stewardship practices.

In short, the essential message of this autobiological analysis is that the traditional agricultural, culinary, and ecological knowledge base of most residents of this region has never been monocultural, and doubtless never will be. Neighboring cultures recognized that they had (or shared) equivalent terms for the same species, management practice, or culinary process. Since this shared knowledge was not necessarily held in a monolingual context, it may pose challenges to the current thinking and emerging policies regarding intellectual property rights for the intangible heritage such as traditional ecological knowledge embedded in particular cultures. Current discourses largely assume that such knowledge evolved internally within a single culture, rather than through protracted interaction among neighboring cultures.

Of the relative richness within the various categories in the lexicon, wild plants foraged for food, found as weeds in fields, and used as indicators of soil and water offered the greatest number of terms (30 percent). This may be because the rates of endemism in desert regions are so high that names for plants used elsewhere on the continent did not adequately describe the many unique species in the borderlands, even in the eyes of farmers and ranchers, let alone foragers. Thus, a regional lexicon for wild plants is one key means through which natives and immigrants adapted to the particular conditions of their locales. Other means are through landscape terms for geomorphic, ecological and pedological conditions (9 percent), weather (1 percent), huntable terrestrial fauna (7 percent), and harvestable fish and shellfish (4 percent).

Agricultural terms such as crop varieties, soil management techniques, and horticultural practices unique to the region comprise 13 percent of the terms in the lexicon, but this grows to 19 percent if terms for water management through spring development and irrigation (6 percent) are included. Ranching terms—aside from those exclusively dedicated to horsemanship, tack, and horse colors—comprise 7 percent of the lexicon.

One significant category in the lexicon is primarily contributed through work traditionally accomplished by women—that of preserving, processing, and preparing foodstuffs for the table (18 percent). A category of terms primarily contributed through men's work has emerged through the pastime of bootlegging, particularly of the various mescals distilled in the region. Roughly 7 percent of the lexicon—the same as hunting terms—comes from the fermenting and distillation of beverages. Finally, 2 percent of the lexicon refers to cooking utensils, as well as farm and ranching tools or implements not commonly used in other regions.

Of course, this autobiological lexicon is biased toward the traditional knowledge held in rural communities of the borderlands, and has largely been collected over the last half-century. Today, the population of the Sun Belt is predominantly urban on both sides of the border, and the average age of residents is under twenty-five. These demographic indicators suggest that land-based vocabularies may be less frequently relied upon by the majority of the region's inhabitants than at any time in the past. It is likely that such time-tried traditional ecological knowledge embedded in regional Spanish and English must be quickly fading here, as it is among indigenous languages.

The documentation and renewed use of many of these terms seems worthy of our attention, time, and passion as ethnobiologists. We certainly do not know what the future holds, but forecasts of both our immediate climatic and economic futures often seem bleak. During recent years, more than fourteen U.S. states and eight Mexican states suffered from extreme drought and heat, triggering federal governments to declare drought disaster area status for more than 2,200 counties and hundreds of *municipios* on the North American continent. It just may be that to adapt to accelerated climate change and economic instability, such reservoirs of ecological knowledge have renewed significance to all of us, not just for desert dwellers alone. Interest in such lexicons of land-based knowledge should not be dismissed as "retro" or "nostalgic." In a world where nonstationarity is bound to be the "new normal," we will need all the help we can get.

REFERENCES CITED

Cassidy, Frederic C. 1985. *Dictionary of American Regional English, Volume 1*. Belknap Press of Harvard University Press, Cambridge.

Cobos, Ruben. 2003. *A Dictionary of New Mexico and Southern Colorado Spanish*. Museum of New Mexico Press, Santa Fe.

Hall, Joan Huston. 2012. *Dictionary of American Regional English, Volume 5*. Belknap Press of Harvard University Press, Cambridge.

Harshberger, John W. 1896. The Purpose of Ethnobotany. *Botanical Gazette* 21:146–58.

Majnep, Ian Saen, Ralph N. H. Bulmer, and Christopher Healey. 1977. *Birds of My Kalam Country*. Oxford University Press and Aukland University Press, Auckland.

Said, Edward W. 1978. *Orientalism*, 25th Anniversary Edition 2003. Penguin, New York.

———. 1993. *Culture and Imperialism*. Knopf/Random House, New York.

Sobarzo, Horacio. 1966. *Vocabulario Sonorense*. Editorial Porrua, Mexico, D.F.

Veteto, James R. 2011. Apple-achia: The Most Diverse Foodshed in the United States, Canada and Northern Mexico. In *Place-Based Foods of Appalachia: From Rarity to Community Restoration and Market Recovery*, eds. James R. Veteto, Gary Paul Nabhan, Regina Fitzsimmons, Kanin Routson, and DeJa Walker, pp. 2–4. University of Arizona Southwest Center, Tucson.

5

SEARCHING FOR THE ANCESTRAL DIET

Did Mitochondrial Eve and Java Man
Feast on the Same Foods?

GARY PAUL NABHAN

T HESE DAYS, IT SEEMS AS THOUGH eating is done with more self-
consciousness than ever before in human history. Most everyone is trying out some "miracle diet," one whose champions claim will keep them
fit, prevent diseases, make them look sexy, and ensure greater longevity. Nearly
everywhere we look, there are TV doctors and nutritional-supplement hawkers,
cookbook divas and sports celebrities trying to hook us on a diet plan that they
claim will cure all that ails us. Many of these miracle diets are based on trendy
theories about what is nutritionally best for *the* human body in this day and age,
given our exposure to an unprecedented set of toxic additives and highly derived
compounds such as transfatty acids. While some of these dietary theories divide
all of humankind up into a few groups with different nutritional needs based on
a handful of blood types or metabolic inclinations, these diets are the exception
rather than the rule. Indeed, the vast majority of these miracle cures tend to
gloss over the ways in which our bodies and our genes and cultures are different
from each other. At present, my body may look like the funhouse mirror distor-
tion of your body, but once we both start eating the latest version of the optimal
diet, its proponents claim that we will look and function the same.

Curiously, some proposals for what the optimal diet may sidestep the peculiar challenges of staying healthy in the current techno-industrial world while encouraging us to delve into the past; these diets want us to remember our bodies' inherent capacities and our minds' predilections for foods that have been shaped over evolutionary time. As nutritional anthropologist Boyd Eaton and his colleagues have recommended for some two decades, we might choose what to eat by paying more attention to the "Paleolithic Legacy" written into our own blood and bones, nucleotides, and genes. By Eaton's reckoning, the very foods that our "first" hominid ancestors ate millions of years ago are still what our metabolisms are best suited to consume.

This evolutionary perspective was later incorporated into a landmark paper, "The Dawn of Darwinian Medicine," in which ecologist George Williams and psychiatrist Randolph Nesse blamed most present-day nutrition-related diseases on the fact that we no longer eat and exercise as we did during the period of human origins. We ignore at our peril, they claim, the fact that "human biology is designed for Stone Age conditions."

As one of Eaton's disciples, paleonutritionist Loren Cordain has written in his popular cookbook, *The Paleo Diet*, that this ancestral cuisine is "*the one and only diet*" that ideally fits our genetic makeup. Just 500 generations ago—and for 2.5 million years before that—*every human on Earth ate this way*. It is the diet to which all of us are ideally suited, and the lifetime nutrition plan that will normalize your weight and improve your health. I didn't design this diet—Nature did. *This diet has been built into your genes*" (emphasis added).

There are now millions of people around the planet who agree with Eaton, Williams, Nesse, and Cordain, and they are attempting to locate and eat the very foods they presume to be most fitting for their Stone Age–designed bodies. Every day, hundreds of thousands of people follow menu plans found in a set of books that collectively inform the "ancestral diet" movement. Most of these menus are based on the tenet that there is but one diet that fits the human metabolism and that is the diet most akin to what our ancestors ate during the earliest eras of human evolution.

However, going as far back as we can toward our common human origins gets many of us off the hook from identifying a single ethnic diet derived from that of our more recent ancestors. With so much ethnic intermarriage these days, many of us grew up exposed to the comfort foods of several different cultures rather than sticking with one cuisine that jived with some simplistic notion of pure-blooded ancestry. Statistically speaking, most of us are mutts rather than blue bloods, which makes it ever more difficult to select one ethnic diet that may speak most directly to our genes, as the diet to which our metabolism is hardwired. This dilemma is especially evident for the 7 million Americans who identify themselves as composites of two or more "races"—whatever a "race" is considered to be today.

Accordingly, it may be more comforting for most of us to eat our way farther back in time, loading our plates with the very same foods that our great-great-great-etc.-grandmother Lucy once served in her camp near the Olduvai Gorge thousands of generations ago. Hundreds of thousands of dieters have aimed to do just this, pledging to spend their budgets on calories, cures, luncheons, and literature that pursue a Paleolithic prescription, one that ignores the nuances of *ethnicity* in exchange for a sense of *antiquity*. They have become hooked on website versions of an ancient cuisine variously referred to as the Cave Man Diet, the NeanderThin™ formula, the Origins Diet, the Stone Age Menu, the Paleo Diet, or the Carnivore Connection.

Dieters following these plans are romantically attempting to reconstruct just what exactly it was that Eve, Lucy, or Java Man may have eaten around the campfire in the olden days, with a few food-preparation shortcuts thrown in. Unfortunately, if you would prefer recipes that are authentically grounded in knowledge derived from paleonutritional, zooarchaeological, and ethnobotanical studies, there are few signposts along the trail to assure that you are truly eating your way back to your roots.

Just what are the contemporary foods acceptable as ingredients in "ancestral" diets that have taken on the aura of lifetime nutrition plans? Can a descriptive reconstruction of past diets be used in a prescriptive manner for today's health problems? Ask a dozen nutritionists, physical anthropologists, and paleoethnobotanists, and you may get two dozen answers. Nevertheless, most proponents of ancestral diets do agree with some basic parameters, which I will try to distill from the writings of the more legitimate scholarly sources:

1. Our hunter-gatherer ancestors may have gained as much as 65 percent of their energy from the meat and bones of vertebrate animals, eating all parts of game and fish, while seldom eating eggs and never consuming milk products.

2. In addition, these foragers consumed in raw forms a variety of fresh fruits, flowers, leaves, and bulbs, many of which are rich in disease-preventing compounds that have since been bred out of most of our cultivated food crops.

3. Our ancestors rarely ate any quantity of cereals and certainly did not finely grind grains and other small seeds into fiber-depleted flours.

4. Neither did they consume quantities of sodium salts, although their diet was
    rich in calcium and potassium salts.

5. As nomads, our ancestors seldom camped in any single place long enough to
    let fruits or other carbohydrate-rich plant parts ferment into ethanol or acetic
    acid (vinegar), and they certainly were not involved in the distillation of highly
    potent alcoholic beverages.

Of all the paleonutritionists, perhaps Eaton himself takes the longest view
of dietary evolution, emphasizing that "the nutritional requirements of contemporary humans represent the *end-result* of dietary interactions between our
ancestral species and their environments extending back to the origins of life on
earth" (Eaton et al. 1996). Nonetheless, Eaton and his disciples have paid particular attention to how our hominid ancestors foraged in wild habitats around
2.5 million years ago. They claim that our ancestors' foraging patterns continued
essentially unchanged for hundreds of thousands of years, shifting substantively
only when farming and livestock raising began some 10,000 to 12,000 years ago.

But if we are to get down to brass tacks—by precisely defining in some detail
what our common ancestors ate that may still be available and palatable to
our modern sensibilities—we must gain some sense of whether there was ever
much place-specific variation in dietary preferences. In other words, what our
single common ancestor (nicknamed "mitochondrial Eve" by geneticists) ate
at one spot in ancient Africa over a lifespan of twenty or thirty years really is
not the issue; it is how much our other ancestors' diets in various regions devi-
ated from her food choices and whether the dietary variation among them had
much influence on the design of our bodies.

My hunch is that most characterizations of ancestral diets woefully simplify
such variation, ignoring incredible levels of dietary diversity that have guided
our evolution in space and in time. So instead of searching for *the* ancestral diet
only where the oldest human remains occur in the Rift Valley of Africa, let us
sail all the way over to Bali and Java, among the farthest places from Africa to
which protohumans strayed long, long ago. These are places that presently fall
within the nation of Indonesia, places that served as the haunts of a wild-food
forager who goes by the name of Java Man.

Java Man was named by Eugene DuBois, an adventurous scientist who first
made his way from the Netherlands to Java and Bali in 1880, when the islands
were still parts of the Dutch West Indies. DuBois knew that orangutans still

survived in the mountains of Java, and so he speculated that the uplands might also harbor skeletal remains of links between orangutan history and ours. He followed several fruitless leads until 1891, when he excavated an ancient skull that suggested he was finally on the right track. It was not until the next year, when he found a thigh bone and a few teeth, that he proclaimed he had indeed found *the* missing link.

In retrospect, it does appear that the skull belonged to one now notorious individual of *Homo erectus* (a.k.a. Java Man) who lived 800,000 to a million years ago. The femur and the teeth, unfortunately, have been determined to belong to two other species. At the time of its discovery, DuBois had asserted that he had uncovered the femur of a primate who had walked around Java in an upright position; that particular fossil is now regarded as the remains of a human individual who lived much later than Java Man. And the teeth . . . well . . . they do not belong to either Java Man or Mr. Upright; instead, they appear to have served a now-extinct orangutan species in his masticatory pursuits. Nonetheless, the highlands of the East Indies had proven to be fertile ground for studies of primate evolutionary history.

When I first traveled to the East Indies, I was constantly trying to determine what foods Java Man may have been exposed to that might still occur on the islands, and what might have changed in the meantime. Within hours of landing on Bali, I was able to travel by bus to a tropical beach where I could scan the eastern horizon for the coastal cliffs and volcanic summits of Java. I recognized that dramatic changes to these islands had occurred over the millennia—not merely affecting their shapes, sizes, and seasons, but their floras and faunas as well. As my hosts offered me a sampling of some flavors characteristic of Bali, I sensed I was tasting foods more akin to what DuBois' Java Man had eaten than to what mitochondrial Eve had ever tried in the Rift Valley of Africa—snake fruit, water apple, melinjo, and rambutan, as well as smoked reef fish wrapped in pandanus leaf.

As I experienced my first dawn within this tropical archipelago, someone pointed out to me the last of some flying foxes coming back to roost in the palm fronds above our heads. Larger than any bat I had ever seen in the Americas or in Africa, the presence of these unique animals made me realize that I— like Java Man millennia before me—had reached into a Southern Pacific realm where a distinctive biota had evolved. Java Man is among the best documented of our hominid ancestors who ranged well beyond the forests and savannas of

Africa. He must have foraged across a wide range of habitats, including those once associated with the Java land mass when it was connected to Eurasia by a land bridge, and neighboring Bali when it was emerging from the ocean. Did he eat the same things everywhere? How then did "his" diet change through time and space?

Sourcing a list of ingredients for a reconstructed ancestral diet to match that of Java Man will, of course, prove difficult. When Java Man's species, *Homo erectus*, took up residency on the land mass that survives today as Java, giant land tortoises, pangolins, and mastodons were among the many large mammals and reptiles that roamed the coastal lowlands. This megafauna was no doubt part of human diets, at least for a while, but on most islands where such giants formerly roamed, humans sooner or later had a hand in their demise. Today a third of the species known to be contemporaneous with Java Man are globally extinct; another third occur elsewhere, but not on Java nor Bali; and the final third (including flying foxes) persist, but in relatively low numbers on these islands.

It is this latter third that interests me, for it indicates that Java Man may have been familiar with some of the very same animals and plants present in today's East Indies. Surprisingly, some of the species are edible ones that I, like pioneering biogeographer Alfred Wallace a century before me, had previously sampled on other land masses. The plants may not grow today in the exact places that Java Man or even Wallace found them, but perhaps they are still within grasp.

Out of the bus window on Bali, I began to spot familiar trees that I had also seen grow wild in parts of Asia and even Europe. The presence of these ubiquitous plants did not mean that they had recently invaded Bali; to the contrary, in prehistoric times, most had naturally been dispersed to Bali, Java, and other islands close to the Asian mainland. This floral exchange with Asia, Europe, and even Africa was what fascinated Wallace, one of the earliest and greatest scientific explorers of the Balinese highlands. Yes, this was the same Wallace who fleshed out the theory of natural selection almost as if it were a malaria-induced hallucination, which came to him in his sick bed, while the more methodical Darwin labored away on the same theory for some thirty years.

Wallace was an astute observer of natural variation and similarity; he was quick to recognize that the berries and wildflowers he spotted in the mountains of Bali were of the same species that he had first learned in the hill country of England, or later, on his holidays to the Alps. Curiously, the edible species that Wallace found in the highlands and on other islands of Indonesia have implications for our understanding of the dietary breadth of early humans. Given the degree to which the northern islands of Indonesia have shared elements of their flora and fauna with Africa and Eurasia, it is not surprising that *Homo erectus*, and later, *Homo sapiens*, spread this far east, encouraged by some overlaps in floral and faunal choices that would have provided a modicum of dietary continuity. After all, any plum looks and tastes somewhat like any other plum, regardless of whether it grows on the banks of the Upper Nile or on the beaches of Bali.

But as I soon learned by venturing out by boat to islands south of Bali, the continuous chain of plant foods that I could find from Africa and Eurasia to Bali went no farther. While my botanical training helped me quickly pick out the few plants on Bali, which were shared with other places I had traveled to, it also prepared me to recognize the huge turnover in plant species that I would see between Bali and the islands reaching south to Australia.

It was Wallace who first grasped the full significance of this discontinuity, although he was not thinking of its significance to human diets. I decided to loosely retrace the trajectory that Wallace had taken more than a century ago, traveling to some islands with plants that look (and taste) very different from those on Bali. With friends, I chartered a sailboat and headed southward toward the islets of Lombagan and Penida, only ten miles off Bali's shores. If paleoanthropologist Mike Morewood is correct, Java Man and his kin could have now and then made such a journey, establishing satellite populations of *Homo erectus* on neighboring islands: "*Homo erectus* was not just a glorified chimp.... We now believe they made sea crossings to reach Flores and other Indonesian islands" (Morewood 1997).

What I could see on Lombagan, just as Wallace had seen on several islands south of Bali and Java, was how abruptly floras as well as faunas could change in a matter of just ten miles, and accordingly, how dramatically the human diet must have had to shift as it adapted to newly occupied habitats. Inevitably, there must have been significant turnovers in the composition of ancestral diets as our progenitors moved through space as well as through time. It was simply not possible for the historic dwellers of Bali and Lombagan to share much of the same diet, whether it was optimal or not. In fact, my visit to Lombagan and other outliers convinced me that very few foodstuffs could have been shared by ancestral peoples who contemporaneously ranged from Africa to what is now the East Indies, since few foods were even shared between folks on the coasts of Bali and Lombagan—people who lived near enough to each other to send smoke signals back and forth.

Here's why. Lombagan and the neighboring isle of Penida are decidedly arid, not tropically moist like most of Bali. Thorny, little-leafed acacias, sennas, mimosas, and straggly tree euphorbias line their coasts, while their inlands are far too small and dry to raise rice-like grasses at all. They are covered not by the lofty, massive canopies of dark green leaves found on Bali, but by dozens of grayish, groundhugging aromatic shrubs—ones loaded with terpines and other aromatic oils. Most of these plants have small, leathery, water-conserving leaves and oily berries that are miniscule in comparison to the hundreds of large tropical fruits I saw in the Balinese highlands.

When I went ashore on Lombagan, I felt caught between the glaring sun and the reflected heat rising from the rocks at my feet. Compared to the way I had nestled deep into Bali's cool, multilayered shade, on Lombagan I felt more exposed, more thirsty, and even prone to heat stroke. It made me visually hungry for Bali's almost excessive abundance of everything green and edible.

It also made me remember Wallace's Line, a tangible example of real geographic barriers that have made the food resources available in one place vastly different from those in another. Wallace had discovered this biogeographic border while venturing from Bali to Lombok, another island to the south that is even more eerily arid than Lombagan and Penida. Wallace's Line is an ancient barrier that effectively halts the further dispersal of plants and animals between the Eurasian and the Australian biogeographic provinces. Whereas Bali and Java share some 97 percent of their bird species, the island of Lombok—some two-dozen miles south—shares only 50 percent of its birds with Bali. When Wallace compared Lombok to Bali's lush, leafy, fruit-laden forests, he described its depauperate thornscrub as "a parched-up forest of prickles . . . the bushes were thorny, the creepers were thorny, the bamboos were even thorny . . . everything grew zigzag and jagged in an inextricable tangle" (Wallace in Van Oosterzee 1997).

An inextricable tangle: that is exactly what happens among the genes, foods, and habitats of plant, wildlife, or human populations when they become even somewhat isolated from other populations in different habitats nearby, whether they live on different islands or at various elevations on the same land mass. Wallace demonstrated that there are hugely different selection pressures placed on plants and animals inhabiting distinctive landscapes just a few miles apart.

Because such populations exist in some degree of reproductive isolation from one another, a second evolutionary mechanism favoring divergence, *genetic drift*, is also active. Genetic drift is the skewing of the frequencies of genes in populations that becomes more pronounced the smaller and more isolated those populations happen to be. Thus, once a gene for dwarfism is introduced to or emerges within an island species, it has a higher probability of spreading and becoming dominant in the small population than it would in a larger population.

And so, most islands have what we might call a skewed set of foods containing a skewed mix of dietary chemicals in them. They are considered to be skewed when compared to what colonizers might have been familiar with in mainland habitats, thanks to the natural selection that has occurred in those dissimilar environments and the larger role that genetic drift plays in small populations. Darwin and Wallace were the first biologists to describe the consequences of plant and animal species' divergence, which biologists now refer to as the process of *adaptive radiation*.

As an insightful observer of patterns in the natural world, Wallace, in particular, recognized the dramatic differences in the floral and faunal composition of islands hardly set apart from one another spatially. Compared to Wallace and other contemporary biogeographers, Darwin's vision was limited in a way that until recently was prevalent among students of evolution. While Darwin surmised evolutionary processes by making comparisons across the relatively short distances he traveled in the Galapagos, he still believed such processes could be observed only as their cumulative effects spanned great stretches of time or space: "It may be metaphorically said that natural selection is daily and hourly scrutinizing, throughout the world, natural variations; rejecting those that are bad, preserving and adding up all that are good; silently and insensibly working, *whenever and wherever opportunity offers* . . . [but] we see nothing of these slow changes in progress, until the hand of time has marked the lapse of ages" (Darwin 1859, emphasis added).

But what is now apparent—both from ecological studies of island plants and animals and from genetic studies of island peoples—is that many of the changes in genetic frequencies do not proceed as slowly as Darwin or even Wallace had assumed. As Harvard-trained science journalist Jonathan Weiner has so vividly elucidated in *The Beak of the Finch*, evolution is observable in "our time" and in "our species." Our bodies' responses to particular diets were not fully shaped 2.5 million years ago during the emergence of the genus *Homo*, nor were they fixed during the period when mitochondrial Eve roamed the savannas of East Africa between 150,000 and 200,000 years ago. They have been constantly reshaped by the peculiar range of food choices, environmental stresses, and diseases that humans face in every place in which they have spent considerable time; and, of course, our reactions continue to be reshaped by our present food choices and disease exposures as well.

Human populations like our own have encountered distinctive sets of food-stuffs and dietary chemicals that interact with our genes wherever we have lived. Perhaps that is the essence of why archaeologists and paleoecologists search through debris for bones of fish, fowl, and game, and for seeds, pits, and plant stems at places on Java or Bali where ancient human bones have been found. It is also why I spent time scanning the leftovers around far more recent human encampments on the beaches of Bali, Lomagan, and Penida. The more campfire rings I saw, the more I noticed what a motley mess of kitchen scraps humans tend to leave behind as trash wherever we camp. At one site, I saw plenty of firecracked clams and charred fish bones, but little else. At another camp a ways inland, there were rotting leaves and shoots of wild vegetables and a few tat-tered fragments of insect carapaces.

Each time that I have visited with archaeologists who sift through the soil at early hominid camps, they seem less certain that there is a single discernible dietary pattern evident among excavated sites. Some scholars have begun to doubt whether Java Man or other populations of *Homo* ever kept to a uniform diet; some even wonder if ancestral diets contained more or less the same pro-portions of fats, proteins, sugars, and fiber. Such a varied diet may simply have resulted because Java Man and his descendants craved different foods as they aged—or became pregnant, sick, or injured—or as they increased or decreased their physical activity in work or in play.

And yet, there may be a deeper reason why Java Man may not have main-tained any one dietary pattern, and accordingly, why there may not be an opti-mal diet for all humans, past and present. One explanation may be that we differ genetically from one another in small but significant ways that not only shape our food preferences, but also are reciprocally shaped by them. Human diversity—the genetic variation within our species—interacts with the diversity of edible plants and animals distributed across this planet in ways we are just beginning to understand. And while *diversity* of any kind is now celebrated in some social circles, its implications for how we eat have largely been ignored. Perhaps this is because of the many times in recent history that supposed physical or psychological differences among human populations have been used politically as a means to deprive one ethnic or "racial" group of opportunities that another "elite" group controls.

Now, however, with the unbelievably rich information suddenly made available to the public by the Human Genome Project, old scientific notions of races have lost much of their credibility. Of course, that does not mean that deep-seated cultural prejudices have suddenly vanished; like the ghosts of evolution mentioned in the previous chapter, they still haunt us whether we choose to see them or not. Nonetheless, it has become abundantly clear that differences in skin color are not well correlated with the way other human traits are distributed within our species. Moreover, eminent geneticists such as Harvard's Richard Lewontin have conclusively demonstrated that more human genetic variation is situated within "racial" or ethnic populations than between these populations. By various calculations, differences between ethnic populations account for only 7 to 15 percent of our species' total heterogeneity.

And yet, much of the popular science literature on human genetics that I read continues to be full of simplistic truisms. One of those is that *99.9 percent of the human genome is shared by each and every one of us and all of our ancestors*, regardless of how we self-identify our racial heritage. If I took this new cliché at face value, I would have to pretend that all significant genetic characteristics of our species became "fixed" quite a long time ago, with few adaptive variations on any evolutionary theme persisting in the human genome. In other words, I would have to assume that the extant genetic variation found in humans living today is about the same as that which could be found among the range of human populations living 100 generations ago. For that matter, some schools assume it may be on the same order as what we may find in other primates—as if there have been no new selective pressures on us for millions of years. If that were true, our contemporary dietary needs for a certain mix of macronutrients should hardly differ from those of our hominid ancestors.

The trouble with this argument is that vertebrate zoologists have found considerable variation in diet and genes even among primate populations of the same species living less than one hundred miles away from one another. There is also considerable genetic variation extant among all of us contemporary humans, and we survive and thrive upon a bewildering diversity of foods. So just how similar are our genetically determined needs for nutritional resources? Are they similar enough that we should all pattern our current diets after those of our common ancestors?

In the pages of the *New York Times Magazine* in 2002, Dr. Sally Satel—a physician with a penchant for delving into the philosophical dimensions of biomedical practice—tried to get a grip on the degree to which genetic determinism should guide us in accepting one-size-fits-all medical and nutritional recommendations:

> What does it really mean to say that 99.9 percent of our content is the same? In practical terms it means that the DNA in any two people will differ in one out of every 1,000 nucleotides, the building blocks of individual genes. With more than three billion nucleotides in the human genome, about 3 million nucleotides will differ among individuals. This is hardly a small change; after all, mutation of a single one can cause the gene within which it is embedded to produce an altered protein or enzyme. It may seem counterintuitive, but the .01 percent of human genetic variation is a medically meaningful fact (Satel 2002).

What does that all mean with respect to our diets? It is doubtful that any set of recipes could be custom-made to meet *all of our* physiological requirements, given how much diversity there is among us. At best, a uniform dietary regimen could try to strike a balance of macronutrients catering to the 2,997,000 nucleotides that may have not changed much since our human origins, an approach that still glosses over our varying needs for micronutrients. At the same time, the mongrelized recipes in the ancestral-diet literature largely ignore the 3 million nucleotides that mark the divergence of all humans currently living from our common female ancestor, mitochondrial Eve, who lived 150,000 to 200,000 years ago. Since her lifetime, many millions of nucleotides have contributed to the diversity found among all humans past and present, 3 million of which continue to be expressed in the physical differences among those living today. Regardless of the intricate branching and intermixing of the human family into the great genetic diversity we see within our species, the recipes found in the ancestral-diet movement focus on the presumed *taproot* of our species, not on the branches. And it is the branches, not the roots, that may indicate just how much nutritional needs of individuals and populations may vary instead of fitting a single pattern.

That single pattern—as the proponents of an optimal Stone Age diet claim in their cookbooks—is that hunter-gatherers nearly always consumed more animal foods than plant foods. Paleonutritionists insist that if you averaged it out over hundreds of thousands of years, the animal to plant ratio of energy intake would tip the balance with two-thirds meat to one-third veggies.

Ironically, when some of these proponents of Stone Age diets publish more scholarly treatises in technical journals, they have belatedly acknowledged how difficult it is to be precise about such ratios for most hunter-gatherer cultures, given the extreme variation that has been found among individuals, families, seasons, years, and habitats. When several of these scholars looked in detail at 229 hunter-gatherer societies, one in seven of these foraging cultures clearly consumed more plants than animal foods. In the *American Journal of Clinical Nutrition* in 2000, Loren Cordain and his colleagues concluded that "our data clearly indicate that there was no single diet that represented all hunter-gatherer societies."

Yes, you heard Cordain's name before, just a few pages ago. Remember what he stated in his popular 2002 cookbook: "The Paleo Diet is *the one and only diet* that ideally fits our genetic makeup. Just 500 generations ago—and for 2.5 million years before that—*every human on Earth ate this way.*"

When I pointed out this discrepancy to him over the phone, Cordain defended this statement by arguing that there were indeed strong commonalities in the trends of macronutrient composition of diets documented among various hunter-gatherer societies. He did, however, agree with me that the micronutrient and secondary compound composition of hunter-gatherer diets varied greatly from landscape to landscape and season to season.

Micronutrients and other, secondary dietary chemicals are the spices of life that vary from place to place, time to time, and in ways that make the study of human diets so fascinating. Of course, wild plants and animals are astonishingly diverse in the chemicals that they contain, and these chemicals can both benefit *and* imperil our health. Many of the more toxic as well as the more protective chemicals that were formerly consumed routinely in wild-food diets around the world have been consciously and unconsciously eliminated by modern crop and livestock breeding, which is ever striving for more palatable, uniform products. But this winnowing away of the chemical diversity found in wild plants and animals had not yet happened when Java Man and our direct ancestors first spread across the face of the Earth. Instead, our predecessors were fully exposed to the astonishing range of plant and animal chemicals found in various habitats. They learned what to forage (as well as what to avoid) from sea level to more than 10,000 feet in elevation on several continents. Each landscape that they entered harbored additional species, each with a different mix of protective chemicals and attractive nutrients.

As an ethnobotanist, I have helped document more than 350 species of plants historically used as food in the Sonoran Desert, a landscape not particularly known for high levels of diversity. On a global scale, however, some 30,000 wild plant species have been documented to have been prehistorically or historically consumed by various ethnic populations. Those plants are not merely sources of the proteins, sugars, and fats that Cordain and his colleagues recorded to use in their reconstruction of dietary ratios for an optimal diet. They are also arsenals of the potent chemicals that botanists call *secondary compounds*, plant chemicals that seem to serve no direct metabolic purpose in photosynthesis, growth, and reproduction. Instead, these chemicals—which comprise unique mixtures in different species and even in different populations of the same species—protect plants against environmental stresses such as drought, freezes, and fires, and from interspecific stresses such as competition, disease, predation, or herbivory.

When consumed by humans, these secondary compounds also give our plant foods their flavors and fragrances, their capacity to poison us or to kill us, their ability to protect against carcinogens or microbes, and their utility as aphrodisiacs or as fertility suppressants. Moreover, it has recently become clear that some chemicals in wild foods are potent enough to cause our own genes to mutate. Fatimah Linda Collier Jackson, the African American nutritional anthropologist mentioned earlier, has pondered the significance of this little-appreciated fact: that human genetic mutations can be induced by some wild herbs, legumes, and tubers that various human cultures have consumed since time immemorial.

As Jackson has elegantly documented, such plants' secondary compounds—especially those called *allelochemicals* for their capacity to reduce herbivory from visiting animals and competition from neighboring plants—can influence human genetic variation in myriad ways. Science writer Bruce Grierson has noted that "dietary chemicals change the expression of one's genes and even the genome itself" (Grierson 2003). He reminds us that not all dietary chemicals get metabolized as calories to fuel our work and play; some of them are transformed to ligands and attach to proteins, forming complex molecules that literally turn on and off the expression of certain genes. As a specific example, Grierson explains that a secondary chemical in soybeans known as genistein binds itself to estrogen receptors and regulates the expression of genes affecting hormonal fluxes. And yet, the consumption of genistein does not affect every woman's estrogen cycle in the same manner, since individuals from different ethnic populations carry different estrogen receptors that respond to genistein and other ligands to varying degrees. In short, there are complex feedback loops between preexisting genetic variability and the influence of secondary chemicals on gene expression and mutation.

With the accumulation of such evidence over the last decade or so, it has become increasingly clear that dietary chemicals are major driving forces for genetic expression, mutation, and selection within our species, not merely a sideshow. Jackson has boldly suggested that these secondary compounds have literally fostered human diversity through their inclusion in traditional diets over millennia.

Let us try to fathom how pervasive the influence of these chemicals in plant foods might be—and why numerous secondary compounds, not just macro-nutrients—have influenced the shapes of human diets and genetic variation through time. Some phytochemists have hazarded the guess that 40,000 to 50,000 secondary compounds have already been described from the 270,000 named plant species, and yet, not even a fraction of the 30,000 edible plant species have been subjects of substantive laboratory analyses. The chemists therefore concede that they have barely scratched the surface in characterizing the structure of these compounds, let alone in understanding their ecological function, their role in nutrition, or their mutagenic capacity (that is, their ability to induce genetic changes).

Nevertheless, there are some things we do know. Just one set of secondary compounds, the bitter-tasting alkaloids, can be found in one out of every five plant species, or some 54,000 of the currently identified species altogether. These species are not uniformly distributed around the planet; some landscapes, such as dry tropical forests, and some families, such as the nightshades (including tomatoes, potatoes, chile peppers, and eggplants), are more loaded with alkaloid-bearing species than others.

Many of the same secondary compounds can be mutagenic at one level of habitual ingestion, carcinogenic at another, and disease preventative at still another. As many Latin Americans are well aware, a culinary herb like epazote (*Dysphania ambrosiodes*, a relative of lamb's-quarters) can be a simple flavoring in a pot of beans, a reducer of flatulence if liberally added to the same beans, or an accidental abortifacient if a pregnant woman happens to ingest too much of the herb. Some wild populations of epazote are intentionally sought out and used by *curandera* herbalists to induce abortions in their human patients or in livestock.

Such properties are not restricted to a peculiar set of medicinal and culinary herbs. They are also found in fruits that are widely distributed around the world; particular plum populations may have their own potent mix of chemicals. Collectively, various wild plums contain as many as 150 known secondary compounds, but their concentrations vary among species and their populations. Some sixty-seven of the secondary compounds identified in edible plums have been found to be bioactive, that is, capable of stimulating a variety of metabolic consequences that affect our health. All sixty-seven compounds may be found in a particular kind of wild plum, but the different beach plums that cover the shores of Bali, Java, Hawaii, and Africa vary greatly in their concentrations of these compounds.

Throw the myriad kinds of plums on Earth into the same plum pudding, observe the effects as we feed it to representatives of the thousands of cultures found around the planet, and we have what ecologists call biocomplexity. Now multiply that complexity by the 30,000 edible plant species on Earth, plus a few thousand edible animal species. It becomes exceedingly plausible that prehistoric Java Man was exposed to a vastly different set of compounds than were his contemporaries in Africa's Rift Valley. Java Man's species, *Homo erectus*, never covered even a fraction of the ground or achieved a fraction of the population size associated with our more recent species of *Homo sapiens*, and yet the evolutionary trajectory of *Homo erectus* was probably set by a dramatically different brew of secondary compounds than we consume today.

These secondary compounds likely fostered the considerable genetic variation in humans and in primates that I alluded to earlier. Although we may never be able to quantitatively reconstruct just how much human genetic diversity has been lost through time, it is probable that there was far more genetic differentiation *between* the populations of our ancestors than there is today. If genetic studies of chimpanzee populations are any indication, there was also greater variability within each breeding population. Curiously, the chimps within one breeding population on a hillside in Africa express twice as much variability in their mitochondrial DNA than do all of the 6 billion humans currently living around the Earth.

By the time I left Bali, I became more aware of just how heterogeneous both our food choices and our own human populations once were, compared to what we experience today. Despite the many plant and animal extinctions that have occurred within this last century, there remain tens of thousands of edible species within our reach, but most of us have narrowed our diets down to a few hundred domesticated species, and most of them have had their potent chemicals culled out by crop breeders. Since colonizing cultures began the spread of agriculture and the conversion of diverse wild landscapes, most human diets have become far more homogeneous than ever before in our species' history. We can only speculate how much more genetically narrow our species has become over the same time period of the last 12,000 years. When prehistoric human populations were widely scattered and exposed to so many distinct plant chemicals, perhaps the variation between such populations was on the order of two or three out of every six genes in the cumulative human genome. Without a doubt, there were greater genetic differences (as well as dietary differences) than we see among contemporary human populations, which only vary from one another in one out of every six genes.

During the Holocene, the consequences of livestock and crop domestication began to dramatically shape some human physiological responses as people adapted to new sets of foods. However, the emergence of agriculture 10,000 to 12,000 years ago was not the only period of time when dietary changes caused shifts in human genetic variation. As Beverly Strassman and her colleagues have concluded, "The forces of evolution (natural selection, gene flow, mutation, and drift) continue to act on human populations and have demonstrably altered allelic frequencies since the origins of agriculture. The best documentation of this is for malaria resistance and lactose intolerance" (Strassman and Duarte 1999).

Strassman further cautions against the view that our nutritional needs and optimal diet were "set" in the Paleolithic, for this view "ignores the fact that human evolution has been mosaic in form; different components of our biology evolved at different stages and rates. Our analysis of the transition to agriculture [from wild foraging] uncovered no empirical evidence that it was a singular watershed between adaptation and maladaptation."

The coevolutionary dance between our genes and our foods began long before the first farmers and herdsmen and continues to this day. The list of gene-food interactions in the introduction (see Table 5.1) include genes that have been documented for some ethnic populations, but not others, making the notion of a single optimal diet for all of humankind an absurdity. The selection for these genes has occurred much more rapidly than the prophets of the Paleolithic prescription initially acknowledged. And that is why *evolutionary gastronomy* celebrates the influence of ethnic cuisines on both natural and cultural evolution *in our time*, as it does in the Paleolithic.

TABLE 5.1. A Registry of Gene-Food Interactions Associated with the Human Family Tree

DISORDER/ ADAPTATION	GENE MAP LOCUS	DEMOGRAPHIC DATA	FOOD/DRUG/ BEVERAGE TRIGGER
Alcoholism	Many, incl. chrs. 4p, 4q22, 17q21, 11q23, 11p15, 22q11	Broad; (Native) America, Asia, Australia	Fermented grains and tubers
Alcohol dehydrogenase (ADH2)	Chr. 4q22, 11s	Broad; (Native) America, Asia, Australia	Fermented grains and tubers
Aldehyde dehydrogenase variant (ALDH1Aa)	Chr. 9q21	Broad; (Native) America, Asia, Australia	Fermented grains and tubers
Aldehyde dehydrogenase variant (ALDH2)	Chr. 12q24	Japan, China, South America	Fermented grains and tubers
Amotrophic lateral sclerosis–Parkinsonia-dementia (ALS-PD)	Chr. 17a21.1	Guam, Kii peninsula of Japan	Cycad seeds; flying foxes, which ingest cycad seeds
Apolipoprotein A	Chr. 11q23	Europe and elsewhere	Vegetable and animal fats
Apolipoprotein B	Chr. 2p24	Europe and elsewhere	Vegetable and animal fats
Apolipoprotein E (APOE2)	Chr. 19q13	Broad; esp. Mediterranean	Vegetable and animal fats
Celiac disease (gluten sensitivity)	Chr. 6p21	Europe, North America	Gluten from wheat, rye, barley
Cytochrome P450 (coumarin 7-hydroxylase)	Chr. 19q13	Many variants; Central Asia, China	Coumarin in herbs, key vegetables, fruits
Diabetes mellitus type 2 (NIDDM)	Many, incl. chrs. 2q32, 11q12, 13q24, 17q25, 20q	Broad, many variants; (Native) America, Australia, Polynesia	Fast-release, fiber-depleted foods
Disaccharide intolerance (sucrose-isomaltose malabsorption)	Chrs. 3q22–q26	Native America, incl. Inuit (Eskimo), Greenland, Siberia	Milk, sucrose, maltose in high concentrations or quantities
Fanconi-Bikel syndrome	Chr. 3q26	Scattered; Swiss Alps, Japan	Galactose sugars
Fructose intolerance	Chr. 9q	British Isles	Fruits
Glucose-6-phosphate dehydrogenase (G6PD, favism)	Chr. Xq28	Mediterranean	Fava beans, anti-malarial drugs, some herbs

continued

TABLE 5.1. *continued*

DISORDER/ ADAPTATION	GENE MAP LOCUS	DEMOGRAPHIC DATA	FOOD/DRUG/ BEVERAGE TRIGGER
Homocysteinemia	Several, incl. chr. 21q22	Broad; Europe, America	Vitamin B12
Homocystinura	Chrs. 21q22, 5p15	Northern Europe, British Isles	Lack of folic acid from greens, beans
Hypercholestrolemia	Chr. 2p24	Northern Europe, British Isles, America	Fast-release, fiber-depleted foods
Insulin resistance	Chr. 11p15	Broad, many variants; (Native) America, Australia, Africa	Fast-release, fiber-depleted foods
Lactose intolerance	Chr. 2q21	Lactase persistence in Northern Europe, Arabia, parts of Africa; deficiency everywhere else	Milk products
Phenylthiocarbamide tasting (PTC tasting/ PROP tasting)	Chr. 5p15	Broad, many variants	Chiles, quinine, certain drugs and bitter herbs
Serum albumin A	Chr. 4q11, chr. 7	Many variants; Eti Turks and others in central Asia, Athapaskan and Uto-Aztecan in the Americas	Coumarin-containing plants and drugs, incl. sage, warfarin
Transferrin	Chr. 3q21	Africa, esp. Zimbabwe	Diets deficient in vitamin C and iron

SOURCE: V. McKusick, Online Mendelian Inheritance in Man database, www.ncbi.nlm.nih.gov/omim.

Legend: *Column 1* lists the common name for a particular medical condition, with its more precise technical or other abbreviation in parentheses; although most physicians consider these conditions to be disorders, some may be place- or diet-specific adaptations to diseases or stresses.

Column 2 cites the gene map loci that confer the condition, noting both the chromosome(s)—chr. or chrs.—and the general or specific location of the gene(s) presumed to be involved. For instance, Aldehyde dehydrogenase variant 1Aa is located on chromosome 9 and the q21 locus. See the OMIM database for more detail, as well as for the published sources that first related these loci to particular medical conditions.

Column 3 indicates, where possible, the human populations with particular geographic distributions that tend to have higher frequencies of individuals carrying the gene(s) or any variants. (Native) America refers to American Indians, Inuit, and related populations, where America refers to a condition also shared with Euro, African, and Asian Americans.

Column 4 lists some but not all of the foods and drugs (or deficiencies of same) that interact with the gene(s) in ways that alter the health status of the carrier individual. Note that in nearly all cases, a single gene in and of itself does not, for example, "cause" alcoholism. Most of these conditions are influenced by multiple genes and by environmental, cultural, and developmental conditions.

REFERENCES CITED

Cordain, L. 2002. *The Paleo Diet*. New York: John Wiley and Sons.

Cordain, L., J. C. Brand-Miller, S. B. Eaton, N. Mann, S. H. A. Holt, and J. D. Speth. 2000. Plant-animal subsistence ratios and macronutrient energy estimations in worldwide hunter-gatherer diets. *American Journal of Clinical Nutrition* 71:682–692.

D'Adamo, P. J., and C. Whitney. 2002. *Eat right for your type*. New York: Riverside Books.

Darwin, C. 1859. *The origin of species by means of natural selection*. Chicago: Encyclopedia Brittanica (reprint 1990).

Eaton, S. B., and M. Konner. 1985. Paleolithic nutrition: A consideration of its nature and current implications. *New England Journal of Medicine* 312:283–289.

Eaton, S. B., M. Shostak, and M. Konner. 1988. *The Paleolithic prescription*. New York: Harper and Row.

Eaton, S. B., S. B. Eaton III, M. J. Konner, and M. Shostak. 1996. An evolutionary perspective enhances understanding of human nutritional requirements. *Journal of Nutrition* 126:1732–1740.

Ehrlich, P. R. 2000. *Human natures: Genes, cultures, and the human prospect*. Washington, DC: Island Press.

Grierson, B. 2003. What your genes want you to eat. *New York Times Magazine*, May 4, 77–79.

Jackson, F. L. C. 1991. Secondary compounds in plants (allelochemicals) as promoters of human biological variability. *Annual Review of Anthropology* 20:505–546.

Lewontin, R. C. 1998. *Human diversity*. New York: Scientific American Library.

———. 2004. *The triple helix: Gene, organism and environment*. Cambridge: Harvard University Press.

Morewood, M. 1997. Quoted in P. Van Oosterzee, *Where worlds collide: The Wallace line*. Ithaca: Cornell University Press.

Olson, S. 2002. *Mapping human history: Discovering the past through our genes*. Boston: Houghton-Mifflin.

Reaven, G., T. K. Strom, and B. Fox. 2001. *Syndrome X: The silent killer*. New York: Simon and Schuster.

Satel, S. 2002. I am a racially profiling doctor. *New York Times Magazine*, April 13, 56–60.

Sears, B. 1999. *The Zone Diet*. New York: Harper-Perennial.

Simopoulous, A. P., and J. Robinson. 1999. *The Omega Diet*. New York: Harper-Perennial.

Somer, E. 2002. *The Origins Diet*. New York: Owl Books / Henry Holt.

Strassman, B. I., and R. I. M. Duarte. 1999. Human evolution and disease: Putting the Stone Age in perspective. In *Evolution in health and disease*, ed. S. C. Sterns, 91–101. New York: Oxford University Press.

Wallace, A. Quoted in P. Van Oosterzee, *Where worlds collide: The Wallace line*. Ithaca: Cornell University Press.

Weiner, J. 1994. *The beak of the finch: A story of evolution in our time*. New York: Alfred Knopf.

Williams, G. C., and R. M. Nesse. 1991. The dawn of Darwinian medicine. *The Quarterly Review of Biology* 66 (1): 1–81.

6

MICROBIAL ETHNOBIOLOGY AND THE LOSS OF DISTINCTIVE FOOD CULTURES

GARY PAUL NABHAN

WHILE ATTENDING A CONFERENCE on the conservation of biological diversity a few years back, a senior microbiologist noticed that my name tag identified me as an ethnobiologist.

"I assume that you study land races of cultivated plants or rare breeds of livestock, am I correct?"

"Yes, at least sometimes," I answered timidly. "And their relationships with particular cultures in specific places," I added as a meager clarification.

"Well, that's a pity, because the microbial world is where the *real* biodiversity lies. . . . And I don't think folk cultures have much to say about microbes, do they? Since they can't see them, they don't name them, do they?"

The assumption was that microbiology was one realm where Western science clearly had a leg up on so-called indigenous science. Its technological tools, from scanning electron microscopes to rDNA sequencers, suggest that there are at least 4×10^{30} microscopic prokaryotic cells on the face of the earth. Gene banks have already begun to cultivate some 30,000 distinctive taxa of bacteria and archaea (Weinbauer and Rassoulzadegan 2007), roughly the same

Originally published as "Ethnobiology for a Diverse World: Microbial Ethnobiology and the Loss of Distinctive Food Cultures," *Journal of Ethnobiology* 30.2 (Fall/Winter 2010): 181–3. Reprinted with permission of *Journal of Ethnobiology*.

order of magnitude as the total number of cultivated plant species on earth (est. 35,000 vascular plant species, including landscape plants, see Khoshbackht and Hammer 2008). In a single water sample taken from the Sargasso Sea, a recent "shotgun approach" to microbial gene sequencing newly identified 1.2 million genes and 1,800 species (Venter et al. 2004).

But the microbiologist's assumption disregarded the fact that most traditional cooks, vintners, picklers, brewers, bakers, and cheese-makers around the world differentiate by taste, smell, sight, and other evidence the minute differences that exist among tens of thousands of microbially fermented food products. Fungi, molds, yeasts, and bacteria have been selected and domesticated to assist in the fermentation of human foods. In the case of Korean kimchis, hundreds of species of *Lactobacillus, Leueconostoc, Sachromyces* and *Streptococcus* may be involved in giving a particular pickled vegetable its distinctive signature of flavors and fragrances (Scott and Sullivan 2008). While traditional managers of fermentation do not necessarily name the microorganisms themselves, they do name and describe in considerable detail the preparation and organoleptic qualities of the derived fermented food products (Katz 2003).

Since the earliest collaborations of ethnobiologists with archaeologists, nutritionists, and geneticists, pioneering ethnobotanists such as Robert Braidwood and Jonathan Sauer have attempted to link plant domestication and the use of pottery vessels with the fermentation of grains into alcoholic beverages (Kavanagh 1994). More recently, ethnobiologists Robert Bye, Jr., Daniel Zizumbo-Villareal, Will McLatchey, among others, have advanced ethnobiological methods to explore prehistoric, historic, and contemporary fermented and distilled beverages in relation to the human and microbial cultures that have nurtured them. It has now been confirmed by collaborations of archaeologists, chemists, and ethnobiologists that fermented beverages were consumed in China as early as 9,000 years ago (McGovern et al. 2004).

Few scientists have explicitly specialized in microbial ethnobiology; nevertheless, the emergence of such a sub-discipline seems to be looming before us. Sandor Katz's (2003) astonishingly rich "ethnography of live-culture foods" from around the world offers young ethnobiologists a point of departure for learning more about these foods among a variety of traditional cultures, as does Ken Albala's book (2010), *The Lost Art of Real Cooking*, and his Cult of Pre-Pasteurian Preservation recently featured on Facebook. Fermented, smoked, and cured foods were featured at the 2010 Oxford Symposium on Food and Cookery. It may be arriving just in time, for microbiologists are now deeply concerned with the real and presumed losses of microbial diversity (Staley 1997; Weinbauer and Rassoulzadegan 2007). Famed food writer Harold McGee (2004)—who takes a science-based approach to food chemistry and preparation—has expressed concern that more than a dozen different microbial taxa, once involved in the fermentation of yoghurt-like milk cultures, may have already disappeared. The reasons for their demise are varied, including the indiscriminate use of antibiotics, anti-bacterial soaps, the narrow temperature range of keeping fermented foods under refrigeration, and the rise of super-sterile foods. This concern has been validated by Spanish microbiologist José Garabal (2007:2):

> Although protection of the world's biodiversity is currently a topic of particular concern, little attention has been given to the preservation of microorganisms and how this is related to the survival of traditional or autochthonous products ... there is increasing risk of loss of diversity in raw-milk microbiota and [as a result] the quality of traditional fermented products is seriously threatened.

Ironically, Ethiopia, one of the poorest countries in the world, appears to be a leader in ethnobiological conservation of such fermented food cultures. On a recent visit to Addis Ababa, I learned that the National Institute of Biodiversity Conservation currently maintains more than 400 microbial cultures collected from peasant kitchens across the country (Nabhan 2008). Nevertheless, the institute has struggled to maintain funding for its microbial conservation efforts, as have many seed banks in the Third World.

Perhaps the most worrisome warning about the potential loss of microbial diversity comes not from the Sargasso Sea or an Ethiopian kitchen, but from a comparison of gut microbiota of children from urbanized parts of Europe and a remote rural village in Burkina Faso, Africa. Due to a number of factors, including the excessive use of antibiotics in Europe, certain elements of gut microbiota commonly found in children living in rural communities of Africa were completely lacking in samples from children living in Europe (DeFilippo et al. 2010). It may be that the loss of beneficial microbes poses a larger health risk than the presence of pathogenic ones. (Miller 2013; Velasquez-Manoff 2012). While such reports must be cautiously evaluated, it is evident that ethnobiologists can play key roles in helping future interdisciplinary teams of scientists contextualize how human cultural and technological change may be affecting our "food cultures"—those in our fermenting vats, sourdough starters, vinegar mothers, and our very own guts.

REFERENCES CITED

Albala, Ken. 2010. *The Lost Art of Real Cooking*. Penguin Group, New York.

DeFilippo, C., D. Cavalieri, M. Di Paola, M. Ramazzotti, J.B. Poullet, S. Massart, S. Collini, G. Pieraccini, and P. Lionetti. 2010. Impact of diet in shaping gut microbiota revealed by a comparative study in children from Europe and rural Africa. *Proceedings of the National Academy of Sciences* 107(33):14691–96.

Garabal, J.I. 2007. Biodiversity and the survival of autochthonous fermented products. *International Microbiology* 10:1–13.

Katz, S. 2003. *Wild Fermentation: The Flavor, Nutrition and Craft of Live-Culture Foods*. Chelsea Green Publishing, White River Junction, VT.

Kavanagh, T.W. 1994. Archaeological parameters for the beginnings of beer. Brewing Techniques Magazine, September-October. Available at: www.brewingtechniques.com/library/backissues/issue2.5/kavanagh.html (Verified October 7, 2010).

Khoshbakht, K. and K. Hammer. 2008. How many plant species are cultivated? *Genetic Resources and Crop Evolution* 55(7):925–28.

McGee, H. 2004. *On Food and Cooking*. Scribner, New York.

McGovern, P.E., J. Zhang, J. Tang, Z. Zhang, G.R. Hall, R.A. Moreau, A. Nuñez, E.D. Butrym, M.P. Richards, C. Wang, G. Cheng, Z. Zhao, and C. Wang. 2004. Fermented beverages of pre- and proto-historic China. *Proceedings of the National Academy of Sciences* 101(51):17593–98.

Miller, D. 2013. *Farmacology*. William Morrow and Company, New York.

Nabhan, G.P. 2008. Of moulds and men. *Resurgence* 250: 68–69.

Scott, R. and W.C. Sullivan. 2008. Ecology of fermented foods. *Human Ecology Review* 15(1):25–29.

Staley, J.T. 1997. Biodiversity: Are microbial species threatened? *Current Opinion in Biotechnology* 8(3):340–45.

Velasquez-Manoff, M. 2012. *An Epidemic of Absence*. Scribner, New York.

Venter, J.C., K. Remington, J.F. Heidelberg, A.L. Halpern, D. Rusch, J.A. Eisen, D. Wu, I. Paulsen, K.E. Nelson, W. Nelson, D.E. Fouts, S. Levy, A.H. Knap, M.W. Lomas, K. Nealson, O. White, J. Peterson, J. Hoffman, R. Parsons, H. Baden-Tillson, C. Pfannkoch, Y.H. Rogers, and H.O. Smith. 2004. Environmental genome shotgun sequencing of the Sargasso Sea. *Science* 304: 66–74.

Weinbauer, M.G. and F. Rassoulzadegan. 2007. Extinction of microbes: evidence and potential consequences. *Endangered Species Research* 3:205–15.

7

ETHNOPHENOLOGY AND CLIMATE CHANGE

GARY PAUL NABHAN

T HE FIRST SEED that we planted in the spring was the sunflower seed,"
Buffalo Bird Woman explained to Gilbert Wilson (Wilson 1917:16),
recalling her early attempts at gardening when she was 18 years of age,
around 1857. She then noted how she and her contemporaries decided when it
was time to plant their floodplain fields along the Missouri River in central-
western North Dakota:

> Ice breaks on the Missouri about the first week in April; and we planted sun-
> flower seed as soon after as the soil could be worked. Our native name for the
> lunar month that corresponds most nearly to April, is Mapí-ócē-mídi, or Sun-
> flower-planting-moon (Wilson 1917:16).

So begins one of the earliest American accounts of *ethnophenology*, the cultural perception of the timing of recurrent natural history events, in this case,
for their use in managing horticultural crops. It was recorded between 1906
and 1916 when Buffalo Bird Woman—known to her Hidatsa kinsmen as

Originally published as "Perspectives in Ethnobiology: Ethnophenology and Climate
Change," *Journal of Ethnobiology* 30.1 (Spring/Summer 2010): 1–4. Reprinted with permission
of *Journal of Ethnobiology*.

Maxidiwiac—was between sixty-seven and seventy-seven years of age. But Gilbert Wilson had asked her to reconstruct "an ethnographic present" that occurred just before the Civil War, when she was living at Like-a-Fishhook Village near old Fort Berthold:

> I take Maxidiwiac (Buffalo Bird Woman) as the typical informant [*sic*]. I take her account of a single year's work, in the main, when she was about eighteen years of age. I follow the seasons with her, getting her always to add all she can or will of personal experiences (Wilson 1917:xix).

Although there were risks in constructing an idealized ethnographic present for the Hidatsa through one elderly woman's recollections half a century later, this may have allowed Buffalo Bird Woman to spatially and temporally situate her experiences with some precision. Let us listen to what she had to say to Reverend Wilson about when the seeds of corn should be planted in mounds:

> Corn planting began the second month after the sunflower-seed was planted, that is in May; and it lasted a month. . . . We knew when corn planting time came by observing the leaves of wild gooseberry bushes. This bush is the first of the woods to leaf in the spring. Old women of the village were going into the woods daily to gather fire wood; and when they saw that the wild gooseberry bushes were almost in full leaf, they said, 'It is time for you to begin planting corn!' (Wilson 1917:22).

If we compare the phenological indicators that Buffalo Bird Woman used to prompt the timing of planting for sunflowers and maize, some complexities are revealed. Sunflower planting was triggered by a hydrological event—the first big breakup of ice on the river, as long as it was in the fourth lunar month of the year—while corn planting was triggered by a biological event, the new vegetative growth on a conspicuous wild perennial food plant. Both, of course, were indirect effects of meteorological (temperature and moisture) trends occurring over the previous months.

We could assume that the triggers for these planting activities are merely the easiest observable phenomena during that period of the year, but rather imperfect correlations with the arrival of optimal planting conditions. In other words, scholars might take the cynical view that such correlations are quaint almanac-like indicators of seasonality, but of little scientific interest. That view might be underestimating the depth of traditional ecological knowledge embedded in such indicators, as well as the potential utility of such place- and time-specific signposts for understanding climate change.

One spring, while involving Seri (Comcaac) para-ecologists and Northern Arizona University graduate students in a desert tortoise survey on the coast of the Sea of Cortés, I overheard an interesting conversation. Humberto Romero Morales, one of the most fieldworthy para-ecologists and hunting guides, was explaining to the American students that the earliest migratory green sea turtles would soon be arriving in the shallow coastal waters below the desert ridges where the desert tortoises had already begun to emerge. How, the students asked, did he know that the time for this migration was soon to begin?

"Well," he replied, "we use the flowering of the ocotillos as a sign . . ."

One student giggled and rolled his eyes. "You mean the sea turtles can see the flowering of desert plants up here?" the student asked.

Humberto shook his head, holding back some frustration, but kindly explained his earlier comment in more detail. My roughly translated paraphrase of what he said follows:

> It's not that the sea turtles see flowers up here, but whatever moves the ocotillo to flower is ultimately the same force that attracts the *cooyam* (first-time migrants) to the shallow shoals along this stretch of coast. We don't know if it's due to temperature, or other forces as well, but our traditions suggest that these events occur together at about the same time . . .

Humberto was proposing an indigenous theory of phenology among his people, one that he did not further elaborate that day, but one that builds on certain kinds of correlations to hypothesize about potential causation. While most Western trained scientists will immediately remind me that correlation does not infer causation, Humberto was suggesting that some co-occurring events are triggered by the same underlying causes. That hypothesis is not only testable; it is particularly interesting to ponder during a time of rapid climate change. What if such correlations are being scrambled, as seasonal temperatures, moisture gradients, and other factors have begun to shift at different rates? The observations of Buffalo Bird Woman may serve as a benchmark from which we can measure change.

Today, hundreds if not thousands of indigenous peoples in various parts of the world are recording their own phenological observations as a means to monitor the impact of climate change on their livelihoods, and the biota upon which their livelihoods depend (Krupnik and Jolly 1987). Some of them are comparing the current timing of events to those in their canon of oral histories, and are finding significant shifts in the timing of phenological events. As Shari Fox has summarized, "These are the things that are really happening" at Nunavut (Fox 2002), whether they are due to global climate change, local heat island effects, or other environmental changes in the Arctic. Igloolik elder Z. Uqalik commented, "There is no question about it, you can tell the big difference in weather patterns from the past" (Fox 2002:13). Indigenous communities of the Arctic have now recorded dramatically different timing for the maturation of berries, and in the emergence or migration of beaver, beluga whales, caribou, cod, foxes, geese, lake trout, marten, muskox, rabbits, and seals. They have observed that certain fish are now skinnier and riverside stands of willows are growing taller.

Such indigenous observations of phenological shifts and climate change have been actively discussed at gatherings of indigenous activists since 2000, if not earlier. In a February 2002 draft declaration on traditional ecological knowledge elaborated by indigenous peoples meeting in Finland, the signatories noted, "Indigenous TEK is a valuable source of information in scientific assessments of climate change and should be recognized as an equal tool of research."

In the April 24, 2009, Anchorage Declaration, a larger gathering of indigenous people expressed deep concern not only that these shifts are accelerating, but that they may be differentially impacting their own homelands:

> We express our solidarity as Indigenous Peoples living in areas that are the most vulnerable to the impacts and root causes of climate change. We reaffirm the unbreakable and sacred connection between land, air, water, oceans, forests, sea ice, plants, animals, and our human communities as the material and spiritual basis for our existence.
>
> We are deeply alarmed by the accelerating climate devastation brought about by unsustainable development. We are experiencing profound and disproportionate adverse impacts on our cultures, human and environmental health, human rights, well-being, traditional livelihoods, food systems and food sovereignty, local infrastructure, economic viability, and our very survival as Indigenous Peoples (Anonymous 2009).

It is clear that indigenous peoples do not want to be seen merely as astute observers of climate change, nor as its passive victims, but as active players in adaptation, mitigation, and resolution of the root causes of these perceived changes. In such cases, it may well be that ethnobiology must recast its value to society not as documentation of past traditions of plant and animal knowledge among the diverse cultures of the world, but instead as the multicultural generator of guideposts and benchmarks for the future. Just as palynologists and dendrochronologists have recast themselves as predictors of future trends, rather than being exclusively focused on retrodiction, ethnobiologists should now entertain engagement in a similar paradigm shift. We owe it to those such as Buffalo Bird Woman who have taught us so much about how the world has worked over the millennia, but we also owe it to future generations.

REFERENCES CITED

Anonymous. 2009. The Anchorage Declaration, April 24, 2009. Indigenous Peoples' Global Summit on Climate Change, Anchorage. Available at: http://www.indig enoussummit.com/servlet/content/declaration.html (Verified March 23, 2010).

Fox, Sheri. 2002. These are things that are really happening: Inuit perspectives on the evidence and impacts of climate change in Nunavut. In *The Earth is Moving Faster Now: Indigenous Observations of Arctic Environmental Change*, eds. Igor Krupnik and Dyanna Jolly, pp. 13–53. Alaska Arctic Research Center, Fairbanks.

Wilson, Gilbert I. 1917. *Agriculture of the Hidatsa Indians: An Indian Interpretation*. University of Minnesota, St. Paul. Reprinted as *Buffalo Bird Woman's Garden* in 1987 by Minnesota Historical Society, St. Paul.

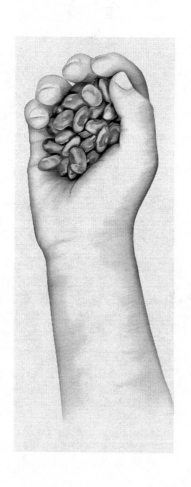

PART II

EXEMPLIFYING HOW ETHNOBIOLOGY SERVES AS A PIVOTAL INTERDISCIPLINE IN BIOCULTURAL CONSERVATION

I N THIS SECOND SECTION, we attempt to "walk the talk" in applying the theoretical precepts sketched out in the first section. More specifically, we wish to demonstrate the heuristic value of combining various methodologies that have emerged over the last quarter century to capture new synergies. The goal of this section is offer tangible examples of the implementation of broader and more unifying theories of biocultural complexity can help us respond to a rapidly changing world. While some of these chapters explicitly deal with the methodologies themselves—such as quantitative analyses from applying island biogeography to the patterns found in island-like cultural landscapes in a desert sea—others focus on these methodologies as means to new ends. For example, they might suggest how applied scholars can get traction on restoring diversity to culturally managed habitats found along the continuum between the fisheries in coastal waters and the multiple strata of intensively harvested garden-orchards in desert oases. They also look at new means to determine the origins and dispersals of domesticated organisms by finding consilience among archaeological, climatic, genetic, eco-geographic, and linguistic data sets.

As for the content of these essays, there is a prevailing emphasis on the restoration and revitalization of plant and animal resources, as well as the inter-generational transfer of traditional knowledge about them. But at a larger level, these papers exemplify how we can build teams with scholars of other disciplines and cultures to create a whole that is greater than the sum of the parts. Such team-building is desperately needed in both our pure and applied pursuits, whether scholarly or oriented toward community service. We sense that ethnobiologists have always been inclined toward such teamwork, but that now it has almost become mandatory with regard to solving certain problems.

Again, we are intentionally focusing on how our interdiscipline can address some of the most pressing issues of our times. Nevertheless, other perfectly valid but less newsworthy topics in ethnobiology may also benefit from more innovative forms of interdisciplinarity as well.

In other words, if biocultural diversity is not your motivating interest, but ethnobotanical education in museums is, then take it and run with it by building a team that brings your shared interests and creative skills to the forefront. If Einstein was correct that "insanity is doing the same thing over and over again and expecting different results," we clearly need to "de-silo" our inquiries, to be more dynamic and innovative in our approaches, even if some of our experimental approaches are ultimately found to be less fruitful than others.

8

SAFEGUARDING SPECIES, LANGUAGES, AND CULTURES IN A TIME OF DIVERSITY LOSS

From the Colorado Plateau to Global Hotspots

GARY PAUL NABHAN, PATRICK PYNES, AND TONY JOE

ABSTRACT

HOTSPOTS OF BIODIVERSITY have become priority areas for land conservation initiatives, oftentimes without recognition that these areas are "hotspots" or clusters of cultural diversity as well. Using the Colorado Plateau ecoregion as a case study, this inquiry (1) outlines the broad geographic patterns of biological diversity and ethnolinguistic diversity within this ecoregion; (2) discusses why these two kinds of diversity are often influenced by the same geographic and historic factors; and (3) suggests what can be done to integrate traditional ecological knowledge of indigenous peoples into multicultural conservation collaborations.

"The diversity of life on earth is under threat; so is the diversity of human cultures. . . . The intriguing question is this: apart from establishing rights over resources, will the local communities bring back some of their earlier cultural traditions of conservation of biological diversity?"
—GADGIL (1987)

Previously published in the *Annals of the Missouri Botanical Garden* 89.2 (Spring 2002): 164–75. Reprinted with permission of the Missouri Botanical Garden Press.

INTRODUCTION

The Colorado Plateau of North America (Fig. 8.1) has received international recognition for nearly a century because of the pioneering efforts there to formally protect its spectacular natural and cultural landscapes (Sellars, 1997). Despite that recognition, the region's resource managers and conservationists have yet to work with much understanding of how biological and cultural diversity have interacted within this four-state region. Since the establishment of Mesa Verde National Park in 1906 and Grand Canyon National Park in 1919 (Burnham, 2000), more than 1.1 million acres of the Colorado Plateau's 130 million acres have been federally protected for their natural and cultural resources. A diverse collection of national parks and monuments, wildlife refuges, recreation areas, conservation areas, preserves, wilderness areas, and national historic parks and sites, these protected lands are managed by the National Park Service, the U.S. Fish and Wildlife Service, the U.S. Forest Service, and the Bureau of Land Management (Tables 8.1 and 8.2). Conservation efforts on the Colorado Plateau were initiated long before our belated recognition that the ecoregion harbors a remarkably high diversity of plants, butterflies, tiger beetles, and mammals, compared to 109 other ecoregions of similar size in North America (Ricketts et al., 1999a, 1999b). Although recent National Monument designations such as the Grand Staircase/Escalante have, in fact, taken into account the area's biodiversity and rich cultural heritage, these two factors have rarely been conceptually linked. More typically, they have been offered as "twin" attractions for ecotourists intrigued by redrock landscapes. Indeed, the 8 to 10 million tourists who annually visit national parks and monuments on the Plateau may receive some unanticipated exposure to this biodiversity and the ancient cultural influences on it, but that is seldom what attracted the majority of them to the parks and monuments of the Painted Desert or Canyonlands in the first place.

OVERVIEW OF BIODIVERSITY

Because about 13.5 percent of the Colorado Plateau's land mass is already protected by federal agencies, the ecoregion's extant biodiversity has not been considered as gravely imperiled as the biodiversity of other regions of North

COLORADO PLATEAU

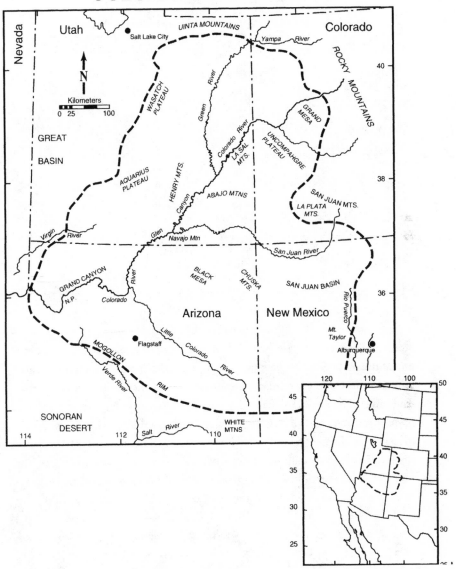

FIGURE 8.1. Boundary of the Colorado Plateau.

TABLE 8.1. National parks of the Colorado Plateau. Source: National Park Service website (http://www.nps.gov)

PARK	STATE	ACREAGE
Arches	Utah	76,518
Black Canyon of the Gunnison	Colorado	27,705
Bryce	Utah	35,845
Canyonlands	Utah	337,597
Capital Reef	Utah	241,904
Grand Canyon	Arizona	1,217,403
Mesa Verde	Colorado	52,121
Petrified Forest	Arizona	93,533
Zion	Utah	146,592
9 National Parks	2 in AZ, 2 in CO, 5 in UT	2,229,218 total acres (2.2 million acres)

America. Nevertheless, Sisk's (2002) recent survey of more than seventy environmental professionals (including Native Americans) working on the Plateau indicates that this ecoregion remains unusually vulnerable to threats such as the damming of rivers; oil, gas, coal, uranium, and aquifer mining; competition from invasive species; mismanagement of wildfire regimes; and the fragmentation of wild-land habitats by rapidly increasing urbanization. Such threats continue to diminish native biodiversity, both within and beyond national parks. The Nature Conservancy (TNC) has therefore ranked the Colorado Plateau within the third tier of hotspots of imperiled biodiversity. At the same time, TNC recognized that this ecoregion's "rarity-weighted species richness" was considered more significant and less well-known than it deserved to be (Stein et al. 2000); in other words, the Colorado Plateau harbors many biological rarities whose vulnerability to threats has not yet been adequately assessed. Consider the fact that the relatively well-endowed Grand Canyon National Park has continued to lose an average of one species per year during the last two decades; the park's current research budget and resource management strategies have somehow not been sufficient to prevent the local extirpation of rare species.

TABLE 8.2. National monuments of the Colorado Plateau. Source: National Park Service and Bureau of Land Management websites (http://www.nps.gov) and (http://www.blm.gov.)

NAME	STATE	MANAGING AGENCY	ACREAGE
Aztec Ruins	New Mexico	NPS	319
Canyon de Chelly	Arizona	NPS (leased from Navajo Nation)	83,840
Canyons of the Ancients	Colorado	BLM	164,000
Cedar Breaks	Utah	NPS	6,154
Colorado	Colorado	NPS	20,453
Dinosaur	Utah	NPS	210,277
El Malpais	New Mexico	NPS	114,277
El Morro	New Mexico	NPS	1,278
Grand Canyon-Parashant	Arizona	BLM	1,014,000
Grand Staircase-Escalante	Utah	BLM	1,900,000
Hovenweep	Utah	NPS	784
Montezuma Castle	Arizona	NPS	857
Natural Bridges	Utah	NPS	7,636
Navajo	Arizona	NPS (leased from Navajo Nation)	360
Pipe Spring	Arizona	NPS	40
Rainbow Bridge	Utah	NPS	160
Sunset Crater Volcano	Arizona	NPS	3,040
Tuzigoot	Arizona	NPS	40
Vermilion Cliffs	Arizona	BLM	293,000
Walnut Canyon	Arizona	NPS	3,579
Wupatki	Arizona	NPS	35,422
Yucca House	Colorado	NPS	33
22 National Monuments	10 in AZ; 3 in CO; 3 in NM; 6 in UT	BLM and NPS lands	3,859,549 total acres

Putting aside for the moment the degree to which current threats imperil the ecoregion's biota, it is clear that the Colorado Plateau is indeed rich in such rarities, including *endemic* species (that is, species with narrow distributions that occur in this ecoregion and nowhere else). Continent-wide floristic analyses by Kartesz and Farstad (1999) have affirmed that the Plateau is the ecoregion of continental North America with the highest rate of vasular plant endemism, reporting 290 species restricted to this ecoregion. For the fauna of the Colorado Plateau ecoregion, David Armstrong (2002) has recently determined that 23.6 percent of the 281 mammals and 36 percent of the rodents in particular exhibit endemism at the levels of species or subspecies.

OVERVIEW OF CULTURAL DIVERSITY

While appreciation of the Plateau's biological uniqueness has grown, recognition of its cultural and linguistic uniqueness still lags far behind. The Colorado Plateau is home to more speakers of Native American languages than all other regions in the United States combined. The ecoregion's indigenous peoples belong to twenty-four different tribes, bands, or dialect communities and represent six different language families (Table 8.3).[1] (English, of course, as well as Spanish and Basque are also spoken here in some communities.) Among the Plateau's indigenous languages, Zuni is a language isolate, or what biologists might call an "endemic" language of the Colorado Plateau. According to many linguists, Zuni (*a:shiwi*) has no close relative in any other language family (Campbell, 1997). In addition to Zuni, the other language families indigenous to the Colorado Plateau include Keres, a family represented by Acoma Pueblo, Laguna Pueblo, and Zia Pueblo; Kiowa-Tanoan, the language family represented at Jemez Pueblo; Uto-Aztecan, the language family to which the Hopi, Ute, and Paiute languages belong; Athabaskan, represented by the Apache and Navajo languages; and Yuman, represented by the Yavapai, Havasupai, and Hualapai tribes on the Colorado Plateau. Figure 8.2 shows the approximate geographic boundaries of these six indigenous language families in 1850, when the Colorado Plateau officially became part of U.S. territory. Tribes and communities who speak a language that belongs to one of the six families have lived in these areas at that point in time. For example, Navajo and Apache speakers occupied lands shown as "Southern-Athabascan" on this historical map.

TABLE 8.3. Status of the Colorado Plateau's indigenous languages.

TRIBE, BAND, OR COMMUNITY	TOTAL TRIBAL LANDBASE (ACRES)	LANGUAGE OR LANGUAGE SUBGROUP	LANGUAGE FAMILY AFFILIATION	TOTAL ENROLLED TRIBAL MEMBERS	APPROXIMATE PERCENTAGE OF FLUENT NATIVE SPEAKERS	APPROXIMATE PERCENTAGE OF FLUENT NATIVE SPEAKERS, AGES 2–18
Jicarilla Apache	879,605	Apache	Eyak-Athabaskan	3,500	23%	<2%
Tonto Apache	85	Apache	Eyak-Athabaskan	110	30%	0%
White Mountain Apache	1,600,000	Apache	Eyak-Athabaskan	15,000	50%	13%
Alamo Navajo	63,000	Apache	Eyak-Athabaskan	2,000	95%	90%
Navajo Nation	17,000,000	Navajo	Eyak-Athabaskan	259,556	57%	<50%
Ramah Navajo	146,953	Navajo	Eyak-Athabaskan	2,463	60%	5%
Tóhajiileehé (Cañocito Band of Navajos)	80,000	Navajo	Eyak-Athabaskan	2,382	75%	50%
Havasupai	188,077	Pai	Cochimi-Yuman	639	98%	90%
Hualapai	1,000,000	Pai	Cochimi-Yuman	2,100	30%	<25%
Camp Verde Yavapai-Apache	636	Pai & Apache	Cochimi-Yuman & Eyak-Athabaskan	1,675	<2%	<2%
Yavapai-Prescott	1,395	Pai	Cochimi-Yuman	158	<2%	<2%
Kaibab Band of Paiute Indians	120,431	Southern Paiute	Uto-Aztecan	240	<2%	0%
Paiute Tribe of Utah	36,000	Southern Paiute	Uto-Aztecan	753	<2%	0%

continued

TABLE 8.3. *continued*

TRIBE, BAND, OR COMMUNITY	TOTAL TRIBAL LANDBASE (ACRES)	LANGUAGE OR LANGUAGE SUBGROUP	LANGUAGE FAMILY AFFILIATION	TOTAL ENROLLED TRIBAL MEMBERS	APPROXIMATE PERCENTAGE OF FLUENT NATIVE SPEAKERS	APPROXIMATE PERCENTAGE OF FLUENT NATIVE SPEAKERS, AGES 2-18
San Juan Southern Paiute	5,000	Southern Paiute	Uto-Aztecan	300	75%	10%
Southern Ute	313,288	Ute	Uto-Aztecan	1,316	15%	5%
Uintah Ouray Ute	4,500,000	Ute	Uto-Aztecan	3,500	33%	<33%
Ute Mountain Ute	606,218	Ute	Uto-Aztecan	2,000	54%	2%
Acoma Pueblo	378,262	Western Keres	Keresan	6,344	50%	2%
Laguna Pueblo	491,387	Western Keres	Keresan	7,696	30%	2%
Hopi Pueblo	1,542,306	Hopi	Uto-Aztecan	10,916	48%	<8%
Hano (Hopi Tewa)		Tewa	Kiowa-Tanoan	600	65%	<2%
Jemez Pueblo	89,619	Towa	Kiowa-Tanoan	3,083	75%	50%
Zia Pueblo	117,000	Eastern Keres	Keresan	773	70%	<2%
Zuni Pueblo	463,270	Zuni	Zuni (no known relatives)	9,690	66%	60%
24 district tribes, bands, or communities in four different states	29,622,532	10 languages	6 language families	335,782		

NOTE: Sources for this chart are shown in the References section. Each source is preceded by an asterisk (*).

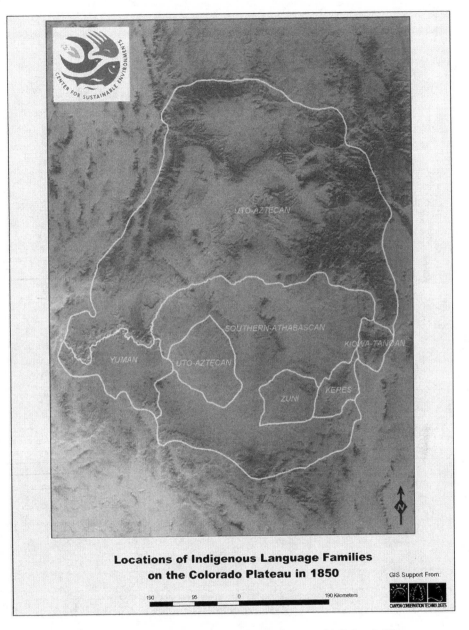

FIGURE 8.2. Locations of indigenous language families on the Colorado Plateau in 1850. (From data developed by the Center for Sustainable Environments.)

PLANNING FOR DIVERSITY

The Colorado Plateau undoubtedly ranks among the top five American regions north of the Tropic of Cancer in terms of linguistic, cultural, and biological diversity, as well as in biological and linguistic/cultural endemism. Nevertheless, there is not a single conservation plan that takes into account both the cultural diversity and the biological diversity of the region. It is as if the historic and geographic relationships between "nature" and "culture" on the Plateau are somehow irrelevant, or too hotly debated to be of value in conservation planning. While it may be reasonable for conservation planners to be skeptical of painting all Native American land and water management practices as "ecologically noble," it is also tragic that so few Native American communities have been involved in planning national parks and monuments adjacent to their current reservations. These federal lands were clearly parts of their historic homelands (Burnham, 2000). As a result, the management of cultural and natural resources have typically been done by different sets of specialists, sometimes involving Native Americans in the former, but nearly always ignoring their traditional ecological knowledge in the latter.

This historic failure of the vast majority of conservation biologists and environmentalists to substantively engage Native American communities in collaborative work based on shared goals is both disappointing and ironic. It is ironic because the long-term residents of the Colorado Plateau have substantial knowledge about the history of the local flora and fauna, which is not available from other sources. Even if all their current hunting, foraging, or farming practices are not considered to be ecologically benign by conservation biologists (Diamond, 1993), this does not negate the value of their traditional ecological knowledge (as defined by Berkes, 2000) about factors influencing plant and animal distributions, densities, and vulnerabilities. [Incidentally, Diamond's (1993) widely cited condemnation of prehistoric peoples of the Colorado Plateau for deforesting the Chaco Canyon area to obtain timber to build multistoried pueblos has been refuted by many anthropologists (McAnany and Yoffee, 2010). Recent strontium isotope evidence demonstrates that the Chaco Anasazi obtained their ponderosa and spruce/fir beams by cutting a single-age class of trees, selected from two large mountain ranges 50 to 75 miles away, and not from the Chaco environment itself (English et al., 2001).] Indeed, the more pertinent question is whether the traditional ecological knowledge of Plateau tribes is being lost at such a rapid rate that it will be of marginal service in biological conservation (Nabhan, 2000a). To date, this rapidly disappearing, orally transmitted knowledge has rarely been systematically taken into account and valued by land managers, who often consider such knowledge to be the quaint but anecdotal or superstitious recollections of scientifically untrained old-timers.

Even contemporary Native Americans' roles in managing the lands of the Colorado Plateau have been chronically underestimated. While the Grand Canyon Trust considers "Indian country" to comprise just a quarter of the Colorado Plateau's 130 million acres (Hecox & Ack, 1996; Wilkinson, 1999), our GIS-based analyses more accurately establish that 29 to 32 percent of the Colorado Plateau is being managed by Native American communities (depending upon which definition of the Plateau's boundaries is used). By virtue of this fact alone, it would be presumptuous, if not impossible, to develop a systematic conservation plan for this ecoregion that did not take into account Native American land stewardship and traditional ecological knowledge of endangered species on the Colorado Plateau (Nabhan, 2000a, b).

In a modest effort to begin to bridge the historic gap between studies of biological and cultural diversity, Northern Arizona University's Center for Sustainable Environments (CSE) has initiated a pilot study with the Grand Canyon Wildlands Council to assess ways to better safeguard and restore both the biological and the cultural uniqueness of springs on the Plateau. In designing this pilot study, we have investigated the potential linkages between biological and linguistic diversity elucidated by the scholars involved in "Terralingua: Partnerships for Linguistic and Biological Diversity," an international nonprofit organization hosted by CSE, which has recently published a global analysis of biocultural diversity (Maffi, 2001). The following discussion emphasizes why efforts to conserve biological and linguistic diversity should be linked, whenever possible, using examples from the Colorado Plateau.

THE BIODIVERSITY ON NATIVE AMERICAN LANDS DESERVES MORE CONSERVATION INVESTMENT

Indian reservations in the United States cover tens of millions of acres of the North American continent, comparable in extent to the acreage that the National Park Service manages for North America's biodiversity. In particular, reservation lands on the Colorado Plateau (Fig. 8.3) cover nearly twice the area that national parks, monuments, preserves, conservation areas, wilderness areas, and wildlife refuges cover in the same ecoregion. Nevertheless, the 29.6 million acres of lands managed by Native Americans on the Colorado Plateau have yet to receive much investment from federal or private sources for the inventory of their biodiversity, monitoring, and recovery of their rare species, or local capacity-building in environmental protection—relative to the considerable support given to those working on adjacent federally protected lands.

If all the species found on Indian lands were also found on lands rigorously protected by the National Park Service or The Nature Conservancy, perhaps this issue would be easier for conservation biologists to ignore. However, the narrowly distributed endemics of the region are often restricted to habitats found only on reservation lands, and not on parklands. The Navajo sedge, *Carex specuicola* J. T. Howell, is an endangered species found around only three springs and seeps used by Diné (Navajo) livestock herders, and one spring used by Hopi farmers. In other words, its range is restricted to the Navajo and Hopi Reservations (D. House, pers. comm.; Nabhan et al., 1991). Similar situations occur for the endemic Hopi chipmunk (*Tamias rufus*), a subspecies of the Spotted Ground Squirrel (*Spermophilus spilosoma cryptospilotus*), the Chuska and Tunitcha Mountain subspecies of Abert's squirrel (*Sciurus aberti chuskensis*), and a subspecies of Stephen's woodrat (*Neotoma stephensi relicta*) found only on Navajo lands. Even if conservation biologists continue to feel ill-equipped to deal with the cultural and legal (sovereignty) issues regarding plants and animals restricted to tribal lands, they can no longer ignore the fact that the only means to sustain these species is by providing Native American land managers with the resources needed to protect or recover these rare populations and their habitats.

THE CONSERVATION COMMUNITY NEEDS TO EMBRACE TRADITIONAL ECOLOGICAL KNOWLEDGE

Until recently, endangered species recovery teams and ecological restorationists disregarded the traditional ecological knowledge found in Native American communities. Perhaps the first formal breakthrough occurred when Diné biologist Donna House incorporated traditional ecological and ethnobiological knowledge about the Navajo sedge into its federal species recovery plan (House in Nabhan et al., 1991), acknowledging that Diné herders had been stewards of

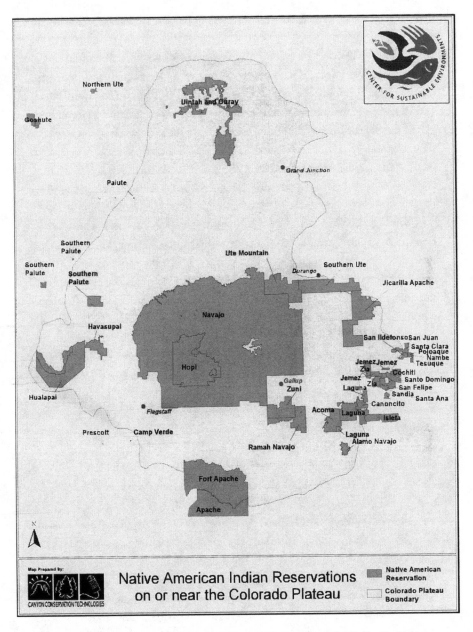

FIGURE 8.3. Native American Indian Reservations on or near the Colorado Plateau.

this plant's habitat for decades and deserved to participate in further efforts to safeguard the sedge.

In addition to their role as habitat managers, some cultural communities on the Colorado Plateau intentionally protect rare species, as is the case with the anomalous sunflower (*Helianthus anomalus* S. F. Blake). Of the twenty-five known localities for this species, at least seven are in or adjacent to Hopi fields and kivas, where farmers and priests spare it from their otherwise rigorous wedding practices (Nabhan & Reichhardt, 1983). Its flowers may be the sole source of a ceremonial facepaint prepared for the *Lakon mana* (maiden) ceremonies of early fall, so that these sunflower populations are protected as a necessity for fulfilling spiritual obligations (L. Masayesva Jeanne, in Nabhan & Reichhardt, 1983).

Traditional ecological knowledge can also be useful in locating and staging rare species reintroductions and habitat restoration. At a time when the California Condor recovery efforts in California were on the verge of failure, Rea (1981) proposed that the recovery team broaden its view and consider reintroductions in the historic refugium near the Colorado River's Grand Canyon, where oral histories from the Hopi recall sightings of the giant bird they call *kwaatoko* (Whiting unpublished, in Seaman, 1993). This has, in fact, turned out to be one of the more successful areas for Condor reintroduction, even though it is outside of California where many biologists erroneously presumed that the California Condor belonged (Rea, 1981).

INVESTMENT IN CONSERVATION CAPACITY-BUILDING FOR NATIVE AMERICANS REMAINS CRITICAL

For decades, the Bureau of Indian Affairs hardly involved Native Americans in so-called "technical decisions" regarding biological resource and land management options on tribal lands. While the number of Native Americans trained in biology and nature resource management increased fivefold between 1970 and 1999, there remains a chronic underinvestment in training Native American professionals in biodiversity conservation on tribal lands, relative to the training available for professionals managing federal lands. The Navajo Natural Heritage Program, first sponsored by The Nature Conservancy, has become an outstanding example of the "conservation payoff" of such investment (Stein et al., 2000). The Hopi, Zuni, and White Mountain Apache tribes have also developed programs that include wildlife management, endangered species recovery, and ecological restoration. In the case of the Zuni, their program to reintroduce beavers as part of the tribe's riparian restoration efforts has involved elders teaching youth about the cultural significance of beavers and other wetland dwellers (Albert & Trimble, 2000).

When both Western academic and traditional ecological knowledge are valued by such programs, it ensures that Indian youth interested in natural history are not forced to choose between their own cultural way of looking at the natural world, and the way of modern science. One superlative example of such capacity-building efforts among Native Americans is the EPA-funded Institute for Tribal Environmental Professionals based at Northern Arizona University, which has already trained more than 500 tribal members from over 200 communities in inventory, monitoring, and restoration techniques for environmental protection. ITEP and AISES (American Indian Science and Engineering Society), founded by Hopi geneticist Frank C. Dukepoo in 1977, have played major roles in training Native Americans for careers in environmental science.

MORE LINKAGES ARE NEEDED BETWEEN ECOLOGICAL RESTORATION AND LINGUISTIC REVITALIZATION

In addition to the many ecological restoration projects recently initiated on tribal lands, most Native American communities on the Colorado Plateau are actively engaged in language stabilization and revitalization efforts (Cantoni, 1996). These language restoration projects often include the elaboration of the entire extant lexicon of a tribe, including its names for plants, animals, and their habitats. In eliciting these names, linguists often do not know the particular scientific taxa the words are describing, but nevertheless record ecological information that may be of use to ecological restoration and species recovery projects (Nabhan, 2000a). For instance, the Diné name for the Indian paintbrush, *Castilleja lanata* A. Gray, is *dah yiitihidaa tsoh*, meaning "big hummingbird's food," to distinguish it from the beardtongue, *Penstemon barbatus* (Cav.) Roth, called *dah yiitihidaa'ts'ooz*, or "food of the slender hummingbird." It may be that Diné elders recognize that these two flowers are frequented by different sizes and species of hummingbirds, and that such information can be integrated into ecological restoration efforts to increase forest understory biodiversity.

CONCLUSIONS: IMPLICATIONS FOR
GLOBAL CONSERVATION STRATEGIES

Over the last decade, tremendous effort has gone into defining, locating, and rapidly assessing the species richness of "hotspots of biodiversity" (Mittermeier et al., 1998; Olson & Dinerstein, 1989; Ricketts et al., 1999a). By some accounts, these hotspots not only capture a large proportion of the planet's biodiversity, but they also define an agenda for conservation investment, which is largely expended on land purchases and infrastructure development for protected areas (Mittermeier et al., 1998). By investing an average of $40 million per year on land purchases in hotspots, rather than on the current "scattergun" approach of current conservation expenditures, these conservation strategists have proposed a new "silver bullet" to biodiversity loss that could protect areas containing a high proportion of the world's species, while business outside the hotspots could be allowed to go on as usual.

Ehrenfeld (2001) has pointed out the serious flaws associated with such an agenda, the most serious being that most hotspots are not only inhabited by diverse cultures, but they are also not for sale. By the mid 1990s prominent ethnobiologists, anthropologists, linguists, and biogeographers had brought attention to the fact that the ten to twenty richest biodiversity hotspots were also extremely rich in cultural diversity, which was typically defined in terms of the richness of extant indigenous languages (Harmon, 1995). For instance, Toledo (1994) observed that of the nine countries considered to have the highest species richness of mammals, six of these were also among the richest in indigenous language groups: Indonesia, Brazil, Mexico, Zaire, India, and Australia.

Three commentaries are typically offered to explain this correlation and to hypothesize its causes (as cited by various authors in Maffi, 2001):

- *Geographic determinism*: Both species and languages diversify in heterogeneous landscapes with formidable geographic barriers.
- *Ecological determinism*: Linguistic diversification occurs in response to high biodiversity, as different cultural groups explore diverse ecological niches for themselves and encode their knowledge of rich biotas in different ways.
- *Historic determinism*: Areas of high linguistic diversity today are "residual," persisting because of their geographical isolation from extensive agricultural development (implying that current impoverished areas were once more diverse).

Clearly, our Colorado Plateau study reiterates a pattern seen on other continents as well: where hotspots of biodiversity or endemism are inhabited by a diversity of cultures, the ways in which these cultures encode traditional ecological knowledge about species in their native languages has tremendous potential for helping to conserve this biodiversity (Nabhan, 2000b). From this frequently observed correlation, several management implications must be considered:

- It may not be feasible or even advisable for government or nongovernmental organizations (NGOs) to purchase the lands within these hotspots for biodiversity protection, because much of the biologically diverse area may be "common lands" held in trust by these cultural communities, such that they cannot be purchased, traded, or condemned. New efforts to conserve biodiversity elsewhere in the world need not make the same mistake the National Park Service historically made on the Colorado Plateau, by stealing, condemning, or finagling the rights to species-rich lands held in trust for future generations of indigenous peoples (Burnham, 2000).

- It is probable that for such high levels of biodiversity to persist in any hotspot until this day, indigenous residents consciously or unconsciously developed active and indirect means of managing particular landscapes, microhabitats, or species guilds to maintain them. The potential utility of such knowledge, skills, and practices is great (Nabhan, 2000b), so much so that species recovery teams and formal land managers should be encouraged to integrate such knowledge into their conservation management plans (Tuxill & Nabhan, 1998).

- It is likely that proponents of biodiversity conservation will forge stronger, more effective collaborations with indigenous residents in biodiversity hotspots if they listen to and respect indigenous concerns about sovereignty, cultural property rights, and secrets associated with esoteric beliefs and ceremonies. Conservationists should attempt to collaborate on community-based projects that foster the continued oral transmission of traditional ecological knowledge, the persistence of indigenous languages, traditional subsistence or ceremonial practices, and the generation of health benefits or income for a broad cross-section of community members. While such community-based conservation efforts are already given lip service from governments and NGOs alike, there remains a disproportionate investment in "top-down" conservation strategies, and only scattered investment in community-based "bottom-up" strategies for maintaining biodiversity.

- Given the fact that traditional ecological knowledge about landscape-level biodiversity itself is being diminished (Berkes, 2000), the fragile relationship between the two needs to be more tangibly explored. While many biogeographers and linguists are already involved in efforts to understand global patterns of biodiversity and cultural diversity, it is hoped that our pilot project to safeguard the uniqueness of the Colorado Plateau will encourage other community-based practitioners to experiment with more practical means of integrating indigenous knowledge into collaborative efforts to conserve the world's hotspots of diversity and endemism.

NOTES

1. The numerous sources for Table 8.3 are found in the Literature Cited, and each source is preceded by an asterisk (*).

LITERATURE CITED

Agnon, S. Y. 1966. Editorial commentary. The Observer 5(1): 6.

Albert, S. & T. Trimble. 2000. Beavers are partners in riparian restoration on the Zuni Indian reservation. Ecological Restoration 18(2): 87–96.

Armstrong, D. M. 2002. Appendix 1: Checklist of native mammals of the Colorado Plateau. Pp.81-4 in G.P. Nabhan, ed. Safeguarding the Uniqueness of the Colorado Plateau. Northern Arizona University Center for Sustainable Environments, Flagstaff, AZ.

*Benson, Gloria. Paiute Tribe of Utah. Telephone interview. December 12, 2000.

Berkes, F. 2000. Sacred Ecology. Yale University Press, New Haven, CT.

Burnham, P. 2000. Indian Country, God's Country: Native Americans and the National Parks. Island Press, Washington, DC.

*Campbell, L. 1997. American Indian Languages: The Historical Linguistics of Native America. Oxford University Press, New York, NY.

Cantoni, G. (ed.). 1996. Stabilizing Indigenous Languages. Northern Arizona University Center for Excellence in Education, Monograph Series, Flagstaff, AZ.

*Cuch, Mariah. Ute Tribe Public Relations. P. O. Box 400, Ft. Duchesne, Utah 84026. Electronic mail correspondence, December 27 and 29, 2000.

Diamond, J. 1993. The Third Chimpanzee. W. W. Norton and Company, New York, NY.

Ehrenfeld, D. 2001. Hot Spots and the Globalization of Conservation. Oxford University Press, Oxford.

English, N. B., J. L. Betancourt, J. S. Dean & J. Quade. 2001. Strontium isotopes reveal distance sources of architectural timber in Chaco Canyon, NM. Proceedings of the Nattional Academy of Sciences 98: 11891-96.

*Eriacho, Wilfred. Bilingual Specialist, Zuni Public Schools. Personal interview, November 17, 2000. Zuni Pueblo, NM.

*Estes, James. October 1999. How Many Indigenous Languages Are Spoken in the United States? By How Many Speakers? National Clearinghouse for Bilingual Education. <http://www.ncbe.gwu.edu/askncbe/faqs/20natlang.htm>.

Gadgil, M. 1987. Diversity: Cultural and biological. Trends in Ecological Evolution 2(12): 369–73.

*Gallegos, Estrella. Culture and Language Department. Ute Mountain Ute Tribe. Telephone interview. November 1, 2000.

*Glassco, Greg. Cultural Resources Office, Hualapai Tribe. Peach Springs, AZ. Telephone interview. December 12, 2000.

*Grimes, B. 1996. Ethnologue: Languages of the World. Dallas: SIL International, updated February 1999 at <http://www.sil.org/ethnologue>.

Harmon, D. 1995. The status of the world's languages as reported in *Ethnologue*. Southwest Journal of Linguistics 14: 1–28.

Hecox, W. E. & B. L. Ack. 1996. Charting the Colorado Plateau: An Economic and Demographic Exploration. Grand Canyon Trust, Flagstaff, AZ.

*Hussey, Jennifer. Assistant Director, Paiute Tribe of Utah Language Department. Cendar City, Utah. Telephone interview. December 20, 2001.

Kartesz, J. & A. Farstad. 1999. Multi-scale analysis of endemism of vascular plant species. Pp. 51–5 *in* T. H. Ricketts, E. Dinerstein, D. M. Olson & C. Loucks, Terrestrial Ecoregions of North America: A Conservation Assessment. Island Press, Washington, DC.

*Krauss, Michael. 1996. Status of Native American Language Endangerment. Pp. 16–21 *in* G. Cantoni (editor), Stabilizing Indigenous Languages. Center for Excellence in Education, Northern Arizona University, Flagstaff, AZ.

Maffi, L. 2001. On Biocultural Diversity. Smithsonian University Press, Washington, DC.

McAnany, P.A. and N. Yoffee. 2010. Questioning Collapse. Cambridge University Press, New York, NY.

Mittermeier, R. A., N. Myers, J. G. Thomsen, G. A. b. Da Fonseca & S. Olivieri. 1998. Biodiversity hotspots and major tropical wilderness areas: Approaches to setting conservation priorities. Conservation Biology 12: 516–20.

Nabhan, G. P. 2000a. Interspecific relationships affecting endangered species recognized by O'odham and Comcaac cultures. Ecological Applications10: 1288–95.

———. 2000b. The Colorado Plateau as a center of diversity. Biodiversity Newsletter, The Consultative Group on Biological Diversity, San Francisco, CA.

———& K. L. Reichhardt. 1983. Hopi protection of *Helianthus anomalus*, a rare sunflower. Southwestern Naturalist 28: 231–36.

———, D. House, H. Suzan, W. Hodgson, L. Hernandez & G. Malda. 1991. Conservation and use of rare plants by traditional cultures of the U.S./Mexico borderlands. Pp. 127–46 *in* M. Oldfield & J. Alcorn (eds.), Biodiversity: Culture, Conservation and Ecodevelopment. Westview Press, Boulder, CO.

*Naranjo, Dorothy. Cultural Preservation Office, Southern Ute Tribe. Ignacio, CO. Telephone interview. December 12, 2000.

Olson, D. M. & E. Dinerstein. 1998. The Global 2000: A representation approach to conserving the world's most biologically valuable ecoregions. Conservation Biology 12: 516–20.

*Pino, Jackson. Middle School and High School teacher. Alamo Navajo Community, Alamo, NM. Telephone interview. November 15, 2000.

*Polacca, Mary. Office of Hopi Tribal Enrollment. Telephone interview. December 10, 2000.

*Poleahla, Anita. Office of Hopi Cultural Preservation. Telephone interview. December 10, 2000.

Rea, A. M. 1981. California Condor captive breeding: A recovery proposal. Environment. SouthW 492: 8–12.

Ricketts, T. H., E. Dinerstein, D. M. Olson & C. Loucks. 1999a. Who's where in North America? BioScience 49: 369–81.

———, ———, ——— & ———. 1999b. Terrestrial Ecoregions of North America: A Conservation Assessment. Island Press, Washington, DC.

*Rollo, Gail. Tribal Administrator. Paiute Tribe of Utah. Telephone interview. September 11, 2000.

*Salari, Nasim. Program Coordinator, San Juan Southern Paiute Tribe. Telephone interview. September 11, 2000.

*Sandoval, Merton. Cultural Preservation Department. Jicarilla Apache Nation. Dulce, New Mexico. Telephone interview. November 13, 2000.

*Saunders, Vanessa. Tribal Secretary, Tonto Apache Tribe. Payson, Arizona. Telephone interview. September 11, 2000.

Seaman, P. D. 1993. Users Guide and Index for the A. F. Whiting Collection. Northern Arizona Anthropological Paper 1, Flagstaff, AZ.

*Secatero, Tony. President of Tonhajilee (Canoncito Navajo). Telephone interview. October 23, 2000.

Sellars, R. W. 1997. Preserving Nature in the National Parks: A History. Yale University Press, New Haven, CT.

Sisk, T.D. 2002. Eliciting perceptions of biocultural diversity on the Colorado Plateau. Pp. 13-26 in G.P. Nabhan, ed. Safeguarding the Uniqueness of the Colorado Plateau. Northern Arizona University Center for Sustainable Environments, Flagstaff, AZ.

*Smith, Joni. Administrative Assistant. Camp Verde Yavapai-Apache Tribe. Telephone interview. September 11, 2000.

Stein, B. A., L. S. Kutner & J. S. Adams. 2000. Precious Heritage: The Status of Biodiversity in the United States. Oxford University Press, Oxford, UK.

*Tohtsoni, Nathan. Who is a Navajo? Navajo Times. August 31, 2000: 1.

Toledo, V. M. 1994. Biodiversity and cultural diversity in Mexico. Different Drummers: Incentives for Protecting North American Biodiversity 1: 16–19.

Tuxill, J. & G. P. Nabhan. 1998. Plants and Protected Areas. World Wildlife Fund Plants and People Manual. Stanley Thornes Publishing, Cheltenham, U.K.

*Vital Affairs Office. White Mountain Apache Nation. Whiteriver, AZ Telephone interview. November 13, 2000. Also <http://primenet.com> (landbase information).

*Wemytewa, Edward. Zuni Department of Game and Fish. Telephone interview. September 11, 2000.

Wilkinson, C. 1999. Fire on the Plateau: Conflict and Endurance in the American Southwest. Island Press, Washington, DC.

*Willis, Lornene. Director of Cultural Center, Jicarilla Apache Nation. Dulce, New Mexico. Telephone interview. November 13, 2000.

*Yavapai Prescott Indian Tribe (brochure). The Yavapai Prescott Indian Tribe, 530 E. Merritt, Prescott, AZ.

9

AGROBIODIVERSITY IN AN OASIS ARCHIPELAGO

RAFAEL DE GRENADE AND GARY PAUL NABHAN

INTRODUCTION

T HE OASES OF THE Baja California peninsula, Mexico, harbor farming systems with crops first introduced by Jesuit missionaries during their political, economic, and ecclesiastical dominance from 1697 to 1768. The oases represent geographies of historic dissemination and hold assemblages of heirloom perennial crop species with origins in six of seven continents. The first Jesuit missionaries to the peninsula documented their agricultural introductions in detail. These historic documents, along with records from subsequent Franciscan and Dominican missionaries, provide a benchmark by which to measure the persistence and/or loss of perennial crop species. Few other locations in the world have such complete historical records of the earliest agricultural transformations occurring with contact between hunter-gatherers and agricultural societies. Using original ethnohistorical manuscripts, combined with thorough field-garden surveys and farmer interviews, we have attempted to measure modern species richness and characterize species persistence within and among the oases of the peninsula.

Studies in agricultural oases in Egypt, Oman, and on the Baja California peninsula show that oases, harboring complex species assemblages, provide unique sites for formal and informal *in situ* crop conservation and associated traditional knowledge (Hammer et al. 2009; Gebauer et al. 2007; Nabhan 2007; Nabhan et al. 2010; Routson 2012). *In situ* conservation maintains agricultural species within the biocultural systems in which they evolved and, is especially applicable to oases agroecosystems, allowing for continuing the adaptation of plants and animals within a social context (Brush 2000; Altieri and Merrick 1987; Nabhan 2007). Traditional oasis agricultural systems support complex agroecosystems with higher levels of native biodiversity than either surrounding natural environments or small household gardens (Nabhan et al. 1982; Pimentel et al. 1992; Thrupp 2000). The agrobiodiversity within these systems—diverse crop and livestock species, crop wild relatives, other associated wild biodiversity, and traditional knowledge—are resources for the future of humanity and natural systems in the face of environmental degradation, climate variability and extreme events, crop disease outbreaks, and a growing world population (Frese et al. 2012; Hammer and Teklu 2008; Lenné 2011; Ortiz 2011). These "islands" of agricultural diversity exist in broader landscapes where agriculture cannot be practiced, urban development has consumed agricultural production, or the systems have changed to large-scale crop monocultures. Oases, or other isolated pockets in the geographies of historical dispersal, however, might only hold small representations of genetic diversity for each species, bottlenecked as many populations are through fragmentation, vicariance, or long-distance dispersal mechanisms. Associated farming and food processing knowledge and practices are equally fragmented and vulnerable to disappearance.

We participated in a collaborative initial investigation into the historical and contemporary dynamics of the species composition, farming systems, and farming communities of the Baja California peninsula oases (Cariño et al. 2013; Nabhan et al. 2010). Using historical records, farmer interviews, agricultural species inventories, and species-area and rank-abundance graphs, we characterized patterns of perennial crop species persistence in the oases. We refined a model of the archipelago of oases as a series of connected refugia to conserve agrobiodiversity on the Baja California peninsula first proposed by our team in 2010 (Nabhan et al. 2010). We built upon the rapid-assessment methodology of this previous work through in-depth studies of twelve of fifteen Jesuit mission oases, including surveys of every field-garden within each oasis and extended interviews with farmers and oasis residents to understand the full complexity of oasis farming systems.

SOCIAL AND ECOLOGICAL CONTEXT
OF THE BAJA CALIFORNIA OASES

The isolation of the peninsula and the oases create agricultural landscapes with unique environmental and social potential for *in situ* conservation. The Baja California peninsula forms a splinter off the southwestern edge of the North American continent, reaching a length of approximately 1,300 kilometers and varying in width from thirty to 240 kilometers between the Pacific Ocean and the Gulf of California (Davis 2006). A series of mountain ranges forms the spine of the peninsula, uplifted and eroded remnants of a geology that predates the formation of the peninsula and others formed from subsequent volcanic activity (Aschmann 1967). The peninsula transitions from a temperate northern region to extreme aridity in its central deserts to the dry, tropical cape. The northern reaches receive more winter rainfall, and the south receives the tailspin of summer tropical cyclones (Adams and Comrie 1997; Comrie and Glenn 1998; Minnich et al. 2000). Climate also transitions west to east, with fog and colder temperatures along the western margin of the peninsula, and higher temperatures and lower humidity along the gulf coast. Annual rainfall on the peninsula varies between 100 to 300 mm (León de la Luz and Cadena 2006).

Although the peninsula has no perennial rivers, a series of springs and seeps along its length create small riparian environments, or oases. Using aerial images, Maya et al. (1997) identified 184 permanent and ephemeral oases in the state of Baja California Sur. The length and varied geography of the narrow peninsula creates an "archipelago" of these oasis environments, each differing in latitude and longitude, microclimate, geology, soil types, hydrology, vegetation, and human influence. The agricultural oases we selected for this study all have perennial springs that support farming villages. They span the lower two-thirds of the peninsula and have vastly different environmental matrices, though they share many of the same agricultural species, farming systems, and traditional practices. These oases were nuclei for the hunter-gathering groups that inhabited the peninsula for thousands of years prior to the arrival of the Jesuit missionaries (Crosby 1994).

During their seventy years on the peninsula (1697–1768), Jesuit missionaries established eighteen missions on the Baja California peninsula to evangelize the native Pericú, Guaycura, and Cochimí tribes and enforce the *"reducción"* of the nomadic peoples to sedentary, agrarian lives (Cariño 1996). The rugged, arid geography of the peninsula limited the ecological niches in which agriculture could be successfully established (Crosby 1994). The missionaries concentrated their efforts within spring-fed oases where they developed terraced fields and *acequia* irrigation systems, and introduced domesticated crop and livestock species (Del Barco 1980; Clavijero 2007; Venegas 1757). Extreme aridity, plagues of locusts, destructive hurricane floods, and the almost complete decimation of native populations through disease and cultural disruption diminished the long-term success of their evangelical objectives.

Despite the fact that these missionaries spent only a handful of decades on the peninsula, their efforts transformed the peninsula landscapes through the processes that Crosby calls "ecological imperialism." Many of the original stone structures and crop species have persisted through the centuries. These missionaries developed the oases into complex agroecological systems with stratified cropping structures, livestock and crop rotations, terraced fields, winding canals, and open spaces between hedgerows of mixed perennials where they planted annual vegetable and grain crops.

The crop repertoire within each oasis embodies cumulative geographies of agricultural and cultural dissemination from around the world. The Jesuit missionaries transported perennial crop species available in Spain at the time as well as those species they found in the landscapes of their New World conquests (Dunmire 2004; Nabhan 2012). These included figs, date palms, pomegranates, grapes, and olives, species that originated in Central Asia, the Middle East, North Africa, and the Mediterranean region, citrus species transported along silk and spice routes from Asia, mango and coconut brought on ships directly across the Pacific, and several New World species introduced across the peninsula, as well as a few native to the peninsula (Mukherjee 1953; Ramón Laca 2003; Rivera et al. 2012; Zizumbo-Villarreal 1996). The oases, spanning the lower two-thirds of the peninsula, have varied climates and microclimates to successfully support a broad range of these introduced food crop species, including tropical fruits such as breadfruit, mangosteen, and cherimoya in the central and southern oasis sites, and more temperate apple, pear, peach, and quince species in the northern oases.

The Mission era and more recently introduced species and farming systems comprise the agrobiodiversity that exists in the oases of the Baja California peninsula. After the Jesuit expulsion in 1768, Franciscan and Dominican missionaries assumed temporary control of the missions and settlers, ranchers, and miners from the mainland arrived on the peninsula. These people formed the basis of the new-ranchero culture that adopted the agriculture of the mission oases on the peninsula. The physical geography and quantity of water and arable land limited the scale at which agriculture could be produced, however, the products exceeded local demand and were exported in national and international markets (Lassépas 1859). While enhanced water extraction technologies and agricultural machinery has allowed mechanized, industrial agricultural production to be implemented in many of the oases, farmers still practice small-scale systems and cultivate many of the original perennial crop species.

METHODS

STUDY SITES

To characterize oasis agrobiodiversity and persistence of Mission era species, we selected twelve of fifteen agricultural oases on the Baja California peninsula inhabited by the Jesuits at the time of their expulsion in 1768 (Figure 9.1, Table 9.1). We excluded three, Santa Maria, Loreto, and San Jose del Cabo, based on their absence of original mission crops and/or agricultural systems. These twelve mission oasis sites all have persistent small-scale agriculture and records of historic agricultural introductions by Jesuit, Franciscan, and Dominican missionaries. These missions were developed under the same religious institution during the Jesuit era (1698–1768) and were interconnected through the secularization of the missions (1833). This early institutional network among the oases ensures that a similar suite of agricultural crops was introduced to each and likely reintroduced following catastrophic events that occurred during the Mission era.

While the environmental matrix within which the oases occur varies greatly from dry temperate desert in the central mountains to subtropical hills on the cape, these mesic systems share many characteristics. Each oasis has one to several springs that emerge in a canyon or drainage, usually where erosion has exposed an impermeable layer of rock or consolidated sediment along which the subterranean water flowed. Most oases have a constructed dam or spring box to catch the water and divert it into a canal that transports the water along the banks of the water channel to downstream fields. The location and size of these fields depend on the topography of the canyons; however, in general the field gardens lie close to or within the arroyos, and the villages are positioned slightly higher on the slopes. Soil types range from dense clays to almost pure sand—the geology of the peninsula cannot be easily generalized, and includes old basement sedimentary and metamorphic from before the split of the peninsula, unconsolidated alluvium, and ancient to very recent volcanic rock.

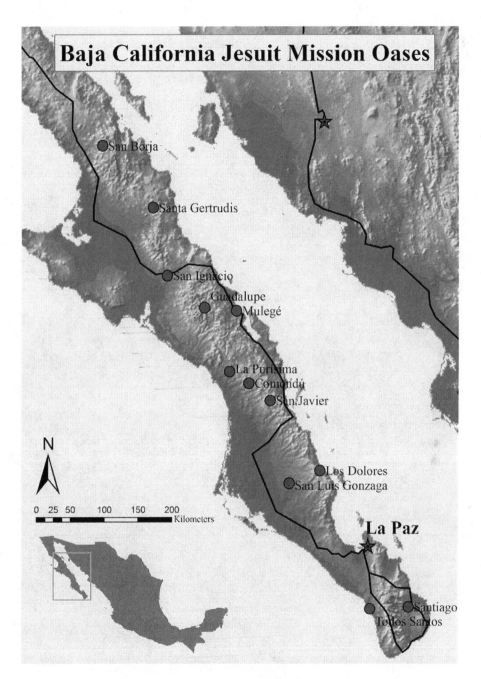

FIGURE 9.1. Twelve of fifteen Jesuit mission oases of
the Baja California Peninsula selected for this study.

TABLE 9.1. Physical data of the Jesuit mission oases included in this study, listed north to south (climate data calculated from CONAGUA 2011).

OASIS	OASIS CODE	LAT/LONG COORDINATES	AVG ELEV.	TEMP. RANGE	ANNUAL PRECIP.	CULTIVATED AREA	FIELD GARDENS
San Borja	SB	N28 44.657 W113 45.255	400m	—	—	6.29ha	2
Santa Gertrudis	SG	N28 03.081 W113 05.097	400m	0°C–42°C	109mm	9.47ha	12
San Ignacio	SI	N27 17.024 W112 53.912	120m	-1°C–45°C	145mm	25.68ha	25
Guadalupe	GU	N26 55.153 W112 24.353	700m	-5.5°C–46°C	239mm	0.50ha	3
Mulegé	MU	N26 53.118 W111 59.159	8m	-1.5°C–45°C	97mm	6.64ha	8
La Purísima	LP	N26 11.422 W112 04.371	100m	0°C–45°C	113mm	75.93ha	43
San José de Comondú	CU	N26 03.583 W111 49.330	280m	0°C–46°C	230mm	65.60ha	43
San Javier	SJ	N25 51.652 W111 32.521	420m	1°C–47°C	255mm	17.01ha	17
Los Dolores	LD	N25 03.333 W110 53.071	55m	1°C–45°C	249mm	13.97ha	3
San Luis Gonzaga	SLG	N24 54.490 W111 17.451	160m	0°C–46°C	191mm	4.60ha	1
Todos Santos	TS	N23 26.991 W110 13.531	41m	3°C–42°C	144mm	153.15ha	55
Santiago de los Coras	SC	N23 28.540 W109 43.041	120m	-2°C–44°C	308mm	45.80ha	29

Likewise, the topography ranges from deep, narrow canyons within the peninsula's mountains to the more gently rolling slopes of the southern tip. Rainfall is highly variable on both spatial and temporal scales; the oases receive from 109mm to 308mm, generally following a pattern of higher precipitation in the more southern latitudes, but this is also subject to coastal proximity and rain-shadow effect. Climatic fluctuations are also variable, though all oases show about a 46-degree range between the minimum and maximum temperatures. The proximity of both water bodies to all of the oases has a tempering effect on the climate, however, interior mountain oases such as San Borja, Santa Gertrudis, San Ignacio, Guadalupe, San Javier, Comondú, and San Luis Gonzaga tend to have slightly more extreme temperature trends more often than those closer to the coasts—Mulegé, La Purísima, Los Dolores, Todos Santos, and Santiago.

Within each mission oasis, we delimited the agricultural sites surrounding the Jesuit missions as the collective body of *huertas*, or agricultural plots within the original *acequia* or canal system, initiated by Jesuit missionaries. For the purposes of this study we define a *huerta* as a field-garden larger than 100 square meters, watered by the *acequia* or canal system or by a well, though not usually associated with a house. The primary purpose of the *huerta* is to grow food for domestic consumption and/or for market, and not to produce the assorted vegetables and culinary herbs for the kitchen. *Huertas* may also supply forage for livestock; farmers grow, harvest, and transport the forage crops to animals, or rotate animals through the *huerta* between growing seasons. Most *huertas* have hedgerows or borders of perennial species, oftentimes in tiered vegetation structure, and open, sunny areas between, to grow annual crops or rows of perennials, such as grapevines or prickly pear (*Opuntia* spp.).

HISTORICAL INVENTORIES

We used several sources to establish the extent of the original crop introductions to the peninsula during the Jesuit Mission era. In particular, we scrutinized the published works of Jesuit and Franciscan missionaries from the peninsula. We also conducted research at the archives of the Arizona State Museum, the Mexican federal *Archivo General de la Nación* (AGN) in Mexico City and state *Archivo Histórico de Baja California Sur Pablo L. Martínez* (AHPLM) at La Paz. We used historical registries, writings, and drawings of the Jesuit missionaries Del Barco (1980), Baegert (1979), and Venegas (1757) as primary sources for inventories of agricultural species and practices introduced during the Jesuit era; however, these records are incomplete and not sufficient for reconstructing an agricultural baseline. The writings of Clavijero (2007) during this same time period also give information about the agriculture of the Baja California peninsula missions, though this missionary never visited the peninsula and his works provide only a partial description.

Crosby (1994) provides the most comprehensive collection of agricultural data from Jesuit missionary writings as well as descriptions of agriculture in the missions today. Vernon (2002) has also collected primary Jesuit agricultural data and described the current condition of mission agriculture on the peninsula. Inventories and descriptions of Franciscan missionary Palóu written in 1772, collected, and translated in Engelhardt (1908) are the first original writings that treat all of the Baja California peninsula missions together and describe the condition of the fields after the Jesuit expulsion. We used a series of Dominican records collected and compiled in 1774 as our baseline for Mission era crop introductions. A thorough review of these in the *Archivo General de la Nación* (AGN) enabled us to complete a partial list developed during our first survey of peninsula agriculture (Nabhan et al. 2010). These writings provide the earliest comprehensive inventories and descriptions of annual and perennial crops, area in cultivation, and amount harvested in the missions. Most of the fruit trees recorded in these inventories are mature, and thus would have been planted during the Jesuit administration of the peninsula, six years earlier. These records also verify the Jesuit's critical role in introducing agricultural techniques, systems, and crops to the missions.

OASIS GARDEN SURVEYS

At each mission oasis, we attempted to survey every *huerta* within the original irrigation systems, though in a few cases, this was not possible. We utilized guides who introduced us to farmers, pointed out the boundaries of the *huertas*, clarified questions on some varieties and species, and served as a connection to the community. We obtained approval through the University of Arizona Human Subjects Protection Program for all methods included in this research (IRB00001751; FWA00004218; Project# 09–0552–02). We collected Global Positioning System (GPS) points for at least two field corners to assist in the delineation of field shape and area using GIS (Geographic Information Systems) technology and aerial photographs. We took GPS points at the mission, springs, wells, and dams in each oasis.

We limited our investigations to cultivated perennial food crop species to characterize current species richness and compare our results with historical inventories. We selected perennials because of their longevity and the likelihood that the species we encountered would be comparable with the species, and in some cases, the varieties described in the historical records. Many of these are clonally reproduced, and if the original trees are not still living, the genetic material vegetatively propagated from them would likely be similar or identical. The few studies we have of Mission figs and Mission grapes show an extraordinarily high level of genetic similarity among parent populations in the Old World and widely dispersed clonal materials still growing in American regions (This et al. 2006; Aradhya et al. 2010). The only case of possible divergence over the last three centuries in this region—noted in a recent study of Mission olives—may in fact be evidence of somaclonal mutations or hybridization with a parent that is no longer present (Soleri et al. 2010).

We recorded scientific names and local names for all perennial food crop species and made photo collections and descriptions based on standards of the International Plant Genetic Resources Institute. For each collection, we recorded site descriptions, tree or plant and fruit characteristics, and GPS points. We collected specific and varietal names from the historic documents, oasis farmers, and Mexican and American horticultural scientists for the perennial food crops in archaic and contemporary Spanish and the corollary English and scientific (Latin) names. For perennial crops that we could not identify in the field, we collected samples for herbarium identification, or sent photos to horticulturalists or species experts. We consulted horticulturalists and botanists from the Baja California peninsula, Mexico City, Spain, and the United States for different agricultural species identifications. Some species still remain in question since the identities of several of the historic crops are difficult to reconstruct with absolute confidence, and we could not accurately identify some of the nopal, agave, and citrus species.

AGROBIODIVERSITY ANALYSES

We combined field data with geo-referenced digital maps of the oases produced from SPOT (*Satellite Pour l'Observation de la Terre*) composite aerial photograph images and aerial photography with a resolution of two meters (WGS84, UTM Zone 12) to calculate the area of each garden. We calculated species-area relationships for the oases using number of species and total area in cultivation for each, and fit a power curve to the data following the Arrhenius power curve calculation ($S = cA^z$, where S = number of species, A = area, c = constant, and z = slope of the species-area curve in log-log space). Both c (constant) and z (slope) are determined from the data by transforming the equation logarithmically (logS = logc + zlogA), which linearizes the relation (Dengler 2009). We then used these coefficients in the original equation to develop a descriptive model or curve of the oasis species-area relationship. We tested individual significance of the species-area relation (total number of perennial crop species and total area in cultivation) for each oasis to the curve using Pearson residuals. We generated calculation sets, one to compare total perennial crop diversity and one with only historic, Mission-era crop species.

To determine trends in oasis agricultural diversity, we calculated rank-abundance relationships for seven oases using species presence/absence and frequency of occurrence in each garden to characterize the total perennial crop diversity within oases. The rank-abundance graphs for the oases show both overall species richness (x axis) and number of gardens (y axis) and demonstrate the frequency of each crop appearing in the oasis gardens. Oases with fewer than ten gardens (SB, GU, MU, LD, SLG; Table 9.1) were excluded from the analyses. The species with highest relative frequency (number of times species occurred/number of gardens in the oasis) were assigned a number 1, and consecutive numbers given to consecutive decreasing values of species relative frequency. Graphs of these relative frequencies represent the distribution of perennial crop species within the oases. The species with the most representation are given the highest scores, while species with low representation lie closer to the x axis. The graphs with the steepest rate of descent are those where only a few species have the most representation in the gardens. The graphs with shallow declines are those where a higher number of species are represented throughout more of the gardens. The sites with the most even descents imply that these oases have the greatest long-term potential of retaining agrobiodiversity because the diversity is more evenly distributed throughout the gardens. We used these data to analyze oasis agricultural diversity, trends, and persistence of historic crops.

OASIS FARMING SYSTEMS AND PRACTICES, POLITICAL ECOLOGY, AND CULTURAL PRACTICES

We selected farmers in each oasis to answer interview questions based on farmer availability, knowledge, and willingness to participate. We conducted one to fifteen farmer interviews per oasis to gather further information on agricultural practices, including history of the garden, information on perennial plant management, irrigation timing and methods, fertilizer inputs, field design, annual crop inventories and cultivation, and livestock management. We also conducted interviews with farmers, as well as supplemental interviews with produce buyers, extension agents, and town authorities related to oasis political ecology, including questions about distance to markets and source areas for seed, fertilizer, and mechanical needs, primary revenues from the agricultural lands and a description of economic chains, and how land tenure, tourism, demography, and water governance of the oasis affected the persistence of perennial crops. Our third set of interviews addressed cultural foodway practices, and symbolic significances associated with heritage crops in the oases. We asked about processing techniques and histories of the different perennial species in the oases, and also questions related to the significance of each species, and its use during religious rites and celebrations, holidays, and daily life. We used the responses to these questions to understand individual and community knowledge repertoires related to the perennial food crop species. In all, we conducted seventy-nine individual and group farmer interviews related to farming practices, eighty-three interviews on oasis political ecology, and ninety interviews related to cultural practices. We acquired human subjects' approval from the University of Arizona, and all methodology followed these institutional standards. We took handwritten notes and translated all interviews, then analyzed them in relation to the agrobiodiversity persistence at each oasis.

RESULTS

HISTORICAL INVENTORIES

We found mention of twenty-one perennial crop introductions to the Baja California missions in the historical documents of Jesuit, Franciscan and Dominican priests, and compiled by later authors (De Mora et al. 1774; Engelhardt 1908; Baegert 1979; Del Barco 1980; Crosby 1994; Del Rio 2003) (Table 9.2).

OASIS GARDEN SURVEYS

Within 241 oasis *huertas* surveyed in the 2010/2011 study, we recorded a total of 89 species of perennial food crops, belonging to 64 genera and 36 families

TABLE 9.2. Crops introduced to the Baja California Peninsula oases by 1774 as recorded by Jesuit, Franciscan, and Dominican missionaries, updated from Nabhan et al. 2010. Updated information is identified in bold.

NAME IN ENGLISH	NAME IN SPANISH	MISSIONS (WHERE NOTED)	SOURCE
Annona: custard apple	*Chirimoya*	San José de Comondú, San Javier	De Mora et al. 1774
Avocado	***Aguacate***	**La Purísima, San José de Comondú**	**De Mora et al. 1774**
Banana	*Plátano*	San José de Comondú, San Javier	De Mora et al. 1774; Crosby 1994; Del Barco 1980
Century plant	*Maguey*	Santiago	Del Barco 1980
Citrus: citron	***Cidra***	**La Purísima**	**De Mora et al. 1774**
Citrus: lime	*Limón*	**La Purísima**, San José de Comondú, San Javier, **San Ignacio**	De Mora et al. 1774; Crosby 1994; Del Barco 1980
Citrus: sweet lime	***Lima***	**La Purísima, San José de Comondú**	**De Mora et al. 1774**
Citrus: orange	*Naranja, naranjo*	**La Purísima**, Todos Santos, San José de Comondú, San Javier	De Mora et al. 1774; Crosby 1994; Del Barco 1980
Coconut	*Coco*	Loreto	Zizumbo-Villareal 1996; Crosby 1994
Date palm	*Dátil, palma*	**Loreto, La Purísima**, San José de Comondú, San Javier	De Mora et al. 1774; Aschmann 1967
Fig	*Higo*	**Loreto, San Gertrudis**, Todos Santos, San José de Comondú, San Javier, **Guadalupe, San Ignacio, San Borja, Santa María**	De Mora et al. 1774; Crosby 1994; Del Barco 1980

continued

TABLE 9.2. *continued*

NAME IN ENGLISH	NAME IN SPANISH	MISSIONS (WHERE NOTED)	SOURCE
Grape	*Uva, parra, zepa, cepa*	**La Purísima, San Gertrudis**, San José de Comondú, San Javier, **Guadalupe, San Ignacio**, Todos Santos, **San Borja, Santa María, San José del Cabo**	De Mora et al. 1774; Crosby 1994; Del Barco 1980
Guava	*Guayabo*	**La Purísima, San José de Comondú**	**De Mora et al. 1774**
Olive	*Olivo, aceituna*	**La Purísima, Santa Gertrudis**, San José de Comondú, San Javier, **Guadalupe, San Ignacio**	De Mora et al. 1774; Crosby 1994; Del Barco 1980
Passion fruit	*Granada china, granadilla*	Santiago?	**Del Barco 1980**
Peach	*Durazno*	**La Purísima**, Santa Gertrudis, **San José de Comondú**	De Mora et al. 1774; Del Barco 1980
Pomegranate	*Granado*	**Loreto, Santa Gertrudis**, San José de Comondú, San Javier, **Guadalupe, San Ignacio**, Todos Santos, **San Borja**	De Mora et al. 1774; Crosby 1994; Del Barco 1980
Prickly pear	*Nopal, tuna*	**La Purísima, San Javier**	**Del Barco 1980**
Sapote, yellow	*Zapote (amarillo)*	**La Purísima**, San José de Comondú, San Javier	De Mora et al. 1774
Sugarcane	*Caña de azúcar*	Todos Santos, San Ignacio, San José de Comondú	De Mora et al. 1774; Crosby 1994
Tamarind	*Tamarindo*	Loreto	**De Mora et al. 1774**

(Table 9.3). All twenty-one species of mission crops noted in the 1,774 inventories were found in the 2010/2011 surveys. In some cases, however, these Mission-era introductions were not associated with the same oases as noted in historical documents. This indicates that the crops were introduced and then lost and reintroduced to the peninsula in other locations, or propagated and dispersed to another oasis, and then lost in the original location (Table 9.4). The genera with the most species represented were *Citrus* (13+ species and distinct hybrids), *Prunus* (5 species), *Annona* (4 species), and *Morus* (3 species). Among the families, Rutaceae (16 genera), Rosaceae (10 genera), Moraceae (6 genera), Anacardiaceae (4 genera), and Anonaceae (4 genera) had the highest number of genera represented. Only three species were found in all twelve of the surveyed oases: sweet orange, date palm, and guava. Eight species were found in eleven of twelve oases: the three previously mentioned and sour lime, fig, mango, pomegranate, and grape. The next most frequently encountered species (found in ten of twelve oases) were papaya, sweet lime, banana, olive, and prickly pear. This last species is problematic, since some of the individuals were clearly *Opuntia* × *ficus-indica* and others may be a distinct *Opuntia* or *Nopalea* species. Nearly one-third (thirty-one species) of the total species were documented in one of twelve oases.

Oasis Todos Santos had the highest number of perennial food crop species (78/89) and families (35/36) recorded and also the highest number of mission species (21/21) (Tables 9.3 and 9.4). Santiago de los Coras, also in the southern peninsula, had the second highest number of species (48/89), families (24/36), and mission species (19/21). San José/San Miguel de Comondú and San Ignacio both had 18 of 21 mission species; San Javier 17 of 21; and Mulegé and Santa Gertrudis 16 of 21 mission species. All oases contained mission perennial crop species, and all had over ten mission species except San Luis Gonzaga, with the fewest species (5), families (5), and mission species (4). Two species found in the *huertas* actively planted and harvested as food crops are native to the peninsula: native cherry and uvalama (Wiggins 1980). Several species are native to continental Mexico and/or Central America and the Caribbean, among them allspice, custard apple-annona, soursop, sugar apple, avocado, agave, chiltepín, guava, mamey sapote, papaya, Spanish plum/red mombin, prickly pear, false prickly pear, sapodilla, black sapote, white sapote, tepeguaje, and vanilla (Dunmire 2004; Janick and Paull 2008; GRIN Database, accessed in August 2013; USDA Plants Database, accessed August 2013).

The twelve oases under consideration in this study are situated along the lower two-thirds of the Baja California peninsula, and differ in latitude,

TABLE 9.3. Total perennial food crop species found in 2010/2011 oasis *huerta* surveys.

ENGLISH NAME	SPANISH NAME	SCIENTIFIC NAME	FAMILY
Ackee	*Ackee*	*Blighia sapida* K.D. Knoenig	Sapindaceae
Allspice	*Pimienta*	*Pimenta dioica* (L.) Merr.	Myrtaceae
Annona: custard apple, cherimoya, anona	*Anona*	*Annona reticulata* L.	Annonaceae
Annona: custard apple, cherimoya	*Chirimoya*	*Annona cherimola* Mill.	Annonaceae
Annona: soursop	*Anona, guanabana*	*Annona muricata* L.	Annonaceae
Annona: sugar apple	*Anona*	*Annona squamosa* L.	Annonaceae
Apple	*Manzano*	*Malus domestica* Borkh.	Rosaceae
Apricot	*Chabacano, albaricoque, alberichigo*	*Prunus armeniaca* L.	Rosaceae
Asparagus	*Esparragos*	*Asparagus officinalis* L.	Asparagaceae
Avocado	*Aguacate*	*Persea americana* Mill.	Lauraceae
Banana, plantain	*Plátano*	*Musa ×paradisiaca* L.	Musaceae
Blackberry	*Mora, zarsamora*	*Rubus* sp.	Rosaceae
Breadfruit	*Arbol de pan*	*Artocarpus altilis* (Parkinson) Fosberg	Moraceae
Cashew	*Castaña de cajú*	*Anacardium occidentale* L.	Anacardiaceae
Century plant	*Maguey, mescal*	*Agave* spp.	Asparagaceae
Cherry	*Cereza*	*Prunus avium* (L.) L.	Rosaceae

continued

TABLE 9.3. *continued*

ENGLISH NAME	SPANISH NAME	SCIENTIFIC NAME	FAMILY
Cherry, native sand	*Capulín o cereza*	*Prunus serotina* Ehrh. var. *virens* (Wooton & Standl.) McVaugh	Rosaceae
Cherry, tropical (Brazilian, Surinam)	*Cereza braziliano*	*Eugenia uniflora* L.	Myrtaceae
Chiltepín	*Chiltepín*	*Capsicum annuum* L. var. *glabriusculum* (Dunal) Heiser & Pickersgill	Solanaceae
Chive	*Cebollín*	*Allium schoenoprasum* L.	Amaryllidaceae
Cinnamon	*Canela*	*Cinnamomum verum* J. Presl	Lauraceae
Citrus: calamondin	*Tanjerina, naranjito*	×*Citrofortunella microcarpa* (Bunge) Wijnands	Rutaceae
Citrus: citron	*Cidra*	*Citrus medica* L.	Rutaceae
Citrus: grapefruit	*Toronja*	*Citrus paradisi* Macfad	Rutaceae
Citrus: rough lemon	*Limón base de injertos*	*Citrus jambhiri* Lush	Rutceae
Citrus: sweet lemon	*Limón real*	*Citrus* hybrid	Rutaceae
Citrus: sour lime (large)	*Limón Americana*	*Citrus limon* (L.) Burm. F.	Rutaceae
Citrus: sour lime (small)	*Limón*	*Citrus* ×*aurantifolia* (Christm.) Swingle	Rutaceae
Citrus: sweet lime	*Lima dulce chichona*	*Citrus limettioides* Tanaka	Rutaceae
Citrus: lime-orange	*Naranja lima*	*Citrus* sp.	Rutaceae
Citrus: mandarin	*Mandarina*	*Citrus reticulata* Blanco	Rutaceae
Citrus: sour orange	*Naranja amarga*	*Citrus aurantium* L.	Rutaceae
Citrus: sweet orange	*Naranja dulce*	*Citrus sinensis* L. (Osbeck)	Rutaceae

continued

TABLE 9.3. *continued*

ENGLISH NAME	SPANISH NAME	SCIENTIFIC NAME	FAMILY
Citrus: pummelo	*Pomelo/toronja*	*Citrus maxima* (Burm.) Merr.	Rutaceae
Clove	*Pomarosa*	*Syzgium aromaticum* (L.) Merr. & L. M. Perry	Myrtaceae
Cacao	*Cacao*	*Theobroma cacao* L.	Malvaceae
Coconut	*Coco*	*Cocos nucifera* L.	Arecaceae
Coffee	*Café*	*Coffea arabica* L.	Rubiaceae
Date palm	*Dátil*	*Phoenix dactylifera* L.	Arecaceae
Fig	*Higo*	*Ficus carica* L.	Moraceae
Ginger	*Jinjibra*	*Zingiber officinale* Roscoe	Zingiberaceae
Grape, mission	*Uva misionera*	*Vitis vinifera* (Roxb.) Benth.	Vitaceae
Guamúchil	*Guamúchil*	*Pithecellobium dulce*	Fabaceae
Guava	*Guayaba*	*Psidium guajava* L.	Myrtaceae
Guava, pineapple	*Guayabo de piña*	*Acca selloviana* (O. Berg) Burret	Myrtaceae
Guava, strawberry	*Guayaba de fresa*	*Psidium cattleianum* Sabine	Myrtaceae
Hibiscus, sorrel	*Jamaica*	*Hibiscus sabdariffa* L.	Malvaceae
Jackfruit	*Yaca*	*Artocarpus heterophyllus* Lam.	Moraceae
Jujube	*Jujube*	*Ziziphus mauritiana* Lam.	Rhamnaceae
Kumquat	*Naranja china*	*Fortunella margarita* (Lour.) Swingle	Rutaceae
Lemon grass	*Té limón*	*Cymbopogon citratus* (DC.) Stapf	Poaceae
Loquat	*Níspero*	*Eriobotrya japonica* (Thunb.) Lindl.	Rosaceae

continued

TABLE 9.3. *continued*

ENGLISH NAME	SPANISH NAME	SCIENTIFIC NAME	FAMILY
Lychee	*Litchi*	*Litchi chinensis* Maiden & Betche	Sapindaceae
Macadamia nut	*Macademia*	*Macadamia integrifolia*	Proteaceae
Mamey sapote	*Mamey*	*Pouteria sapota* (Jacq.) H. E. Moore & Stearn	Sapotaceae
Mango	*Mango*	*Mangifera indica* L.	Anacardiaceae
Mangosteen	*Mangostín*	*Garcinia mangostama* L.	Clusiaceae
Moringa	*Moringa*	*Moringa oleifera* Lam.	Moringaceae
Mulberry, black	*Mora negra*	*Morus nigra* L.	Moraceae
Mulberry, red	*Mora roja*	*Morus ruba* L.	Moraceae
Mulberry, white	*Mora blanca*	*Morus alba* L.	Moraceae
Olive	*Olivo misionero*	*Olea europaea* L.	Oleaceae
Papaya	*Papaya*	*Carica papaya* L.	Caricaceae
Passion fruit	*Granadilla*	*Passiflora ligularis* Juss.	Passifloraceae
Peach	*Durazno*	*Prunus persica* (L.) Batsch	Rosaceae
Pear	*Pera*	*Pyrus communis* L.	Rosaceae
Pecan	*Pecan*	*Carya illinoinensis* (Wangenh.) K. Koch	Juglandaceae
Pineapple	*Piña*	*Ananas comosus* (L.) Merr.	Bromeliaceae
Plum	*Chabacano*	*Prunus domestica* L.	Rosaceae
Plum, Spanish, red mombin	*Ciruela roja/amarilla*	*Spondias purpurea* L.	Anacardiaceae
Pumb, Spanish, yellow mombin	*Ciruela anaranjada*	*Spondias mombin* L.	Anacardiaceae

continued

TABLE 9.3. *continued*

ENGLISH NAME	SPANISH NAME	SCIENTIFIC NAME	FAMILY
Pomegranate	*Granada*	*Punica granatum* L.	Lythraceae
Prickly pear	*Nopal, tuna*	*Opuntia ficus-indica* (L.) Mill.	Cactaceae
Prickly pear, false	*Nopalillo*	*Nopalea cochenillifera* (L.) Salm-Dyck	Cactaceae
Quince	*Membrillo*	*Cydonia oblonga* Mill.	Rosaceae
Rosemary	*Romero*	*Rosmarinus officinalis* L.	Lamiaceae
Rue	*Ruda*	*Ruta graveolens* L.	Rutaceae
Sapodilla	*Chico sapote*	*Manilkara zapota* (L.) P. Royen	Sapotaceae
Sapote: black	*Zapote negro/prieto*	*Diospyros digyna* Jacq.	Ebenaceae
Sapote: white/yellow	*Zapote amarillo*	*Casimiroa edulis* Llave & Lex.	Rutaceae
Spearmint	*Yerbabuena*	*Mentha spicata* L.	Lamiaceae
Star fruit	*Carambola*	*Averrhoa carambola* L.	Oxalidaceae
Sugarcane	*Caña de azúcar*	*Saccharum officinarum* L.	Poaceae
Tamarind	*Tammarindo*	*Tamarindus indica* L.	Fabaceae
Tepeguaje	*Tepeguaje*	*Leucaena leucocephala* (Lam.) de Wit	Fabaceae
Uvalama	*Uvalma*	*Bumelia peninsularis* Brandegee	Sapotaceae
Vanilla	*Vanilla*	*Vanilla planifolia* Andrews	Orchidaceae
Walnut	*Nogal*	*Juglans regia* L.	Juglandaceae
Yuca/cassava	*Yuca*	*Manihot esculenta* Crantz	Euphorbiaceae

TABLE 9.4. Presence/absence data for perennial food crop species in 2010/2011 oases surveys.

CROP	OASIS CODE												N (%)
	SB	SG	SI	GU	MU	LP	CU	SJ	LD	SLG	TS	SC	
Ackee											X		1 (8.3)
Allspice											X		1 (8.3)
Annona: custard apple; annona*							X		X		X	X	4 (33.3)
Annona: custard apple; cherimoya							X						1 (8.3)
Annona: soursop											X	X	2 (16.7)
Annona: sugar apple											X	X	2 (16.7)
Apple	X	X	X			X	X	X			X	X	8 (66.7)
Apricot		X											1 (8.3)
Asparagus											X		1 (8.3)
Avocado*	X	X	X				X	X	X		X	X	8 (66.7)
Banana, plantain*	X	X	X		X	X	X	X	X		X	X	10 (83.3)
Blackberry											X		1 (8.3)
Breadfruit											X		1 (8.3)
Cashew											X		1 (8.3)
Century plant*		X	X		X			X	X		X	X	7 (58.3)
Cherry			X								X		2 (16.7)

continued

TABLE 9.4. continued

CROP	OASIS CODE												N (%)
	SB	SG	SI	GU	MU	LP	CU	SJ	LD	SLG	TS	SC	
Cherry, native sand											X		1 (8.3)
Cherry, tropical (Brazilian, Surinam)											X	X	2 (16.7)
Chiltepín			X		X	X	X	X			X	X	7 (58.3)
Chive						X					X		2 (16.7)
Cinnamon											X		1 (8.3)
Citrus: calamondin					X		X	X			X	X	5 (41.7)
Citrus: citron*											X		1 (8.3)
Citrus: grapefruit		X	X		X		X	X	X		X	X	8 (66.7)
Citrus: rough lemon					X		X						3 (25.0)
Citrus: lemon sweet		X	X		X	X	X	X	X		X		8 (66.7)
Citrus: sour lime (large)			X		X	X	X	X	X		X	X	8 (66.7)
Citrus: sour lime (small)*	X	X	X	X	X	X	X	X	X		X	X	11 (91.7)
Citrus: sweet lime*	X	X	X	X	X		X	X	X		X	X	10 (83.3)
Citrus: lime-orange	X		X	X	X	X	X	X			X	X	9 (75.0)
Citrus: mandarin	X		X		X		X	X	X		X	X	8 (66.7)
Citrus: sour orange		X	X		X	X	X	X	X		X	X	9 (75.0)

continued

TABLE 9.4. *continued*

CROP	OASIS CODE												N (%)
	SB	SG	SI	GU	MU	LP	CU	SJ	LD	SLG	TS	SC	
Citrus: sweet orange*	X	X	X	X	X	X	X	X	X	X	X	X	12 (100)
Citrus: pummelo			X	X	X	X	X	X	X		X	X	9 (75.0)
Clove											X		1 (8.3)
Cacao											X		1 (8.3)
Coconut*			X		X		X		X		X	X	5 (50.0)
Coffee											X	X	2 (16.7)
Date palm*	X	X	X	X	X	X	X	X	X	X	X	X	12 (100)
Fig*	X	X	X	X	X	X	X	X	X		X	X	11 (91.7)
Ginger											X		1 (8.3)
Grape*	X	X	X	X	X	X	X	X	X		X	X	11 (91.7)
Guamuchil			X		X	X	X	X	X		X	X	8 (66.7)
Guava*	X	X	X	X	X	X	X	X	X	X	X	X	12 (100)
Guava, pineapple											X		1 (8.3)
Guava, strawberry											X		1 (8.3)
Hibiscus						X					X	X	3 (25.0)
Jackfruit					X						X		2 (16.7)
Jujube												X	1 (8.3)

continued

TABLE 9.4. *continued*

CROP		SB	SG	SI	GU	MU	LP	CU	SJ	LD	SLG	TS	SC	N (%)
	OASIS CODE													
Kumquat													X	1 (8.3)
Lemon grass											X	X		2 (16.7)
Loquat								X				X		2 (16.7)
Lychee												X	X	2 (16.7)
Macadamia nut									X			X		2 (16.7)
Mamey sapote												X		1 (8.3)
Mango		X	X	X	X	X	X	X	X	X		X	X	11 (91.7)
Mangosteen												X		1 (8.3)
Moringa												X		1 (8.3)
Mulberry, black			X	X				X						3 (25.0)
Mulberry, red				X			X	X						3 (25.0)
Mulberry, white				X		X								2 (16.7)
Olive*		X	X	X	X	X	X	X	X			X	X	10 (83.3)
Papaya		X	X	X		X	X	X	X	X		X	X	10 (83.3)
Passion fruit*						X			X			X	X	2 (16.7)
Peach*		X	X	X				X	X	X		X	X	9 (75.0)
Pear				X					X			X	X	4 (33.3)

continued

TABLE 9.4. *continued*

CROP						OASIS CODE							N (%)
	SB	SG	SI	GU	MU	LP	CU	SJ	LD	SLG	TS	SC	
Pecan											X		1 (8.3)
Pineapple											X		1 (8.3)
Plum					X						X	X	3 (25.0)
Plum, Spanish, red mombin					X	X	X	X	X		X	X	7 (58.3)
Plum, Spanish, yellow mombin							X					X	2 (16.7)
Pomegranate*	X	X	X	X	X	X	X	X	X		X	X	11 (91.7)
Prickly pear*	X	X	X	X	X	X	X	X		X	X	X	11 (91.7)
Prickly pear, false			X		X	X	X	X			X	X	7 (58.3)
Quince	X												1 (8.3)
Rosemary		X	X				X				X		4 (33.3)
Rue												X	1 (8.3)
Sapodilla					X		X				X		3 (25.0)
Sapote: black											X	X	2 (16.7)
Sapote: white/yellow*		X	X	X	X	X	X	X			X	X	9 (75.0)
Spearmint		X						X			X		3 (25.0)

continued

TABLE 9.4. *continued*

CROP	OASIS CODE												N (%)
	SB	SG	SI	GU	MU	LP	CU	SJ	LD	SLG	TS	SC	
Star fruit											X		1 (8.3)
Sugarcane*		X	X				X	X			X	X	5 (41.7)
Tamarind		X	X		X		X	X	X		X	X	8 (66.7)
Tepeguaje		X			X	X	X	X			X	X	7 (58.3)
Uvalama						X							1 (8.3)
Vanilla											X		1 (8.3)
Walnut											X		1 (8.3)
Yuca/cassava											X		1 (8.3)
N of species[1]	19	27	37	14	36	28	42	36	25	5	78	48	
Percent of species[2]	21	30	42	16	40	32	47	41	28	6	88	54	
N of ME species[3]	13	16	18	11	16	11	18	17	15	4	21	19	
Percent of species[4]	61	76	86	52	76	52	86	81	71	19	100	91	

* Mission-era crop introduction.

1. Number of perennial food crop species found in each oasis.

2. Percent of total number (N=89) of perennial crop species found in all oases.

3. Number of Mission Era (ME) food crop species found in each oasis.

4. Percent of total number (N=21) of Mission era crop introductions.

longitude, and their proximity to the Gulf of California and the Pacific Ocean. This produces a gradient of climatic, topographic, and other physical factors, which inform the type of perennial crop species that can survive in the oases. While the natural mesic environment of the oasis, as well as human alterations and constructions, can create microclimates, the data show slight differences in the species found in the northernmost and southernmost oases. A visual scan of the presence/absence data (Table 9.4) combined with farmer interview questions related to crop selection, reveal that perennial species that thrive best in cooler climates or require chill hours, such as pears, quinces, pomegranates, grapes, and olives, were found more often in the northern oases than in the southern oases. Tropical introductions such as cherimoya, soursop, and bread-fruit were found in higher frequency in the southernmost oases. This did not seem to hold true for tropical crops such as mangos, sugarcane and avocados, which were distributed throughout the oasis archipelago. Soil type also limited the species: coconuts were found mostly in the oases close to the coast, and in the oasis of La Purísima, farmers said that the soil was not suited to olive trees.

SPECIES-AREA RELATIONSHIPS

Our findings confirm that agricultural species within oasis-gardens tend to follow the classic species-area power curve used for wild species in natural habitats, with the number of domesticated perennial crop species increasing with area in cultivation. Total perennial crop diversity and Mission-era crop diversity differ with respect to species accumulation, with increasing area when each are plotted out on a log-log scale (Total species/area slope (z) = 0.316; Mission-era species/area slope = 0.137, Figures 3a and 4a). Slope (z) values for Total species are comparable to those observed for island-archipelago communities (0.25–0.35; Rosenzweig 1995), whereas the slope value for Mission-era species alone falls within the range of slopes observed for species on continents or subdivisions (0.12–0.18; Rosenzweig 1995). The reasoning for this is simple: the Mission-era species were introduced three centuries ago and 1) are presumably the perennial crop species the Jesuits found to be most adapted to the peninsula climate and oasis environments; 2) were dispersed among all of the mission oases in this study during the Mission era; and 3) are more deeply woven into the cultural fabric of the peninsula oases.

The slope also demonstrates the number of species shared among the sample plots. Plots that share many of the same species will have a more shallow slope than plots that share few species, which have slopes of higher values (Collins et al. 2002). In the Mission-era species graph (Figure 9.3a), the slope of the line is shallower, indicating that all of the oases share many of the mission crops, and the sites in the Total species graph (Figure 9.2a) share fewer species (as would be expected). Also in the Total species slope, the number of species continues to increase with area at a higher rate than the Mission-era species slope, indicating that levels of mission crops reach saturation quickly in the oases, and larger oases do not hold many more mission species than smaller oases.

Applying this information to oasis agrobiodiversity conservation, we suggest that a reduction in area for "island," or total species (Figures 9.2a and 9.2b) lowers the diversity more than a reduction of area does for "mainland" or mission species (Figures 9.3a and 9.3b). This indicates that "losing" one or more of the oases will result in a greater loss of newer species introductions than in a loss of the mission species. Again, because many of the newer species introductions are limited to a single garden or oasis, they are more vulnerable to social and environmental stochasticity. These data show that to preserve the total perennial crop diversity and the associated farming systems and knowledge, the oases should be considered as interdependent and interconnected sites, where some oases may serve as source areas for those "sink areas" more vulnerable to species loss.

Analyzing the oases individually against the two predictive species-area power curves (Total species and Mission-era species), we see that the oases show more variation with respect to the total species diversity than with respect to the Mission-era species (Figures 9.2b and 9.3b; Tables 9.5 and 9.6). In other words, while all perennial crop species in the oases tend to increase with area in cultivation, our data indicate that calculations of only the Mission-era crops in the oases more closely align with the species-area power curve than calculations for the total perennial crop species. This can be seen in the number of oases that show significant relationships when we tested the individual fit of each oasis to the Total Perennial Species and Mission-era descriptive power curves using Pearson residuals (Tables 9.5 and 9.6).

For the Total Species analysis, eight of the twelve oases demonstrate a significant relationship with the predictive species-area curve at the 95-percent confidence level (Figure 9.2b; Table 9.5). Four of the sites did not show significance with the predictive model—two above the curve, and two below. The sites that show no significance above the curve are Mulegé and Todos Santos. Tourist development in Mulegé has expanded on much of the arable land and the remaining few gardens are small, but they maintain a relatively high number of

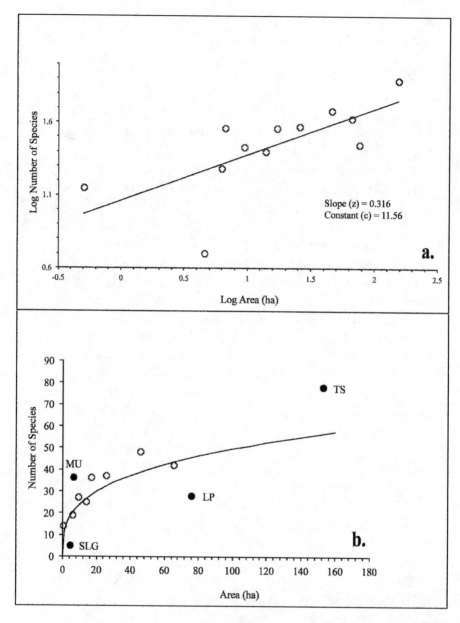

FIGURE 9.2. Total perennial food species–area relationship (LogSpecies: LogArea) (a) and curve (Species: Area) (b). In Figure 9.3b, the black dots are those oases that do not demonstrate a significant relationship to the curve. Mulegé and Todos Santos are above the curve, and San Luis Gonzaga and La Purísima are below the curve.

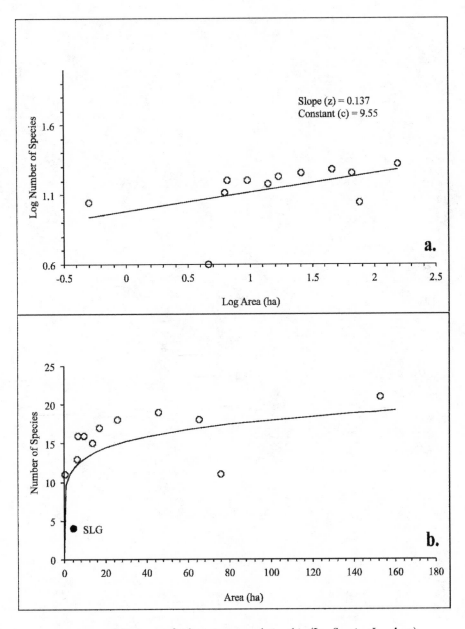

FIGURE 9.3. Mission era food species–area relationship (LogSpecies: LogArea) (a) and curve (Species: Area) (b). In figure 9.4b, San Luis Gonzaga, which shows no significant relationship to the curve, is shown as a black dot.

TABLE 9.5. Statistical results for oasis total perennial crop species-area curve. Results that show no significance are bolded (p < .05).

OASIS	AREA IN CULTIVATION	NUMBER OF SPECIES	PREDICTED VALUE	PEARSON RESIDUAL	P VALUE
SB	6.29	19	20.7	-0.37	0.3556
SG	9.47	27	23.5	0.71	0.2382
SI	25.68	37	32.3	0.83	0.2032
GU	0.50	14	9.3	1.53	0.0624
MU	**6.64**	**36**	**21.0**	**3.26**	**0.0006**
LP	**75.93**	**28**	**45.5**	**-2.59**	**0.0048**
CU	65.60	42	43.4	-0.22	0.4141
SJ	17.01	36	28.3	1.44	0.0750
LD	13.97	25	26.6	-0.32	0.3763
SLG	**4.60**	**5**	**18.7**	**-3.17**	**0.0008**
TS	**153.15**	**78**	**56.8**	**2.81**	**0.0024**
SC	45.80	48	38.8	1.48	0.0690

TABLE 9.6. Statistical results for oasis Mission era species-area relationship. Results that show no significance are bolded (p < .05).

OASIS	AREA IN CULTIVATION	NUMBER OF SPECIES	PREDICTED VALUE	PEARSON RESIDUAL	P VALUE
SB	6.29	13	12.3	0.20	0.4206
SG	9.47	16	13.0	0.83	0.2035
SI	25.68	18	14.9	0.80	0.2127
GU	0.50	11	8.7	0.78	0.2172
MU	6.64	16	12.4	1.03	0.1525
LP	75.93	11	17.3	-1.52	0.0645
CU	65.60	18	17.0	0.25	0.4016
SJ	17.01	17	14.1	0.77	0.2199
LD	13.97	15	13.7	0.34	0.3652
SLG	**4.60**	**4**	**11.8**	**-2.27**	**0.0117**
TS	153.15	21	19.1	0.44	0.3294
SC	45.80	19	16.2	0.71	0.2396

species; the ratio of total species to total area in cultivation is much higher than predicted by the curve. Todos Santos graphs much higher than the expected on the species-area curve because this oasis had by far the highest number of total perennial crop species with many exotics and recent crop introductions due to its tropical climate, high foreign population, and number of professional horticulturalists and nursery owners living in the oasis. The gentle topography of Todos Santos does not constrain arable land and the region has very productive springs. Indeed, despite the 150 hectares in cultivation, excess spring water flows directly into the ocean.

San Luis Gonzaga falls below its expected value because it has only one garden and five perennial crop species remaining due to land tenure disputes and a damaged dam and *acequia* system. La Purísima also lies below its expected value on the curve because of water issues—much of the spring water historically used in this oasis has been diverted to the upstream community of San Isidro, leaving many of the field-gardens fallow. The spring water that does reach La Purísima is salty and intermittent, leading to a decline even in the number of untended crops that grow along the irrigation canal.

When the same calculations are applied only to species introduced during the Mission era (Figure 9.3b; Table 9.6), all oases except San Luis Gonzaga demonstrate significance with respect to the predictive species-area curve. All oases surveyed held some or all of the twenty-one Mission-era species, and larger oases tended to hold more than smaller oases. While total species richness within the oases is influenced by many factors, including proximity to highways, urban development, tourism, agricultural market integration and other social, political, economic, and environmental factors, these analyses indicate that such factors do not have as strong an influence on mission species richness within oases, which tends to increase simply as area in cultivation increases.

RANK-ABUNDANCE RELATIONSHIPS

We differentiate three general patterns in species distribution in the gardens: 1) oases that show relatively even descent lines (San Javier, Comondú, and San Ignacio); 2) oases that show steep, short descent patterns (Santa Gertrudis and La Purísima); and 3) oases that show initial steep declines and then flatten out to include many other species (Santiago and Todos Santos) (Figures 9.4a–g).

The oases with the most even descent lines, and therefore the greatest long-term potential of retaining agrobiodiversity because the diversity is more evenly

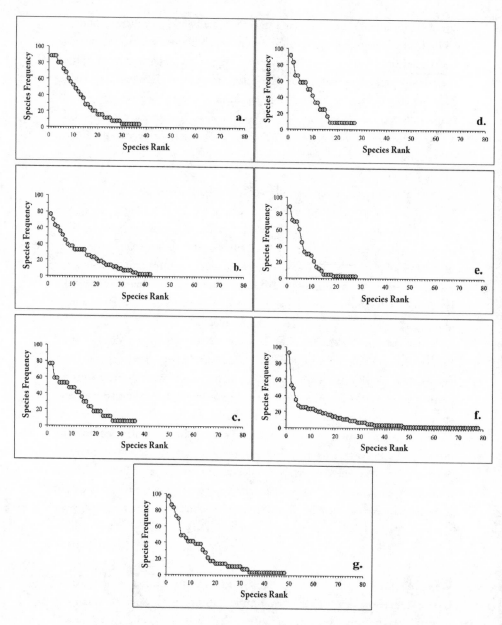

FIGURE 9.4. Rank-abundance curves for San Ignacio (a); Comondú (b); San Javier (c); Santa Gertrudis (d); La Purísima (e); Todos Santos (f); and Santiago (g).

distributed in the gardens, are San Javier, Comondú, and San Ignacio (Figures 9.4a–c). These oases will be more resilient in the face of environmental and social stochasticity because farmers tend to each cultivate a diversity of species and "share" the responsibility of species conservation. These are all mid-sized oases, ranking in the middle of the species-area curve, and they are also located in the middle of the peninsula—meaning central in latitude and at the midpoint between the Pacific and gulf coasts. All are somewhat accessible—neither too isolated, nor too integrated; both of these extremes tend to result in species and farming system disappearance (De Grenade and Nabhan 2013). These oases were located far from markets and agricultural resource centers, and had limited access to seed, fertilizers, and machinery, and thus had little industrial agricultural development. Their location distance from either coast tends to conserve traditional farming methods because the oases receive fewer foreign tourists and residents.

The oases with both low species richness and low species ubiquity among the gardens are represented by rank-abundance graphs with short, steep declines (Santa Gertrudis and La Purísima, Figures 9.4d–e). These would be the most vulnerable to species loss because they have relatively few species to begin with, and few farmers, and many species are found in only a few of the gardens. These are the oases where conservation measures might have highest priority. Corroborating this finding, we noted one species fewer in Santa Gertrudis between our 2010 rapid surveys and the 2011 surveys (Nabhan et al. 2010).

Those oases with steep initial declines, but higher overall species diversity (Santiago and Todos Santos, Figures 9.4f–g), have few species with high frequency and many species with lower occurrence rates in the gardens. Both of these oases lie in the southern peninsula where arable land and water are abundant, supporting many gardens and high species diversity. Both towns have large populations, including many foreign residents who bring in new species, and strong agricultural economies based on a few export crops. These oases would also be vulnerable to losing single species, though the systems here are more robust in general because of the high species richness and high number of farmers and gardens.

OASIS FARMING SYSTEMS AND PRACTICES

Based on our observations of the Baja California peninsula oases, we found that the oases comprise an archipelago of unique agroecological landscapes developed for and through the specific geography of the oases and the peninsula. The landscape informs the design of the fields, especially in narrow canyons. The slope and track of the canal system also influence the location and extent of the arable land. Topography and soils give the gardens their slope and substrate, though terracing and soil development moderate these factors. In some of the ranch gardens, farmers had hauled soil in using mules to create gardens in the rocky canyon sides. These oasis gardens show structural diversity and an integrated native and domesticated animal and plant agricultural system both within and among the oases. They are also, in most cases, small-scale farming systems that utilize crop rotation, livestock integration, mixed annuals and perennials, and structural diversity or crop stratification. In many of the gardens, perennial fruit plants grow along the irrigation ditches and form hedgerows between fields, providing shade, windbreaks, and attraction for predatory species and pollinators. In open areas between the hedgerows, farmers cultivate forage crops, grains, legumes, vegetable crops, or are planted in rows of perennial fruit crops or vineyards. Livestock, including cattle, burros, hair sheep and goats are grazed in the gardens during fallow periods, or tethered to tall trees in the *huertas* and fed grass and herbacious plants harvested by sickle. These mixed-method systems offer a defense against pest epidemics, drought, and floods and enable long-term viability of the farms and the farm families.

The systems integrate wild and introduced species in highly interactive, though not truly mutualistic relationships; date palms along with native California fan palms grow in the riparian ecosystems, providing food resources to temporary and permanent resident species, ecosystem structure for nesting and habitat sites, shade for understory species, and organic matter that alters soil composition and moisture. Grapevines, pomegranate bushes, and fig trees introduced from the Old World serve as understory species in the agrosystems; they also provide food and habitat resources as well as contribute to the agroecosystem structure and function. Rosenzweig (1995) noted in wild systems that the more species share a particular space, the more habitats they distinguish within the space; in oasis-gardens, the more complex the garden structure, the more agriculture species likely to be found. Rosenzweig also notes that the highest levels of biodiversity are often correlated with intermediate disturbance.

Within oasis-gardens, our general observations show that the highest agrobiodiversity and biodiversity are often associated with traditional management systems where little if any mechanization is utilized in the garden. Small sections of fields are tilled by hand for annual crops, and other sections left with perennial fruit trees, vines, and forage crops. The fields with the lowest biodiversity are those almost abandoned and those converted to extreme industrial agricultural practices. When considered as an archipelago or interconnected system, the series of oases—with the range of industrial agricultural and small-scale agriculture sites, the combinations of irrigation systems, and the abandoned to heavily managed spaces—represent higher compositional, structural, and functional diversity than systems of only small-scale agriculture.

The farmers interviewed also gave us a range of agricultural perceptions and knowledge and utilized many different types of practices, from traditional to highly mechanized. These are elaborated in Routson (2012). In general, we found many shared techniques and methods described by farmers in all oases. The pool of agricultural knowledge in the oases is representative of a short agricultural history (three centuries) and a limited population of farmers connected through trade and intermittent travel to festivals. The methods that survived over the isolation and distance may be simple techniques, which were easy to remember and transfer orally or by demonstration.

As examples of specific traditional farming practices shared among the oases, most farmers pruned mission grapevine spurs to "two buds" in February, and did not prune fruit trees within the field-gardens at all except to remove dead branches. In the southern commercial citrus and mango orchards in Santiago and Todos Santos, farmers pruned more rigorously in the spring, either before flowering (mangos) or following harvest (citrus). Most described similar methods reproducing perennial fruit trees and vines—either separating the young plants from the mother tree at or near the base and planting them in other locations, or taking the trimmings of the branches or vines and keeping them moist, in a mix of soil, sand, and organic matter until roots sprout, and the cuttings become individual plants. Other methods utilized include air-rooting techniques of wrapping moist soil and organic material around a higher section of a branch and then parting the branch when roots sprout inside the soil ball, or bending a branch to the ground and pinning it to the moist earth until roots sprout, called acodo. Most gave importance to the stage of the moon, but many gave opposite recommendations (planting and pruning on the full moon or new moon), or simply could not remember. In general, farmers did not practice grafting. Farmers also used seeds of perennial trees as a means of reproduction, especially if the seeds were large and did not require difficult processes or treatment for the seeds to germinate. These techniques were all those that could be easily transferred among farmers or through generations of farmers.

The knowledge described showed more variation among individual farmers than among oases, though many of the people interviewed had lived for three to five generations at the same oasis. Often traditional methods using hand and animal labor and mechanized cultivation methods were both utilized in the oases, though the oases with better access to highways tended to have more mechanized agricultural, more use of synthetic fertilizers, and greater orientation toward commercial production. We found that traditional farming methods were better preserved in some of the small and mid-sized, more isolated oases because limited land and/or water resources had made it not worth developing industrial agriculture within the oases, and they had limited access to the agricultural resource centers.

OASIS POLITICAL ECOLOGY

Interviews related to our framework of oasis political ecology reveal that the agrobiodiversity in the oases is partially shaped by many factors, but determined absolutely by no single factor. We noted several driving factors, including the physical geography of the oasis, geographical isolation and access to markets, industrialization of agriculture, urban development, water quantity and quality limitations, proximity to cities, highways, airports, and ports, and area of arable land. Oases on either spectrum of geographic isolation—those too isolated or too urbanized, both demonstrated an absence of heritage crop species and traditional farming systems (De Grenade and Nabhan 2013). Otherwise, proximity to resource centers, highways, ports or airports, and the coast tended to increase the overall species richness, but not the frequency of occurrence. This finding is partially due to tourists, foreign residents, and those from the Mexican mainland with second homes on the peninsula, commercial agricultural production, and the immigrant laborers introducing more perennial crops species within individual field-gardens, but these species have not had time to disperse within or among the oases. Land tenure type and conflicts over land ownership were most likely the cause of the low diversity in San Luis Gonzaga, and to some degree in Comondú and Santa Gertrudis, whereas private property ownership was correlated with higher total perennial crop diversity in San Ignacio, Mulegé, Todos Santos, and Santiago de los Coras.

Problems in water access, quality, and quantity were the primary cause of low species diversity in La Purísima and noted by community members to have affected crop diversity in Mulegé. Water governance is the power management structure that most closely matches the scale of the oases, a form of governance internal to them. Higher levels of agrobiodiversity and vibrant agroecosystems exist where there is governance at the oasis scale, because the community has more control over its degree of autonomy and integration. Autonomy in oases requires self-governance; the degree of organization within the self-governing bodies allows them to negotiate the modes of connectivity, while maintaining solidarity. It is the relative autonomy of these oases that allows them to retain agrobiodiversity. This provides insights into governing oases more generally; if governance matches the ecological and agricultural scale, the integrity of the oasis can be maintained.

We discovered that the oasis agrobiodiversity is produced through both intentional and unintentional actions. It is a combination of that which is actively managed and cultivated and that which survives a historical moment, that which is planted and maintained, and that which grows or survives because of the natural mesic environment or the inefficiencies in the system. Species that were once in demand as export crops continue to thrive in the oases even after demand and commercial production has ceased, and similarly, species that once held important cultural roles now grow almost wild along irrigation ditches, self-propagating through clones or seeds dispersed through animals.

OASIS CULTURAL PRACTICES

All oases surveyed demonstrated persistence of heritage Mission-era species and intact cultural practices and food knowledge. Oral history and interview data revealed common perceptions of oasis and peninsula identities, pride in oasis culture, and memories of foodways, harvesting and food processing techniques and recipes, and descriptions of the importance of cultural events such as festivals in maintaining these practices. Refer to Routson (2012) and De Grenade and Nabhan (2013) for an expanded discussion of the Baja California oasis cultural ecology. One key finding is as with the farming practices, most of the processes of preparing and processing these food resources are similar throughout the peninsula, with more variation among individuals than among the oases. This indicates that the peninsula landscape, or interconnected archipelago of oases, has undergone more independent cultural evolution than the individual oases, and that the oases operate together as a collective unit of agricultural and cultural practice and knowledge sites.

The degree of active cultural practices did vary among oases. Wine making, though the process was common knowledge in all oases surveyed, was only actively practiced in San Ignacio, Comondú, and La Purísima. This was partly connected to the presence of sufficient quantities of grape vines in these missions; for example the missions of Todos Santos and Santiago in the south of the peninsula were too tropical to produce grapes, though residents did speak of the practice of making wine from the wild grapes that grow in the mountains. The missions of San Javier, San Luis Gonzaga, Los Dolores, Guadalupe, and Mulegé, historically areas of grape production, did not have any sizeable grape vineyards. In a few cases, residents gave personal reasons for not producing wine, such as abstinence from alcohol or a lack of desire to undertake the rigorous process any longer.

Processing of sugarcane followed similar patterns. Sugar mills only existed in the oasis of Comondú, though residents in both La Purísima and San Ignacio had access to nearby mills. Otherwise, residents said that only a few remote ranches and smaller oases had mills and actively milled and processed sugarcane. Unlike grapes, which are limited by climate, sugarcane was historically grown in all oases, especially in Todos Santos, Santiago, and Mulegé—three of the most urbanized oases that we surveyed, and all distinctly lacking in this traditional practice as well as in large cultivated areas of sugarcane. The practice of making dulces was more widespread and documented and described in all oases surveyed except San Luis Gonzaga and Guadalupe, both where the number of living fruit trees were few.

Importantly, the small and mid-sized, mid-peninsula oases (San Borja, Santa Gertrudis, San Ignacio, La Purísima, Comondú, and San Javier) that also showed the most potential for heritage crop persistence on the rank-abundance graphs and strong traditional farming practices, all showed a high retention of traditional food processing practices. These data indicate that active cultural practices are directly tied to the presence of crops within the oases and oasis-gardens. The higher prevalence of crops within the oasis-gardens offers community members more access, and this in turn relates to the prevalence of the traditional foodways practices. Memories tended to be less tied to the actual trees—many of the agricultural changes within the oasis occurred since the construction of the trans-peninsula highway in the 1970s, and residents are at most two generations removed from times when most of these practices were commonplace.

Many of the techniques, recipes, and traditions are still held in living memory if not actively practiced. All of the oases tended to be connected by familial networks and pilgrimages for annual religious celebrations where families and oasis residents can "re-source" traditional practices in the same way that they can re-source agricultural species.

DISCUSSION

We confirm that Baja California oases harbor Mission-era and modern crop introductions (89 total perennial food crop species, with twenty-one Mission era species) and demonstrate a strong tendency to retain historically introduced perennial food crop species over time. Compared to the agrobiodiversity of Sonoran oases first reported at Quitouac three decades ago by Nabhan et al. (1982), these oases on the other side of the Gulf of California remain far more biologically diverse and structurally complex. They show a diversity of structural, compositional, and functional complexity in their cultural management of the agricultural systems and integrated use of native and domesticated plant and animal species.

Our decision to focus on perennial species instead of varieties or land races, however, might be underestimating or possibly obscuring the broader range of genetic and cultural resources that these oases hold. Many of the oasis farmers we interviewed also distinguish annual crop varieties by color, size, ripening time, and flavor; of course, some perennial varieties are well-recognized clones of a single parent type, some distinct types reproduced by seed, others seedling types from heterogeneous species or progeny of cross-pollination between varieties that have not been widely cloned or recognized. In addition, our surveys of crop species and varieties were not detailed enough to distinguish such unique selections as the original sweet orange, reproduced by seed from the mission times, from the standard grafted varieties, present now in many commercial orchards within oases.

We offer these baseline "snapshots" of agrobiodiversity at particular places and times to encourage others to further document the genetic diversity represented in these heritage species. The relatively short cultivation history and the clonal propagation techniques do not facilitate varietal evolution or adaptation to the region; however, this does not rule out the possibility for some small degree of genetic difference, or the development of different land races or distinct hybrids that are selected over time for environmental or cultural characteristics as Soleri et al. (2010) suggest for Mission olives in the nearby Catalina Islands off Alta California. These oases are likely to retain genetic material that while once common in other areas of the world, may have been lost in their source areas, just as some arcane forms of Medieval Iberian Spanish are still utilized here in a manner similar to the linguistic and food crop relicts well-known from Appalachia (Veteto 2010). The Baja California peninsula oases represent a series of "end of the line" agricultural landscapes that may collectively function as a genotype repository just as they serve as an agroecological and cultural repository of traditional farming and foodways practices. These are not merely valuable from a historical perspective but may provide options for a more sustainable agricultural future in the face of an increasingly arid climatic scenario projected for the next century (Nabhan 2013).

Our decision to focus on perennial food crops, which allows us to analyze the existence of Mission-era species and varieties, also limits our ability to compare total diversity within the mission oases to other agroforestry and agrobiodiversity studies. For instance, Gebauer et al. (2007) found 107 total species in Omani oasis-gardens, including annual and perennial fruit, forage, vegetable, grain, medicinal, and ornamental crops. Many authors have addressed species richness in tropical agroforestry systems. Kabir and Webb (2008) recorded 419 total species in Bangladeshi home-gardens, including native, cultivated, and exotic perennials and annuals. Hemp (2006) recorded 520 vascular plant species in Chaga home-gardens in the Mount Kilamanjaro region, including ninety-nine cultivated species. Nevertheless, all oases surveyed on the Baja California peninsula showed retention of some of the original mission species, indicating that these oases are sites worthy of protection as historic agroecological landscapes and reservoirs or refugia of relict heritage folk taxa.

The patterns of species richness per area among oases are notable—species-area curve calculations reveal that larger oases do not favor the retention of mission species any more than small oases. Patterns of agrobiodiversity within oases, addressed through rank-abundance curves, show that the oases with the most even distribution of species and therefore the highest potential of species persistence are the mid-sized, mid-peninsula oases of San Javier, Comondú, and San Ignacio, which also closely fit the traditional species-area curve. The smaller, more isolated oases tended to have the lowest overall agrobiodiversity and be the most vulnerable to species loss. The two southern oases demonstrated the highest numbers of total species—of old and new introductions together—due to increased accessibility, foreign interest, industrialization of the agriculture, and strong agricultural economies. The mid-sized, mid-peninsula oases showed the greatest potential of heritage crop species retention, as well as strong traditional farming practices and cultural foodways practices.

CONCLUSIONS

The critical conservation-oriented finding in this research is that the high diversity of perennial food crops are partitioned among several oases so that conservation efforts focused on one or a few key sites will likely *not* retain as much of the total crop diversity represented on the peninsula as an "archipelago approach" might do. Oases are dynamic landscapes due to the frequency of hurricanes and floods, droughts, and human population changes, as well as the nature of the sites as "source and sink" populations of heritage crops (Pulliam 1988). The geographic diversity of these oases, that is, the physical structure, distance from one another, and location on the peninsula with respect to urban development, highways, and industrialized agricultural production areas, produces the very differences needed to maintain agricultural diversity over long time periods and dispersed spatial patterns. We see farmers differentially engaging with environmental, political, economic, and cultural processes, and these same factors differentially working on or shaping the farmers, the oases, and the gardens. The geography of these oases as agroriparian landscapes on the Baja California peninsula, isolated by desert and saltwater and connected through families, migration, and transportation and communication networks, creates a chain of similar, yet distinct agricultural nuclei. This island biogeographic pattern analysis strongly suggests that oases should be considered components of an interconnected system or archipelago of heritage sites.

The Baja California archipelago of cultivated oases cumulatively (or collectively) feature and retain unique crop assemblages and traditional knowledge and practices that substantively differ from other sets of cultivated desert oases in Central Asia, the Middle East, and North Africa. As such, they have been publicly promoted as sites of informal and formal *in situ* conservation of farmer-bred genotypes and traditional ecological knowledge of unique enough value, which may interest international programs such as UNESCO, Bioversity,

FAO and GIAHS. As of summer 2015, it appears that Mexico's CONANP agency, with technical input from CONABIO, has recommended the Sierra de la Giganta and its agricultural oases at Comondú, to become Mexico's first area to be protected for its agrobiodiversity and its wild biodiversity. If such international protection and recognition are to proceed, we suggest that *Californio* farmers, gardeners, and home cooks be engaged with every step of decision-making, from formulation, definition, designation (or not), benefits-sharing, and landscape-level management. The three-century, shared history of agriculture in the oases has generated a *Californio* culture that continues to inform peninsula residents, shape identity, and support the persistence of heritage crop species and traditional agricultural practices. Promoting the oases as unique cultural landscapes through direct interaction with oasis and ranch families, conservation efforts through governmental and non-governmental organizations, and generating international recognition of the spaces, which function as biologically and culturally diverse refugia, are critical conservation decisions to consider as the peninsula becomes more urbanized, globalized, and tourism-driven.

At the same time, we see an emerging need for cross-cultural and geographic comparisons of agrobiodiversity that use the same measures, methodologies, and ethics. A recent paper of the measurement of agrobiodiversity (Love and Spaner 2007) is a partial start toward this, but a more effective and lasting means to foster such comparisons is by "open source" sharing of methodologies and related computational software, as well as farmer-researcher ethical protocols that allow these comparisons to function across time and space. We look forward to being part of such a larger discussion.

ACKNOWLEDGMENTS

This research would not have been possible without the academic and technical guidance of Dr. Exequiel Ezcurra, Dr. Paul Robbins, Dr. Steve Yool, Dr. Micheline Cariño Olvera, Dr. Stuart Marsh, and Dr. Suzanne Fish. We wish to express our gratitude to Dr. Robert Krueger at the National Clonal Germplasm Repository for Citrus and Dates, David Karp and Dr. Ben Wilder at the University of California, Riverside, Dr. Michael Rosenzweig at the University of Arizona, Dr. Marc Baker of Southwest Botanical Research, Dr. Robert Bye at the Universidad Nacional Autónoma de México, Dr. José Luis León de la Luz at Centro de Investigaciones Biológicas del Noroeste at La Paz, Jesus García at the Arizona-Sonora Desert Museum, and Jaime Gil, agricultural engineer of the Canary Islands. We thank the researchers in the networks of RIDISOS and Cultura del Oasis for collaboration, research advice, information and technical support. Science Foundation Arizona, Fulbright-COMEXUS, the Philanthropic Education Organization, Universidad Autónoma de Baja California Sur, and the University of Arizona's School of Geography and Development and Southwest Center provided the institutional support and funding for this doctoral research. Our deepest gratitude to Jaime de Grenade, Don, Rebecca, Kanin, and Cody Routson, Jack and Eileen Routson, Laurie Monti, Ellery Kimball and Becca Munro, and those who provided the encouragement and support necessary for this extensive process.

REFERENCES CITED

Adams, D. K. and A. C. Comrie. 1997. The North American monsoon. *Bulletin of the American Meteorological Society* 78: 2197–213.

Altieri, M. A. and L. C. Merrick. 1987. In Situ conservation of crop genetic resources through maintenance of traditional farming systems. *Economic Botany* 41:86–96.

Aradhya, M.K., E. Stover, D. Velasco, and A. Koehmstedt. 2010. Genetic structure and differentiation in cultivated fig (*Ficus carica* L.). *Genetica* 138:681–94.

Aschmann, H. 1967. *The Central Desert of Baja California: Demography and Ecology.* Manessier Publishing Company, Riverside, CA.

Baegert, J. J. 1979. *Observations in Lower California.* University of California Press, Berkeley, CA. Available at: http://ark.cdlib.org/ark:/13030/ft5r29n9xv/. Accessed May 2012.

Brush, S. B. ed. 2000. *Genes in the Field: On-Farm Conservation of Crop Diversity.* Lewis Publishers, Boca Raton, FL.

Cariño Olvera, M. M. 1996. *Historia de las Relaciones Hombre/Naturaleza en Baja California Sur, 1500–1940.* Centro de Investigaciones Biologicas del Noroeste, A.C., 2nd edition, UABCS SEP, La Paz, México.

Cariño Olvera, M.M., A. Breceda, A. Ortega, and L. Castorena. 2013. *Evocando El Eden: Conocimiento, Valoracióny Problemática del Oasis de Los Comondú.* Icaria Editorial, Barcelona, Spain.

Clavijero, F. J. 2007. *Historia de la Antigua o Baja California.* Editorial Porrú a, México, D.F.

Collins, M.D., D. P. Vázquez, and N. J. Sanders. 2002. Species-Area curves, homogenization and the loss of global diversity. *Evolutionary Ecology Research* 4:457–64.

Comrie, A. C. and E. C. Glenn. 1998. Principle components-based regionalization of the precipitation regimes across the Southwest United States and Northern Mexico, with an application to monsoon precipitation variability. *Climate Research* 10: 201–15.

CONAGUA. 2011. Comisión Nacional de Agua. La Paz, México. Information requested in May 2011.

Crosby, H. W. 1994. *Antigua California: Mission and Colony on the Peninsular Frontier, 1697–1768.* University of New Mexico Press, Albuquerque, NM.

Davis, L. 2006. Baja California's paleoenvironmental context. In *The Prehistory of Baja California: Advances in Archeology of the Forgotten Peninsula*, edited by D. Laylander and J. D. Moore. University of Florida Press, Gainsville, FL.

Del Barco, M. 1980. *A Natural History of Baja California.* Dawson's Bookshop, Los Angeles, CA.

De Grenade, R. and G. P. Nabhan. 2013. Baja California peninsula oases: An agro-biodiversity of isolation and integration. *Journal of Applied Geography* 41:24–35.

De Mora, Fr. V., D. Gines, and M. Perez. 1774. *California Antigua: Padrones y Noticias de Estado de Las Misiones en el Año del 1774.* Archivo General de la Nacion, México. Provincias Internas (092)/Vol 166. Accessed on March 1–4, 2011.

Del Rio, I. 2003. *El Regímen Jesuítico de la Antigua California.* Universidad Nacional Autónoma de México; Instituto de Investigaciones Históricas, México, D.F.

Dengler, J. 2009. Which function describes the species-area relationship best? A review and empirical evaluation. *Journal of Biogeography* 36:728–44.

Dunmire, W. W. 2004. *Gardens of New Spain: How Mediterranean Plants and Foods Changed America.* University of Texas Press, Austin, TX.

Engelhardt, Z. 1908. *The Missions and Missionaries of California, Vol. I. Lower California.* The James H. Barry Company, San Francisco, CA.

Frese, L., G. K. Bjørn, F. Franca, B. V. Ford-Lloyd, C. U. Germeier, J. M. Iriondo, A. Katsiotis, S. P. Kell, V. Negri, and M. A. A. Pinheiro de Carvalho. 2012. Genetic reserve conservation of European crop wild relative and landrace diversity. In *Agrobiodiversity Conservation: Securing the Diversity of Crop Wild Relatives and Landraces*, edited by N. Maxted, M. Ehsan Dulloo, B. V. Ford-Lloyd, L. Frese, J. Iriondo, and M. A. A. Pinheiro de Carvalho, pp. 1–6. CABI International, Wallingford, UK.

Gebauer, J., E. Luedeling, K. Hammer, M. Nagieb, and A. Buerkert. 2007. Mountain oases in northern Oman: An environment for evolution and In Situ conservation of plant genetic resources. *Genetic Resources and Crop Evolution* 54: 465–81.

GRIN: Germplasm Resources Information Network [Online Database]. National Germplasm Resources Laboratory, Beltsville, Maryland. Available at: http://www.ars-grin.gov. Accessed August 2013.

Hammer, K., J. Gebauer, S. Al Khanjari, and A. Buerkert. 2009. Oman at the crossroads of inter-regional exchange of cultivated plants. *Genetic Resources and Crop Evolution* 56: 547–60.

Hammer, K. and Y. Teklu. 2008. Plant Genetic Resources: Selected issues from genetic erosion to genetic engineering. *Journal of Agriculture and Rural Development in the Tropics and Subtropics* 109:15–50.

Hemp, A. 2006. The banana forests of Kilimanjaro: Biodiversity and conservation of the Chagga homegardens. *Biodiversity and Conservation* 15:1193–217.

Janick, J. and R. E. Paull. 2008. *The Encyclopedia of Fruits and Nuts*. CAB International, Wallingford, UK.

Kabir, Md. E. and E. L. Webb. 2008. Can homegardens conserve biodiversity in Bangladesh? *Biotropica* 40:95–103.

Lassépas, U. U. 1859. *Historia de la Colonización de la Baja California*. Decreto de 10 Marzo de 1857. Vicente Garcia Torres, México, D.F.

Lenné, J. M. 2011. Food security and agrobiodiversity management. In *Agrobiodiversity Management and Food Security: A Critical Review*, edited by Lenné, J. M. and D. Wood, pp. 12–25. CAB International, London, UK.

León de la Luz, J. L. and R. D. Cadena. 2006. Hydrophytes of the oases in the Sierra de la Giganta of Central Baja California Sur, México: Floristic composition and conservation status. *Journal of Arid Environments* 67:553–65.

Love, B. and D. Spaner. 2007. Agrobiodiversity: Its value, measurement, and conservation in the context of sustainable agriculture. *Journal of Sustainable Agriculture* 31:53–82.

Maya, Y., R. Coria, and R. Dominguez. 1997. Caracterización de Los Oasis. In *Los Oasis de La Península de Baja California*, edited by L. Arriaga and R. Rodríguez Estrella, 5–26. Centro de Investigaciones Biológicas de Noroeste, La Paz, BCS, México.

Minnich, R.A., E. F. Vizcaíno, and R. J. Dizzani. 2000. The El Niño/southern oscillation and precipitation variability in Baja California, México. *Atmósfera* 13:1–20.

Mukherjee, S. K. 1953. The mango: Its botany, cultivation, uses and future improvement, especially as observed in India. *Economic Botany* 7: 130–62.

Nabhan, G. P. 2007. Agrobiodiversity change in a Saharan Desert oasis, 1919–2006: Historic shifts in Tasiwit (Berber) and Bedouin crop inventories of Siwa, Egypt. *Economic Botany* 61:31–43.

———. 2012. *Desert Terroir: Exploring the Unique Flavors and Sundry Places of the Borderlands.* University of Texas Press, Austin, TX.

———. 2013. *Growing Food in a Hotter, Drier Land: Lessons from Desert Farmers on Adapting to Climate Uncertainty.* Chelsea Green Publishing, White River Junction, VT.

Nabhan, G.P., A. M. Rea, K. L. Reichhardt, E. Mellink, and C. F. Hutchinson. 1982. Papago influences on habitat and biotic diversity: Quitovac ethnoecology. *Journal of Ethnobiology* 2:124–43.

Nabhan, G.P., J. Garcia, R. Routson, K. Routson, and M. M. Cariño Olvera. 2010. Desert oases as genetic refugia of heritage crops: Persistence of forgotten fruits in the mission orchards of Baja California, México. *International Journal of Biodiversity and Conservation* 2:56–69.

Ortiz, R. 2011. Agrobiodiversity management for climate change. In *Agrobiodiversity Management for Food Security: A Critical Review,* edited by Lenné, J. M. and D. Wood, pp. 189–211. CAB International; London, UK.

Pimentel, D., U. Stachow, D. A. Takacs, H. W. Brubaker, A. R. Dumas, J. T. Meaney, J. A. S. O'Neil, D. E. Onsi, and D. B. Corzilius. 1992. Conserving diversity in agricultural/forestry systems. *Bioscience* 42:3354–62.

Pulliam, H. R. 1988. Sources, sinks and population regulation. *The American Naturalist* 132:652–61.

Ramón Laca, L. 2003. The introduction of cultivated citrus to Europe via Northern Africa and the Iberian Peninsula. *Economic Botany* 574: 502–14.

Rivera, D., D. Johnson, J. Delgadillo, M. H. Carrillo, C. Obón, R. Krueger, F. Alcarez, S. Ríos, and E. Carreño. 2012. Historical evidence of the Spanish introduction of date palm (*Phoenix dactylifera* L., Arecaceae) into the Americas. *Genetic Resources and Crop Evolution* 60:1433–52. DOI 10.1007/s10722-012-9932-5.

Rosenzweig, M. L. 1995. *Species Diversity in Space and Time.* Cambridge University Press, Cambridge, UK.

Routson, R. J. 2012. *Conservation of Agrobiodiversity in Baja California Desert Oases.* Unpublished Doctoral Dissertation, Department of Geography, University of Arizona, Tucson, AZ.

Soleri, D., A. Koehmstedt, M. K. Aradhya, V. Politi, and K. Pinney. 2010. Comparing the historic olive trees (*Olea europaea* L.) of Santa Cruz Island with contemporaneous trees in the Santa Barbara, CA area: A case study of diversity and structure in an introduced agricultural species conserved in Situ. *Genetic Resources and Crop Evolution* 57:973–84.

This, P., T. Lacombe, and M. R. Thomas. 2006. Historical origins and genetic diversity of wine grapes. *Trends in Genetics* 22:511–19.

Thrupp, L. A. 2000. Linking agricultural biodiversity and food security: The valuable role of agrobiodiversity for sustainable agriculture. *International Affairs* 76:265–81.

USDA (United States Department of Agriculture) Plants Database [online database]. Available at: http://plants.usda.gov. Accessed August 2013.

Venegas, M. 1757. *Noticia de la California: y De Su Conquista Temporal, y Espiritual Hasta el Tiempo Presente*. Viuda de M. Fernandez, Madrid, Spain.

Vernon, E. W. 2002. *Las Misiones Antiguas: The Spanish Missions of Baja California, 1683–1855*. Viejo Press, Santa Barbara, CA.

Veteto, J. R. 2010. *Seeds of Persistence: Agrobiodiversity, Culture and Conservation in the American Mountain South*. Unpublished Doctoral Dissertation, Department of Anthropology, University of Georgia, Athens, GA.

Wiggins, I. L. 1980. *Flora of Baja California*. Stanford University Press, Stanford, CA.

Zizumbo-Villareal, D. 1996. History of the coconut in México: 1549–1810. *Genetic Resources and Crop Evolution* 43:505–16.

10

PASSING ON A SENSE OF PLACE AND TRADITIONAL ECOLOGICAL KNOWLEDGE BETWEEN GENERATIONS

GARY PAUL NABHAN

INTRODUCTION

MANY COMMUNITIES, ESPECIALLY THOSE on Indian reservations near rapidly growing urban areas, have demonstrated their commitment to ensuring that their cultural sense of place, as well as their traditional ecological such knowledge and values about native plants and animals, continue to be passed on to their children. The passing on of knowledge by word of mouth, and the passing on of values and skills associated with traditional cultures, while still continuing, has often been disrupted by a number of external pressures. Contemporary children's attitudes, knowledge, and behaviors toward animals, plants, and their habitats may therefore be very different from those of the generations preceding them (Kellert and Westervelt 1977; Nabhan 2003).

Instead of being regularly involved in learning from community elders about their people's traditional ways of living well in the deserts, forests, mountains, or coastal habitats, most children today spend more time in schools, in transit to and from schools, or on the Internet and TV (Nabhan and St. Antoine 1993).

This chapter is taken from the online series sponsored by World Wildlife Fund's *People and Plants Handbook* edited by ethnobiologist Gary Martin of the Global Biodiversity Foundation based in Morocco.

Over the last fifty years, more parents have abandoned traditional subsistence activities to work away from home for wages, and therefore have less time to teach their children their native language, customs, and skills (Zitnow 1990). It also appears that Native American children in the binational Southwest now spend less time alone or with peers in the desert, directly involved with the plants and animals native to their homeland (Nabhan 1997; Rosenberg 1997).

In a recent survey of twenty-seven Tohono O'odham schoolchildren in southern Arizona, only 37 percent of the eight to fourteen year olds claimed that they had ever gathered wild foods, and just 44 percent said they had been hunting with their parents or grandparents. However, 78 percent said that they had watched TV shows about wildlife, 56 percent had read books about wildlife within the previous year, and 74 percent have been to zoos, museums, or botanical gardens in the last two years (Nabhan and Tanner, unpublished data). These and other indicators suggest that children—even those living in the most remote rural areas—are now influenced by many sources of conventional and digital information about the natural world, over and above what their parents and grandparents teach them, or what they learn by direct hands-on experience. We analyzed data from a cross-cultural comparison of Anglo, Mexican, O'odham, and Yaqui American students living in rural areas of southern Arizona and adjacent Sonora, all within miles of national parks. These preliminary data clearly indicate that today's schoolchildren do not necessarily experience the full range of activities on which their cultures' traditional sense of place was formerly based.

It has been widely debated whether that traditional farming, hunting, fishing, and gathering skills are as necessary for cultural survival as they once were (Brody 2001; Pretty 2014). Yet some communities have recognized that such family-based activities serve as the most important vehicles for teaching native language, traditional stories, and community values that reinforce a distinctive sense of place (Ohmagari and Berkes 1997). Skills such as traditional food gathering and processing, or basket making and hide tanning, can only be learned by "hands-on" instruction from elders, and there are specialized vocabularies, which go with each of these activities. It appears that the use of native terms associated with place-based subsistence activities, such as tanning hides or crafting wood implements, is the realm within native languages that is most rapidly being lost (Zepeda 1983). Put in the context that 90 percent of the world's native languages will be lost within the next century (Krauss 1992), the outlook for linguistically encoded traditional knowledge about place is not at all good.

There are numerous programs around North America that are encouraging native language retention, but few of them reinforce native language use in conjunction with traditional knowledge about the local environment through community visits to sacred places, plant gathering grounds, hunting camps, or springs. The Sense of Place Project of the Arizona-Sonora Desert Museum has recently sponsored such outings in collaboration with Seri, O'odham, and Hispanic communities, in some cases taking children to such culturally significant places for the very first time in their lives. The Sense of Place Project is committed to recognizing, celebrating, and reinforcing local knowledge of place, plants, and animals in the Sonoran Desert borderlands. In particular, one of our objectives has been to work with communities wishing to pass on traditional ecological knowledge, and to reinforce it through their own communities' institutions, such as tribal museums and cultural preservation programs.

However, there are few communities that know the extent to which traditional knowledge about place, plants, and animals is still being passed on from generation to generation or, conversely, the magnitude of loss of language, knowledge, and hands-on experience, which has already occurred (Ohmagari and Berkes 1997; Zent 1999). There is currently no standard methodology for determining the rate or extent of traditional knowledge retention or loss about place, nor any surefire techniques for preventing or mitigating such losses that work in all communities (Ohmagari and Berkes 1997). Nevertheless, by carefully choosing one or more of the intergenerational survey methods suggested below, and establishing a benchmark assessment, communities can better determine the challenges they face in ensuring that effective culturally sensitive environmental education occurs.

DETERMINING GOALS, CHOOSING APPROPRIATE METHODS

There are several possible objectives that a community may have for sponsoring an intergenerational survey of traditional knowledge retention or loss. Each objective may require a different kind of survey, or a combination of several different kinds of interviews and assessments. We will list some of the many possibilities below, providing short synopses of appropriate methods to go with them.

RETENTION OF NATIVE TERMS FOR PLANTS, ANIMALS, AND PLACES

As part of comprehensive community-based surveys of native language loss or retention, language educators may wish to see if there is differential loss of terms relating to the local environment, to its biota, and to traditional subsistence skills (Zepeda 1983; Zepeda and Hill 1995). For O'odham speakers, Hill and Zepeda presented a scrapbook of over a hundred photos from magazines and books, which illustrated local plant and animal life and subsistence activities, then asked native speakers in O'odham to name or describe the objects and organisms while being tape-recorded. More than eighty plants and animals were pictured. They compared the names given by different ages of women to come up with a measure of lexemic (name) loss, but also analyzed the extent to which dialect distinctions were maintained, or loan words used.

One flaw with this method was that some of the photos were not detailed enough for interviewees to distinguish and name different species of prickly pear, or different kinds of beans. In addition, some sets of photos were used to elicit names of life forms (such as fish) as opposed to showing local species (such as desert pupfish).

Similarly, in a pilot survey of O'odham children paired with their grandparents in the Ajo, Arizona area, Nabhan and St. Antoine (1993) used a booklet of twenty line drawings of common plants and animals. However, it was difficult for all those interviewed to determine which "black bird" was illustrated—a boat-tailed grackle, a common raven, or a Brewer's blackbird. If photos or drawings are to be used in such surveys, they should be of plants or animals not closely related to other local species. For instance, showing drawings of jojoba and saguaro might prove more productive than showing two kinds of mesquite trees, since the traits by which O'odham elders distinguish the two mesquites cannot often be seen in photos. For Rosenberg's (1997) interviews of Seri children, Arizona-Sonora Desert Museum photo archives were searched to obtain forty color photos that showed distinctive local (often endemic) species close-up, with most distinguishing features visible. Even so, the identities of certain species of lizards remained so difficult to determine that the Seri had no consensus about their names (Rosenberg 1997), although Nabhan (2003) later found they are identified as much by behavior and habitat as by morphology.

In order to overcome problems posed by using photos and drawings, Zent (1999) took Piaroa schoolchildren on walks through a five-yard wide and

150-yard long transect of old growth forest located thirty minutes (by foot) from their town. There, he marked fifty different kinds of plants, and asked those interviewed to name and discuss the cultural significance of each marked plant along the transect. His forty-four respondents sorted into two groups, with a much higher competence level displayed among those over thirty years of age who grew up in such forests. Thus, the older the respondent, the more competent the person was in knowing Piaroan names for plants; however, the more one participated in formal (Spanish-language) education, the less likely it was that the person would have the same level of naming competency that an unschooled person of the same age retained. In general, Zent (1999) concluded that showing respondents live plants growing in the local environment meant that methodological problems in obtaining near-perfect identifications for all species were virtually eliminated.

Nevertheless, such surveys show that even O'odham women in their twenties and thirties recall only a fraction of the native names for plants and animals, which older women in their communities still recall (Zepeda and Hill 1995). In the pilot survey near Ajo, O'odham children knew only a third of the native names that their grandparents knew for the most common plants and animals in their local environments (Nabhan and St. Antoine 1993). These initial surveys had small sample sizes and should be done in more communities before any final conclusions are made regarding ethnobiological knowledge retention among the O'odham. Nevertheless, they suggest that losses are occurring even in a group such as the O'odham, which continues to have thousands of native language speakers. Fortunately, programs such as Tohono O'odham Community Action are giving young people opportunities to reacquaint themselves with native names for basketry and food plants, and for processing skills (Reeder 1997).

RETENTION OF TRADITIONAL KNOWLEDGE AND VALUES OF LOCAL WILDLIFE

Educators may wish to know whether the way in which science is taught in schools is changing children's values and perceptions of local animals. For example, a science teacher may lecture students about how horned lizards are harmless animals, but the children's grandparents may simultaneously teach them that these creatures are psychically or spiritually dangerous and may cause human illness such as "staying sickness" if mistreated.

Rosenberg (1997) and Nabhan (2003) have devised a productive means of eliciting and comparing information from children and their elders in the Seri community with regard to such knowledge, beliefs, and values. She asked interviewees
to sort photos of animals into groupings of which animals were good, beautiful,
or liked, versus those which are considered bad, ugly, dangerous, or hated. She also
asked the Seri which animals were considered edible or poisonous. Finally, with
regard to ceremonially important animals such as the leatherback turtle, she asked
if children had been to the ceremony, whether they believed that leatherbacks can
talk with the Seri, and whether leatherbacks can or should be eaten. Only two
children under twenty had participated in the ceremony; among the twenty to
thirty-nine year olds, only 10 percent think that leatherback meat is eaten at ceremonies; this percentage increased to 44 percent in the next age group (40–59), and
to 50 percent among those over sixty years of age (Rosenberg 1997). These trends
held up with a larger sample undertaken several years later by Nabhan (2003).

Where there are differences of opinion—especially among different age
groups—the usual assumption is that the eldest group's answer is the "correct
one." However, there may even be differences of opinion among elders, as there
is in this fifty/fifty split among Seri elders. A shift in opinion between generations is not necessarily "loss." Rosenberg (1997) did not attempt to use consensus analysis (Romney, Weller and Batchelder 1986) to determine what answer
is shared by most members of a culture, but this additional analytical tool has
proven useful in other studies (Zent 1999). However, it may be valid to give
more weight to consensus among elders, relative to consensus among schoolchildren, for certain kinds of esoteric cultural information.

RETENTION OF TRADITIONAL ECOLOGICAL
KNOWLEDGE ABOUT NATURAL RESOURCES

Traditional hunters, gatherers, herbalists, and farmers know far more than the
mere names of plants and animals; they also know a lot about the ecological
relationships among plants and animals, and how certain ecological processes
such as fire or flood affect their distributions. Although all these relationships
and processes are not necessarily given names, they are known in a way that can
be elicited by interviews. Simple questions, such as "Where does this animal
live?" or "What animal eats this plant?" can help document such traditional
ecological knowledge. In addition, Rosenberg (1997) asked children to compare
the hunting and nesting habits of selected species (ospreys and pelicans) that

are locally abundant. Because a single species of animal may eat many things or nest at different places within its territory, the range of answers may be different for children who stay close to a single home, versus adults who had a more mobile lifestyle while growing up. Any differences in outcomes from different age groups should be carefully interpreted.

RETENTION OF TRADITIONAL SUBSISTENCE SKILLS

One universal—if there are any at all—is that the major means by which all traditional ecological knowledge is transmitted is through hands-on involvement in food-getting, basket-making, and land management. Accordingly, Ohmagari and Berkes (1997) and Nabhan (2003) have focused on how, when, and to what extent children are learning the "bush skills" associated with their community's heritage. They cite a learning sequence that they believe most children go through in learning the land- or water-based traditions of their community. The child becomes familiar with the fact that elders participate in an activity such as hunting waterfowl or harvesting willow for basketry; they then observe the hunting or harvesting. Next, they take initial steps in participation, assisting with the most basic tasks. They are then explicitly shown the entire sequence of a process by an elder, and are next asked to perform the sequence under the supervision of an adult. Finally, they begin to experiment with innovations to personalize the task, and they become equal partners with their instructors.

In two rural Cree communities, Ohmagari and Berkes (1997) asked women three questions about each of 93 particular "bush skills" involved in foraging, fishing, hunting, and crafts-making:

Did you learn the particular skill?
If yes, who was your major teacher?
How old were you when you learned the skill?

Historically, most Cree girls learned such skills from their parents, grandparents, and aunts. Today, it is becoming more common for women to learn these skills only after they have married, and then it is from their in-laws who remain most active in subsistence activities. It may be that a revival of interest in traditional ecological skills and knowledge is now going on among Cree individuals who missed exposure to such activities while they were young. Ironically, boarding school students were among those most active in learning these skills when they came home on vacation for extended periods, while the children who stayed at home and went to local schools tended to take the skills for granted.

For better or worse, many subsistence skills tend to be taught within a single gender, from mother or mother-in-law to daughter or daughter-in-law. There are exceptions of course; both O'odham boys and girls have learned certain kinds of basketry-making techniques. Nevertheless, it may be relevant in some communities to discuss with boys and girls different lists of traditional skills, with some items on both lists. It is clear that there are cultural gender issues with regard to learning some skills, stories, and ethical precepts (Nabhan 2003).

The following list is offered as examples of questions about some traditional subsistence skills commonly found throughout rural communities:

When is the best time of year to harvest roots and leaves for baskets?

How do you prepare gourds for making rattles, ladles, or masks?

What is the best wood to burn for baking clay pottery?

Why shouldn't you hunt rabbits during the summertime?

When is the best time of year to cut wood for making termite-resistant posts?

When can tortoises be found sleeping in caves or crevices?

How can you remove spines or stickers from food plants so that you can eat them?

How big should wild greens (*quelites*) be when you pick them?

If you harvest a plant for medicine, do you take the root, the flowers, or the green branches?

These skill sets are learned by doing, rather than through simple oral transmission (Nabhan 2003).

RETENTION OF TRADITIONAL SONGS, STORIES, AND VERNACULAR MAPS THAT REINFORCE A SENSE OF PLACE

Traditional stories about places and songs, plants and animals, continue to be shared in most communities, whether or not they are still offered in native dialects. In certain cases, these cannot be shared with outsiders, at least not during all seasons. Nevertheless, it is possible to simply ask children and adults if they themselves have sung songs or told stories about coyotes, tortoises, eagles, cacti, or other species. Often, the younger generation only gets the general gist of a song, since it may be rendered in an archaic dialect (Nabhan 2003).

When permissible, asking for a description or summary of the song or story helps to verify that children are speaking of the same narrative that elders are speaking of, and not one from a Coyote and Roadrunner cartoon. Rosenberg (1997) was able to determine that Seri elders knew two and a half times as many songs about animals as did the children, even though there was not nearly as much difference in their competency in simply naming the animals in Seri. Only a third of the children and teens could say a tongue twister about coral snake coloration that was performed by virtually all Seri over the age of forty. Importantly, such knowledge is almost exclusively transmitted between generations while they are engaged in subsistence activities in the field and not at home or in schools (Nabhan 2003).

With regard to sense of place, it is not merely the names of particular locations that matter; it is also the events that took place there and the stories about them (Basso 1996). Certain elements, which modern mapmakers would never include, have great prominence on hand-drawn "vernacular" maps by traditional peoples (Hine and Hill 1986). For instance, eighteen of twenty-four Seri mapmakers marked the area where their afterbirth was buried, and ten of them centered their maps of their land (*terrêno*) on the exact place where their afterbirth was buried. Prominent features on the horizon and along the coast were more important than nearby towns, geopolitical boundaries or even roads (Hine and Hill 1986). It would be interesting to interview Apache youth regarding their knowledge of the stories recorded by Basso (1996) for the hundreds of place names in the Cibecue area. However, recent place-name work with the Hia C-eḍ O'odham in southwestern Arizona suggests that few individuals under fifty years of age have ever had access to the majority of traditional sites in their former homeland, since much of it has become a bombing range where public access is restricted.

When asking community members to draw maps of their homeland, it is best not to give them a base map, or to predetermine which kinds of cultural or natural features should be mapped. The more open-ended the invitation is, the closer the drawn map may be to the individual's own cognitive map.

EVALUATING RESULTS, DETERMINING EDUCATIONAL INTERVENTIONS

Regardless of which methods are used to determine the degree of intergenerational retention of traditional knowledge, it should be explained to the communities involved that these surveys are only first approximations intended to stimulate more reflection, discussion, and educational action. Ultimately, the community's collective feelings—not the statistics alone—are the best way to determine whether traditional sense of place and relationship to other creatures is being lost, retained, or revived. Interviews and surveys should be thought of as means to catalyze more community discussion of the importance of language and land-use traditions, and what is at risk if these traditions are lost.

Communities need not despair if they become aware that changes are occurring at a much more rapid rate than they had previously assumed. Many communities have recently begun to experiment with means to slow or avert the losses of traditions. Immersion schools and after-school tutorials with elders have proven effective in slowing native language loss, or even reviving language use. Summer camps and field trips focused on teaching children native traditions have been successful among a variety of cultures, from the Gwichi'in on the Arctic Circle in Alaska (Gildart 1997), the Haisla on the Pacific temperate rainforest coast of British Columbia, and the Tohono O'odham in southern Arizona deserts. The Arizona-Sonora Desert Museum and Prescott College's Kino Bay Center have sponsored a series of field trips to traditionally significant places, where Seri elders knowledgeable about songs and stories of those places shared them with children who had never before had access to those places (Nabhan 2003).

Obviously, there are many other strategies for preserving cultural traditions about place other than the ones briefly mentioned here. And yet, we see many community organizations—such as TOCA on the Tohono O'odham Reservation—embracing the notion that neither native language nor stories can survive unless traditional interactions with the natural world persist to give them context, their sense of place. As TOCA's Tristan Reader (1997) has written,

> ... it is not enough to preserve a language, its words and its linguistic structures, its images and grammar. In order for a language to be truly alive and vital, we must also preserve the subjects of discussion. A living language means a language that is lived, a language that grows out of the ways in which people make their living and their meanings. . . . Cultural preservation requires that we rejuvenate traditional food systems, local economies and ways of interacting with the natural world.

A growing number of indigenous communities, their schools and museums, are sponsoring means by which their children learn not only their native language, crafts, and ceremonies, but also the subsistence activities in the natural world from which these artistic expressions emerged. The Sacred Sites and Gathering Grounds Initiative of Northern Arizona University is but one of several activities and programs that have been successful in helping elders pass on their traditional knowledge and sense of place to younger generations (Trujillo, Monti, and Jarratt-Ziernicki 2005). Initiatives also underscore the need to keep such gathering grounds and touchstones of tradition accessible to future generations.

LITERATURE CITED

Basso, K. 1996. *Wisdom Sits in Places*. Albuquerque, University of New Mexico Press.

Brody, H. 2001. *The Other Side of Eden: Hunters, Farmers and the Shaping of the World*. Farrar, Straus and Giroux, New York.

Edwards, J. 1995. *Multilingualism*. New York, Penguin Books.

Gildart, R. C. 1997. Gwich'in: We are the people. *Native Peoples* 11(2): 76–82.

Hine, C., and J. Hill. 1986. *Seri Concepts of Place*. Unpublished paper presented at the Southwestern Anthropological Association's annual meeting, Las Vegas, Nevada, March 28, 1986.

Kellert, S., and M. O. Westervelt. 1977. *Children's Attitudes, Knowledge and Behaviors Toward Animals*. Phase V. U.S. Fish and Wildlife Service, Washington, DC.

Krauss, M. 1992. The world's languages in crisis. *Language* 68(1): 4–10.

Nabhan, G. P. 1997. Children in touch, creatures in story. Pages 59–80 in *Cultures of Habitat*. Washington, DC, Counterpoint Press.

Nabhan, G. P., and S. St. Antoine. 1993. The loss of floral and faunal story, the extinction experience. Pp. 229–50 in S. R. Kellert and E. O. Wilson, editors, *The Biophilia Hypothesis*. Washington, DC, Island Press.

Nabhan, G. P., and T. Tanner. n.d. *Results from O'odham High School Student Biology Survey*, 1992, Sells, Arizona. Unpublished data.

Nabhan, G. P. 2003. *Singing the Turtles to Sea*. University of California Press, Berkeley, CA.

Ohmagari, K., and F. Berkes. 1997. Transmission of indigenous knowledge and bush skills among the Western James Bay Cree women of subarctic Canada. *Human Ecology* 25(2): 197–222.

Plotkin, M. 1997. Personal communication, Arlington, Ethnobiology and Conservation Team.

Pretty, J. 2014. *The Edge of Extinction: Travels with Enduring People in Vanishing Lands*. Cornell University Press/Comstock Publishing Associates, Ithaca, NY.

Reader, T. 1997. *Recontextualizing culture: Some reflections on the material roots of language and culture*. Paper presented to the Lannan Foundation by Tohono O'odham Community Action (TOCA), Tucson, Arizona.

Romney, A. K., S. C. Weller, and W. H. Batchelder. 1986. Culture as consensus: A theory of culture and informant accuracy. *American Anthropologist* 88(2): 313–38.

Rosenberg, J. 1997. *Documenting and Revitalizing Traditional Ecological Knowledge: The Seri Curriculum Project*. Tucson, University of Arizona master's thesis.

Rosenberg, J., and G. P. Nabhan. 1997. Where ancient stories guide children home. *Natural History* 7: 263–68.

Trujillo, O., L. Monti, and K. Jarratt-Ziernicki. 2005. *The Sacred Sites and Gathering Grounds Initiative: Strategies for Protecting Traditional Native Places on Federal, State and Private Lands*. Pp. 126–28 in T. Schaaf and C. Lee, eds. *Conserving Cultural and Biological Diversity: The Role of Sacred Natural Sites and Cultural Landscapes*. UNESCO, Paris, France.

Zent, S. 1999. The quandary of conserving ethnoecological knowledge: A Piaroa example. Pp. 90–124. In T. Gragson and B. Blount, eds., *Ethnoecology: Knowledge, Resources and Rights*. Iowa City, University of Iowa Press.

Zepeda, O. 1983. *A Papago Grammar*. Tucson, University of Arizona Press.

Zepeda, O., and J. Hill. 1995. *Papago Dialect Survey*. Unpublished, Tucson, University of Arizona.

Zitnow, J. D. 1990. A comparison of time Ojibway adolescents spend with parents/elders in the 1930s and 1980s. *American Indian and Alaska Native Mental Health Research* 3(3): 7–16.

11

BIOCULTURAL AND ECOGASTRONOMIC RESTORATION

The Renewing America's Food Traditions Alliance

GARY PAUL NABHAN, DEJA WALKER,
AND ALBERTO MELLADO MORENO

OVER THE LAST DECADE, there has been a convergence of interest among restoration ecologists, native food activists, chefs, and ethnobiologists on two related issues. The first is the recognition of the historic role played by foragers, hunters, and small-scale horticulturists in regenerating habitats in ways that allowed sustainable harvests of plants and animals for food (Anderson 1996, 2006, Daggett 2005). The importance of this historical role has been acknowledged and underscored by the former editor of *Ecological Restoration*, William R. Jordan III (2003), who noted that some strategies now being used by ecological restorationists mimic those hunters and gatherers have practiced for millennia:

> Besides being a kind of agriculture and a way of doing ecological research, restoration includes the experience of gathering and, to some extent, even hunting as well.... The realization that the restorationist is at times a gatherer and at times a hunter completes an evolutionary catalog of human experience, recapitulating the principal modes of our relationship with nature. (p. 89)

This article first appeared in a 2010 issue of *Ecological Restoration*, Vol. 28, Number 3, pp. 266–79.

The second focus of convergence has been in recognizing the need to restore historically depleted habitats and to recover food-producing species if these place-based heritage foods are ever again to be reintegrated into sustainable regional economies that advance local food security (Nabhan 2008). Again, Jordan (2003) has been intrigued that today salmon stream restoration, bison recovery in restored prairies, and the regeneration of nut-bearing forests are all being done with *economic* and *cultural* as well as ecological goals in mind:

> Like fishing, forestry provides excellent opportunities to integrate human econo-
> mies with local ecologies, in part because both actually integrate forms of hunting
> and gathering—economies based on direct exploitation of a natural ecosystem
> and therefore dependent on its well-being. (p. 77)

Of course, not all restoration ecologists may necessarily feel comfortable with this convergence, in the sense that it opens up the possibility of harvest and consumption from restored streams, prairies, forests, and wetlands. If over-harvesting has contributed to the historic decimation of populations of the passenger pigeon, bison, sturgeon, agave, or mariposa lily, why would conservation biologists or restorationists want to see such pressures on other species? Jordan (2003), among others, has stopped short of endorsing "consumptive" harvests of species selected directly from restored ecosystems, raising the question of whether this may risk further population depletion and habitat degradation. And yet, there are ecological, economic, and cultural reasons to reconsider the role sustainable harvests of wild foods may play in restoration, and to solve the potential problems noted by Jordan.

AN ALTERNATIVE VIEW OF RESTORATION'S ULTIMATE GOALS

Many traditional land stewards, indigenous and otherwise, feel that restoration and sustainable use of wild resources have been and should be positively linked. Indeed, the very methods that some restorationists now use (such as burning, pruning, transplanting, thinning, and waterspreading) were initially used by hunters, gatherers, and even farmers from indigenous communities of North America to stimulate plant and animal yields for harvesting, or were consequences of their means of harvest (Anderson 2006, Deur and Turner 2005). It has even been argued that the depletion of some species and decline in habitat quality of some vegetation types occurred as a consequence of federal land managers forcing the cessation of these regenerative processes by Native American harvesters, who had long been functioning as active resource managers (Anderson 1996, Nabhan 2003a).

Today, theorists of restoration ecology such as White and Jentsch (2004) acknowledge that certain intensities of disturbance—such as those historically generated by traditional hunting and gathering communities—dynamically function on temporal and spatial scales that enable restorative processes to proceed rather than decline:

> Although restoration ecologists may conceive of disturbance as limited to the period before restoration begins, disturbance actually plays two roles: it creates the initial conditions for change, and it produces the continuing dynamics that control the establishment and turnover of individuals and species. Thus the culling or harvest of particular plant and animal populations (including ones to be used for food) during particular phases of the ecological restoration process may be necessary for restoration to advance. (White and Jentsch 2004, p. 342)

This insight is welcomed by native food activists, indigenous restorationists, and applied ethnobiologists now intent on recovering a number of wild foods formerly depleted by habitat loss, contamination, or overharvesting. While acknowledging certain potential risks inherent in their strategies, these groups aim not merely for the recovery of species or populations and their habitats, but for renewed and sustainable use as well. In their views, it would be ironic to restore a habitat so that wildlife may once again be sustained by foraging there while denying that same opportunity for our own species. As Lauren Lester (2006) has explained for tribal conservation goals, tribes wish to "protect the fish and eat them too." They are working to restore these foods to their cultures' diets and economies for a number of reasons: to reduce their vulnerability to nutrition-related diseases from which traditional diets formerly protected them, to reassert tribal food sovereignty, and to incorporate traditional ecological knowledge to generate new sources of income for impoverished rural communities.

Some food species like bison, salmon, or chestnuts not only served as ecological keystones that shaped habitats used by many other species, but they also functioned as cultural keystones, imbued with spiritual and symbolic significance that remains potent to this day. Recovering these species and restoring them to their "rightful place" in the landscape is therefore seen as a spiritual

FIGURE 11.1. Map of the foodsheds of North America for the purposes of discussion, revision, and alternative naming by communities in these various ecoregions. Concept by RAFT partners, with drafting by Mark Wegner.

and moral imperative. Again, William Jordan III (2003): "In this way a single species (in this case actually a genus) can become not just the basis for an economy, but a totem for an entire region, guiding and inspiring the work necessary to ensure its well-being" (p. 115). As a case in point, hundreds of thousands of indigenous and immigrant residents of the Pacific Northwest have formally pledged allegiance to *Salmon Nation*—what we prefer to call the *Salmon* or *Pacific Northwest Foodshed* (Figure 11.1).

Rather than using the term *Food Nation*, we now prefer *foodshed*, out of deference to First Nations' food sovereignty efforts, which are attempting to underscore their nationhood status to other Americans (Nabhan 2006). (By foodshed, we are describing the traditional area or landscape from which a culture or multicultural set of interacting communities have historically gained most of their nourishment.) These foodshed activists directly support not only stream recovery for wild salmon, but also boycott farm-raised, transplanted Atlantic salmon, and feature salmon as a cultural symbol or totem in public events and artistic and literary expressions (House 2002, Woody 2006). As Bottom (1995) has succinctly put it, "Without the bond of salmon traditions, Northwestern rivers, forests and fishermen become expendable. The interdependence of cultures and ecosystems lends a certain urgency to restoration" (Bottom 1995: 167).

It is therefore timely for the members of the Society for Ecological Restoration International to consider what its role should be in offering its skills, talents, theories, and practices in service to the ecological and cultural restoration of traditional foods. To understand the opportunities as well as the challenges that such an endeavor may raise, it may be worth reviewing the progress of one of the many collaborative efforts working toward the ecological, cultural, and culinary restoration of place-based heritage foods. The focus will be on a decade of trinational efforts in partnership through the Renewing America's Food Traditions Alliance. In particular, we will feature its survey and promotion of efforts across North America to foster *ecogastronomic restoration*.

RENEWING AMERICA'S FOOD TRADITIONS: HISTORY AND GOALS

The Renewing America's Food Traditions (RAFT) Alliance emerged in 2003 as an effort to link ecological restoration, genetic conservation, species recovery, and the market recovery of place-based heritage foods. The Center for Sustainable Environments (CSE) of Northern University was, at that time, involved in providing technical assistance to a number of Native, Hispanic, and Anglo American communities interested in spring, wetland, and woodland restoration on the Colorado Plateau and in the Sonoran Desert. It also advised communities and agencies on the sustainable harvest, use, and marketing of place-based foods, fiber, and other non-timber forest products.

These seemingly disparate research and extension efforts began to converge as participating community members explored such synergies as using

Navajo-Churro sheep as browsers in projects to restore forests and reduce fire risk; restoring sacred springs and wetlands to provide aquatic and riparian plants for food, medicine, and ceremonial uses; and reviving production and pursuing niche-marketing of place-based heritage foods, both wild and cultivated, at the request of ranchers and foragers. Staff at CSE also initiated the country's first community-supported wild foraging project, which assisted some ongoing ecological restoration projects by removing edible non-natives (Himalayan blackberry [*Rubus discolor*], horseradish [*Armoracia rusticana*], and crayfish [*Oronectes* spp.]) so that native species recovery could proceed.

As CSE staff began to assist rural communities with these income-generating efforts, it sought assistance from two national nonprofits, Chefs Collaborative and Slow Food USA. It became clear that the biological recovery of some species could be tangibly linked to how their food products were harvested and marketed, and by whom. After forming some bilateral partnerships, we invited the American Livestock Breeds Conservancy, the Cultural Conservancy, Native Seeds/SEARCH, and the Seed Savers Exchange to join our incipient coalition, which thereafter became known as the RAFT Alliance. As stated in its first nationally released publication:

> The coalition is dedicated to documenting, celebrating, and safeguarding the unique foods of North America—not as museum specimens, but as elements of living cultures and regional cuisines. . . . The RAFT campaign will explore novel means to support traditional ethnic [and indigenous] communities that are striving to make these foods once again part of their diets, ceremonies and local economies. (Nabhan and Rood 2004, viii)

After rich input and reflection derived from numerous regional workshops allowed us to amplify and expand that publication five years later, we took the opportunity to circumscribe the tasks needed to ethically and operatively advance the ecological and cultural restoration of place-based foods through what we nicknamed the seven "Rs" (Nabhan 2008):

1. *Recognizing* which place-based foods are most at risk.
2. *Recovering* their species, varieties, stocks, or populations.
3. *Restoring* their habitats in both wild and agricultural landscapes.
4. *Rescuing* and passing on local traditional knowledge about their stewardship and cultural uses.
5. *Recuperating* markets and local infrastructures to support their production.

6. *Rewarding* and actively supporting the original stewards of these resources with market-based incentives, recognition of "farmers' rights" or "foragers' rights," and cross-cultural reinforcement.

7. *Reducing* or altogether eliminating contamination, both chemical and genetic, of these foods.

In virtually all publications and presentations made by RAFT partners, we have insisted that such initiatives should not move economic (market) demand ahead of ecological restoration and implementation of best practices for sustainable harvests. In other words, we would refrain from generating market demand or encouraging human consumption of a species, subspecies, or variety until it has biologically recovered (and been legally delisted), or until contamination and development pressures on its habitats have abated.

Recently, we profiled ninety-three "threatened or endangered foods"; among them, thirty-four wild species, subspecies, or ecotypes (genetically unique populations adapted to a local environment) needing more investment in genetic recovery and ecological restoration (Nabhan 2008). Among those traditional foods profiled, a number are already being integrated into ecological restoration efforts. However, there has never been a comprehensive survey of how many of the wild species, stocks, or ecotypes used as place-based heritage foods in North America are at risk, in need of habitat restoration and genetic recovery, or already involved in ecological restoration efforts. The following analysis addresses those issues for the first time in print.

METHODS FOR IDENTIFYING THE CONSERVATION STATUS OF PLACE-BASED FOODS

We created a comprehensive list of all North American wild species, subspecies, stocks, and ecotypes documented to be edible, historically used, and at risk. Tables 11.1–11.4 are a subset of this comprehensive list, including only those species, subspecies, stocks or populations affected by active ecological restoration or population recovery efforts. We included Canada, the continental United States, and Mexico north of the Tropic of Cancer. The tables and comprehensive list were developed through an incremental sorting process that included several steps. Since that time, we have added longer lists for Appalachia and the Gulf Coast, which were not included in this analysis.

TABLE 11.1. List of fish used as place-based, edible, and historic foods in North America. E stands for endangered and T for threatened, as listed in the Renewing American Food Traditions compilation. Abbreviations for Canadian provinces and territories and Mexican and U.S. states indicate the current geographic distribution. Shaded rows (indicating *reported* species) are fishes known to be included in restoration projects from personal field visitations by the authors, unpublished reports at regional or national conferences, or personal communications by professional ecological restorationists. Unshaded rows (*documented*) are species, populations, or stocks known to be included in ecological restoration projects that have been reported in the pages of this journal.

TYPE	VARIETY NAME	SCIENTIFIC NAME	RARITY	DISTRIBUTION	FOODSHEDS
Chub	Boneytail	*Gila elegans*	E	AZ, UT	Great Basin and Rockies
	Humpback	*G. cypha*	E	AZ, CA, UT, NV	Great Basin and Rockies, Desert Southwest
Croaker	Totoaba	*Totoaba macdonaldi*	E	BCN, BCS, SON; CA	Desert Southwest
Pike-minnow	Colorado River	*Ptychocheilus lucius*	E	BCN, SON; AZ, CA, NV, UT	Desert Southwest
Rockfish	Acadian redfish, rockfish	*Sebastes fasciatus*	E	NB, NL; ME	New England Seaboard
Salmon	Atlantic, Gulf of Maine	*Salmo salar*	T	NL, NS; ME	New England Seaboard
	Chinook, coastal California	*Oncorhynchus tshawytscha*	T	CA	Pacific Northwest
	Chinook, some Columbia River runs	*O. tshawytscha*	E	CA, OR, WA	Pacific Northwest

continued

TABLE 11.1. *continued*

TYPE	VARIETY NAME	SCIENTIFIC NAME	RARITY	DISTRIBUTION	FOODSHEDS
Salmon (*cont.*)	Chinook, Central Valley spring run	*O. tshawytscha*	T	CA	Pacific Northwest
	Chinook, Central Valley winter run	*O. tshawytscha*	T	CA	Pacific Northwest
	Coho, northern California	*O. kisutch*	T	CA	Pacific Northwest
	Coho, central coast	*O. kisutch*	E	CA	Pacific Northwest
Smelt	Delta	*Hypomesus transpacificus*	T	CA	Pacific Northwest
Sturgeon	Atlantic	*Acipenser oxyrinchus*	T	NB, NL, NS; CT, MA, ME, NJ, NY, PA	New England Seaboard
	Green	*A. medirostris*	E	OR, WA	Pacific Northwest
	Lake	*A. fulvescens*	T	NY, PA, WV	New England Interior
	Shortnose	*A. brevirostrum*	E	NB, NL, NS; MA, ME, NH	New England Seaboard, Southeast Coast and Piedmont
	White	*A. transmontanus*	T	BC; CA, OR, WA	Pacific Northwest

continued

TABLE 11.1. *continued*

TYPE	VARIETY NAME	SCIENTIFIC NAME	RARITY	DISTRIBUTION	FOODSHEDS
Sucker	Razorback	*Xyrauchen texanus*	E	AZ, CA, CO, NM, NV, UT, WY	Great Basin and Rockies, Desert Southwest
Trout	Apache	*Oncorhynchus gilae apache*	T	AZ	Great Basin and Rockies
	Gila	*O. gilae*	E	AZ, NM	Great Basin and Rockies
	Greenback cutthroat	*O. clarkia stomias*	E	CO, WY	Great Basin and Rockies
	Lahontan cutthroat	*O. clarkii benshawi*	T	CA, NV, OR	Great Basin and Rockies
	Little Kern golden	*O. mykiss whitei*	T	CA	Great Basin and Rockies
	Steelhead, central coast	*O. mykiss*	T	CA	Mediterranean California
	Steelhead, Central Valley	*O. mykiss*	T	CA	Mediterranean California
	Steelhead, northern California	*O. mykiss*	T	CA	Pacific Northwest
	Steelhead, south-central California	*O. mykiss*	T	CA	Mediterranean California

We first cross-referenced the online threatened and endangered species lists for Canada, Mexico, and the United States with lists of useful plants and animals of North America (many of them now integrated into the www.natureserve .org databases). Next, we targeted those species or subspecies globally ranked according to NatureServe as G-1 to G-3 (most at risk); plant taxa were compared to those listed in Moerman's (1998) *Native American Ethnobotany* as traditional food sources, while animals were compared to faunal collections, such as Collette and Klein MacPhee's (2002) *Fishes of the Gulf of Maine* or Minckley and Marsh's (2009) *Inland Fishes of the Greater Southwest*. These steps provided us with a target list that we shared at a series of workshops of regional food experts, who reviewed the inventories and deleted, added, or qualified the inclusion of particular foods. These regional experts were not only conservation biologists from agencies and universities, but also included foragers, farmers, fishers, chefs, food historians, and environmental historians.

After each regional workshop, we typically spent a year following suggestions and leads, compiling, reviewing information, and rechecking against www .natureserve.org and regional ethnobotanical and ethnozoological treatises. Finally, we shared a draft list with the regional experts to check and revise. We then released the provisional regional foodshed lists online and in printed form at regional and national meetings to obtain more feedback. Revised regional and continental inventories of foods that are at risk both biologically and culturally can now be found at www.albc-usa.org/RAFT/resources.html

The last criterion—that a food may be biologically depleted but not formally listed as threatened or endangered by conservation biologists and policymakers—is a critical one to consider. If the food has been depleted or contaminated to the degree that it is no longer harvestable, we included it as threatened or endangered in our RAFT "Red List." In most cases, such foods have fallen out of gastronomic use and, in a few cases, they are no longer being marketed or traded anywhere that we could identify. We have also included some uncommon edible species or subspecies, for which the loss of traditional ecological knowledge about how and when to harvest has led to the demise of culinary uses.

Once we determined which foods were at risk, we attempted to identify the state, foodshed, or ecoregion where the food remains, and whether it was currently being targeted for species recovery and ecological restoration. We surveyed the first twenty-six volumes of *Ecological Restoration* to identify wild, place-based heritage foods for which restoration efforts have been published (Tables 11.1–11.4).

Because many restoration projects benefit multiple species and cultures too numerous to mention, we humbly acknowledge that this list is in now way comprehensive or exhaustive; it is merely suggestive of a larger and more diffuse grassroots movement toward biocultural restoration that has also generated benefits to communities.

GEOGRAPHIC AND TAXONOMIC PATTERNS OF FOODS AT RISK

Of the 267 wild species, subspecies, stocks, or ecotypes of place-based foods at risk in North America, 42 may be broadly classified as wild game (including 12 birds, 20 mammals, and 10 reptiles), 82 as wild-foraged plants, 40 as shellfish, and 103 as fish. Because fish and shellfish stocks, more than wild plants and game, tend to be "overclassified" as ecotypes with distinctive flavor and texture characteristics, we wish to point out that the following discussions do not always use species as the unit of comparison, as most discussions of biodiversity tend to do. It is clear that different populations of the same species—for example, sugar maples (*Acer saccharum*) in Vermont—tend to offer different taste and texture profiles, depending on whether the sugar bushes grow on limestone, shale, or pelitic schist (Trubek 2008). Thus the ecogastronomic unit of concern may not be the species, but a population or ecotype, such as the bay scallops of the Peconic Bays (Tettlebach and Smith 2009) or the Olympia oysters of Puget Sound (Jacobsen 2009).

Of 267 place-based heritage foods in our survey, fewer than a dozen have been extirpated as species, subspecies, or populations. Fortunately, forty-five (17 percent) are the subjects of genetic recovery and habitat restoration, as noted in previous articles and abstracts featured in *Ecological Restoration*. If we take into account all the restoration efforts for place-based foods at risk that have been reported in *Ecological Restoration* and in recent oral communications to us, a minimum of 38 percent of North America's wild foods at risk may be on the way to recovery at one or more sites (Tables 11.1–11.4).

The geographic distribution of North America's at-risk foods is not random. Two regions—the Pacific Northwest ("Salmon Foodshed"), with 55 threatened or endangered foods, and New England Interior ("Clambake Foodshed")— have many more recorded foods at risk than other foodsheds. Mediterranean California ("Acorn Foodshed"), the Great Basin and Rockies ("Pinyon Foodshed"), the Southeast Coast and Piedmont ("Crabcake Foodshed"), and the

TABLE 11.2. List of shellfish used as place-based, edible, and historic foods in North America. E stands for endangered, T for threatened, and X for extinct, as listed in the Renewing American Food Traditions compilation. Abbreviations for Canadian provinces and territories and Mexican and U.S. states indicate the current geographic distribution. Shaded rows (*reported* species) are shellfish known to be included in restoration projects from personal field visitations by the authors, unpublished reports at regional or national conferences, or personal communications by professional ecological restorationists. Unshaded rows (*documented*) are species, populations, or stocks known to be included in ecological restoration projects that have been reported in the pages of this journal.

TYPE	VARIETY NAME	SCIENTIFIC NAME	RARITY	DISTRIBUTION	FOODSHEDS
Abalone	Black	*Haliotis cracherodii*	E	BCN, BCS; CA	Mediterranean California, Desert Southwest, Pacific Northwest
	Flat	*H. walallensis*	T	CA	Mediterranean California
	Pink	*H. corrugata*	T	CA	Mediterranean California
	Pinto	*H. kamtschatkana*	T	BC, YT; BCN; BCS; AK, OR, WA	Mediterranean California, Pacific Northwest, Desert Southwest
	Red	*H. rufescens*	T	BCN; CA, OR	Mediterranean California, Pacific Northwest
	White	*H. sorenseni*	E	BCN, BCS; CA	Mediterranean California, Desert Southwest
Crab	Blue, Chesapeake and Delaware Bays	*Callinectes sapidus*	T	DE, MD, VA	Southeast Coast and Piedmont
Crawfish	Shasta	*Pacifastacus fortis*	E	CA	Pacific Northwest
Oysters	Callawassie Island	*Crassostrea virginica*	T	SC	New England Seaboard
	Cape Cod/Martha's Vineyard	*C. virginica*	T	MA	New England Seaboard

continued

TABLE 11.2. *continued*

TYPE	VARIETY NAME	SCIENTIFIC NAME	RARITY	DISTRIBUTION	FOODSHEDS
Oysters (*cont.*)	Chesapeake Bay subtidal	*C. virginica*	E	MD, VA	Southeast Coast and Piedmont
	Great Bay/Piscataqu River	*C. virginica*	T	NH	New England Seaboard
	New Haven	*C. virginica*	E	CT	New England Seaboard
	Olympia, Puget Sound	*Ostrea conchaphila*	T	WA	Pacific Northwest
	Olympia, San Francisco Bay	*O. conchaphila*	X	CA	Pacific Northwest
	Olympia, Tomales–Drakes Bay	*O. conchaphilia*	T	CA	Pacific Northwest
	Perth Amboy	*Crassostrea virginica*	E	NJ	New England Seaboard
	Raritan Bay	*C. virginica*	E	NJ, NY	New England Seaboard
	Rockaway	*C. virginica*	E	NJ	New England Seaboard
	Sea of Cortés	*C. corteziensis*	T	BCN, BCS, SON	Desert Southwest
Quahog	Chesapeake Bay	*Mercenaria mercenaria*	T	MD, VA	Southeast Coast and Piedmont
	Great South Bay	*M. mercenaria*	T	DE, NJ, NY	Coastal New England
Scallop	Bay scallop, Cape Cod/ Martha's Vineyard	*Argopecten irradians*	T	CT, MA	Coastal New England
	Bay scallop, Peconic Bay	*A. irradians*	T	NY	Coastal New England
	Bay scallop, Pine Island Sound	*A. irradians*	T	FL	Gulf Coast
	Bay scallop, Tampa Bay	*A. irradians*	T	FL	Gulf Coast
	Pen shell, callo de hacha	*Pinna rugosa*	T	BCN, BCS, SON	Desert Southwest
	Purple-hinged or rock	*Crassadoma gigantea*	T	CA, OR, WA	Pacific Northwest

Desert Southwest ("Chile Pepper Foodshed") also have more than twenty foods at risk in their wildlands, rivers, estuaries, springs, and streams. We now know that Appalachia ("Chestnut Foodshed") retains more diversity in traditional crops, and wild foods are at risk more than all the other regions of North America combined (Veteto and Nabhan 2011).

Because the foodsheds are not of equal size, caution must be used in overanalyzing these patterns. However, one hypothesis that RAFT partners wish to test empirically is whether the levels of wild plant and animal endangerment in North America are directly correlated with what Wendell Berry (1978) termed "the unsettling of America." Our proposal for a new law of biogeography (which we call Berry's Rule) is that the greater the proportion of human population involved in recent (post–World War II) arrival or departure from a region, the greater the depletion of biodiversity and the more severe the disruption of place-based food traditions and land stewardship practices. We hypothesize but cannot yet prove that the high rates of human migration for a region are positively correlated with high levels of endangerment among the wild biota (Nabhan 2003b).

To understand the processes by which ecological and cultural restoration of a wild food are integrated, we present four recent initiatives that may provide models or best practices for future restoration efforts.

SEA OF CORTÉS OYSTER AND SCALLOP RESTORATION AMONG THE SERI OF SONORA, MEXICO

Native populations of bivalve mollusks once nourished most coastal peoples of North America, but they have declined dramatically along many shorelines of the continent during the past century owing to habitat degradation, contamination, overfishing, disease, and changing densities of predators (Tettelbach and Smith 2009). In addition, native oysters, such as the Olympia and Sea of Cortés species, have in many places suffered from competition, replacement, and habitat usurpment by introduced Asian oysters (Jacobsen 2009).

In 2005, after hurricanes damaged shellfish beds and fish nurseries in the Estero Sargento coastal lagoon on the Sea of Cortés coast of Sonora, Mexico, the Comcaac or Seri Indian community of Desemboque del Sur was encouraged to rent its estuarine coastlands to large-scale industrial shrimp-farming operations. Instead, they opted to initiate hatchery and restoration efforts for native oysters (*Cassostrea corteziensis*) and scallops (*Atrina maura* and *A. tuberculosa*) in open waters of their lagoons in order to move them toward "native aquaculture" as an income-generating and food-producing activity. These native aquacultural initiatives, they affirmed, should be fertilizer and antibiotic free so as not to disrupt wild fisheries. To advance these efforts, the tribe sought technical advice from Rob Garrison (a consultant for the Wampanoag tribe and the First Nations Aquaculture Program), Northern Arizona University's Center for Sustainable Environments (CSE), and the Aquaculture Institute of the state of Sonora, Mexico.

One of us, Seri tribal member Alberto Mellado Moreno (see plate 1), stepped up to lead this project after receiving an aquaculture science degree and gaining additional training at the Sonoran Aquaculture Institute's hatchery in Kino, Sonora. He is now using traditional ecological knowledge from his own people and scientific data, as well as approaches from his university training, to guide native shellfish production and marketing from his family's ancestral gathering grounds. Recruited from the Desemboque community, twelve to fifteen certified aquaculture technicians work to sustainably harvest the native oysters and release more captive-bred scallops to the same waters from which they were derived. After letting populations grow to sufficient sizes, the shellfish have been sold to restaurants in the Seri communities and Sonoran beach towns and used for feasts associated with ecotourism events. The collaboration has grown to include the Seri youth environmental group Grupo Tortuguero Comcaac, which has been honored with a World Oceans Day award from the National Geographic Society, the Cousteau Society, and Ocean Revolution. While other scallop and oyster populations along the Sonoran coast are still being overharvested or threatened by pollutants and introduced diseases, those in Seri coastal waters have stabilized and are increasing.

CAMAS RESTORATION IN THE WILLAMETTE VALLEY, OREGON

Camas (*Camassia camas*), wapato (*Sagittaria* spp.), biscuit-roots (*Lomatium* spp.), and other roots, tubers, and corms played a historically important role in the diet and rituals of the First Nations of the Pacific Northwest (Moerman 1998). As reported by Smith and Farque (2001), the indigenous communities of Siletz and Grande Ronde have been engaged in revitalizing these traditions by transplanting camas bulbs and burning prairies to stimulate camas production.

The camas regeneration and recovery efforts in wetlands of the Willamette Valley of Oregon are nested within larger efforts working toward the goals of biocultural restoration and place-based environmental education, particularly aimed at First Nations youth. These efforts place youth in contact with tribal elders so that traditional ecological knowledge about camas and other food plants can once again be transmitted intergenerationally. This approach, pioneered by the Cultural Conservancy, one of RAFT's founding partners, has now been adopted by numerous indigenous and multicultural groups, who are concerned not only with biodiversity but also with cultural diversity and food sovereignty.

A camas baking oven has been constructed in the West Eugene Wetlands Ethnobotany Resource Area, based on evidence of historic camas ovens found at this site, and nearby. These activities encouraged a nonprofit research organization, the Institute for Culture and Ecology, based in Portland, Oregon, to bring local tribal elders and schools into a restoration and education collaboration sponsored by the Willamette Resource and Education Network and the U.S. Forest Service. A multicultural workshop during summer 2008, which featured presentations by Eric Jones, Dennis Martinez, Gary Nabhan, and tribal elders, brought in broader support for this cross-cultural effort to link ecoculinary and biocultural restoration.

Camas restoration itself is not technically difficult, and so it is being integrated into broader efforts to revive food, medicine, basketry, plants of the wetlands, mesic grasslands, and oak savannas, which may require periodic burning for the plants to flourish. Native American students from charter schools can listen to both tribal elders and restoration ecologists about the role of the plants in their cultures and in the ecosystem—and taste the harvests as well. Culturally adapted curriculum materials are also being developed. While the initial, direct food use of the recovered camas populations has been largely for the purposes of tribal environmental education, the partnerships among agencies, tribes, schools, nonprofits, and food activists have been bearing additional fruits in the Willamette Valley communities.

FREE-RANGING BISON RECOVERY TO RESTORE GREAT PLAINS LANDSCAPES

Bison (*Bison bison*) were undoubtedly among the most important traditional foods for people in the midcontinent before cattle-introduced diseases, overhunting, and habitat conversion decimated bison numbers in the late 19th century (Isenberg 2000). Today, the half-million bison left in North America inhabit less than one percent of the former range; many are in feedlots or small, fenced pastures; and most exhibit some genetic contamination from introgression with cattle. While there may be no immediate need to breed 100 percent genetically pure bison, there is growing interest in seeing more grass-fed bison meat produced from large native pastures, rather than from dry feedlots or small, fenced pastures dominated by Eurasian plants. This growing interest includes that of thirty-three Native American tribes engaged in the Intertribal Bison Cooperative. The tribes cite their reasons for being engaged in bison recovery as the following (in order of decreasing importance): spiritual and cultural, health and diet, financial, ecological, and novelty (Zontek 2007).

At a 2007 conference organized by the Wildlife Conservation Society, Kent Redford led some two hundred scientists, activists, ranchers, and native-food promoters in envisioning alternative futures for bison and the landscapes where they historically ranged (Sanderson et al. 2008). Given earlier criticisms of the "Buffalo Commons" proposals by Frank Popper, Deborah Popper, and Ernest Callenbach (e.g., Pfeiffer 1996), the RAFT Alliance proposed a modified, eco-culinary "Bison Commons" initiative focused on achieving regional food security through carbon-neutral production of native foods. This modified approach has both economic and gastronomic possibilities for revitalizing native-food diversity, which were not fully explored in the original Buffalo Commons debate (Nabhan and Kindscher 2006). It is also supportive of efforts of eleven tribes that have established their bison herds in the interests of improving the health and diet of their community (Zontek 2007). Many "slow-release" native foods are now needed by tribes suffering from adult-onset diabetes in order to manage their blood glucose and cholesterol levels, and to reduce soaring health costs.

Although we agree with Pfeiffer's (1996) conclusion that bison and cattle may have some comparable ecological influences, depending upon how they are managed, it is also true that grazing of bison in large, unfenced landscapes could uniquely regenerate the kinds of buffalo wallows historically known as breeding sites for prairie chickens (*Tympanuchus* spp.), prairie turnips (*Pediomelum esculentum*), American groundnuts (*Apios americana*), Jerusalem artichokes (*Helianthus tuberosus*), and other native foods and wildlife. Thus the restoration focus should not be on bison alone, but on the suite of ecological associates of bison-generated microhabitats that have served as traditional foods. The Intertribal Bison Council, American Bison Society, National Bison

TABLE 11.3. List of wild game used as place-based, edible, and historic foods in North America. E stands for endangered and T for threatened, as listed in the Renewing American Food Traditions compilation. Abbreviations for Canadian provinces and territories and Mexican and U.S. states indicate the current geographic distribution. Shaded rows (*reported* species) are game known to be included in restoration projects from personal field visitations by the authors, unpublished reports at regional or national conferences, or personal communications by professional ecological restorationists. Unshaded rows (*documented*) are species, populations, or stocks known to be included in ecological restoration projects that have been reported in the pages of this journal.

TYPE	VARIETY NAME	SCIENTIFIC NAME	RARITY	DISTRIBUTION	FOODSHEDS
Bird	Attwater's greater prairie chicken	*Tympanuchus cupido pinnatus*	E	LA, TX	Great Plains
	Greater sage-grouse, Rockies	*Centrocercus urophasianus*	T	CO, ID, MT, ND, NV, WY, UT	Great Basin and Rockies
	Masked bobwhite	*Colinus virginianus ridgwayi*	E	SON; AZ	Desert Southwest
	Western sage-grouse	*Centrocercus urophasianus phaios*	T	BC; OR, WA	Pacific Northwest
Mammal	Beaver, Southwest desert populations	*Castor canadensis*	T	AZ, NM	Great Basin and Rockies, Desert Southwest
	Free-ranging, Plains bison	*Bison bison*	T	AB, SK; MT, WY	Great Plains
	Key deer	*Odocoileus virginianus clavium*	E	FL	Gulf Coast
	Sonoran pronghorn antelope	*Antilocapra americana sonoriensis*	E	SON; AZ	Desert Southwest

continued

TABLE 11.3. *continued*

TYPE	VARIETY NAME	SCIENTIFIC NAME	RARITY	DISTRIBUTION	FOODSHEDS
Mammal (*cont.*)	Wood bison	*Bison bison athabascae*	T	AB, MB, NT, SK, YT	Canadian Shield
	Woodland caribou	*Rangifer tarandus caribou*	T	AB, BC, MB, ON, QC, SK; ID, WA	Pacific Northwest, Canadian Shield, Great Lakes
Reptile	American crocodile	*Crocodylus acutus*	E	FL, Caribbean	Gulf Coast
	Atlantic green sea turtle	*Chelonia mydas*	T	DE, MD, NJ, NY	New England Seaboard, Southeast Coast and Piedmont, Gulf Coast
	Desert tortoise	*Gopherus agassizii*	T	AZ, CA, NV, UT	Desert Southwest
	Hawksbill sea turtle	*Eretmochelys imbricata*	E	DE, MD, NJ, NY	New England Seaboard, Southeast Coast and Piedmont, Gulf Coast
	Kemp's ridley sea turtle	*Lepidochelys kempii*	E	AL, GA, MS, LA, NC, SC, VA, TX	New England Seaboard, Southeast Coast and Piedmont, Gulf Coast
	Leatherback sea turtle	*Dermochelys coriacea*	E	DE, MD, NJ, NY	New England Seaboard, Southeast Coast and Piedmont
	Loggerhead sea turtle	*Caretta caretta*	T	DE, MD, NJ, NY	New England Seaboard, Southeast Coast and Piedmont

FIGURE 11.2. Award-winning chef Fernando Divina, coauthor
of *Foods of the Americas* and principal menu consultant for
the Mitsitam Café at the National Museum of the American
Indian, shown here with his native food preparations at the
2007 American Heritage Picnic hosted by Slow Food Seattle.
Photo courtesy of the RAFT Alliance, Gary Paul Nabhan.

Association, Slow Food USA, and many other organizations have endorsed
and are promoting this broader sense of bison recovery for the Great Plains, or
"Bison Foodshed."

Healthful meat is already being distributed in tribal communities as a result
of the collaborations, but the degree to which bison are playing significant roles
in the landscape-level recovery of other, diverse wild foods varies from reservation to reservation.

AMERICAN CHESTNUTS

Like the passenger pigeon, the American chestnut (*Castanea dentata*) was once so abundant and integral to native and immigrant cultures that few 19th-century inhabitants of this continent would have ever fathomed that it might one day disappear (Freinkel 2007). But by 1904, a blight-causing fungus had been introduced from Asia to eastern forests. The blight rather dramatically infested an estimated four billion trees over some 81 million hectares, reducing the forest canopy of Appalachia by at least a quarter in a matter of decades. Although an occasional tree infested with the blight resprouted, the dominance of chestnuts in American forests was eliminated, as were the boiled nuts that provided Captain John Smith and his contemporaries from the First Nations "both broth and bread for their chief men at their greatest feasts."

Three-quarters of a century after the blight devastated chestnuts and their related culinary traditions, Charles Burnham founded the American Chestnut Foundation to restore this ecological and cultural keystone species to its historic range. Although university researchers focused on advancing a backcrossing program of plant breeding that introduced fungus resistance to American chestnut germ plasm, Burnham found willing propagators of these trees and established state and local chapters to advance chestnut recovery and forest restoration. Federal and state agencies, as well as nonprofits and unaffiliated volunteers, became keen on seeing American chestnuts bear fruit within their lifetimes on reclaimed mining lands and in secondary growth on abandoned farmlands (McCarthy et al. 2008). These cooperative efforts involve diverse stakeholders engaged in the Appalachian Regional Reforestation Initiative, including environmental and horticultural nonprofits, tribes, the coal industry, the Office of Surface Mining, private landowners, and universities. More importantly, perhaps, these on-the-ground restoration efforts refamiliarized many Americans with the shapes and sizes of chestnut trees and the status of the former habitats. Within two decades, the foundation began receiving from its cadre of supporters reliable reports and photos that verified how some trees had indeed survived the blight.

It now appears that some of the outlying survivors in Alabama and Georgia may be ancient natural hybrids between the American chestnut and the chinquapin (*Chrysolepis chrysophylla*), a congener known for its immunity to the blight (Minor 2006, Nabhan 2008). While this may be just one more source

TABLE 11.4 List of wild plants used as place-based, edible, and historic foods in North America. E stands for endangered and T for threatened, as listed in the Renewing American Food Traditions compilation. Abbreviations for Canadian provinces and territories and Mexican and U.S. states indicate the current geographic distribution. Shaded rows (*reported* species) are game known to be included in restoration projects from personal field visitations by the authors, unpublished reports at regional or national conferences, or personal communications by professional ecological restorationists. Unshaded rows (*documented*) are species, populations, or stocks known to be included in ecological restoration projects that have been reported in the pages of this journal.

TYPE	VARIETY NAME	SCIENTIFIC NAME	RARITY	DISTRIBUTION	FOODSHEDS
Fruit	Four-petal pawpaw	*Asimina tetramera*	T	FL	Southeast Coast and Piedmont
	Mountain cranberry	*Vaccinium vitis-idaea*	E	Broad range	Great Lakes
	Northern black currant	*Ribes hudsonianum*	T	Broad range	Great Lakes
	Okeechobee gourd	*Cucurbita okeechobeenisis*	E	FL	Gulf Coast
Grain	Wild rice, river rice	*Zizania aquatica*	T	Broad range	Great Lakes
Herb	Camas, prairie camas	*Camassia quamash*	T	AB, BC; CA, CO, ID, MT, NV, OR, UT, WA	Pacific Northwest
	Running buffalo clover	*Trifolium stoloniferum*	E	AR, IL, IN, KS, KY, OH, MO, WV	Central Prairies and Woodlands, Appalachia
	Thread-leaved bluedicks	*Brodiaea filifolia*	T	CA	Mediterranean California

continued

TABLE 11.4. *continued*

TYPE	VARIETY NAME	SCIENTIFIC NAME	RARITY	DISTRIBUTION	FOODSHEDS
Herb (*cont.*)	Tiburon Island mariposa lily	*Calochortus tiburonensis*	T	CA	Mediterranean California
Nut	American chestnut	*Castanea dentata*	E	Broad range	New England Seaboard, New England Interior
	Beaked hazelnut	*Corylus cornuta*	T	Broad range	Great Lakes
	Butternut	*Juglans cinerea*	T	Broad range	Great Lakes
	California scrub oak	*Quercus dumosa*	T	CA	Mediterranean California
	Northern butternut	*Juglans cinerea*	E	Broad range	Appalachia, New England Seaboard, Central Prairies and Woodlands, New England Interior, Canadian Shield, Great Lakes
	Monterrey pine	*Pinus radiata*	T	CA	Mediterranean California
	Torrey pine	*Pinus torreyana*	T	CA	Mediterranean California
Root, Corm, Bulb, and Tuber	Canadian milkvetch	*Astragalus canadensis*	T		Great Lakes

of fungal resistance that can be employed in the chestnut recovery program, it promises to offer an all-American solution to the blight problem that may help bring true forest restoration—not just chestnut plantations—to the American landscape. The broad support for the "rebirth" of this quintessential American tree crop among conservationists and native-food enthusiasts alike is one reason that it has been boarded onto the Slow Food Ark of Taste—an international registry of traditional foods believed to be at risk of loss from the food system and in need of market recovery. To be "boarded" onto the Ark of Taste by Slow Food International, the foods must be delicious or unique in their culinary use, able to be produced sustainably under well-defined protocols, associated with a particular place or culture, and associated with a historical tradition or production community.

CONCLUSIONS

Tremendous momentum is now evident among the many efforts to integrate the ecological restoration, species or stock recovery, cultural recovery, and culinary revival of place-based heritage foods in North America. Some community-based projects have been generated exclusively by First Nations or tribes seeking to reestablish their food security, self-sufficiency, and sovereignty, but most of these initiatives are cross-cultural and intergovernmental in nature. This is fitting, since many of these species and stocks require habitats extensive enough to cross political or administrative boundaries. Moreover, both traditional ecological knowledge and academic scientific knowledge may offer valuable perspectives needed for full recovery. In nearly all of these projects, the goal of restoration is not merely the recovery of a single species, but also of the cultural values associated with healthy habitats, diverse species, and traditional foods.

From our modest survey, it appears that ecogastronomic and biocultural restoration efforts are underway for more than forty-five wild food species, populations, or stocks unique to North America. These projects are the first to challenge the prevailing paradigm of ecological restoration since Aldo Leopold, as outlined by Jordan (2003): *restore it then leave it alone*. The ecogastronomic and biocultural restoration paradigms have potential risks because they may increase market pressures on scarce resources. On the other hand, they may nourish human communities involved in ecological restoration not merely in an intellectual and spiritual sense, but in a nutritional, gastronomic, and cultural sense as well.

As David Bottom (1995) has noted, the ultimate success of such biocultural restoration efforts "depends on nurturing by people with firsthand memories and shared traditions who are willing to commit themselves to the task. Subsequent generations without the bond of such memories will likely have other priorities," (Bottom 1995; p. 167). Flavors and fragrances are lodged deep within such motivating memories, and they appeal to people who may never read this book, nor formally join a restoration-oriented alliance. As such, the ecogastronomic and biocultural approaches to restoration broaden the range of values through which we can engage stakeholders from various constituencies in society at large to support nature's restoration in all of its dimensions (Friederici 2006).

REFERENCES

Anderson, M. K. 1996. Tending the wilderness. Restoration and Management Notes 14:154–63.

———. 2006. Tending the Wild: Native American Knowledge and Management of California's Natural Resources. Berkeley: University of California Press.

Berry, W. 1978. The Unsettling of America. San Francisco: Sierra Club Books.

Bottom, D. L. 1995. Restoring salmon ecosystems: Myth and reality. Restoration and Management Notes 13:162–70.

Collette, B. B., and G. Klein-MacPhee. 2002. Bigelow and Schroeder's Fishes of the Gulf of Maine. Washington, DC: Smithsonian Institution Press.

Daggett, D. 2005. Gardeners of Eden: Rediscovering Our Importance to Nature. Reno: University of Nevada Press.

Deur, D., and N. J. Turner. 2005. Keeping It Living: Traditions of Plant Use and Cultivation on the Northwest Coast of North America. Seattle: University of Washington Press.

Freinkle, S. 2007. American Chestnut: The Life, Death and Rebirth of a Perfect Tree. Berkeley: University of California Press.

Friederici, P. 2006. Nature's Restoration: People and Places on the Front Lines of Conservation. Washington, DC: Island Press/Shearwater Books.

House, F. 2002. Totem Salmon: Life's Lessons from Another Species. Boston: Beacon Press.

Isbenberg, A. C. 2000. The Destruction of the Bison: An Environmental History, 1750–1920. New York: Cambridge University Press.

Jacobsen, R. 2009. The Living Shore: Rediscovering a Lost World. New York: Bloomsbury USA.

Jordan III, W. R. 2003. The Sunflower Forest: Ecological Restoration and the New Communion with Nature. Berkeley: University of California Press.

Lester, L. 2006. Protecting the Fish and Eating Them, Too: Impacts of the Endangered Species Act on Tribal Water Use. Tucson: Udall Center for Studies in Public Policy.

McCarthy, B. C., J. M. Bauman, and C. H. Keiffer. 2008. Mine land reclamation strategies for the restoration of American chestnut. Ecological Restoration 26:292–94.

Minckley, W. L., and P. C. Marsh. 2009. Inland Fishes of the Greater Southwest: Chronicle of a Vanishing Biota. Tucson: University of Arizona Press.

Minor, E. 2006. Rare American chestnut trees discovered. Washington Post, May 19. www.washingtonpost.com/wp-dyn/content/article/2006/05/19/AR200 6051901548.html.

Moerman, D. E. 1998. Native American Ethnobotany. Portland, OR: Timber Press.

Nabhan, G. P. 2003a. Destruction of an ancient indigenous cultural landscape: An epitaph from Organ Pipe Cactus National Monument. Ecological Restoration 21:290–95.

———. 2003b. The geography of endangerment. Conservation in Practice 4(3):3.

———. 2006. Renewing Salmon Nation's Food Traditions. Portland, OR: Ecotrust.

———. 2008. Renewing America's Food Traditions: Saving and Savoring America's Most Endangered Foods. White River Junction, VT: Chelsea Green Publishing.

Nabhan, G. P., and K. Kindscher. 2006. Renewing the Food Traditions of Bison Nation. Brooklyn: Slow Foods USA.

Nabhan, G. P., and A. Rood, eds. 2004. Renewing America's Food Traditions. Flagstaff: Center for Sustainable Environments, Northern Arizona University.

Pfeiffer, K. E. 1996. Book review: Bring Back the Buffalo! A Sustainable Future for America's Great Plains. Restoration & Management Notes 14:199–200.

Sanderson, E. W., K. H. Redford, B. Weber, K. Aune, D. Baldes et al. 2008. Ecological future of the North American bison: Conceiving long-term, large-scale conservation of wildlife. Conservation Biology 22:252–66.

Smith, A. C., and T. Farque. 2001. The Camas Prairie restoration project re-establishes an indigenous cultural landscape (Oregon). Ecological Restoration 19:107–08.

Tettlebach, S. T., and C. F. Smith. 2009. Bay scallop restoration in New York. Ecological Restoration 27:20–22.

Trubek, A. B. 2008. The Taste of Place: A Cultural Journey into Terroir. Berkeley: University of California Press.

Veveto, J.R. and G.P. Nabhan. 2011. Place-Based Foods of Appalachia: From Rarity to Community Restoration and Market Recovery. RAFT/Northern Arizona University, Flagstaff, AZ. www.albc-usa.org/RAFT/resources.html.

White, P. S., and A. Jentsch. 2004. Disturbance, succession, and community assembly in terrestrial plant communities. Pages 342–66 in V. K. Temperton, R. J. Hobbs, T. Nuttle and S. Halle (eds.), Assembly Rules and Restoration Ecology: Bridging the Gap Between Theory and Practice. Washington, DC: Island Press.

Woody, E. 2006. Speaking to our roots. Pages 36–07 in G. P. Nabhan (ed.), Renewing Salmon Nation's Food Traditions. Portland, OR: Ecotrust.

Zontek, K. 2007. Buffalo Nation: American Indian Efforts to Restore the Bison. Lincoln: University of Nebraska Press.

12

CONSERVATION YOU CAN TASTE

Heirloom Seed and Heritage Breed
Recovery in North America

GARY PAUL NABHAN

ABSTRACT

O VER THE LAST three decades, more than 100,000 plant and animal
varieties and species have become endangered around the planet,
many of which formerly provided humankind with food or bever-
ages. This has translated to increasing homogeneity in global food supplies, with
adverse consequences for food security and public health (Khoury et al. 2014).
At the same time, a promising counter trend has occurred in America's gardens
and orchards, and on its farms and ranch pastures.

Although virtually unnoticed in some circles, more than 15,000 unique vegetable, fruit, legume, and grain varieties and dozens of livestock and poultry
breeds have returned to U.S. foodscapes, farmers markets, restaurants, and
home tables over the last quarter-century.

Remarkably, this survey documents that at least 640 species are now on the
plates of Americans participating in alternative food networks, not counting the
many North American edible species of fish, game, shellfish, and wild plants.

This essay along with several case studies of successful seed or breed recovery by my collaborators, appeared as a monograph of the Renewing America's Food Tradition Alliance, and was
released to commemorate the twentieth anniversary of Chefs Collaborative in Charleston,
South Carolina, in November 2013.

Curiously, most of these 800-some species had been pushed out of the marketplace over the previous century as industrialized agriculture and national grocery store chains, consciously or unconsciously, reduced the *food biodiversity* available to nourish our families, friends, and communities. And yet, after suffering at least a half-century of endangerment, some foods such as the range-fed lamb grown by by Diné and Hispanic herders of flocks of Navajo-Churro sheep are again gracing the tables of restaurants daily.

To be sure, no single individual or organization is responsible for such culinary comebacks; it has taken a village of collaborators. And yet, it is fair to say that the innovative farmers, ranchers, chefs, co-ops, distributors, and collectives engaged with this food diversity have been supported more by a dozen national nonprofits and regional grassroots alliances than by government agencies, national conservation organizations, or universities. America's repertoire of meats, fruits, grains, vegetables, spices, and beverages have been re-diversified, one foodshed at a time.

In particular, the market recovery of what are popularly known as *heritage foods*—including *heirloom vegetables*, grains, and fruit trees, as well as *historic breeds of livestock* and flocks of so-called *poultry antiquities*—has been nothing short of miraculous. As you will see documented over the following pages, varieties and breeds considered close to extinction a half-century ago are once again being grown by thousands of small-scale farmers, and are back on the tables of fine restaurants, brew pubs, and home kitchens in every state in the union.

It is our contention that dollar for dollar, the heritage foods revival has accomplished one of the highest returns on investment for philanthropic foundations, private businesses, and society at large of any public effort to conserve biodiversity anywhere in the world. Although some nonprofits in the movement have received philanthropic support for part of their work, most of these efforts have been done by farmers, foragers, chefs, and eaters themselves.

The purposes of this survey are threefold. First, we wish to document the extraordinary growth in the production, sales, and use of America's heritage foods over the last half-century. We will give particular attention to those species and varieties that were on the edge of extinction, when certain *biocultural conservation* efforts and *ecogastronomic restoration* strategies began to emerge a quarter-century ago.

Second, we wish to discern the best practices that food producers, distributors, marketers, journalists, chefs, and food activists discovered in advancing the market recovery of particular heritage foods. We include here a number of case studies of particular plant varieties and livestock breeds, which have recovered from the brink of extinction. We highlight the testimonies of early adopters and innovators who nurtured their process of recovery. We also wish to highlight necessary cautions and avoid pitfalls that certain food recovery efforts have encountered. In other words, we hope to learn from our mistakes (and remedy them), as well as learn from the successes that appear to be potentially transferable to other foods at risk.

Third, we wish to propose that new driving factors are emerging, which are likely to propel heritage food recovery and food system diversification in new and unforeseen directions over the next quarter-century. New challenges are emerging as well. So instead of thinking of food system diversification as a rather "retro" effort in historic preservation or genetic conservation, we predict that future advances will take more dynamic and multicultural approaches.

These novel approaches are likely to link these rare seeds and breeds to urban as well as rural food security, seed sovereignty, adaptation to climate change, alternatives to bioengineering and genetic contamination, and the quest for flavor, color, and nutritional value. The latter factor will be given special attention in the face of accelerating rates of obesity, diabetes, and heart disease among American youth.

While we have no crystal ball, we feel it is morally necessary to broaden the discussion about heritage food recovery so that the needs of the poor, food insecure, nutritionally challenged, and politically marginalized populations are more fully taken into account. Thank you for joining us on this journey.

INTRODUCTION: WHAT IS FOOD BIODIVERSITY AND WHY DOES IT MATTER?

Although the term *biodiversity* was not even coined until 1985, the more particular term *food biodiversity* now helps us describe the cornucopia of distinctive kinds of fruits, nuts, vegetables, tubers, greens, herbs, and oilseeds that we intuitively associate with flavor, nutrition, food security, abundance, and health. In a broad sense, the actual number of food varieties that we eat is but a fraction of the total *agricultural biodiversity* on farms and ranches required to assure that food crops and livestock are fed, protected from winds or floods, and supplied with adequate water, forage, nutrients, pollinators, and other beneficial insects to assure a harvest. As noted in the book, *Where Our Food Comes From,*

Agricultural biodiversity is embedded in every bite of food we eat, and in every field, orchard, garden, ranch and fish pond that provide us with sustenance and with natural values not fully recognized. It includes the cornucopia of crop seeds and livestock breeds that have been largely domesticated by indigenous stewards to meet their nutritional and cultural needs, as well as the many wild species that interact with them in food-producing habitats. Such domesticated resources cannot be divorced from their caretakers. These caretakers have also cultivated traditional knowledge about how to grow and process foods; such local and indigenous knowledge—just like the seeds it has shaped—is the legacy of countless generations of farming, herding and gardening cultures.

Close to 7,000 species of plants have been cultivated as food crops worldwide, and 200 or so species of mammals, birds, reptiles, amphibians, fish, and invertebrates have been raised on farms and ranches. However, just 103 crop plants and seven livestock species feed most of the world's population today, and only fifty-two commodity crops provide an ever-increasing proportion of calories and protein consumed in the globalized economy (Khoury et al. 2014). Since 1973, when the first major study of the genetic vulnerability of our global food supply was published, this narrow genetic base has alarmed many scientists and food security planners, especially as the homogeneity in national/cultural diets increased by 16.7 percent between 1961 and 2009 (Khoury et al. 2014).

But what most global surveys have failed to take into account is the tremendous momentum that has been made, at the grassroots level in North America and elsewhere, in not only conserving but also revitalizing the uses of rare food plant and animal varieties. For example, in 1985, members of just one grassroots organization—the Seed Savers Exchange (SSE)—offered to one another the seeds, tubers, and cuttings of about 5,000 distinctly listed varieties of food plants. By 1999, the number of unique food plant listings offered for exchange among SSE members broke 20,000—a fourfold increase in less than a decade and a half—and has generally stayed above 20,000 plant variety offerings since then.

Over roughly the same time period, the number of cultivated plant varieties of vegetables, grains, legumes, and tubers offered in American seed catalogs has increased from 4,989 to well over 8,500 distinctive varieties. On a decade-by-decade basis, this amounts to an average increase of 31 percent in heirloom and old-standard food plant varieties becoming available to American gardeners. Similar trends, to be discussed below, are occurring for access to fruit and nut trees, and berry vines from nurseries, and in the registries of livestock breeds. All

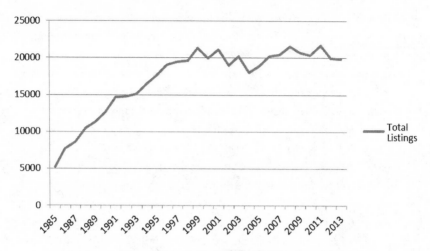

FIGURE 12.1. The number of vegetable, fruit, and grain varieties in
North America available in seed or nursery catalogs or on the Internet by
year, as reported in annual publications of the Seed Savers Exchange.

in all, we now have over 628 species of cultivated food plants and fourteen species
of large livestock and poultry raised in American foodscapes. That is in addition
to over 4,000 wild plants and perhaps 250 wild animal species, which have historically been used as food on the American continent, many growing in open spaces
on farms and ranches, or in the ponds, streams, or rivers that run through them.

This astonishing level of diversity is not simply produced in American gardens, orchards, farms, and ranches, but is more available than ever before to
consumers, home cooks, and chefs. In 1994, there were only 1,775 farmers markets in the United States, but two decades later, there are more than 8,150, with
one in every twenty farmers and ranchers in the country direct marketing at
least a portion of their production to neighbors.

Obviously, not many of us will ever have the chance to taste even a fraction
of the 5,000 species of food sources on this continent, so why do they matter?
Here are a few reasons why they will matter if we are to achieve food security
that nourishes our poor, elderly, and children, along with sustaining the long-
term productivity of our foodscapes.

A. Maintaining a diversity of plants and animals on the land and in our waters
   may be one of the best bet-hedging strategies we have to buffer ourselves from
   climate uncertainty.

B. Harboring biodiversity on farms allows these plants and animals to provide "ecosystem services," which stabilize yields and reduce required inputs, over and above the calories they produce.

C. A neglected "food rule" to guide our healthy eating patterns is that eating a diversity of varieties of the same foodstuff—apples or salad greens—provides us with a greater diversity of nutrients, probiotics, textures, and flavors to keep us well-nourished and protected from disease.

Perhaps the conservation of flavor options and the very pleasure of eating are the least-discussed reasons for attempting to sustain food biodiversity. The following case studies—highlighted as sidebar features scattered throughout this report—remind us that when we conserve food diversity, we are not just saving genes, breeds, or species, but we are saving taste, culture, and livelihoods. We hope that you will now dive into the details of these conservation success stories, for they are truly examples of *conservation you can taste.*

VEGETABLES, LEGUMES, GRAINS, AND ROOT CROPS

As of 2005, when Monsanto took control of Seminis, its new subsidiary had already cornered an estimated 40 percent of the U.S. vegetable seed market and 20 percent of the world market. In other words, one company [Seminis] alone provided the patented or PVPA-certified seed stocks for 85 percent of chili and bell peppers, 75 percent of tomatoes, and 55 percent of lettuce on U.S. super-market shelves, in addition to having a prominent position in seed production for beans, broccoli, cabbage, cucumbers, melons, peas, spinach, and squash. At both the national and international levels, large U.S.-based seed companies have consolidated power over much of the genetic materials on which our fresh vegetable supplies and our food security depend. To date, a proposed $47 billion takeover of Syngenta by Monsanto has not been actualized, but it threatens to continue a trend toward consolidation if not monopolization within the global seed industry.

Nevertheless, there at least 275 other vegetable seed companies in the United States and Canada, up from an all-time low of just 215 companies in 1987. From 1984, when ninety-nine vegetable, grain, legume, tuber, and herb varieties were listed in North American seed catalogs, diversity rose 31 percent to 6,483 varieties in 1994, and increased another 31 percent to 8,494 in 2004. Many online, niche market seed listings have cropped up since 2004, making it almost too difficult to track the growth of the seed outlets which are dramatically diversifying the alternative food networks of North America.

But how are the food networks from farm to restaurant or home kitchen actually diversifying? With data available from the last twenty-two years of Seed Savers Exchange archives, we tracked sixteen of the once-rarest annual heirloom crop varieties that have boarded onto the Ark of Taste, from Amish Deer Tongue lettuce to White Sonora wheat. In 1981, most of those categories were available from only one or two seed catalogs and only a handful of backyard seed savers grew them, let alone many commercial farmers. Today, these sixteen heirloom varieties are offered by an average of 113 commercial growers who post their produce inventory on localharvest.org, an average of six catalogs, and online "mail-order" inventories.

Some of the recoveries are nothing short of miraculous. Amish Deer Tongue lettuce seed is now offered by twenty-three seed catalogs and its fresh greens are found on at least 441 commercial farms. Radiator Charlie's Mortgage Lifter tomato was only offered by Southern Exposure Seeds in the early 1980s, but is now sold by seventeen different seed catalogs, and is grown on 301 commercial farms in the United States.

When we try to discern the driving factors of this re-diversification, it is clear that for the heirloom vegetables, legumes, tuber, and grains we selected, the links to local identity, culture, and community was important for most (twelve) varieties, while taste options for industrialized food (ten), and promoting diversity in backyard production in urban or suburban settings were key.

While the pace of the genetic engineering of transgenic crops, their patenting and licensing, and potential contamination of open-pollinated vegetable and grain crops continue to worry food-justice activists, potential solutions to some of these problems are now emerging. For example, the Open Source Seed Initiative has engaged the Organic Seed Alliance, small seed companies, universities, and nonprofits in seeking means to keep vegetable, grain, legume, and tuber varieties in the public domain, rather than being further privatized. In the meantime, planting a diversity of crop species—most of them still free of any risk of GMO contamination—is the best bet for keeping variety in our produce in North America.

FRUIT, NUTS, AND BERRIES

The number of orchards maintained in the United States has suffered a precipitous decline over the last century. For example, there were over 200 million apple trees in home and commercial orchards in the United States a century ago, and by 1950, there were less than 50 million apple trees left in the United States. Today there are only 7,500 commercial apple orchards in the country, and their acreage has declined by 15 percent since 1997. Today, 90 percent of all apples sold in U.S. chain grocery stores come from just eleven varieties of the 3,000 varieties still available through online sources or catalogs. Six of the major apple juice producers in the United States have gone out of business since 2001, leaving only two U.S.-based companies to compete with China for providing our populace with both apple juice and frozen purée. Similar statistics could be shown for other fruits and nuts.

Despite such consolidation and outsourcing, there were at least 275 fruit, nut, and berry nurseries companies with catalogs or online listings in the United States and Canada by 2009, up from 248 companies in 1987. These 275 inventories offer over 8,750 fruit, nut, and berry varieties to American and Canadian orchard-keepers in North America today.

While hundreds of independently owned nurseries have closed their gates due to the proliferation of "pseudo-nursery" garden centers attached to big box stores, other modes of fruit and nut tree exchange have emerged. Today, thousands of orchard-keepers come to exchange scion wood and learn grafting techniques at seasonal events sponsored by the Home Orchard Society in the Northwest, MOFGA in Maine, the Worcester County Horticultural Society in Massachusetts, the Midwestern Fruit Explorers, and California Rare Fruit Explorers.

The driving factor that appears most important to the re-diversification of fruit and nut orchards is the opportunity to access taste options not available in a few standard varieties; adding diversity to home orchards with urban and suburban areas is also catching wind. These taste options not only include the flavor profiles of fresh dessert apples, but also a revival of hard cider and fruit-brandy making in the United States. Many apples and pears that fell out of fashion during Prohibition for lack of shipability or fresh eating quality are now being rediscovered by cider makers and brandy distillers. If it were not for the interest of apple brandy makers at Germain-Robin artisanal distillers near Ukiah, California, the Sierra Beauty apple would have little value-added market distinction. The artisanal cider makers and distillers emerging all across North America will often pay twice the value per ton of fruit than orchard-keepers can garner from groceries or at roadside stands. As such, artisanal processing of ciders and spirits—like heirloom-focused farmers markets and festivals—are literally keeping dozens of fruit varieties alive that might otherwise go extinct.

Of the fourteen fruits, nuts, and berries now boarded on the Ark of Taste, which we selected for study, the average number of nurseries carrying them is 2.6, and an average of 11.5 growers are now making part of their livelihoods by direct-marketing these fruits or their value-added products to the public. The Meyer Lemon is being offered through the largest number of nurseries (seventeen), and it also has the most growers who list on localharvest.org (seventy-three), while most other heirloom rarities still have less than ten growers nationwide. The Mission olive of California and Arizona is next in importance, with seventeen growers, most of whom cold-press extra virgin olive oil. Because of the longer time to maturation and harvest for tree crops than for field vegetables, it is not surprising that the pace of recovery of fruits, nuts, and berries lags far behind that of annual field crops. They are also more vulnerable to climate change, since many of them are typically long-lived so can suffer dramatic changes in climate over their lifetimes.

LIVESTOCK AND POULTRY BREEDS

We now live in a nation where the top five meat processing and packaging companies control 78 percent of the U.S. market, and just four of them control 80 percent of all beef slaughtered. They primarily sell to the top ten grocery store chains—whose supermarkets control 55 percent of their market—and to the top ten fast food/restaurant chains, which control 45 percent of their market. In 1987, there were about 2,500 companies that produced egg-laying hens in the United States; now, less than 200 companies in the United States produced 95 percent of all laying hens. Similarly, just four turkey-breeding companies produce 95 percent of all of the world's turkey poults, and they are exclusively the highly uniform White turkey.

This has left little room in the commodity markets for subdominant breeds of livestock and poultry. According to the *Encyclopedia of Historic and Endangered Livestock and Poultry Breeds*, there are 191 breeds of rare or endangered poultry and livestock breeds (including equines) in North America and the British Isles, including fifty-three breeds of poultry with eggs or meat that are marketed, sixty-one breeds of large livestock with meat or milk that is marketed in North America. Of these, the American Livestock Conservancy now considers fifty-two of the breeds of food-producing animals (other than equines) critically endangered, and thirty-five of them threatened. That means that over three-quarters of America's distinctive breeds of cattle remain in the two most endangered categories.

And yet, thanks to the many minor breed registries and technical support groups like the American Livestock Conservancy, the recovery trends for many of the rarest poultry and livestock breeds boarded on the Slow Food Ark of Taste look very good.

Of ten of the rarest livestock breeds, eight have shown modest population recovery since 1999; for poultry breeds, nine of the rarest thirteen poultry breeds have also shown tremendous levels of recovery since then. The differences in recovery rates are related to the differences in fecundity rates and lifespan, particularly between large livestock and poultry. Today, there are at least 263 producers in the United States selling meat, milk, or cheese from these recovering breeds of livestock, and another 1,064 producers selling eggs or meat of recovery poultry breeds.

One of the first collaborative efforts toward market recovery of rare poultry breeds brought Frank Reese and his Good Shepard Turkey Ranch network together with Slow Food USA and the American Livestock Conservancy (then known as ALBC). Slow Food USA's first director Patrick Martins then went on to co-found Heritage Foods USA, which now moves into the market place an average of 50,000 pounds from about 200 pigs of heritage breeds per week. Heritage Foods also features once-a-year mail order campaigns that move 6,000 to 7,000 turkeys of heritage breeds each November in advance of Thanksgiving, 1,000 heritage goats each October, 1,500 heritage ducks and geese each December in advance of Christmas, Chanukah, and New Year's, and close to 1,000 half-lamb packages of four heritage breeds in March in advance of Passover and Easter. These collaborations with Heritage Foods USA now provide the primary source of income from thirty to thirty-five farming families across the country. Martins attributes much of his success in fostering the market recovery of rare breeds to the commitment many chefs have made to paying a fixed price per pound to the farmers and ranchers who maintain populations of these rare but recovering livestock breeds:

> "The chefs have really rallied behind the notion of restaurant supported agriculture. They have helped maintain a beautiful landscape all across America, through which something akin to an 'underground railroad' functions to keep these imperiled heritage breeds alive."

EMERGING CHALLENGES, OBSTACLES, AND THREATS

The previous sections suggest that over the last quarter-century, the recovery of heritage food biodiversity has been one of the most cost-effective investments that private citizens, communities, philanthropic foundations, nonprofit organizations, and grassroots alliances have made in collaborative conservation over the last century. But despite recent successes, there are many emerging challenges, obstacles, and threats that must still be dealt with. Among them are:

A. Climate change and the displacement or destruction of rare crop and livestock populations after catastrophic weather events.

B. Expanding distributions for pests, toxic weeds, and diseases that may affect the health of rare plant or animal populations.

C. Potential genetic contamination by GMOs of heritage varieties of corn, rice, or other crops.

D. Loss of pollinators required to assure seed and fruit set of rare food plants.

E. "Green washing" in the commodity marketplace, hoping to capitalize on the buzz associated with heritage foods or heirloom vegetables.

F. Unethical cultural appropriation, patenting, or trademarking of heritage foods that potentially disrupts the food sovereignty of indigenous communities, or of immigrant communities of traditional farmers.

G. Unintended effects of food safety and zoning regulations limiting the production of heritage plants and animals, which local artisans prepare into value-added products.

H. Scarcity of trained livestock breeders or backyard/on-farm plant breeders required to keep heritage plants and animal populations dynamic, rather than having them relegated to the status of static museum pieces.

I. Scarcity of small- and medium-scale processing facilities, particularly for livestock, to allow artisanal fabrication, and curing of heritage foods.

J. Scarcity of training programs to recruit more young nurserymen for tree grafting and more horticulturists for seed increases of rare varieties.

BEST PRACTICES

At the same time, there are many challenges facing the conservation of agricultural biodiversity and the market recovery of heritage foods, there are many best practices embedded in the case studies presented here that could potentially help the recovery of other heritage foods:

1. Most successful heritage food recovery efforts have required a collaborative conservation mentality to recognize that it may "take a village" of heterogeneous participants—farmers, breeders, marketers, chefs, etc., of all political

persuasions and ethnic or racial backgrounds—to help recover a variety, species, or food tradition. Collaborative rather than command-and-control behaviors will likely work best over the long haul. Tribal and ethnic self-determination with regard to breed and seed sovereignty are of paramount importance in shaping such collaborations.

2. Many heritage food recovery efforts simply start with confidence-building between farmers and chefs who share common values; the building of cross-sectoral relationships and lasting friendships matter perhaps more than any other social factor in assuring success.

3. Newly recruited chefs or consumers are ultimately attracted to a heritage food by its flavor, color, texture or shape, and how the person resonates with its story. People are not only willing to pay for the caloric value of these foods; they are willing to pay for their cultural and ecological value. Tell the rich backstory of the food, its related foodways, and its producers.

4. Focus on means to make the seeds and food they produce not only accessible but also affordable. The free seed library movement in North America now engages more than 200 U.S. and Canadian communities in voluntary sharing of garden seeds. Heritage food promoters should not shirk from finding innovative means to reintroduce these foods to markets where consumers have the ability to purchase them at just prices. For instance, Wholesome Wave's double-the-value program for SNAP program recipients can be used to purchase seeds, seedlings, or cuttings of food plants at farmers markets. If low-income families are most nutritionally at risk, it may be more cost-effective to subsidize their access to these foods, rather than pay rising health costs later as a result of the absence of such foods in their diets.

5. Citizen scientists who are organized at the neighborhood, community, or regional scale can help to observe the conditions under which these heritage foods grow best; we need to build a community of "amateur" experts who exchange their insights regarding how to best propagate, breed, manage, harvest, process, store, and utilize these foods.

6. As the recovery and production of a heritage food ramps up, it will be important for a community to plan and invest in milling or processing facilities, storage facilities, and food distribution hubs, which allow these foods to move through short but efficient supply chains.

7. It is critical to seek out mentors, specialists, and technicians who have helped recover similar heritage foods, so that we do not reinvent the wheel each time. They can help you develop a grow-out toolkit as Chefs Collaborative did following its 2009 and 2010 grow-outs in New England that guided farmers and

gardeners to best meet the horticultural needs of rare heritage plants, and to form partnerships with chefs and farmers markets necessary to bring these varieties to the marketplace.

8. It is also worthwhile to develop tasting protocols, as American Livestock Conservancy and the Slow Food Ark of Taste Committee have done, to provide a vocabulary for describing, evaluating, and ranking a foodstuff's flavors, fragrances, and textures, and for exploring its best culinary uses.

9. While avoiding price fixing of any kind, it is important for producers, processors, and chefs to share data on the true cost of producing, marketing, and using a heritage food in scarce supply, and to collectively come to an agreement about an acceptable price range. It is also critical to understand that as supply and demand change through time, the collective spreadsheet will undoubtedly need reworking.

10. Finally, each heritage food may have embedded within its history multiple stories, which appeal to different kinds of people at different times in the food's recovery. Match the most appropriate story with the particular person and moment, so that the person is truly inspired to become engaged in furthering the recovery of the food itself and its associated foodways.

REFERENCES

Dohner, J. V. The Encyclopedia of Historic and Endangered Livestock and Poultry Breeds. New Haven: Yale University Press.

Khoury, C. K., A. D. Bjorkman, H. Dempewolf, J. Ramirez-Villegas, L. Guarino, and A. Jarvis. Increasing homogeneity in global food supplies and the implications for food security. Proceedings of the National Academy of Sciences III (11): 4001–06.

Nabhan, G. P., ed. 2008. Renewing America's Food Traditions. White River Junction, VT: Chelsea Green Publishing.

Nabhan, G. P., ed. 2013. Conservation You Can Taste. Tucson: University of Arizona, Southwest Center, in collaboration with Slow Food USA.

Whealy, K., and J. Thuente. 2001. Fruit, Nut and Berry Inventory. Decorah, IA: Seed Savers Exchange.

Whealy, K., and J. Thuente. 2004. Garden Seed Inventory. Decorah, IA: Seed Savers Exchange.

PLATE 1. Seri Indian aquaculturist and paraecologist Alberto Mellado Moreno holds a cluster of Sea of Cortés native *callo de hacha* scallops propagated in Estero Sargento along the coast of Sonora, Mexico, in 2009. Photo by Gary Paul Nabhan. See chapter 11.

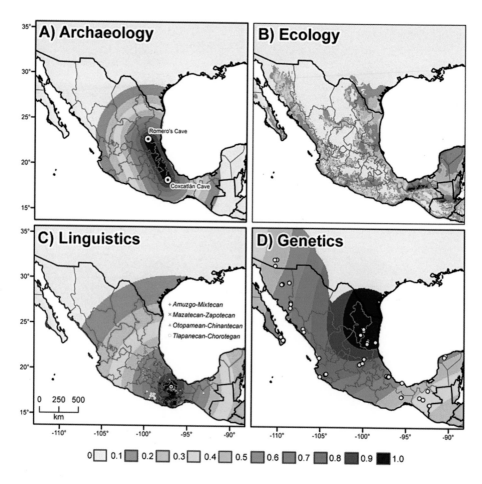

| 0 | 0.1 | 0.2 | 0.3 | 0.4 | 0.5 | 0.6 | 0.7 | 0.8 | 0.9 | 1.0 |

PLATE 2. Possible area of Mexico for *Capsicum annuum* domestication based on (A) archaeological, (B) paleoclimatic, mid-Holocene, (C) linguistic, and (D) genetic data. In addition to the strength of evidence (between 0 and 1), the maps show: (A) Location of the oldest archaeological remains of chili: Romero Cave, Ocampo, Tamaulipas; Coxcatlán Cave, Tehuacán Valley, Puebla. (C) Location of the homeland of Proto-Otomanguean (dotted circle) and of the four subgroups of current Otomanguean languages (see Fig. S5 legend and Table 1; for a more detailed view of the subgroup distribution, see Fig. S5). Open circles represent approximate locations of protolanguages with a reconstructed word for chili. (D) Open circles indicate the location of the wild chili samples used in the genetic distance analysis (29). For explanation of values, see *Materials and Methods* in chapter 13.

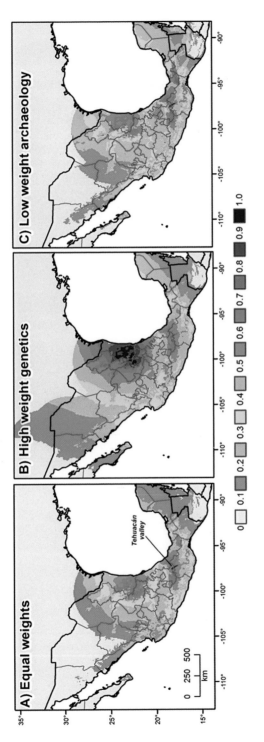

PLATE 3. Consensus models of the likelihood that cultivated chili pepper originated in an area. The models were obtained by combining the four lines of evidence for the origin of domesticated chili pepper (Fig. 1). (A) equal weights; (B) genetics ½ weight; and (C) archaeology ⅓ weight. After combining, the values were scaled between 0 and 1 and then squared to give more weight to the higher values. See chapter 13.

PLATE 4. A Quichuan woman living in the vicinity of the
Parque de la Papa in Peru selling diverse tubers in an open-air
marketplace. Photo by Gary Paul Nabhan. See chapter 17.

13

MULTIPLE LINES OF EVIDENCE FOR THE ORIGIN OF DOMESTICATED CHILE PEPPER, *CAPSICUM ANNUUM,* IN MEXICO

KRAIG H. KRAFT, CECIL H. BROWN, GARY P. NABHAN, EIKE LUEDELING, JOSÉ DE JESÚS LUNA RUIZ, GEO COPPENS D'ECKENBRUGGE, ROBERT J. HIJMANS, AND PAUL GEPTS

EDITOR'S NOTE

Since the publication of this paper in PNAS, a lively debate has ensued among linguists regarding the current understanding of the relationships among the Otomanguean languages and the reconstruction of the Proto-Otomanguean term(s) for chiles. While new evidence may iteratively change some of the tentative conclusions made in this article regarding the linguistic context of chile origins and diffusion, this general model of combining genetic, paleolinguistic, biogeographic, archaeological, and climatic patterns still has hueristic value.

━━━━━━━━━━
━━━━━━━━━━

THE STUDY OF CROP ORIGINS has traditionally involved identifying geographic areas of high morphological diversity, sampling populations of wild progenitor species, and the archaeological retrieval of macroremains. Recent investigations have added identification of plant microremains (phytoliths, pollen, and starch grains), biochemical and molecular genetic

A version of this paper originally appeared in the *Proceedings of the National Academy of Sciences,* Volume III, Number 17:6165–6170.

approaches, and dating through ^{14}C accelerator mass spectrometry. We investigate the origin of domesticated chile pepper, *Capsicum annuum*, by combining two approaches, species distribution modeling and paleobiolinguistics, with microsatellite genetic data and archaeobotanical data. The combination of these four lines of evidence yields consensus models indicating that domestication of *C. annuum* could have occurred in one or both of two areas of Mexico: northeastern Mexico and central-east Mexico. Genetic evidence shows more support for the more northern location, but jointly all four lines of evidence support central-east Mexico, where preceramic macroremains of chile pepper have been recovered in the Valley of Tehuacán. Located just to the east of this valley is the center of phylogenetic diversity of Proto-Otomanguean, a language spoken in mid-Holocene times and the oldest protolanguage for which a word for chile pepper reconstructs based on historical linguistics. For many crops, especially those that do not have a strong archaeobotanical record or phylogeographic pattern, it is difficult to precisely identify the time and place of their origin. Our results for chile pepper show that expressing all data in similar distance terms allows for combining contrasting lines of evidence and locating the region(s) where cultivation and domestication of a crop began.

The analysis of plant macroremains, morphological variation in crop varieties, and identification of wild progenitor species (as determined through their ability to hybridize with the crop) constitute traditional methods for studying crop origins (1, 2). Currently, analysis of microremains such as starch grains, accelerator mass spectrometry (AMS) ^{14}C radiocarbon dating, along with biochemical and molecular genetic analyses of wild and domesticated populations are also used to date and locate geographic areas of domestication (3, 4).

This set of approaches is extended here with two additional methods, species distribution modeling and paleobiolinguistics, integrating these in a comprehensive study of the origin of domesticated chile pepper, *Capsicum annuum* L., the world's most widely grown spice. *C. annuum* is one of five domesticated pepper species, which also include *Capsicum baccatum* L., *Capsicum chinense* Jacq., *Capsicum frutescens* L., and *Capsicum pubescens* Ruiz & Pav. The ~30 species of *Capsicum* are all native to the Americas (5). Comparing karyotypes of wild and domesticated *C. annuum* (var. *glabriusculum* and var. *annuum*, respectively), Pickersgill (6) identified Mexico as the general region of domestication of this pepper. Loaiza-Figueroa et al. (7) used allozyme similarity to identify putative wild ancestral populations for chile pepper in a larger collection of wild and domesticated populations. They narrowed the likely domestication area to the eastern Mexican states of Tamaulipas, Nuevo León, San Luís Potosí, Veracruz, and Hidalgo. Since these investigations, others have sought to determine genetic relationships among wild and domesticated populations of chile pepper (8, 9).

The oldest macroremains unambiguously identified as *Capsicum* pepper were retrieved from preceramic strata of dry caves in two states of Mexico: Puebla (Tehuacán Valley; refs. 10, 11) and Tamaulipas (Ocampo caves; ref. 12) (see plate 2A). These were found with macroremains of maize (*Zea mays*), squash (*Cucurbita* spp.), and other species used by humans, all of which, at both sites, were indirectly dated through associations in archaeological strata, suggesting a rough date for the chile pepper macroremains of around 9000–7000 B. P. (13). Subsequently, remains of maize from Tehuacán were dated directly by AMS and found to be more recent, 5600 y calibrated B. P. (14). AMS dating applied to bottle gourd and squash from Ocampo also yielded more recent ages, 6400–6000 y calibrated B. P. (15). Whereas no AMS dates have been recorded for the Tehuacán and Ocampo remains of chile pepper, remains from Guilá Naquitz and Silvia's Caves in the arid eastern valley of Oaxaca state were dated indirectly by AMS to 1400–500 B. P. (16). Rock shelters in the seasonally dry tropical forest of the Central Balsas watershed (state of Guerrero) have produced phytoliths and starch grain residue for domesticated maize and squash (*Cucurbita*) dated by association to around 9000 B. P. (17). However, no remains of *Capsicum* pepper have been found at that site.

Species distribution modeling (SDM) can be used to predict areas that are environmentally suitable for a species from the sites where it is known to occur (18). In SDM, locations of the known current distribution of a species are compiled; values for climatic predictor variables at these locations and a large set of random (background) locations are extracted from spatial databases; and the climatic values are used to fit a model that estimates the similarity of the climate in any location to climatic conditions at known occurrence locations, using a machine-learning algorithm such as MaxEnt (19). The model is then used to predict the climatic suitability for a species across an area of interest. This prediction can be made using current climate data, but the model can also be "transferred" in time, by using past or future climate data simulated by global climate models (GCMs). This approach has been used for many purposes, including to predict the effect of climate change on the geographic distribution of crop wild relatives (20) and to successfully locate unknown *Capsicum* populations (21).

Crop origins can also be studied using paleobiolinguistics (PBL), which employs the comparative method of historical linguistics to reconstruct the biodiversity known to human groups of the remote, unrecorded past (22–24). By comparing words for a species in modern languages, terms for plants and animals in ancestral languages can be retrieved. The presence of words for a species in an ancestral language is an indication of the species' significance to speakers of that language (25, 26), if not their status as domesticated plants. PBL uses Automated Similarity Judgment Program (ASJP) chronology for estimating the latest date at which a protolanguage was spoken based on lexical similarity (27). Lexical similarity found among related languages is calibrated with historical, epigraphic, and archaeological divergence dates for 52 language groups. In addition, the general area in which an ancestral language was spoken, i.e., the protolanguage homeland, can be approximately determined by locating the area where its modern descendant languages are found to be most diverse (28).

In this paper, we complement existing archaeobotanical data with ecological, paleobiolinguistic, and molecular diversity data to identify the region of initial intensification of human interest in chile pepper that led to crop domestication. The novelty of our approach resides in the addition of SDM and PBL to this type of analysis and the expression of all lines of evidence in comparable spatially explicit units (distance to the area of origin), which allows for their integration into a single prediction.

MATERIALS AND METHODS

ARCHAEOLOGY

We used two locations for which there is evidence of the earliest use of chile: Romero's Cave (near Ocampo, Tamaulipas) and Coxcatlán Cave (Tehuacán Valley, Puebla) (see plate 2A). We connected these locations by their shortest path, and then computed the distance d (in kilometers) to this path for cells on a raster with 1-km2 spatial resolution. We truncated the distances at 1,000 km and used an inverse squared distance decay function, scaled between 0 and 1, $(1 - (d/1,000))$ as a measure of the likelihood that chile was domesticated in a location (grid cell).

SPECIES DISTRIBUTION MODELING

We used SDM to assess spatial variation in suitability for wild *C. annuum* var. *glabriusculum*, the ancestor of domesticated *C. annuum* (6), during climatic conditions of the mid-Holocene (about 6,000 y ago) (see plate 2B). Locations where wild *Capsicum* populations currently occur were from collections made in the fall of 2006 and 2007 (29) and from additional records obtained from the Global Biodiversity Information Facility (GBIF). We used the SDM algorithm MaxEnt (19) to predict suitability during the mid-Holocene according to nine global climate models (*SI Materials and Materials*).

PALEOBIOLINGUISTICS

The different languages considered are listed in Table 13.1 and the respective information sources are compiled in *SI Materials and Methods*. Protolanguage dates (Table 13.1) were calculated through use of ASJP chronology (27). The center of phylogenetic diversity of Otomanguean languages was located from the distribution of places where Otomanguean languages are currently spoken (50), by determining the area where languages spoken in close geographic proximity to one another are affiliated with the largest number of major divisions of the family.

GENETIC DISTANCE ANALYSIS

Genetic distance between 139 wild and forty-nine domesticated pepper accessions were assessed with data from seventeen microsatellite markers (SSRs) developed before this study.

CONSENSUS MODEL

All four data sources were used to create a spatial model on a common raster. All models had values between 0 and 1, with higher scores indicating that a location is more likely to be the area where domestication occurred. We combined these four sources of data into a single consensus model by assigning weights to each indicator. To get a more pronounced differentiation between sites, we squared the values, after first rescaling them between 0 and 1.

RESULTS

ARCHAEOLOGICAL EVIDENCE

The remains from Tehuacán and Ocampo constitute at present the oldest macrobotanical evidence for preceramic chile pepper in the New World. Although these chile specimens cannot definitely be identified as cultivated

TABLE 13.1. Reconstruction of terms for *Capsicum* in selected protolanguages of Mesoamerica and abutting areas.

YEARS BEFORE PRESENT	PROTOLANGUAGE†	RECONSTRUCTED WORD FOR CHILE‡	LOCATION OF MODERN DESCENDANT LANGUAGES	GENETIC AFFILIATION
6591	Otomanguean	*ʔki³	Mexico	Otomanguean
5976	Eastern Otomanguean	*(h)saH³, *ki	Mexico	Otomanguean
5498	Popolocan-Zapotecan	*ki	Mexico	Otomanguean
5357	Amuzgo-Mixtecan	*nʔsah³	Mexico	Otomanguean
4542	Mixtecan	*(H)yaʔ, Hyah, HƟaʔ²	Mexico	Otomanguean
4274	Totozoquean	NR	Mexico	Totozoquean
4018	Uto-Aztecan	NR	U.S. Southwest, Mexico, Central America	Uto-Aztecan
3654	Otopamean	*(m)ʔi	Mexico	Otomanguean
3472	Southern Uto-Aztecan	NR	Mexico, Central America	Uto-Aztecan
3434	Kiowa-Tanoan	NR	U.S. Southwest	Kiowa-Tanoan
3149	Zapotecan	*ki:ʔnaʔ	Mexico	Otomanguean
3036	Poplocan	*hña	Mexico	Otomanguean
3000	Lencan	NR	Central America	Lencan
2774	Misumalpan	kuma	Central America	Misumalpan

continued

TABLE 13.1. *continued*

YEARS BEFORE PRESENT	PROTOLANGUAGE[†]	RECONSTRUCTED WORD FOR CHILE[‡]	LOCATION OF MODERN DESCENDANT LANGUAGES	GENETIC AFFILIATION
2576	Northern Uto-Aztecan	NR	U.S. Southwest	Uto-Aztecan
2445	Chiapanec-Mangue	*niː-ⁿgiʔ	Mexico	Otomanuguean
2400	Sonoran	*koʔokoLi	Mexico	Uto-Aztecan
2220	Mayan	*iːhk	Mexico, Central America	Mayan
1935	Chinantecan	*ʔu^{HL}	Mexico	Otomanuguean
1865	Yuman	NR	U.S. Southwest	Yuman
1737	Numic	NR	U.S. Southwest	Uto-Aztecan
1587	Takic	NR	U.S. Southwest	Uto-Aztecan
1509	General Aztec	*čiːl	Mexico	Uto-Aztecan
1435	Totonacan	*piʔn	Mexico	Totozoquean
1407	Mixe-Zoquean	*niːwi	Mexico	Totozoquean

NR, not reconstructable.

† Sources for each language are listed in *SI Materials and Methods* under *Paleobiolinguistics*.

‡ Explanations for phonetic representation of pepper words are listed in *SI Materials and Methods* under *Paleobiolinguistics*.

or domesticated, their archaeological association with domesticated remains of important crops, such as maize and squash, is strongly suggestive of ancient intensive human interaction with if not management of chile in these areas. Based on this evidence, we assumed that the nearer a place may be to either of these sites, the more likely the location was part of the region where the crop was first grown and domesticated (see plate 2A).

ECOLOGICAL EVIDENCE

Wild chile pepper (*C. annuum* var. *glabriusculum*), the ancestor of domesticated *C. annuum* (6), is a perennial shrub that produces dozens of erect, pea-sized fruits. (51) The fruits are consumed and dispersed by frugivorous birds, which pass the seed through their digestive system. Generally found in the northern half of Mexico, the wild chile pepper is associated with a nurse plant—often a hackberry (*Celtis pallida* Torey), a mesquite (*Prosopis* sp.), or cacti (51). As one travels further southward, wild chile pepper is found more frequently in human-disturbed landscapes—fence rows, home gardens, and roadsides (29). Based on our own collecting localities and those of herbarium specimens and gene bank accessions (29), we estimate that wild chile peppers grow currently in environments with a median annual average temperature of 24 °C and between 20 °C and 26 °C for 90 percent of the locations. The coldest locations with known wild pepper populations are mostly in the central Mexican highlands, the warmest locations in the southern coastal regions of Mexico and Guatemala. The median annual rainfall of these locations is 907 mm, and between 495 and 2,253 mm for 90 percent of the locations, with the driest locations in the northwestern part of the distribution (e.g., Baja California and the Sonoran Desert) and the wettest locations in southeastern Mexico.

The MaxEnt species distribution model had an internal (training) fit area under the curve (AUC) of the receiver operating characteristic (ROC) curve of 0.89. The average cAUC (bias corrected) obtained with fivefold cross-validation was 0.80, which suggests that the model has very good predictive power (30). The two most important predictor variables (based on permutation importance) were mean temperature of the coldest quarter (53 percent), followed by annual precipitation (14 percent).

Under the climate conditions of the mid-Holocene (about 6000 B.P.), the regions predicted to be most suitable for wild chile pepper include areas along the western and eastern coasts of Mexico, southeast Mexico and northern

Guatemala (see plate 2B). The central highlands were clearly unsuitable for this species during this period. The correlation coefficient between the predicted suitability for the current climate and the mid-Holocene climate was 0.92. Despite this overall similarity, there were important differences between these predictions, with areas in the southeast of Mexico more suitable and areas in the northeast less suitable during the mid-Holocene.

PALEOBIOLINGUISTIC EVIDENCE

Brown (22) surveyed the reconstructed vocabularies of 30 protolanguages of Mesoamerica (southern half of Mexico and northern Central America) and abutting areas for terms for forty-one different crops, including chile pepper. His survey presented for each protolanguage the estimated date it was spoken at the latest, making it possible to stratify reconstructed words for crops chronologically (Table 13.1) (27, 28).

Proto-Otomanguean is the oldest (~6500 B.P.) protolanguage of the New World for which a word for chile pepper reconstructs (31). All daughter languages of Proto-Otomanguean, as defined by Kaufman (32), show reconstructed terms for chile pepper (Table 13.1). Given that estimated dates are to be understood as the latest dates at which ancestral languages were spoken, it is plausible that speakers of Proto-Otomanguean actually had a word for chile pepper hundreds, if not thousands, of years before ~6500 B. P. The oldest protolanguage of Table 13.1 not belonging to the Otomanguean family is Proto-Totozoquean (~4300 B.P.), for which a term for chile pepper does not reconstruct. Non-Otomanguean languages for which a term for chile pepper reconstructs are Proto-Misumalpan (~2800 B.P.), Proto-Sonoran (~2400 B.P.), and Proto-Mayan (~2200 B.P.). Thus, the earliest non-Otomanguean dates for *Capsicum* in Mesoamerica and abutting regions are over 3,700 y more recent than the oldest date, suggesting that speakers of a prehistoric Otomanguean language or languages may have been among the first cultivators or domesticators of chile pepper. Note that the current word—chile—is derived from the General Aztec language, Nahuatl, which reconstructs to a much more recent date (~1500 B.P.; Table 13.1).

The area of maximum diversity of a language family has been viewed traditionally by linguists as suggestive of the location of a family's ancestral language (e.g., ref. 28). We use this phylogenetic diversity information in locating the Otomanguean homeland by identifying where languages of the four subgroups of the family—Mazatecan-Zapotecan, Amuzgo-Mixtecan, Tlapanecan-Chorotegan, and Otopamean-Chinantecan (32)—are currently spoken in closest proximity (see plate 2C).

GENETIC EVIDENCE

During the fall of 2006 and 2007, expeditions were conducted in the southern United States and throughout Mexico to sample populations of wild *C. annuum* (29). This provided the most complete set of wild *C. annuum* from Mexico available to date. Based largely on this set, 139 wild types distributed over the entire exploration area were chosen, as were forty-nine domesticated types that are endemic landraces (*ancho*, *puya*, and *guajillo*) (33). This collection was screened with seventeen simple sequence repeat (SSR) DNA markers (34, 35). These markers were chosen for this study because of their consistency of amplification and polymorphism within our sample. For each wild plant, a distance was calculated to the domesticated group based on the average proportion of shared SSR alleles. These distances were then spatially interpolated to produce in each grid cell an estimated genetic similarity between wild pepper populations (if any occurred in the cell) and the group of domesticated chile peppers (regardless of where they occurred). This molecular-marker–based analysis of genetic similarity between wild and domesticated types revealed a broad area of high similarity in the northeastern quadrant of Mexico (see plate 2D), including the states of Tamaulipas, Nuevo León, San Luís Potosí, and Veracruz. In contrast, genetic similarity between wild and cultivated types was generally low in southern and northwest Mexico, confirming earlier results (7).

CONSENSUS MODEL

The four lines of evidence—archaeological, ecological, paleobiolinguistic, and genetic—were all expressed as a spatial model. They can therefore be combined into a single consensus model represented geographically through mapping. Each type of evidence has its particular strengths and weaknesses, discussed below, which need to be taken into consideration when producing a consensus model. Because these merits and demerits are difficult to quantify (some are simply unknown), assigning differential weights to each line of evidence is problematic. Our solution is to present a number of different consensus maps based on several different weighting combinations (see plate 3). (As new evidence in any four of the lines is obtained it can be integrated into this open-ended or iterative model.)

The first map, plate 3A, was established using equal weighting for each type of evidence (each weighted as making a 1/4 contribution). According to this model, areas in central-east Mexico and northeastern Mexico are the most likely area of origin of chile pepper. The second model assigned a high weight to genetic evidence (weighted 1/2) and equal but lower weights to the other three lines of evidence (each weighted 1/6). This assumes that genetic data might be superior to one or more of the other lines of evidence used because, for example, it might suffer less from sampling bias. This results in primary support for northeastern Mexico and only secondary support for central-east Mexico (see plate 3B). The third approach assigned a low weight to archaeology (1/10) and equal higher weights to the other three lines of evidence (each weighted 1/3). This weighting was motivated by the observation that the current archaeological data are assembled from macroremains of only two sites in Mexico. This weighting produces a consensus model resembling the equal weighting of plate 3A because both central-east Mexico and northeastern Mexico result as equally plausible geographic candidates for chile pepper domestication (see plate 3C). Additional information, from other sites and microremains, yet to be discovered, would justify a stronger weighting for archaeobotanical data.

Another weighting strategy produces different models based on randomly assigning combinations of weights for the four types of evidence. This approach allows us to explore the universe of possible weight combinations given different interpretations of the individual lines of evidence. The resulting maps suggest again that either central-east Mexico or northeastern Mexico or, conceivably, both areas were locations of the domestication of *C. annuum*.

DISCUSSION

We have embraced the template of multidisciplinary approaches to study crop origins proposed first by de Candolle (36) and later by Harlan and de Wet (37). Confidence in a crop-origin hypothesis is increased when supported by multiple, independent lines of evidence, and improved understanding comes from new evidence in each field and concomitant predictions in other fields (38). Our multidisciplinary approach depends on the independence and strength of evidence from the different fields, each of which has its strengths and weaknesses.

Current archaeobotanical data for chile pepper is mainly based on macro-remains from only two sites. In addition to the identification of ancient chile remains at additional sites, our understanding could benefit from the investigation of microfossil data such as starch grains (39) in Mesoamerican sites. Availability of microfossils may provide information on the more ancient distribution and importance of chile peppers and potentially also help distinguish domesticated from non-domesticated remains (as in the case of maize) (40).

The quality of species distribution models depends on having a representative sample of the current distribution of the wild species, the quality of climate data, particularly the modeled past climate data, and the algorithm used. Our sample size was large and the species is widespread, suggesting that the SDM approach should work well (41), as confirmed by a high cAUC score (30). Back-casted climate data for the mid-Holocene is, of course, uncertain; furthermore, we did not consider climate variation during that period. Nevertheless, because we use an ensemble of climate models, our predictions should be relatively robust (42).

Utilization of linguistic data assumes an understanding of language development, including information relating to language origin, dispersal, and diffusion of traits across languages that is still emerging as new computer approaches are increasingly applied in linguistic analysis (43, 44). PBL provides an assessment of when species acquired substantial salience for prehistoric groups, whether they were merely harvested, cultivated, or eventually domesticated. If a word for a biological species reconstructs for a protolanguage, this is evidence that the species was known to and probably of considerable importance to speakers of the language as shown by Berlin et al. (25) for two closely related Mayan languages, Tzeltal and Tzotzil (Tzeltalan) and by Balée and Moore (26) in a study of plant names in five Eastern Amazonian Tupi-Guaraní languages.

Genetic data are generally based on the analysis of contemporary populations of the wild ancestor of the crop. The wild populations included in this study constitute the largest and most widespread sample used in genetic analyses for this species (29). However, we do not know to what extent the distribution and genetic structure of these populations have changed over the past 6,000 y. Hence, we modeled the past distribution of wild chile peppers based on the assumption that their climatic requirements are the same as today's wild chile pepper population. Correlation between the suitability scores for ancient and current distributions is high (0.92), suggesting that, whereas climate change over the past 6,000 y has likely shifted the species distribution, for the most part, the historical and current ranges of this species overlap. Another potentially confounding factor is gene flow between domesticated and wild chile peppers, which may cause similarities, which are not due to ancestor–descendant relationships (45). However, this would not seem very important for chile peppers because they are mostly a self-fertilizing species with minimal outcrossing, which is confirmed by the high levels of homozygosity observed for wild chile pepper populations analyzed here.

The concept of origin of *C. annuum* used in this study encompasses a predictable sequence of wild plant protection, management, cultivation, and domestication. Within this continuum of increasingly close interaction between humans and plants, distinguishing among these four stages for most crops is difficult. However, with respect to chile pepper, the fact that a Proto-Otomanguean word for the crop was retained in daughter languages attests to its high salience for speakers of the protolanguage. Furthermore, Proto-Otomanguean speakers may have been actively engaged in cultivation, as suggested by the reconstruction of words for a range of plants, including staple crops such as maize and squash, but also other crops such as avocado and prickly pear (22). Plausibly, then, the saliency of chile pepper among Proto-Otomanguean speakers reflects cultivation and perhaps incipient domestication and not merely use of a wild plant species.

When analyzed separately, our four lines of evidence do not all suggest the same geographic area as being the most likely place of chile pepper origin. Nevertheless, we identify central-east Mexico as a likely region of initial cultivation or incipient domestication because that interpretation most parsimoniously reconciles all evidence (see plate 3A). This area extends from southern Puebla and northern Oaxaca to southern Veracruz and encompasses the valley of Tehuacán (see plate 3A). The Coxcatlán Cave from which preceramic macroremains of chile pepper have been recovered (13) is situated in this valley. Species distribution modeling shows that many parts of the identified area were suited for the wild progenitor of *C. annuum* around the time of first cultivation or domestication in the mid-Holocene and there are currently populations of wild chile pepper that are genetically similar to the domesticated species (see plate 2D). Near to the valley is the likely center of the Otomanguean homeland. Proto-Otomanguean, spoken in mid-Holocene times some 6,500 years ago, appears to be the oldest ancestral language of the New World for which a term for chile pepper reconstructs. Speakers of contemporary Otomanguean languages live in or close to the region. Otomanguean people, then, may have been the first in the New World to transform wild chiles into the domesticated spice and condiment so widely enjoyed today.

By expressing all data as a distance, whether geographical (archaeological and linguistic data), climatic, or genetic, we have developed a method to bring together different lines of evidence about crop origins into a single framework of analysis. This approach has led to the discovery that the origin of domesticated chile peppers may have been located further south than previously thought (7) and in different regions of Mexico than proposed for common bean (46) or maize (47). Thus, our data do not suggest a single, nuclear area for crop domestication in Mesoamerica, but rather a multiregional model as suggested also for the Southwest Asian (48) and Chinese (49) centers of agricultural origins.

ACKNOWLEDGMENTS

Suzanne K. Fish, Eric W. Holman, and Søren Wichmann provided help for this project in its early phase. Holman and Wichmann also read and commented on the manuscript, as did Gene Anderson, Roger Blench, Eric Campbell, Charles Clement, Norman Hammond, Matt Hufford, Sarah Metcalfe, Barbara Pickersgill, Anthony J. Ranere, Brian Stross, and Eric Votava. K. H. K. thanks Horacio Villalón and Sergio Hernández Verdugo for contributions of wild Capsicum; Heather Zornetzer for assistance during field collection; and Derek van den Abeelen, Raúl Durán, Tiffany Chan, Jonathan Kong, and James Kami for assistance in the laboratory work for the genetic analyses; and the Fulbright program, the University of California Institute for Mexico and the United States (UC MEXUS), and the Department of Plant Sciences (Graduate Student Research assistantship) for funding. We thank the World Climate Research Programme's Working Group on Coupled Modelling (CMIP5) and the climate modeling groups for making their model output available.

REFERENCES

1. Smith, B. (1995) *The Emergence of Agriculture* (Scientific American Library, New York).

2. Gepts, P. et al. (2012) *Biodiversity in Agriculture: Domestication, Evolution, and Sustainability* (Cambridge University Press, Cambridge, UK), p. 630.

3. Gepts, P. (2004) Domestication as a long-term selection experiment. *Plant Breeding Reviews* 24(Part 2):1–44.

4. Burke, J.M., Burger, J.C., Chapman, M.A. (2007) Crop evolution: From genetics to genomics. *Current Opinion in Genetics and Development* 17(6):525–32.

5. Bosland, P.W. (1994) Chiles: History, cultivation and uses. *Spices, Herbs and Edible Fungi*, ed. Charambous, G. (Elsevier, New York).

6. Pickersgill, B. (1971) Relationships between weedy and cultivated forms in some species of chili peppers (genus *Capsicum*). *Evolution* 25:683–91.

7. Loaiza-Figueroa, F., Ritland, K., Cancino, J.A.L., Tanskley, S.D. (1989) Patterns of genetic variation of the genus *Capsicum* (Solanaceae) in Mexico. *Plant Systems Evolution* 165:159–188.

8. Aguilar-Meléndez, A., Morrell, P.L., Roose, M.L., Kim, S.C. (2009) Genetic diversity and structure in semi-wild and domesticated chiles (*Capsicum annuum*; Solanaceae) from Mexico. *American Journal of Botany* 96(6): 1190–1202.

9. Votava, E.J., Nabhan, G.P., Bosland, P.W. (2002) Genetic diversity and similarity revealed via molecular analysis among and within an in situ population and ex situ accessions of chiltepin (*Capsicum annuum* var. *glabriusculum*). *Conservation Genetics* 3(2):123–29.

10. Smith, C.E. (1967) Plant remains. *The Prehistory of the Tehuacan Valley*, ed. Byers, D.S. (University of Texas Press, Austin, TX), pp. 220–55.

11. Smith, C.E., Jr. (1987) Current archaeological evidence for the beginning of American agriculture. *Studies in the Neolithic and Urban Revolutions, The V. Gordon Childe Colloquium*, ed. Manzanilla, L. (British Archaeological Reports, Oxford, UK), pp. 81–101.

12. Mangelsdorf, P.C., McNeish, R.S., Willey, G.R. (1965) Origins of Middle American agriculture. *Natural Environment and Early Cultures*, ed. West, R.C. (University of Texas Press, Austin, Texas), pp. 427–45.

13. McClung de Tapia, A. (1992) The origins of agriculture in Mesoamerica and Central America. *The Origins of Agriculture: An International Perspective*, eds. Cowan, C.W., Watson, P.J. (Smithsonian Institution Press, Washington, DC), pp. 143–71.

14. Long, A., Benz, B., Donahue, D., Jull, A., Toolin, L. (1989) First direct AMS dates on early maize from Tehuacán, Mexico. *Radiocarbon* 31:1035–40.

15. Smith, B.D. (1997) Reconsidering the Ocampo Caves and the era of incipient cultivation in Mesoamerica. *Latin American Antiquity* 8(4):342–83.

16. Perry, L., Flannery, K.V. (2007) Precolumbian use of chili peppers in the Valley of Oaxaca, Mexico. *Proceedings of the National Academy of Sciences USA* 104(29):11905–09.

17. Ranere, A.J., Piperno, D.R., Holst, I., Dickau, R., Iriarte, J. (2009) The cultural and chronological context of early Holocene maize and squash domestication in the Central Balsas River Valley, Mexico. *Proceedings of the National Academy of Sciences USA* 106(13):5014–18.

18. Elith, J., Leathwick, J.R. (2009) Species distribution models: Ecological explanation and prediction across space and time. *Annual Review Ecology, Evolution, Systematics* 40(1):677–97.

19. Phillips, S.J., Anderson, R.P., Schapire, R.E. (2006) Maximum entropy modeling of species geographic distributions. *Ecology Modelling* 190(3–4): 231–59.

20. Jarvis, A., Lane, A., Hijmans, R.J. (2008) The effect of climate change on crop wild relatives. *Agriculture, Ecosystems and Environment* 126(1–2):13–23.

21. Jarvis, A. et al. (2005) Use of GIS for optimizing a collecting mission for a rare wild pepper (*Capsicum flexuosum* Sendtn.) in Paraguay. *Genetic Resources and Crop Evolution* 52(6): 671–82.

22. Brown, C.H. (2010) Development of agriculture in prehistoric Mesoamerica: The linguistic evidence. *Pre-Columbia Foodways: Interdisciplinary Approaches to Food, Culture and Markets in Ancient Mesoamerica*, eds. Staller, J.E., Carrasco, M.D. (Springer, Berlin), pp. 71–107.

23. Fowler, C.S. (1972) Some ecological clues to Proto-Numic homelands. *Desert Research Institute Publications in the Social Sciences* 8:105–17.

24. Hill, J.H. (2001) Proto-Uto-Aztecan: A community of cultivators in central Mexico? *American Anthropology* 103:913–34.

25. Berlin, B., Breedlove, D.E., Laughlin, R.M., Raven, P.H. (1973) Cultural significance and lexical retention in Tzeltal-Tzotzil ethnobotany. *Meaning in Mayan Languages*, ed. Edmonson, M.A. (Mouton, The Hague), pp. 143–64.

26. Balée, W.L., Moore, D. (1991) Similarity and variation in plant names in five Tupi-Guarani languages (Eastern Amazonia). *Bulletin of the Florida Museum of Natural History* 35(4):209–62.

27. Holman, E.W. et al. (2011) Automated dating of the world's language families based on lexical similarity. *Current Anthropology* 52(6):841–75.

28. Wichmann, S., Muller, A., Velupillai, V. (2010) Homelands of the world's language families: A quantitative approach. *Diachronica* 27(2):247–76.

29. Kraft, K.H., Luna-Ruiz, J.D., Gepts, P. (2013) A new collection of wild populations of *Capsicum* in Mexico and the southern United States. *Genetic Resources and Crop Evolution* 60(1): 225–32.

30. Hijmans, R.J. (2012) Cross-validation of species distribution models: Removing spatial sorting bias and calibration with a null model. *Ecology* 93(3):679–88.

31. Brown, C.H., Clement, C.R., Epps, P., Luedeling, E., Wichmann, S. (2013) The paleobiolinguistics of domesticated chili pepper (*Capsicum* spp.). *Ethnobiology Letters* 4:1–11.

32. Kaufman, T.S. (1990) Early Otomanguean homeland and cultures: Some premature hypotheses. (University of Pittsburgh Working Papers in Linguistics 1), pp. 91–136.

33. Kraft, K.H., de Jesús Luna-Ruíz, J., Gepts, P. (2010) Different seed selection and conservation practices for fresh market and dried chile farmers in Aguascalientes, Mexico. *Economic Botany* 64(4):318–28.

34. Lee, J.M., Nahm, S.H., Kim, Y.M., Kim, B.D. (2004) Characterization and molecular genetic mapping of microsatellite loci in pepper. *Theoretical Applications in Genetics* 108(4):619–27.

35. Minamiyama, Y., Tsuro, M., Hirai, M. (2006) An SSR-based linkage map of *Capsicum annuum*. *Molecular Breeding* 18(2):157–69.

36. de Candolle, A. (1882) *L'Origine des Plantes Cultivées [The Origin of Cultivated Plants]* (Appleton, New York), pp. 468.

37. Harlan, J.R., de Wet, J.M.J. (1973) On the quality of evidence for origin and dispersal of cultivated plants. *Current Anthropology* 14:51–62.

38. Ammerman, A.J., Cavalli-Sforza, L.L. (1984) *The Neolithic Transition and the Genetics of Populations in Europe* (Princeton University Press, Princeton, NJ), pp. 176.

39. Perry, L. et al. (2007) Starch fossils and the domestication and dispersal of chili peppers (*Capsicum* spp. L.) in the Americas. *Science* 315(5814):986–8.

40. Holst, I., Moreno, J.E., Piperno, D.R. (2007) Identification of teosinte, maize, and Tripsacum in Mesoamerica by using pollen, starch grains, and phytoliths. *Proceedings of the National Academy of Sciences USA* 104(45):17608–13.

41. Wisz, M.S. et al. (2008) Effects of sample size on the performance of species distribution models. *Diverse Distributors* 14(5):763–73.

42. Araújo, M.B., New, M. (2007) Ensemble forecasting of species distributions. *Trends in Ecology and Evolution* 22(1):42–7.

43. Perreault, C., Mathew, S. (2012) Dating the origin of language using phonemic diversity. *PLoS ONE* 7(4):e35289.

44. Bouckaert, R. et al. (2012) Mapping the origins and expansion of the Indo-European language family. *Science* 337(6097):957–60.

45. Papa, R., Gepts, P. (2004) Asymmetric gene flow and introgression between wild and domesticated populations. *Introgression from Genetically Modified Plants into Wild Relatives and Its Consequences*, eds. Den Nijs, D., Bartsch, D., Sweet, J. (CABI, Oxon, UK), pp. 125–38.

46. Kwak, M., Kami, J.A., Gepts, P. (2009) The putative Mesoamerican domestication center of *Phaseolus vulgaris* is located in the Lerma-Santiago basin of Mexico. *Crop Science* 49(2): 554–63.

47. Matsuoka, Y. et al. (2002) A single domestication for maize shown by multilocus microsatellite genotyping. *Proceedings of the National Academy of Sciences USA* 99(9):6080–84.

48. Fuller, D.Q., Willcox, G., Allaby, R.G. (2011) Cultivation and domestication had multiple origins: Arguments against the core area hypothesis for the origins of agriculture in the Near East. *World Archaeology* 43(4):628–52.

49. Cohen, D.J. (2011) The beginnings of agriculture in China: A multiregional view. *Current Anthropology* 52(S4):S273–S93.

50. Avila-Blomberg, A. de, Moreno-Díaz, N.G. (2008) Distribución de las lenguas indígenas de México [Distribution of the indigenous languages of Mexico]. Comisión Nacional para el Conocimiento y Uso de la Biodiversidad, Mexico, DF.

51. Tewksbury, J. L., Nabhan, G. P. (2001) Seed dispersal: Directed deterrence by capsaicin in chiles. Nature 412(6845):403–404.

14

TRADITIONAL ECOLOGICAL KNOWLEDGE AND ENDANGERED SPECIES

Is Ethnobiology for the Birds?

GARY PAUL NABHAN AND DENNIS MARTINEZ

PERHAPS THE MOST OFTEN-CITED QUOTE in biological conservation circles is this ominous warning from E. O. Wilson (1990:182): "The one process now going on that will take millions of years to correct is the loss of genetic and species diversity by the destruction of natural habitats. This is the folly our descendants are least likely to forgive us." If there is a cultural corollary to Wilson's principle, it is that the loss of and disregard for traditional ecological knowledge may regrettably keep us from maintaining or recovering the species now at risk due to habitat destruction, fragmentation, or mismanagement. Nonetheless, there remains sufficient indigenous knowledge about endangered species, their life histories and habitats, to give us hope that it can guide both species recovery and habitat restoration in order to prevent the further loss of biodiversity.

This hope is grounded in our discussions with tribal elders and indigenous resource managers who retain detailed oral histories of the behavior and habitats of critically endangered species such as the "California" condor (*Gymnogyps californianus*), a species that was never geopolitically restricted to California

Originally published in *Journal of Ethnobiology* 32.1 (Spring/Summer 2012): 1–5. Reprinted with permission of *Journal of Ethnobiology*.

alone. This North American condor is one of 1,253 species of birds considered to be threatened with extinction by the International Union for Conservation of Nature (IUCN); another 853 avian species are considered "near threatened" as well. Together, the birds in these two categories amount to roughly 20 percent of all avian species already described by Western science.

But something remarkable has happened to condors in North America over the last quarter-century, something which flies in the face of global trends regarding other endangered birds. While the conservation status of nearly all of the IUCN Red Listed birds at risk has deteriorated since 1988 (Butchart et al. 2004), condor numbers have increased from the twenty-two individuals captured in 1987, to over 386 individuals in 2012. At least 237 free-flying condors, and 435 condors as of May 2015, now live and thrive in the wilds of Arizona, Baja California, California, and Utah.

Notably, both ethnobiologists and keepers of traditional knowledge have played roles in the recovery of condors in North America, and we believe they will continue to do so. It was the Society for Ethnobiology's first elected president, Amadeo Rea, who first discovered that lead poisoning had been playing a disproportionately large role in condor deaths. He was also the first scientist who "recommended the Grand Canyon region as the best place to reestablish the beleaguered condor" (Osborn 2007:48), thereby fostering their reintroduction into portions of their former range beyond the highly disrupted reaches of central and southern coastal California. Rea was well aware of paleontological records of the presence of condors in the Grand Canyon (Rea 2000); of historic observations of condors in the canyon made by early scientist-explorers through the 1920s (Rea 1981); and of traditional knowledge embedded in Hopi oral histories of condors (*kwaatoko*) in the Grand Canyon region (Hopi Dictionary Project 1998). Later, he also played a celebrated role in the reintroduction of condors into the mountains of Baja California Norte in Mexico.

It was in northern Mexico that one of us (G.P.N.) was recently stunned and pleased to learn that traditional knowledge regarding condors remains in currency among the Comcaac or Seri Indians of Sonora. An old friend from the Comcaac community of Punta Chueca, Alfredo Lopez Blanco, had just come back from the Baja California peninsula, where he identified certain petroglyphs found inland in the Sierra San Francisco as signs of ancient Seri clans, which in his mind, supported the Comcaac origin narrative that his Seri ancestors had migrated to the Mexican mainland from the peninsula. Alfredo was paging through Crosby's (1997) beautifully illustrated book on the rock art of

Baja California, when he stopped to show a group of us the animals painted in a particular cave he had visited in the area.

"Do you know the birds in this painting?" he asked.

We looked at the image, and one of us replied that they appeared to be either black vultures or turkey vultures, scavengers that are common in Baja California, as well as in Sonora.

"No, look at them more closely. I believe they are condors!" Alfredo suggested.

"Condors! How do you know condors?" There are no good historic records of condors in Sonora, and the last to inhabit the Sierra Juárez and San Pedro Mártir in northwestern Baja California disappeared by the late 1930s.

"Well, my in-laws saw them on Isla Tiburon in the '30s, way up near the highest point on the island. They were so big and so different from vultures that they told us the details of that encounter many times . . ."

We stood there amazed. A few hundred miles from where they were last seen in Mexico, on the largest island in the Sea of Cortés, condors had escaped the attention of biologists, but had been tangibly identified by indigenous hunter-gatherers, within their final decade, across widely ranging Mexican terrain.

On the other hand, the long-term retention of traditional knowledge about such charismatic avifauna among indigenous peoples should not surprise us. Narratives regarding condors have also persisted among the Chumash, Western Mono, Yokut, Central Miwok, Luiseno, Viyot, and Yurok of California. Both oral and written histories have proven invaluable in shaping the Yurok Tribe Condor Program, managed by wildlife biologists Chris West and Tiana Williams. This program carefully documents the need for establishing California condor release sites within Yurok Ancestral Territory near the Klamath River in northwestern California. According to Chris West, when it comes time to convince the U.S. Fish and Wildlife Service that the Yurok community has the justification for and capacity to manage a reintroduced condor population, it will need letters from both ethnobiologists and conservation biologists supporting its case.

Perhaps the most important contribution that indigenous restorationists and ethnobiologists have made is that condor recovery will ultimately be successful only if land managers return to the kinds of burning practices, which we now know were routinely maintained by First Nations within the condor range (Stewart 2002). Over the last half-century, Western scholars and activists involved in condor recovery may have missed one of the most important reasons for the near extinction of the condor. The zoologist Raymond Cowles and recent work by Dennis Martinez and Chuck Striplen (Amah Mutsun Ohlone; the San Francisco Estuary Institute) have linked the fire suppression policies of the last century to condor starvation (Martinez and Striplen in prep).

According to this hypothesis, California condors have become rare in the central portion of their range because fire suppression has led to higher densities of the "hard chaparral" vegetation type, which reduced food access for condors. As he first proposed in a 1958 paper, Cowles argued that condors were disappearing because modern fire exclusion had resulted in older, taller, and thicker chaparral, which caused a decline in jackrabbits and other small mammals that were favored prey. This, in turn, may have forced the condors to forage almost exclusively in more open foothill habitats of the inner Coast Ranges, Tehachapis, and Sierra Nevada of central California surrounding the San Joaquin Valley.

In addition, condors in tall chaparral had difficulty taking off after gorging on carcasses, or when they became trapped in small openings in dense chaparral. They also lost access to any remaining brush rabbits, which favored the thicker, almost impenetrable chaparral that followed decades of fire suppression.

Of course, there are other possible reasons for the near-extinction of California condors: poisoning from lead buckshot and bullets, raven predation of nestlings and eggs, electrocution by power lines, strychnine poisoning, and target practice by unscrupulous hunters. Notwithstanding these pressures, there is growing evidence of a fundamental shift in territorial foraging use by California condors over the past century or longer in southern California from chaparral and other habitats to the open foothills of the San Joaquin Valley (Snyder and Snyder 2000:139–143). A threshold may have been crossed that precipitated a population crash in a species with already historically low population numbers, a reproductive rate of only one chick every two years, and the longest juvenile dependency stage (five to six years) of any raptor. Except for nesting sites, California condors may have gradually stopped using coastal mountain chaparral for foraging because, as Cowles (1958, 1967) conjectured, they could no longer find sufficient food.

Additional insights regarding the nutritional requirements and foraging habits of condors, put forth later by Mundy and Ledger (1977), show that vultures (and condors) must regularly collect small bone fragments to meet their needs for calcium, and that this may have proven increasingly difficult in closed-canopy chaparral. They hypothesized that endangered Cape Griffon vultures of South Africa, which similarly suffered from lack of calcium, lost access to calcium from the extirpation of hyenas that crushed bones into small enough fragments to be swallowed easily by vultures. It is possible that the extirpation and/or reduction of large predators in California may have had, in part, a similar effect on lack of access to calcium by California condors.

While the evidence for Cowles' starvation hypothesis is circumstantially derived from historic data, and should be seen in the context of a number of other factors that may have contributed to the decline of California condors, it deserves consideration. There is, however, little scientific doubt that dense chaparral currently serves as quality wildlife habitat for very few vertebrate species (Longhurst 1978). Studies consistently show that wildlife prefer habitats with repeating ecotones—fire-induced patchy, fine-grained mosaics made up of a variety of shrub age classes (including mature and old-growth chaparral) and grassy openings rich in forbs. There can be no doubt that fire formerly played a keystone role in shaping and maintaining quality habitat for almost all wildlife, including California condors (Martinez and Striplen in prep; Timbrook et al. 1982). It is clear that current condor recovery efforts will face ongoing challenges unless they are more deeply nested in an understanding of the cultural landscapes in which condors historically thrived.

And yet, until Martinez and Striplen visited Pinnacles National Monument and spoke to staff handling condor releases, Pinnacles researchers had never thought of fire suppression negatively affecting condor survival, but they reacted favorably to the possibility. The Amah Band of the Mutsun Ohlone, led by Striplen, is working with Pinnacles and is pursuing a fire-history study funded by the Joint Fire Science Agency.

In essence, they have collectively posed the following hypothesis: tribes can influence patterns of fire occurrence and resulting vegetation in the coastal mountain regions of Central California. Project partners will include the Bureau of Land Management and the National Park Service, University of California, and California State Parks. Park researchers are beginning to appreciate that as hard chaparral reaches high densities because of fire suppression, the condors they are releasing will inevitably follow the same pattern that led to their near-extinction in the first place and will once again be forced to range into the foothills of the San Joaquin Valley, exposing themselves to the same dangers as before. Traditional ecological knowledge, together with Western science, may yet prevail and show how Indian fire has contributed and can again contribute to the survival of the California condor.

As with many issues in ethnobiology, a detailed understanding of the cultural influences on historic landscapes and populations can help lead us into a future where biodiversity and cultural knowledge are revived, valued and given their rightful place in our society. Ethnobiology is not merely a historic science, but a predictive science that can potentially integrate cultural values with scientific information to undo some of the damage that has occurred to our world and its many life forms. In an era when many species remain in decline, it would behoove wildlife biologists to add indigenous land managers, restorationists and ethnobiologists to their recovery teams. Ethnobiology is not merely "for the birds" such as condors; it can inform our decisions regarding the entire range of life on earth.

REFERENCES CITED

Butchart, Stuart H.M., Alison J. Stattersfield, Leon A. Bennun, Sue M. Shutes, H. Resit Akc̗akaya, Jonathan E. M. Baillie, Simon N. Stuart, Craig Hilton-Taylor, and Georgina M. Mace. 2004. Measuring Global Trends in the Status of Biodiversity: Red List Indices for Birds. *Public Library of Science Biology* 2(12): e83.

Cowles, Henry. 1958. Starving the Condor. *California Fish and Game* 44:175–81.

———. 1967. Fire Suppression, Faunal Changes and Condor Diets. *Proceedings of the Tall Timers Fire Ecology Conference.* 217–24. Tallahassee, FL.

Hopi Dictionary Project. 1998. *Hopi Dictionary: A Hopi-English Dictionary of the Third Mesa Dialect.* University of Arizona, Tucson, AZ.

Longhurst, William M. 1978. Responses of Bird and Mammal Populations to Fire in Chaparral. *California Agriculture* (October):9–12.

Martinez, Dennis and C. Striplen. in prep. Indian Fire, Chaparral, and Condor Survival in the Prehistoric Coastal Mountains of Central and Southwestern California.

Mundy, P. J. and J. A. Ledger. 1977. Griffon Vultures, Carnivores and Bones. *South African Journal of Science* 72:106–10.

Osborn, Sophie A. H. 2007. *Condors in Canyon Country: The Return of the California Condors to the Grand Canyon Region.* Grand Canyon Natural History Association, Grand Canyon, AZ.

Rez, Amadeo M. 1981. California Condor Captive Breeding: A Recovery Proposal. *Environment Southwest* 492:8–12.

————. 2000. Orden Falconiformes: Condor Californiano. In *Las Aves de Mexico en Peligro de Extincion*. Gerardo Ceballos and Laura Márquez Valdelamar, eds. Pp. 100–05. CONABIO, Instituto de Ecología de la UNAM and Fondo de Cultura Econoómica, Mexico City.

Snyder, Noel and Helen Snyder. 2000. *The California Condor: A Saga of Natural History and Conservation*. Academic Press, San Diego, CA.

Stewart, Omer Call. 2002. *Forgotten Fires: Native Americans and the Transient Wilderness*, eds. Henry T. Lewis and M. Kat Anderson. University of Oklahoma Press, Norman, OK.

Timbrook, J., J. R. Johnson, and D. D. Earle. 1982. Vegetation Burning by the Chumash. *Journal of California and Coast Basin Anthropology* 4(2):163–86.

Wilson, E. O. 1990. *Biophilia*. Harvard University Press, Cambridge, MA.

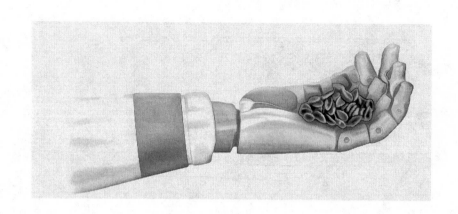

PART III

WRITING ETHNOBIOLOGY FOR BROADER APPEAL AND IMPACT

ALTHOUGH THE ESSAYS SELECTED for this session may it first appear to be random or outside the norms of scholarly writing conventions, they were explicitly chosen to address the issues of "translational science," that is, how do ethnobiologists communicate in ways other than "preaching to the saved?" In other words, how do we begin to engage others who may not ever pick up a copy of our technical journals?

Building upon experimental approaches to ethnographic writing initiated by Basso, Clifford, Geertz, Marcus, Nelson, Shostak, and the Tedlocks in the 1980s, I have attempted to demonstrate literary means of addressing some of the enduring issues in our field and their relevance to the future of life on this planet. Other ethnobiologists might prefer ethnographic films, interactive websites, or oral performance arts, with good cause. But all of these experiments attempt to more deeply connect the ancient past with the present and future, forming a dialectic between archaeology, paleontology, and ethnohistory on one hand, and rewilding, restoration, utopian, or dystopian possibilities on the other.

In these chapters, I have struggled to use one of our most enduring means of communication—narrative prose rather than expository prose or dogmatic graphs—to tell stories that may potentially challenge, change, or reassure some of our most tightly held values. I have opted to offer offer memorable imagery and dialogue that highlight the trajectory of change in a particular person or habitat of pivotal significance to a particular culture. Some of these speak to larger ethical and philosophical issues or conflicts in ethnobiological fieldwork that I have by no means resolved in my own mind.

In fact, my assumption is that many who do ethnobiological fieldwork have personal stories as good as or far better than the ones presented here, but feel suppressed from sharing them (at least in print) with their own colleagues, students, and communities. For that reason, these essays are postcards inviting other ethnobiologists to bear witness to the most profound experiences which have occurred to them while in the field or in the archives. We need to open the floodgates impeding the *acequia* of stories running from our hearts to our mouths, and renew the primacy of story in fostering cultural understanding.

While ethnographic writing has greatly advanced since Clifford Gertz, James Clifford, George Marcus, and Dennis Tedlock offered new directions, ethnobiological writing has lagged behind, seldom offering us as much powerful prose or poetry as our field deserves. The final piece, co-written with my friend and colleague Jim Veteto, reminds us why all this matters: the future may not end up like most neo-liberal logical positivists think (or wish) it should, so ethnobiologists honestly need to help society imagine alternative futures. By joining forces with other cultural creatives besides writers of narratives—oral poets, visual artists, performance artists, musicians, filmmakers, chefs, and intermedia artists—our own interdiscipline may eventually create a timeless literature that must inevitably become less colonial, more relevant, and inclusive.

15

GUADALUPE LOPEZ BLANCO

Reflections on How a Sea Turtle Hunter Turned
His Community Toward Conservation

GARY PAUL NABHAN

WHENEVER I REMEMBER Guadalupe Lopez Blanco, I remember his
feet and his eyes. His feet were somewhat like flippers or fins, made
for clinging to slippery rocks barely above the tidal reach. He never
looked comfortable on dry land, or for that matter, wearing any kind of shoe.
His feet never really needed any of the shoes and boots that his nieces always
insisted that I bring him; Lupe the fisherman looks as silly in footwear as farmers look in three-piece suits. It seemed that his toes and arches held to a moist
surface as tenaciously as the tentacles of an octopus; he could stand on the prow
of a panga in the roughest of seas, and never stumble or fall. I had a strange
feeling that each of his feet had its own gyroscope.

When I first met him—back when he was the most formidable Seri Indian
hunter of sea turtles in the entire Sea of Cortés—he could stand, thirty-foot
harpoon in hand, for hours on end, as his old wooden boat motored him up the
coast of Tiburón Island in search of loggerheads or hawksbills. At that time, I
presumed that he was simply representative of the many sea turtle hunters of
his people, the last hunter-gatherers in all of Mexico who had eschewed agriculture and Catholicism. And yet, I gradually sensed that there was something
exceptional about him, something that transcended the fact that he was a Seri

Originally published in *Connotations*, journal of the Island Institute, Sitka, AK.

who was born when only a couple hundred of his people still stood on this earth and spoke their bafflingly complex language, *Cmique Iitom*. I noticed that there was something *singular* about him, distinctively different from even his own brother and sister, both of whom I adored.

You could feel that difference most when he was standing on the prow of a small fishing boat. He would seem poised there, as if lost in deep contemplation, his harpooning arm ready to spring into action, his long braids flying in the air behind him, his weight shifting effortlessly as each wave jostled the fiberglass *panga* along on its killing course, his ears alert to even the most subtle splash of a turtle's flipper, his eyes always on the water.

I remember those eyes, soft brown eyes, filled with tears at times. Some two decades after I had originally met him, I encountered an altogether different countenance, though his watery eyes were more-or-less the same. That second encounter, I found a gray-haired man—his hair still in pigtails—but he was a man who had been broken by time, whose profession, if not his passion, had become anachronistic. By the time I tracked him down, all five species of sea turtle had declined so precipitously that the Mexican government had tried to ban the killing of *caguamas* for any reason; and so, Lupe had suddenly lost his lifework, his possession of an outboard motor, and finally his last boat, for he lacked enough income to pay the bills. He had become too old and poor to take up commercial fishing, a pursuit that he had always thought trivial, compared to hunting turtles. More surprising, perhaps, was that most everyone around him had forgotten that he had been the greatest turtle hunter of their century. And so, he hid out under a tree in his sister's backyard, carving miniature harpoons out of ironwood, toy boats out of elephant trees, and shaping metal fishhooks out of discarded auto parts.

Around this time, I sought him out to give him a message from a mutual friend, a former housemate of mine who had hunted with Lupe back when we were twenty-five and Lupe was a virile forty-five. But when I surprised him in his little tarpaper hovel under the salt cedar tree behind his sister's house, he had become such a recluse that he seemed uncommunicative, and perhaps a bit dingy.

When I first mentioned our mutual friend's name, he hardly looked up from his carving. And so I mentioned that the friend and I had once encountered a dead leatherback female, strangled by a fishing net in the Upper Gulf, not too far south from the Colorado River delta.

It was then that he looked up at me, as if coming out of a dream, and I could see his long, almost feminine eyelashes batting, as if he were holding back tears. He stopped his carving, looked straight into my own eyes, and spoke as if he were noting the death of a family member:

> Leatherbacks were scarce to begin with, and now there are hardly any left in the sea at all. I worked my entire adult life as a sea turtle hunter, but I was never lucky enough to arrive in time for the full four-day ceremony that happens whenever we sing to migrating leatherbacks and invite them in to visit us on shore. All my life, I made it to only one ceremony, and I came to that one way too late, for one of these creatures was so weak in the heat that he dried up and died, while the other cried until we released her back into the sea . . .

He did not call the leatherback by its usual name in his language, *mosnipol*, but referred to it figuratively as *xica cmotomanoj*, "the fragile one," or "the one whose eyes well up with tears." Because of the capacity of leatherbacks to weep, they were classified in Lupe's language as another kind of human being, not simply as a kind of animal.

It was Lupe's eyes that had initially given him his job as a turtle hunter, which permanently took him away from his childhood home back in the desert interior, and out onto the seas where turtles flocked in great numbers back then. He had grown up at Coyote's Well, a *rancheria* six miles in from the sea, where antelope jackrabbits, packrats, desert tortoises, sidewinders, and an occasional mule deer were the regular dinner fare. When he was still a boy, he learned to use dogs to sniff out the caves where desert tortoises were hibernating, to bring them back to camp to roast over the coals of an evening campfire.

Sometimes he would stay out hunting well past dark, and even on moonless nights, Lupe always made it back to camp without a light. When his parents asked him if the darkness made it difficult to find his way back home, Lupe simply remarked that he didn't see the night he had heard them speak of, that he could see as clearly at midnight as he could at noon. His mother noted that assertion, and loaned Lupe out to a brother-in-law on the coast who loved hunting sea turtles by the light of the moon. Lupe would become his uncle's *pollero* or gaffer, hooking and hauling in any sea turtle that his uncle harpooned. But he soon became his uncle's scout, that is to say, *his eyes went to work at sea*, for long before any other crew member could glimpse a sea turtle swimming near the boat, Lupe had spotted it, moon or no moon, bio-luminescence spark-ling across the ocean surface above the cold dark waters. At age fifteen—the same year that Steinbeck and Ricketts wrote their *Log of the Sea of Cortez*, based on a brief journey they took to the home-waters of the Seri—Lupe had sud-denly become the most sought-after crew member among his people's sea turtle hunters. By age twenty, he himself was heaving sixteen to twenty-foot long harpoons into the salty waters, and hitting descending turtles smack dab in the middle of their shells. By age forty, he was killing as many as twenty or thirty sea turtles in a twenty-four hour period, sometimes working day and night without sleep.

And then the only world he ever knew as an adult came crashing down all around him. In the mid-1970s, Mexican fishermen learned from Lupe's Indian kin that a certain special population of green sea turtles does not migrate to the south but they overwintered in their waters, hibernating on the bottom of the shallow shoals of the treacherous *Canal del Infiernillo*. Most of the time, these sluggish turtles were easy catches, for they stayed in torpor, only occasionally coming up for air before settling into the sand again. The Mexican fishermen learned where to find them during the winter months, but unlike the Seri hunt-ers, who only took a few of these sleepers when other food sources were scarce, they wiped out most of the turtles found in these overwintering grounds in less than a decade. After thousands of years of the Seri community keeping the secret of overwintering to themselves, a covenant had been broken.

Suddenly there weren't enough turtles left for a hunter to make a living. Mexican government officials banned the commercial sales of sea turtle prod-ucts, even as some continued to eat sea turtle soup in their private clubs. Lupe was forced into retirement by new laws, shifting values, and shaky economies. He resorted to making memorabilia—crafts for tourists—as a means of keep-ing himself fed. And yet his heart was not in it; he grew so thin that his nieces forced him to eat at least something with them every evening, so that he would stay alive.

It was around this time that several of us lured Lupe out of retirement—not to resume the killing of *caguamas*—but to go out onto the waters to find them for the purpose of conserving them. We first invited him to lecture some two-dozen young Seri men who wanted to become wildlife technicians and para-ecologists. We were bringing to their villages some of the most accom-plished Western scientists working on sea turtle recovery in Latin America, and wanted their biological knowledge to be complemented by a traditional Seri perspective. Lupe agreed to come, and we translated to him the first biologist's lecture, as thirty of us sat together on the shores of the Sea of Cortés.

When it was Lupe's turn, he went through the same topical sequence as the biologist had done—sea turtle's life from its own birth to mating and reproduction—but he did so for each species and population that came into his ancestral waters. We translated back to the biologists, and they were stunned.

From years of chasing turtles, Lupe had surmised what different kinds of *caguamas* ate at each stage in their development, how deeply they dived in pursuit of particular foods, how their diet expressed itself in their stomach contents, the taste and color of their flesh, and the very smell of their bodies. The biologists got up and congratulated Lupe for the richness of his lecture, then pulled him aside to ask him questions about sea turtles for which they had not figured out the answers.

The students immediately understood what was happening—the detailed knowledge of one of their elders had trumped that of the visiting scholars; their own traditions could be used to contribute to conservation, and not to hinder it. Within a year's time, the students had Lupe back in the water with them on a regular basis, finding and tagging turtles on their old wintering grounds. Their efforts led not only to the reduction of mortality of adult sea turtles, but to the discovery and protection of recolonized nesting grounds on beaches in Seri territory. Within two years, they were publishing their results in international journals of zoology and attending global conferences on marine turtle conservation. Within four years, some of Lupe's nephews and nieces had formed a community-based turtle conservation organization, *Grupo Tortuguero Comcáac*, and in 2006, those Seri Indian youth were presented with a World Oceans Day Conservation Award at the National Press Club in Washington, D.C., by activist-grandson of Jacques Cousteau, a National Geographic biologist, and U.S. Representative Sam Farr. As the congressman noted at the National Press Club ceremony, "We are honoring native peoples for showing us that all politics is local, and for what they see of value there—not only as a natural value but a cultural value as well—to help the oceans and living creatures of the oceans. That lesson is being brought to us from 'off the shore' of Mexico by people who are actually doing something [tangible] to protect ocean life." They have since organized an all-indigenous sea turtle conservation network with tribes from four continents. The work of this group of indigenous youth conservationists has been featured in films, best-selling books on conservation, websites, and posters.

Lupe did not much care about such accolades, but he did find deep satisfaction in learning that leatherback turtles had returned to his homeland. He also discovered something just as remarkable when he came out of retirement and went onto the water once again.

For his entire career as a sea turtle hunter, he had always wondered where male green sea turtles overwintered, for he knew of some two-dozen hibernation sites frequented by females, but not a single one for males. He had puzzled over this riddle for many years, but had never stumbled on the answer.

Then one day, when we were listing and mapping all of the overwintering sites that he could recall—perhaps twice as many as other Seri elders could remember—he closed his large almond-shaped eyes for a moment, shuffled his bare feet in the sand, and quietly said to me,

I think I have figured it out. We have a legend about the only sea turtle hunter of our culture who was a woman. There is a shallow bay named for her—*Cmaam Quiscáma Quih Iti Hascáma Ihíip*—"Place Where the Woman in a Balsa Kayak Went to Hunt Turtles"—and that must be where the male sea turtles gather. Do you see? She is the only woman we know of who hunted at sea, and her secret was that she knew the only place where the male turtles gathered. I have known of this place name for more than fifty years, but I never understood until now that it held a secret. It is the secret refuge of the male turtles, hidden in a place name so that they would be protected.

And then he told me this story, one that I cannot easily explain, but one that I will leave with you to ponder:

There once was a man among us who was a great sea turtle hunter, a man who also cared deeply for his wife and his children. He developed an illness that he knew would kill him, but he tried to keep the secret of this illness from his family as long as he could. Finally, he mentioned to his wife that should he die before her own death came, she should bury his body in the sand. If she and their children were to become hungry, he instructed her to go and dig up his skull, rest it on the front of their boat, and go out at night to hunt for food. His spirit would then lead her to where some male sea turtles would come to gather around her, and she could take as many as she needed to feed her family.

He soon died, and his widow buried him in the desert not far from the sea. She was in grief, and for a while, so distracted that she did not notice that her children

were starving. When she finally realized that she must find them some nourishment, she went out at night, dug up her deceased husband's skull, rested it on the prow of their boat, and went out into the sea that evening. As she paddled along, her husband's ghost materialized at the front of the kayak, and began to guide her toward a shallow bay somewhere off the shores of Tiburon Island. Once they arrived there, he told her to sing an ancient song for attracting turtles, and soon the caguamas gathered around her to listen. Several offered themselves to her, and she loaded them up on the boat, and paddled home before dawn came and her children awakened. By the time they rose from their night's sleep, she had grilled sea turtle meat and boiled up a delicious turtle soup for them to eat. After that, they were never hungry.

But there came a time when she herself grew tired of eating nothing but sea turtle flesh. The neighboring women were also getting suspicious, because there were always six or seven carapaces of recently killed sea turtles around her camp, and they wondered whether she had taken a lover from among their men. Her husband had also been a deer hunter, so she guessed that his power might guide her to mule deer in the desert just as it guided her to turtles at sea. One night, she carried his skull out into the desert behind their home, and she spotted a buck with giant antlers. As it came toward her, she killed it, quartered its carcass, and began to carry the venison home with her in the dark, along with the skull of her husband. But soon she was tiring of the great burden she was carrying, and began to stumble in the darkness. Before she realized what was happening, the skull of her husband fell from where she had pressed it up against her breasts, and it hit a rock, shattering into a dozen pieces. The venison suddenly disappeared from her grasp, and she walked home empty-handed.

From that evening on, she ate only sea turtle meat, but to secure it, she had to rely on her own skill and intelligence, not that of her deceased husband. She never became greedy again, but took only what she and her family needed. To this day, she is remembered as the greatest sea turtle hunter her people have ever known.

Few people who live outside Guadalupe's village still remember Lupe, his watery eyes and "prehensile" feet; fewer still have heard of the widow who went out to hunt sea turtles at night. If someone today is interested in the natural history of the Sea of Cortés, it is more likely that they will associate the names of John Steinbeck and Doc Ricketts with this place of desert and sea, even though the two spent just a few weeks of their entire lives exploring the area while Steinbeck's marriage fell apart and World War II began.

If one is interested in the human history of the desert islands there, it is likely that they will have read the hundred-some pages written by Teddy Roosevelt's friend W. J. McGee, who went out to Isla Tiburón, but never met any Seri there during his entire stay. But what about the old pigtailed man who never married; what about the widow who hunted alone—guided by a ghost—night after night? What might such distinctive individuals reveal to us about what lies hidden in the various and sundry places of our own world?

REFERENCES

Anonymous. 2006. Seri Indian conservation collaboration receives international award for World Oceans Day. Northern Arizona University Center for Sustainable Environments, Flagstaff, AZ. Press release, www.garynabhan.com.

Felger, R.S., K. Cliffton, P. J. Regal. 1976. Winter dormancy in sea turtles: Independent discovery and exploitation in the Gulf of California by two local cultures. Science 191:283–85.

Nabhan, G. P. 2002. ed. Singing the Turtles to Sea: The Comcáac (Seri) Art and Science of Reptiles. Berkeley: University of California Press.

Seminoff, J.A., Alvarado, J. L, Lopez, and G. Hoeffer. 2002. First direct evidence of a green sea turtle migration from Michoacán, México, to a feeding ground on the Sonoran Coast of the Gulf of California. Southwestern Naturalist 47(2): 314–16.

16

PALEOZOOLOGIST PAUL MARTIN, THE GHOSTS OF EVOLUTION, AND THE REWILDING OF NORTH AMERICA

GARY PAUL NABHAN

WHEN I LOOK OUT ACROSS a landscape dominated by mesquite and acacia, I sometimes catch a glimpse of ghosts. Ghosts of former mentors who guided me into the practice of desert natural history, and ghosts of evolution. One moment I see that life inside the gathering of trees called the *mesquital* is still and silent. A moment later, a dust devil has risen up from some disturbance on the desert floor and is raising holy hell, roaring like a banshee and covering everything in its wake with a fine layer of dry talcum-like powder. Ghosts take various shapes. They are chimerical, and for that reason alone, magical. And while not all ghosts are particularly scary, most challenge our ordinary perceptions of how the world works.

These are the ghosts whom I wish to address.

For the last few days, the ghost of my old teacher, Paul Martin, has frequently confronted me. Paul was a polio victim, a paleoecologist, a palynologist, prober of pack rat and sloth dung, the ethnozoological proponent of Pleistocene extinctions occurring at the hand of man, and a prolific writer right up until the time of his death. He was a tall and lanky man, standing six feet and four inches despite his crippled left leg. He typically took the long view of things, but he did it in a manner that made ordinary folks in his midst uneasy.

He was in fact, wondrously off-kilter. He glanced off to the side of mainstream science to see things some of us had not noticed at all. He was the first scientist

I came to know who not only studied plants like mesquite as if they were evolutionary riddles, but also intuitively tapped into the deeper roots of this desert tree.

By deeper roots, I mean that Paul sought to understand the evolutionary and cultural forces that shaped mesquite and the landscapes it dominated. Paul and his students were the first to figure that mesquite's distribution range and densities ebbed and flowed with the movements of climate, cultures, and large mammal populations that once roamed this continent. They discerned that mesquites were beginning to arrive north of the present day U.S.-Mexico border before the end of the Late Pleistocene "Ice Age" around 12,500 years ago.

That geeky little fact might not seem like a big deal to most people, but when Paul was done elaborating its implications, he had given us a longer view of the history of the Americas than most history teachers will ever dare to teach. It is a history jammed full of catastrophes, anomalies, violence and cooperation, extinction, adaptation, and possible resurrection. Paul looked at the history of our continent like it was an epic narrative as archetypal and as expansive as *The Lord of the Rings*, but he used tree rings, pollen grains, hacked-up bones, and tiny seeds in rodent feces to stitch his story together.

Paul began to piece together the history of mesquite from early dispositions of pollen grains, as well as seeds and stems found in packrat dung from Maravillas Canyon Cave in the Big Bend of Texas. From those meager clues, honey mesquite may have arrived north of the Rio Grande at least 13,000 years ago, when now-extinct megafauna still roamed the West. It appears that the other major Southwestern species, the velvet mesquite, first appeared in the Waterman Mountains of Arizona 1,000 years or so later, spreading up from the Gulf of California coast and the Colorado River delta.

From Paul's view, mammoths, mastodons, giant camels, and ground sloths may have had a hand, foot, trunk, or gut in fostering these dispersals. He reckoned that they were among the most voracious consumers and defecators of mesquite pods, for the fossil feces of theirs that he found were filled with seeds that had once been ready for germination. Paul loved to tease apart still-intact seeds caked in the fecal matter he found in caves. They were the archives that he built his epic around, just as J. R. R. Tolkien built his own saga around his deep knowledge of ancient languages and legends.

Curiously, once these super-sized creatures went extinct on the North American continent, the northward dispersal of mesquite into the deserts and semi-arid plains from the subtropics seems to have slowed. It appears to have taken another 5,000 years for sizeable velvet mesquite trees to spread throughout the

Sonoran Desert, and for honey mesquite to form hummocks on the sand dunes near the delta.

Around 10,000 years ago, the Chihuahuan Desert's honey mesquite pods became relatively common in packrat nests found in rock shelters at Hueco Tanks, a place that is now a Texas State Park east of El Paso. By 9,000 years ago, honey mesquite were further disseminated up the Rio Grande past the present location of Las Cruces and then north, toward Albuquerque.

About the time Paul and his collaborators were engaged in this biogeographic detective work, I met him on one of his many trips down to the Research Ranch in Elgin, Arizona. That's where I was studying the effects of browsing animals on the giant soap tree yuccas of the Sonoita Plains. I was immediately in awe of him.

It must have been around 1975, at a time in my life when I was thirsty for some inspiration and intellectual stimulation. I had been living alone, making a meager living raking up tumbleweeds from corrals, painting ranch houses, grading roads, and fixing fences. I was paid $175 a month, given free board and access to all the yucca flowers and mesquite pods I could eat. In addition, I was granted the chance to meet some of the country's best grassland ecologists, many who talked about Paul as if he were a living legend. So when someone invited me to a small dinner party where this world-famous ethnozoologist would be—along with a table full of foods that were well beyond my means—I jumped at the chance to go.

Not wanting to embarrass myself making small talk, I went up to Paul and before even introducing myself, brashly asked if he knew anything about the evolutionary history of the towering arborescent yuccas. I asserted that I was hell-bent on figuring out how their morphology was influenced by their inter-actions with wildlife. Paul was silent for a moment, then simply stated his case in so many words:

Well, it's probably not just the contemporary fauna that shaped their stature. I'd bet that when they were emerging from the denser canopies of the sub-tropics, they were selected for such heights and for the elevated presentation of their fruit by a number of the species in the Pleistocene megafauna. Unfortunately, those creatures are no longer physically present to allow us to observe their foraging strategies. Think about it: there are several species of yucca here that display their fruits at heights well out of reach of nearly all contemporary creatures that reach up to eat fruits while keeping all four of their feet firmly planted on the earth.

I had not yet entertained that possibility of explaining what I had been observing in yucca patches, although I had been reading Paul's essays in *Natural History* magazine. One of his widely celebrated articles was about the role he believed humans had played in driving the "charismatic megafauna" of the Ice Age to extinction. His memorable essay made it into the all-time "best-of" anthology from *Natural History* magazine.

The term megafauna, of course, simply refers to the "big dogs "on the block, whether they are herbivores, frugivores, carnivores, or omnivores. But Paul had a particular interest in the herbivores and frugivores—the grazers, browsers, and fruit-eaters—and their interactions with plants. Paul surmised that before the end of the Ice Age, mesquite pods were voraciously consumed by giant camelids, hippopotamus-or rhinoceros-sized notoungulates, and elephant-like stego-mastodons as they ranged northward out of the subtropical thornscrub. Moreover, Paul hypothesized that these browsers shaped the evolutionary history of mesquites and acacias, along with those of dozens of other thorny trees with enormous pods or fleshy fruits. Then, beginning around 11,500 years ago, these mammoth-sized creatures began to disappear from the Americas.

By 10,000 years ago, virtually all of those super-sized animals had disappeared from North America. As far back as 1780, when Thomas Jefferson described the fossilized bones of a mammoth "six times the size of an elephant" found in Virginia, American naturalists had been debating the causes of the extinction of such mammals. Paul and his closest colleagues had helped to locate sites where there was detailed evidence of intentional killing of such animals by Paleolithic hunter-gatherers. They mapped the distributions of these killing and processing of the megafauna. They also radiocarbon-dated their bones in labs when the faunal remains revealed evidence of projectile points or butchering marks. Paul, in particular, collected their enormous turds from dry caves and rummaged through them, searching for seeds.

On the first day that I took a class from Paul, he led us into a lab where we could scratch and sniff at fossilized feces of giant sloths, camels, and bison larger than any of their kin left on the planet today. In polite parlance, they were called coprolites. These "relaxed fit" turds were some of the most prized collections that Paul kept in his paleoecology lab. He had dissolved many such coprolites in flotation vats full of special chemical solutions, which allowed him to sort the seeds from the chaff the animals had consumed. This allowed him to reconstruct not only their diets but their past habitats. Among the many seeds these feces offered up were the pods or seeds of several species of mesquite and catclaw acacia, proof that the plants had once been directly consumed by the megafauna.

Curiously, most seeds in mesquite pods that passed through the gut of a large mammal more or less intact are prone to germinate in the warm, moist dung the animal leaves behind. But if the pods fall from the tree canopy to the ground, or are merely nibbled on by small mammals, they seldom germinate. It took some sleuthing by one of Paul's collaborators, insect ecologist Dan Janzen, to figure out why.

The pods of mesquite, acacias, and other legumes are typically attacked by bruchid beetles and other seed predators as the pods begin to ripen on the tree. Most pods that drop to the ground become pockmarked with holes of beetles depositing eggs onto the pods, or the seeds inside them. Their larvae usually devour enough of the seeds to keep them from ever germinating.

Almost all pods, which have passed intact through the guts of large mammals, have been freed of their seed predators and parasites. Janzen discovered that their larvae have been killed by the gastric brew of enzymes and microbiota found in the digestive tracts of most super-sized land mammals.

Connie Barlow, a field biologist and science writer from New Mexico, once received a package in the mail from Paul. It contained dozens of pods that had fallen from a tree in Tucson, where no large herbivores had a chance to devour them. As Connie reported in her fine book, *The Ghosts of Evolution*:

> All the pods I received in February were marred by at least one little hole, chewed away by an adult bruchid beetle exiting the pod. Some specimens had a hole over every seed. . . . [In contrast, before they were extirpated], megafauna prevented seed predators and parasites from devastating the crop. . . . By scattering dung over a wide area, fruit-eating mammals help seeds elude seed predators and parasites. Spread out, and sometimes buried deep within dung, the seeds are more difficult to find. In addition, some predators and parasites are deterred by the dung itself. . . . They cannot oviposit on seeds deeply embedded in the dung.

With proof in hand that implied mesquite pod coevolution with the gigantic vegetarians of the late Pleistocene, Paul began to hypothesize about the role these animals played in mesquite evolution. He proposed that the thorns on these trees had evolved to reduce the severity of trampling and branch breakage by herbivorous quadrupeds, which no doubt relished the tree's sweet, meaty pods of mesquite. Alas, many of their branches did get ripped to shreds by these browsing behemoths, so mesquite evolved a tenacious capacity to re-sprout from the base of its broken trunks.

Paul surmised that before their extinction, the mixed herds of megafauna inadvertently increased the density of mesquite near water holes. At the same time, it is possible that the animals' browsing and trampling—among other factors—kept in check the expansion of mesquite into surrounding habitats. Of course, some viable seeds would be dispersed in their feces as they traveled to the edges of other springs, seeps, or lakes, but cooler winters during that era may have also inhibited the ubiquity of mesquite during the late Pleistocene.

In Paul's way of thinking, the megafauna had co-evolved with mesquite through numerous means. Prior to their extinction, these browsers had profoundly influenced the very shapes of mesquite trees, the size and sweetness of the pods, their capacity to re-sprout or to survive germination in dung, and their geographic distribution. Mammoths and sloths are gone from our midst, but their influence on mesquite and acacias linger on, especially at the desert's edge. Biologist Connie Barlow calls these ecological anachronisms "the ghosts of evolution," for their features seem nonsensical if we try to explain them by looking only at their interactions with the present wildlife of desert regions.

If you were not at all aware of their missing partners, the mesquite pods, yucca fruits, Osage oranges, pawpaws, giant prickly pears, and calabash trees would seem more like monstrosities that a pot-smoking Dr. Seuss had invented for an island-like world of his own, rather than species marvelously fitted to the arid subtropical expanses of the Americas.

Soon after my first dinner and class with Paul, my favorite Lebanese American aunt sent me newspaper clippings about a "crazed Dr. Martin," as a way to warn me of such weirdoes at the university I was attending. The newspaper articles implied that Paul was a mad scientist because he asked the federal government to spend millions putting out a fire in Rampart Cave, down in the Grand Canyon. The fire was consuming the dung balls of the extinct Shasta's Giant Ground Sloth that Paul and his colleague Austin Long had meticulously studied.

When the fire was discovered, Paul had called a press conference. He wanted to alert decision-makers of the scientific value of those smoldering deposits of Shasta sloth dung with mesquite seeds embedded in them. He referred to them as ecological archives equivalent in value to all the books in the Library of Congress. I am surprised that he did not say they were more valuable than all the art in the Sistine Chapel, since the Grand Canyon itself had recently been likened to that treasure trove of world heritage.

A few days after the clippings arrived in the mail, my aunt made a rare long-distance call from her home in Indiana.

"Do you read those stories I sent about that mad man running loose on your campus, honey?" my Aunt Rose said.

"What mad man? Oh, Paul? Well, he actually can't run very easily, given the condition of his leg," I answered.

"So you know this scientist who is wasting all our taxpayers' money studying prehistoric B.S.?" She cackled.

When I told her that I was indeed studying with Paul, there was a long silence. Then a kind of disgusted moan flowed out of my phone receiver.

"Don't you know how hard your parents worked to give you a good education? And you're going to waste it all to study with someone who is trying to save old dinosaur poop from burning up?"

"Well, it's not actually dinosaur poop, Aunt Rose," I replied, "It's sloth shit. And don't worry, it doesn't smell much anymore, given that it's been thousands of years since it was dumped in the cave. In fact, it's rather hard to the touch, just like any fossil—"

"I just don't care what you call it. It is still *poop*. Keep your hands off of it."

My dear aunt hung up on me. Thankfully, she never brought up the subject again.

It was not until years after I met him that I realized Paul's gift could not easily be separated from his disability. The Mexican strain of poliovirus that had severely stricken his left leg earlier in life forced him to look at everything off to the side, from a vantage point different from that of other scientists. Metaphorically and figuratively, he towered above his peers like the Leaning Tower of Pisa. For me, hanging out with Paul was like spending time with the Abraham Lincoln of field biologists. A certain brilliance and errant quality came through in just about everything he said.

Years later, when I shared a day with him in Alamos, Sonora, he reminded me why mesquite mattered to him so very much. Our friend Sandy Lanham, a MacArthur Award-winning bush pilot of great skill and daring, had taken Paul up in her little plane to survey the transition zone between the deserts and the tropics that morning. He was still in awe of what he had seen, just after the first dawn light, because it was such rugged country that he would never be able to walk far back into it.

Before he even fully greeted me, he offered a classic Martinesque commentary, much of which I can recall to this day:

I love this place, this ecological edge. I can finally see how our Sonoran Desert flora emerged right out of the tropical deciduous forests and subtropical thorn-scrub that run from here all the way down to Costa Rica in one unbroken chain. And while dozens of acacias dominate the lowlands to the south of here, it is mesquite—not the few acacias that moved northward with them—that dominate the deserts from here on up to the Grand Canyon. The mammoths, mastodons, camels, giant asses, and sloths could have so easily carried them northward, savoring their sweet, fat, juicy pods much more than the dry papery pods of our spindly little acacias.

He continued, "Perhaps that's why we found so many mesquite seeds in the dung balls of Shasta ground sloths up in the Grand Canyon—they are among the northernmost expression of the fruits the gomphotheres and ground sloths ate all the way down through the subtropics."

Paul gazed up toward the crest of the volcanic hills behind me, where the desert and the tropics intersected. I cast my own eyes downward, because I realized he had made me see for the first time the ghosts that had long haunted him. He noticed I was silent.

At last he spoke up: "Gary, how are you doing? I heard that you've recently gone through a breakup, you know, a separation from your wife."

"We just weren't growing in the same direction. I dunno, maybe she felt overshadowed by me, like we were competing or something. I never felt that way, but I did get claustrophobic around her family, like there was no place in the room for me."

My mouth got dry and I stopped talking.

"Do you see those two trees over there, right at the base of the next ridge over?" Paul asked. I thought he was abruptly changing the subject, as if he regretted making any mention of my still open wound. "Here, take my field glasses, look at that pair of trees. Now think about them, their history there. They probably germinated about the same time, within a few feet of one another, and grew side by side at the same pace for a good number of years."

"But then, after a point, one is shading out the other for part of the day, and vice versa. They may be competing for nutrients. Or the ants on one are cutting a little branch off the other when it crosses their path.

"Is it any wonder that they start growing in different directions, seeking out the sun? But what a wonderful miracle it is that they grew in tandem, peaceably, for so many years.

"Savor that, Gary. Savor the memory of all the years you grew up, side by side."

Paul's digression from talking about vegetation to talking about human relationships at first seemed like a radical detour to me, one that embarrassed me at first. But as I later thought back on that brief but poignant conversation, I realized that he, like most of the best ecologists I know, had a hard time unhinging one part of the world from another. He metaphorically used the structure of ecological relationships to help him understand human relationships, and vice versa. For Paul, there were few tangents that did not reveal something about the core issues of life.

During the very last trip I took with Paul, he seemed to be having a post-polio syndrome rebound, which made it increasingly difficult for him to walk with just a cane. Soon he would need crutches or a walker, and later, a motorized wheelchair. But for the moment, he was back at one of those fascinating tension zones, or *ecotones*, between the deserts and tropics, this time near Gomez Farias, Tamaulipas, where he had done the fieldwork for his master's thesis a half century earlier.

"It must feel great to be here again," I said, as we arrived at the edge of a deep gorge. A somewhat deteriorated suspension bridge of rotting wooden slats and two guy wires stood between us and the other side of the gorge. I assumed that we could go no further. We'd savor the moment of being right smack dab on the Tropic of Cancer.

"What do you mean 'great to be here again'? We're not there yet. My thesis sites were on the other side of the gorge. I'm going across."

My Mexican friends looked at him like he was crazy, given the condition of the bridge and his own leg. Then they looked at me as if I could, or would, try to stop him. Before any of us could speak, Paul dropped his cane and lumbered out onto the suspension bridge, which was already swaying wildly with his every move. We watched in disbelief as he placed his good leg forward, grasped onto the waist-high cables above the bridge and swung his other leg sideways to move it forward, rocking the bridge as he went.

It took him five minutes to cross over and another eight to return. His shirt was drenched in sweat and his face was beet red, but Paul was grinning from ear to ear. It was as if he had crossed over some geographic gap like the Bering Bridge, just as some of the megafauna had done many thousands of years ago.

"I just had to do that," he said, panting. "I had to know I could still do that."

To still do that, to cross over to a place that not many other people would ever care to know, let alone venture to.

That is why Paul Martin is one of the ghosts who still haunt me today. As I sit under a mesquite and read a few passages of his last book, *Twilight of the Mammoths: Ice Age Extinctions and the Rewilding of America*, it is as if he has laid out another rickety suspension bridge before us, spanning what seems to be an un-crossable chasm to most people. The book boldly proposed that to make North American ecosystems healthy again, we needed to repopulate them with mixed herds of herbivores—the closest living relatives of the ones the continent had lost during the Pleistocene extinctions. Paul could live with being teased about the likeness of his vision to *Jurassic Park*, if it woke people up to taking a longer view. He wanted us all to move forward from a deep understanding of ecological history, to a richer imagined future on the other side. He was not concerned about how hazardous the journey would be. Paul just knew we had to try to get to the other side.

REFERENCES

Barlow, C. 2000. The Ghosts of Evolution: Nonsensical Fruit, Missing Partners and Other Ecological Anachronisms. New York: Basic Books/Perseus Group.

Martin, P. S. 2007. Twilight of the Mammoths: Ice Age Extinctions and the Rewilding of America. Berkeley: University of California Press.

17

PARQUE DE LA PAPA

Vavilov's Dream for Potatoes?

GARY PAUL NABHAN

F OR A QUARTER CENTURY, the breed of ethnobotanists I've hung with have proposed through countless lectures and publications that crop diversity can best be conserved in situ, in the cultural landscapes managed by the traditional farmers who have long been its stewards. Now, in the highlands of Peru, a dream has come true, one that would have made the late Russian seed conservationist Nikolay Vavilov giddy with delight. Vavilov himself visited the Andes some seventy years ago, during an era when there was no "formal" in situ conservation reserve for potatoes anywhere in the world.

But today, there is such a place, simply known as the Parque de la Papa—the Potato Park. I had the pleasure to visit the park with ethnobotanist Alejandro Argumedo, and listen to the Quechuan farmers just after their "winter" solstice of 2008.

To arrive at the Parque de la Papa, you leave Cusco's high elevation urbanity at 11,000 feet, and you climb, climb, climb. It seems as though you might leave the altiplano behind altogether, for you wind up dirt roads toward the Andes' snow-capped peaks until you can see above you only azure skies as deeply blue as a mountain lake. You must leave behind your earlier elevation sickness known as *soroche* by drinking the tea and chewing coca leaves, and by going slow. Indeed it is important to set your pace through the highlands slow enough

Originally published as a blog post for Island Press on https://islandpress.org/node/193 and on the author's blog at http://garynabhan.com/i/archives/513.

FIGURE 17.1. A market vendor in Cuzco brings
native potatoes and other tubers in from highland fields. Photo by Gary Paul Nabhan.

for your mind to reconnect with farming traditions that have remained resilient
for millennia. Families here grow potatoes on stone-lined terraces, with many
skills and insights that their ancestors accumulated over dozens of generations.

When you are done meandering up switchbacks on a wheezing, teetering
bus, you come to where Quechuans are harvesting their potatoes. There, you find
yourself in front of a large billboard that proclaims that you have entered the
Parque de la Papa. What it does not mention is that this is the only "park" in the
world fully dedicated to the in situ conservation of native crops. The six Quechuan

communities there have dedicated their future to the "repatriation, restoration and sustainable management of the native agrobiodiversity of the potato, and to the traditional knowledge shared within the communities associated with it."

The six agrarian communities, which have rallied around their shared interest in potato diversity, are known as Chawaytiré, Sacaca, Kuyo Grande, Pampallaqta, Paru Paru, and Amaru. They did not always feel united with one another; in fact, in the years prior to the Potato Park, there had been some bloodshed between two of the communities over a contested boundary between their farming and grazing lands. Instead of staying entrenched in such territorial disputes, they agreed to be part of a grassroots initiative facilitated by Argumedo, one of the founders of Asociación Andes based in Cusco. These agrarian communities agreed that they had more to gain by banding together in defense of their sustenance—potato culture—than they could ever realize by struggling against one another or working in isolation.

And so, they began to form institutional linkages not only with NGOs such as Asociación Andes, but with networks including other indigenous communities struggling to define and maintain their own food sovereignty as well. In 2002, the six communities were confident enough to declare some 10,000 hectares of their lands the Parque de la Papa, which was soon followed by an agreement with the International Potato Center (CIP) in Lima, Peru, that allowed the repatriation of some 420 varieties of potatoes previously collected by CIP for the purposes of plant breeding.

Repatriation literally means to bring something back to the fatherland, taking into custody something that once belonged to your cultural community. There have been other instances of crop repatriation—notably the dozens of Hopi crop varieties relocated, documented, and returned to the Hopi Cultural Preservation Office in 2002. This was facilitated by members of what is now called the Renewing America's Food Traditions collaborative, including the Seed Savers Exchange, Native Seeds/SEARCH, and the Center for Sustainable Environments.

Nevertheless, the repatriation of Peruvian potatoes for in situ conservation has been unprecedented both in scale and in its acceptance by one of internationally funded crop conservation and improvement centers (collectively known as CGIAR). Key scientists at the International Potato Center (CIP) had become convinced that such a community-based conservation strategy was indeed worth supporting. Some two decades before, however, CGIAR administrators such as Trevor Williams formally dismissed in situ conservation strategies as impractical, costly, and unproductive. Today, CIP's more forward-thinking scientists provide technical assistance upon request to farmers in the Potato Park who wish to gain advice on the best ways to cultivate, fertilize, and manage their many varieties of native tubers. At the same time, the leaders of the Parque de la Papa have requested that the U.N. Food and Agriculture's International Undertaking on Plant Genetic Resources formally recognize their cultural landscape as a "gene bank" of equal importance and status of that of the International Potato Center.

Today, the Quechuan farmers in the Potato Park maintain some 1,200 varieties of potatoes named in their own language, in addition to *razas criollas* (land races) of maize, oca, quinoa, fava beans, and wheat. When you visit them, you are at first dazzled by the sheer splendor of colors woven into their caps, ponchos, pants, or dresses; these are folks that understand beauty. But color is not merely ornamental; the many varieties of potatoes range from black and purple to brown and yellow; they are knobby, curvilinear, oblong, round, or shaped like a hen's egg. Each has its own identity, its own flavor, its own texture; some even have their own "voice."

Quechuan farmer Ricardo Paco Chipa of the village of Paru explained to me how one potato variety was found to have its own voice. It is now known as a "guardian potato" that collaborates with human guardians or stewards of potato diversity to protect this diversity from outside threats.

"The guardian potato is known as Santo Ruma. It began to speak one time when a thief came to rob all the potatoes from a field; it scared away the thief, and woke up the people to defend the field. Of course, it is rare for a potato to speak," Ricardo added soberly, "but by doing so, it saved the others. Those of us who are appointed as human guardians of the potatoes must recognize this."

I was intrigued by the notion that at least some of the potato varieties were perceived by the Quechuans as embodying qualities that the rest of us might attribute only to humans. Ricardo was straightforward in his defense of this notion:

"Potatoes are part of our family. We keep them in our homes with us."

An elder several decades older than Ricardo added that one should never cut a potato with a knife, because the potato is alive. Such empathy with the sentience of potatoes is complemented by detailed technical knowledge about the plants themselves, and the environments in which they grow. One of the Quechuan farmers of the Potato Park wanted to affirm to academically trained biologists the veracity of his community's knowledge:

"We want the world to know that we ourselves are scientists of the potato. We have detailed knowledge about the life of these plants. We read their flowers, their leaves, their vines. We read the soil, the weather; we see how the plants respond to the winds. They are our books."

This has made the Quechuan farmers particularly attentive to the effects of climate change on the microhabitats where each potato variety can be planted. Ricardo Paco Chipa says his father constantly reminds him that the elevational amplitudes of potatoes today are far different than those that were common when he first farmed a half century ago. Certain varieties cannot grow as low as they once did, because of the heat they would suffer in those places today. At least four cold-tolerant varieties once planted at the highest levels have recently become rare, for lack of any habitats today that are free from the heat during their six-month-long growing season. One black and white variety which Ricardo called *luqui* was once commonly used for making *chuno*, the freeze-dried potatoes that can be rehydrated for soups and purees:

"There is less snow each year, less water, and hotter seasons. Now we must plant each variety higher and higher from year to year. The varieties adapted to the very coldest country below the peaks now have hardly any place to grow."

And yet, these Quechuan farmers are not passive victims of climate change; they are dynamically responding to such changes by employing their crop diversity and their traditional knowledge to meet such challenges. Ricardo was clear that this was among their primary motivations for engaging in the collective mission of the Potato Park:

"We are not only bringing back a diversity of potato varieties to our fields, but the traditional knowledge about how and where to grow them—and prepare them—as well."

This was not always the case. In the 1960s, the Peruvian government and international agricultural agencies lured Ricardo's forefathers into adopting new agricultural practices and concentrating on a few "improved" potato varieties. But these imported techniques, technologies and hybrids did not necessarily suit the conditions found in highlands surrounding Cusco. One Quechuan farmer—Justicio Ucra—smirked as he explained what happened:

"We found that the improved varieties not only did poorly in the marketplace, but they were bad for the soil and bad for your health."

Gradually, the farmers returned to the time-tried varieties that they had not already abandoned; with the repatriation of other varieties collected by CIP's plant explorers in the 1970s, and others gifted to them by farmers in other parts of Peru, they now collectively cultivate over a thousand varieties each year. This not only offers them a modicum of food security from year to year; it is also allowing the farmers to move toward the goal of true food sovereignty:

"We have to go beyond mere food security to food sovereignty and sustainability because that is the only way we can have a good relationship with Pachamama, a good relationship with the land . . ."

In the meantime, the farmers' wives—who also sow, harvest, and ceremonially bless the potatoes—are busy experimenting with how to better use their great diversity of potatoes. They've formed "the Gastronomic Work Group" (*Maruja*, see plate 4) with other women from the six communities to document traditional recipes and innovate around them:

"What we do is not unlike the kind of innovation with food that our grandmothers did. We combine particular potato varieties with various medicinal plants and other herbs from the wild used in making sauces. We evaluate them on whether they are both tasty and healthy."

In the park's co-op restaurant called Papamanka, the food they offered us met both of those criteria. It also had a rich sense of cultural heritage that may still not be apparent in many Novo-Andino restaurants in the city. Argumedo explained just why that might be:

"Our intent has been to integrate all aspects of managing or sustaining a landscape and its food diversity through cultural means. This has been our basis not only for conserving potato diversity, but also for sustaining traditional livelihoods. . . . We had the faith that if we stayed true to the notion of cultural integrity—with the symbol of the potato to unite us under one sombrero— we would achieve not just one objective, but many at the same time."

The people of the Potato Park—including the potatoes themselves—have done just that.

REFERENCES

Argumedo, A. 2013. Collective trademarks and biocultural heritage: Towards new indications of distinction for indigenous peoples in the Potato Park, Peru. International Institute for Environment and Development.

Nabhan, G.P. 2009. Where Our Food Comes From: Retracing Nikolay Vavilov's Quest to End Famine. Washington, DC: Island Press/Shearwater Books.

Silberner, J. 2008. Parque de la Papa: In Highland Peru, a Culture Confronts Blight. National Public Radio. October 2. https://colonos.wordpress.com/2008/10/02/parque-de-la-papa-in-highland-peru-a-culture-confronts-blight/

18

WHY POETRY NEEDS ETHNOBIOLOGY

Hawkmoth Songs and Cross-Pollinations

GARY PAUL NABHAN

> *Bilinguals may have a more flexible approach to the*
> *world . . . from a meta-linguistic awareness of arbitrary,*
> *nonphysical aspects of words and the effect of*
> *context on the meaning of words. Thus bilinguals may*
> *find it easier to encode and access knowledge in diverse*
> *ways, and have greater tolerance for ambiguity.*
> —TODD I. LUBART, *HANDBOOK OF CREATIVITY*

A DATURA FLOWER, IF LEFT UNPOLLINATED, is a sad spectacle to behold during the days following the decline of its blooming. It has wilted down to a flaccid, twisted, withered rag—a far cry from the silky evening gown that excited hawkmoths only a few hours before. That is how I feel about some pursuits of the human mind, which, if kept out of reach of cross-cultural and interdisciplinary exchanges, languish like a withered flower, never to bear fruit.

This is the story of a song-poem that was saved from such a fate only by the wedding of poetry and ethnobiology. By cross-pollinating the linguistic, ethnographic, and poetic understanding of the song with insights from field ecology and neurobiology, we can now celebrate the song-poem in all of its dimensions. We can be thrilled by the loveliness of its imagery and astonished by how it embodies an empirical understanding of plants and animals that modern scientists have only recently gained by other means. Had it not been for a fortuitous convergence of interests among several scholars in the 1980s and 1990s, the

---

Originally published as "Why Poetry Needs Science: Decoding Songs That Can Help Us to Heal" in *Milkweed Editions*.

multiple layers of meanings for a cluster of O'odham songs would have never been recovered. These songs had come from the dreams of an Akimel O'odham shaman who lived more than a century ago in what is now called the Gila River Indian community. But before we hear one of those songs and explore its many dimensions, I must reflect a moment on the historic events that obscured its multiple meanings, and which later brought them to light.

This song-poem was first written down around 1901, translated from the northern Piman dialect of the O'odham language by José Louis Brennan. Also known as José Lewis, this Tohono O'odham folklorist and self-taught linguist let ethnologist Frank Russell use the poem in his comprehensive study of the Pima Indians of Arizona, which was first published in 1908; he later became the first of his people to prepare texts for the Smithsonian Institution on O'odham language, culture, and ritual oratory. When the poem was recorded, it was considered part of a sequence of jimsonweed or thornapple songs performed by an old Piman singer, Vishag Voi'i, or Prairie Falcon Flying. With Russell's help in selecting English equivalents, Brennan transcribed the song in the O'odham language as best he could, then offered a crude literal translation as well as a more poetic translation in English, which follows:

Pima Jimsonweed Song
At the time of the White Dawn;
At the time of the White Dawn,
I arose and went away.
At Blue Nightfall I went away.
I ate the thornapple leaves
And the leaves made me dizzy.
I drank thornapple flowers
And the drink made me stagger.
The hunter, Bow-remaining,
He overtook and killed me,
Cut and threw my horns away.
The hunter, Reed-remaining,
He overtook and killed me,
Cut and threw my feet away.
Now the flies become crazy
And they drop with flapping wings.
The drunken butterflies sit
With opening and shutting wings.

Unfortunately, the first translators of this song glossed the term *ho'okimal* as *butterfly* instead of *night moth*, inadvertently obscuring how the song's imagery moves back and forth between the moths, their horned caterpillars, and the leaves and flowers of thornapple (jimsonweed). That is because the O'odham term *ho'okimal* broadly refers to all lepidoptera, including both nocturnal moths and diurnal butterflies, but by using the latter term, the plant is divorced from its true (nocturnal) pollinator, a hawkmoth. Unfortunately, every version of this poem printed over the following nine decades has retained the word *butterfly*. This biological imprecision has inadvertently obscured certain layers of meaning, which are critically important to understanding the song as a whole.

On the other hand, we can be grateful that Brennan and Russell correctly noted that this *kotadopi ñe'e* (datura song) was considered by the Pima to be related to a genre of *pihol ñe'e* (peyote button songs), both about narcotic plants ceremonially used by the Pima and their relatives to the south. It appears that these songs were introduced from more southerly, Uto-Aztecan tribes in Mexico, who chanted them to bring success to their hunting sacred deer. Both songs, then, dealt with the power of plant hallucinogens to mediate hunters' relationships with animals. These songs were employed in curing rituals during which *mamakai* (shamans, medicine men, or spiritual healers) attempted to remove the causes of vomiting and dizziness from a sick person's body and soul. In the 1980s, linguistic anthropologist Donald Bahr began to explore these and other O'odham curing songs as part of his interpretation of Piman shamanism and oral traditions. To his credit, Bahr invited our mutual friend, the late Pima elder Joseph Giff, to help him retranslate the jimsonweed song word by word, and to relate it to other butterfly songs from the same genre. This work provided fresh insights into the songs and offered more linguistic and ethnographic precision than did the original translation.

Unfortunately, Bahr's brilliance as a linguistically rigorous translator is not matched by much literary intuition or interest in the natural world, the very subject of many of the songs and speeches that he has attempted to translate. Bahr's translations have become notorious among both Pima speakers and desert biologists for their lack of ecological precision, generated by his confusing butterflies with moths, ponds with nectar pools, trash with flood-washed organic detritus, and peacocks with macaws. Like many scholarly translators of his generation, Bahr failed to achieve a deeper understanding of the poetic traditions he analyzed, simply because he lacked familiarity with the flora and fauna that inspired these poems. It appears that Bahr understood so little of the desert ecology well known to O'odham speakers that he could not even ask them appropriate questions about the rich naturalistic imagery in this and other songs. Unfortunately, Joseph Giff, who taught me to understand many interactions between plants and animals from the perspective of a Pima farmer, was never asked to comment on the biological content of the song by Bahr.

Following years of venturing into the Sonoran Desert with O'odham speakers who knew its flora and fauna as well as Joseph Giff did, I soon learned that the songs were not at all about butterflies visiting some weed, but they were about the intriguing interactions between the dangerously beautiful daturas and hawkmoths. Although adult hawkmoths visit datura flowers at dusk, dawn, and throughout the night, the larvae feed on datura foliage around the clock. Many O'odham are curious about both the adult and the larval forms of *Manduca* hawkmoths, for they visit sacred datura flowers as larvae and the leaves as adult moths. The O'odham consider *kotadopi* to be a plant that can cause their people to go crazy with hallucinations. The late Laura Kerman—an O'odham woman who would regularly visit my home even into her nineties—would not even brush against the datura plants in my driveway nor inhale their perfumes for fear of going crazy. And yet she was fascinated that certain moths and caterpillars visited such a dangerous plant whenever it was available to them.

Curiously, academically trained desert ecologists didn't devote much attention to the pollination ecology of datura for the first century that they explored the Sonoran Desert. Only within the last three decades did ecologists "discover" that, like monarchs and their milkweeds, *Manduca* moths coevolved with sacred daturas. Their caterpillars are the only creatures known to be capable of consuming and detoxifying the powerfully narcotic alkaloids produced by daturas. The hawkmoth larvae called tomato and tobacco hornworms not only ingest the usually toxic datura leaves, but they sequester the plant's atropine and scopolamine in their flesh to deter potential predators, who suffer greatly if they eat the smallest bit of the moths' alkaloid-laden bodies. Oddly enough, when adult moths ingest alkaloids from datura, it stimulates a pronounced dizziness, if ecologists have correctly interpreted the behaviors they witness after *Manducas* forage in and around datura flowers. It was not until 1983—eight decades after Prairie Falcon Flying's song was published—that pollination ecologists Verne and Karen Grant described in the scientific literature the dizzy, drunken behavior of adult hawkmoths hovering around datura blossoms—perhaps the same behavior that is alluded to in the O'odham song. The Grants presumed that the moths were hallucinating after having imbibed alkaloids present in datura flower nectar.

However, after reading the Grants' report, many ecologists wondered whether the Grants themselves had hallucinated! These scientists were skeptical that the potent secondary chemicals found in datura foliage and fruit could ever be present in the nectar and pollen of the blossoms. The herbivore-deterring chemical compounds found in the vegetative tissues of desert plants are seldom present in their reproductive tissues, since such an expensive chemical arsenal is hardly ever needed to protect their sexual organs. But when I suggested to several well-known pollination ecologists that the O'odham song corroborated the Grants' study, they scoffed at the suggestion. They thought it highly unlikely that any insects visiting datura flowers could absorb significant doses of alkaloids unless they were also foraging on datura foliage.

Then in 1999 and again in the year 2000, these ecologists humbly admitted that new information had forced them to change their views. Two reputable teams of scientists from other parts of the world reported that humans had suffered mental and physical disorders after consuming honey produced by wasps that had visited (and foraged within) datura blossoms. Their observations confirmed that psychotropic alkaloids are indeed taken up by insect visitors in sufficient quantities to affect animal (including human) behavior. It now seems plausible that the composer of this O'odham song had witnessed such aberrant behavior among pollinators visiting datura blossoms, for his observations predated by at least a century those of the scientists who confirmed this chemically mediated relationship.

And so this convergence of indigenous poetic knowledge and ecological scientific knowledge seems to me to be something worth celebrating. It sent me back to the original O'odham transcript of Prairie Falcon Flying's song, and to Joseph Giff's word-by-word translation of it, for I wanted to arrive at a translation that was at once ecologically precise and literary. With some refinements, it builds on the translation that appears in my chapbook of poems, *Creatures of Habitat*, and in my book of essays, *Cultures of Habitat*:

Sacred Datura–Hawkmoth Song
I.
Stopping for a while in the white of dawn,
Stopping for a while in the white of dawn,
Then rising to move through the valley,
Then rising to move through the valley,
Remembering when the green of the evening fell away,

When the green of the evening falls away:
Sacred datura leaves, sacred datura leaves,
Eating you, I dizzily staggered, drunkenly crawled,
Sacred datura blossoms, sacred datura blossoms,
Drinking your nectar, I dizzily, drunkenly flew away:
2.
As I hovered, he pursued me, his bow looming larger,
His arrow overtaking me, shooting right through me,
My horns were cut off, and thrown away.
As I was pierced by the arrow, my guts were spilled,
I fell from the air until my fluttering was stilled,
The horns severed from me had fallen away.
3.
They are bugging me now, crazily buzzing,
bugs are swarming, driving me crazy,
I'm diving, swooping, my wings tucked away,
A night moth drunk on nectar,
I'm so drunk on datura nectar,
I shudder and flutter till it all goes away.

Two years after beginning this translation, I stumbled upon a description of the physiological effects and psychiatric consequences of human ingestion of atropine and scopolamine, the chemicals in datura, which are considered to be poisons as well as powerful drugs. I realized that to a remarkable extent the behaviors alluded to in the O'odham song-poem parallel the responses of those who have lived to describe datura-induced hallucinations. I am more and more convinced that Prairie Falcon Flying or some unknown O'odham shaman-poet before him composed this song under the spell of datura's wild chemicals.

As I learned from psychiatric studies, and from interviewing intentional and accidental consumers of datura, it is probably not coincidental that a Pima poet felt as though he were flying and staggering. This happens to most folks who have ingested datura, some of whom claim that they witnessed night skies turning an iridescent green. As the drug takes effect, those under its spell become dizzy and nauseous. They soon begin to suffer from a sort of paranoia, aroused sometimes by the unanticipated appearance of even the slightest of creatures. They may fear being attacked by flies, mosquitoes, or miniscule insects, whose buzzing is both amplified and distorted in their ears. At the peak of their hallucinations, some victims of datura poisoning feel that they have been splayed open, burnt, or brought into the flaming world of the dead. The victims who are fortunate enough to escape both death and permanent disability have described their escape from the dead and delivery into a brief period of ecstasy. There, they experience the intense pleasure of being immersed in a kaleidoscopic world before they lose consciousness and fall into a coma-like state that lasts for hours.

It is not surprising, then, that the creature dwelling in this song-poem—the one who has imbibed datura nectar and leaves—recalls a sense of flying in the green light before dawn, of being chased by a force that tears him apart, of being tortured by buzzing insects, and of being left to flutter helplessly to the ground before closing down.

We will never know whether Prairie Falcon Flying himself ingested datura, or whether another deer singer set down this poem. We do know from oral tradition that O'odham spiritual healers have long known how to prepare datura roots to induce visions, although most contemporary medicine men consider the plant to be so dangerous that it is rarely worth using. However, these healers may still sing datura songs for children or young adults who have become sick with nausea, dementia, insomnia, or dizziness. Through complex cultural methods of diagnosis, the healers determine that the victims have at one time or another violated the spirit power of datura flowers, the moths that visit them, or other powerful beings. These violations may have occurred even when the victims were toddlers and unaware of the potential consequences of their actions. One account tells how young O'odham girls used the silky white blossoms of datura to fashion dresses for their dolls. Datura flowers could often be found in the desert washes and hedgerows where O'odham youngsters played, and they made such lovely gowns that they must have been irresistible. And yet when the girls were found playing with datura, their parents scolded them and hastily confiscated the dolls' dresses. While some children might simply become momentarily saddened or frightened by this reprisal, it appears that others were left with a prolonged feeling of deeper emotional distress.

If this stress later generated psychosomatic maladies, O'odham spiritual healers were brought in to detect the cause of the trouble and to relieve it. They did so by singing a set of songs that acknowledged the violation of some ethical and ecological condition essential to their well-being. The songs often began with a staccato cacophony that recreated the sense of emotional turmoil felt at the time of the scolding, followed by a haunting melody overlaid with words forming a metaphorical riddle, one which could not be consciously solved.

Oftentimes, the final images of the song and the final melodic theme sublim-inally suggested that a peaceful solution could be found. At the same time, the singer took images of flowers and moths cut from deerskin and applied them to the victims' bodies, further encouraging their healing by returning them to peaceful engagement with the creatures of the wilderness world.

I have recently learned that curing songs inhabited by moths, datura, pey-ote, or deer are common to most cultures forming the Uto-Aztecan family of languages, a family that includes not only the O'odham or Pima, but Yaqui and Huichol as well. In other words, the healing power of restoring relationships with these particular plants and animals was recognized so long ago that it is not restricted to the contemporary O'odham. Nor was it peculiar to the Yaqui shamanism that was distorted and popularized by the late Carlos Castaneda. Yaqui deer singer Felipe Molina, folklorist Larry Evers, and linguists Ofelia Zepeda and Jane Hill have collectively demonstrated how such songs are used to evoke the Wilderness World. This is also known as the Flower World, the place where ancestral spirits still dwell. The spirits there love the movements of brightly colored and iridescent beings: wildflower blossoms, hummingbirds and butterflies, moths and stars, wildfires and rainbows, dawns and sunsets. To remember and give pleasure to their deceased ancestors, the O'odham, Yaqui, Huichol, and Tarahumara all sing of the dance of pollinators amidst brilliant flowers, of spinning, drifting, and shining objects, of deer bedecked with bou-quets and ribbons, standing at peace in the Wilderness World.

Since the words for wildness, health, curing, and healing have the same roots in the O'odham language, Pima medicine men may have selectively used datura-induced contacts with wild creatures to promote a deep healing within those who had been traumatized earlier in their lives. Ironically, modern medical practitioners have recently begun to prescribe small doses of alkaloid extracts from datura to their patients. They offer light doses of these drugs to quell the same intensities of nausea and gastrointestinal spasms that can be triggered by overdosing on datura. Psychiatrists, I suspect, could learn much about the effects of potent plant drugs like atropine and scopolamine simply by more deeply reflecting upon oral traditions regarding datura, still extant among Native Americans. Just as some pollination ecologists have come to appreciate the knowledge of plant-pollinator interactions encoded in datura song-poems, so may neurobiologists.

Indeed, I feel fortunate to live in a time when a growing number of scientists are increasingly inclined to consider the work of poets, and vice versa. And yet,

I often wonder why they ever fell out of dialogue with one another at all. For complex reasons, many scientists during the latter half of the twentieth century must have believed that they were the only scholars who could legitimately elucidate the world's truths. At the same time, many poets, novelists, and literary critics became disenchanted with the stories of the wild world; that is to say, natural history became marginal to their core interests. A tide of disengagement between the arts and the sciences rose sometime after World War II and began to ebb around Earth Day in 1970, although its undertow still pulls down some postmodern poets and scientists. My sense is that the rift between those engaged in scientific and literary pursuits reached its widest dimensions between 1940 and 1970. At that time, only a few agile individuals found ways to straddle the two diverging worlds—Edward Ricketts, Loren Eiseley, Vladimir Nabokov, Archie Carr, Rachel Carson, Peter Matthiessen, and Ursula Le Guin, among others. Perhaps this rift can be likened to the kind of differential pressure found along a geological fault line, where part of a landscape has been forced to slide away, deepening the divide between two sides of a canyon.

One explanation for how this rift formed can be found in Michael Brenson's *Visionaries and Outcasts*. Brenson reminds us of the deep sadness, grief, anger, and alienation felt by many poets and artists after American scientists unleashed the atomic bomb on Japanese civilians and soldiers at the end of World War II. During the Cold War, American bullishness led to additional, almost unbridled, investment in science and technology, while support for aesthetic and moral expressions by artists and writers lagged far behind. The political ideologies of the space race fueled further growth of scientific institutions, but nothing so lavish was offered to the arts and humanities to foster creativity in their domains. By 1968, the U.S. government was investing more than $16 billion a year in resources for scientists and engineers, but less than $8 million a year in opportunities for artists, writers, dancers, and musicians. When contrasted with governmental investment in the National Science Foundation, NASA, and the National Institutes of Health, support for the National Endowment for the Arts and the National Endowment for the Humanities appeared to be a belated, token attempt to keep artists, poets, and social scholars from starving.

And then, as Brenson documents, in the early 1960s a counterbalancing force gained some momentum. Advocates for the arts successfully convinced President Kennedy that extravagant investment in the sciences had created a disequilibrium in America that had diminished its citizens' creative and moral status in the world at large. Beginning with Kennedy and continuing through

several more presidencies, political leaders entertained the premise that free-
dom of artistic expression set America apart from other nations, so that the arts
could serve as an indicator of how mature and sophisticated the United States
had become.

To gain long-overdue support for fellowships that benefited poets and
painters, their supporters argued that outstanding artists, like good scientists, deserved the resources to enable them to experiment and to explore the
unknown. Compare, for example, the statements in the 1970s of biomedical
researcher Albert Szent-Györgyi with arts advocate James Melchert.

A Noble Prize winner, Szent-Györgyi asserted that "research means going
out into the unknown with the hope of finding something new to bring home.
If you know what you are going to do, or even find there, then it is not research
at all . . ."

Not long after Szent-Györgyi's plea for more support for open-ended experimentation among scientists, Melchert explained to Congress, "What a great
many artists do is investigate. For that matter, art can be thought of as aesthetic
investigation. Where would science be without research? The same question can
be said about art."

By the mid-1980s, artists, writers, and critics found that the National
Endowment for the Arts had begun to divert its limited resources away from
individual artistic experimentation. Some poets and artists found that by
engaging with others in public arts projects that explored the perception of
natural environments, they could dip into some of the philanthropic sources
that had only supported scientists up until that time. In particular, I think of the
re-photography projects in the arid West, where arts photographers went to the
very same spots where government-supported documentary photographers first
ventured to demonstrate how these pioneers had constructed a peculiar image
of the West. While the aesthetic attraction to the natural world felt by many
poets, photographers, and painters remained as steadily expressed as it had been
for decades, a new dimension emerged in their work: deep moral concern over
the ever-more-prevalent desecration of lands and waters they held sacred, and
the accelerating extinction of species.

Poets and novelists soon offered up eulogies for fallen species and despoiled
places. Some rallied together in defense of the earth and began to embrace
the many fresh ecological insights about biodiversity that were emerging out
of field research. Instead of further distancing themselves from the sciences,
certain artists and writers marveled at all that biologists and physicists were

learning about nature. They read all they could about fractals and biomimicry, and their art began to reflect a new scientific literacy.

Around the same period, a few literary critics began to take an interest in the writing of scientists, especially those who displayed an occasional metaphorical flair. By the time the Association for Study of Literature and Environment (ASLE) convened its first international conference in 1995, it seemed as though the Great Rift had disappeared.

This too was cause for celebration, as I sensed at the site of ASLE's first massive gathering of its green literati, at Fort Collins, Colorado. I had already been on the Colorado State University campus for several days before the ASLE conference began, attending the Board of Governors' meeting of the Society for Conservation Biology. Fortuitously, I heard that another group of environmentalists—literary ones—would be meeting next door. When I stumbled into an assembly hall filled with 600-odd aficionados of nature writing, I felt as though I had metamorphosed and ascended into heaven. As SueEllen Campbell, John Elder, and Larry Buell offered their welcoming words at the plenary sessions, I could sense that a critical mass of poets, literary scholars, and environmental historians were no longer wary of being in dialogue with natural scientists. I only wished that more of my colleagues from the conservation biology constituency had gone truant that day and come over to ASLE to hear its leaders' encouraging words about the marriage between poetry and science in service to the other-than-human world.

While many scholars of literature, culture, and history acknowledged the ways they had benefited from reading literary naturalists and natural scientists, I sensed that the percentage of biologists, geologists, or hydrologists who found their work enhanced by reading (or writing) poetry and novels was likely to be far lower. I no longer doubted that those who read, loved, and interpreted Native American literature would appreciate the insights into Prairie Falcon Flying's song-poem that were offered by pollination ecology and neurobiology. But to put it bluntly, I still worried whether pollination ecologists or psychiatrists would find the sacred datura song-poem of much value to their own work, or to their own hearts and souls.

If I were to convince any scientists that their own worldview might be enriched by a greater familiarity with poetry, I would have to demonstrate to them that the fostering of creativity is essential to the advancement of science and that without it modern science will wither like an unpollinated flower. And so I began to ask myself, what has my own practice of science tangibly gained from my own forays into creative writing and my frequent reading of leading poets? Are these pastimes mere diversions, which ultimately distract me from fully exercising the rigors of scientific thought? Or might my interest in other languages, and more specifically in language play, somehow serve to prepare me to be more deeply engaged in metaphorical thinking? If so, does some capacity in metaphorical thinking actually help me generate novel hypotheses to test, or freshly interpret, field conditions and experiments in ways I might not otherwise entertain? As I pondered the possibility that an engagement with poetry might be of value to scientific inquiry, a preposterous question crossed my mind: Has a hawkmoth ever wondered what good it is to a datura blossom?

REFERENCES

Lubart, T. I. "Creativity Across Cultures" in Handbook of Creativity, ed. Robert J. Sternberg (Cambridge: Cambridge University Press, 1999), 344.

Suzán H., G. P. Nabhan and D. T. Patten. 2002. Nurse Plant and Floral Biology of a Rare Night-Blooming Cereus, Peniocereus striatus (Brandegee) F. Buxbaum Conservation Biology 8(2):461–70.

Nabhan, G. P. and J. L. Carr, eds. 1994. Ironwood: an Ecological and Cultural Keystone of the Sonoran Desert. Washington, DC: Conservation International Occasional Papers in Conservation Biology/University of Chicago Press.

Brennan, J. L., trans. 1975. "Pima Jimsonweed Song," in The Pima Indians by Frank Russell (Tucson: University of Arizona Press), 299–300.

Szent-Györgyi, A. 1963. The Science of Life: A Picture History of Biology by Gordon Rattray Taylor. London: Thames and Hudson.

Melchert, J., quoted in Brenson, M. 2001. Visionaries and Outcasts. New York: New Press, p. 158.

Poincaré, H. 1924. The Foundations of Science, trans. George Bruce Halsted. New York: Science Press.

19

AROMAS EMANATING FROM THE DRIEST OF PLACES

GARY PAUL NABHAN

I AM FOLLOWING *a scent across the desert.*

I meander my way up the slope between boulders of limestone, ones that are almost too hot to touch. I am dodging dwarfed trees and shrubs that all have spiny branches. They are tortuously twisted and punctuated by greasy but fragrant leaflets. A few spindly milkweeds with toxic sap cling to the cliff face beside me.

As I stop for a moment to catch my breath, I let my eyes scan the arid terrain rolling high to the south of me, up the mountain plateau that is called Jabal Samhan in Arabic. I am witness to a stark and largely unpopulated landscape. Jabal Samhan might not be totally barren, but most farmers and city dwellers from around the world would declare it to be "empty." By that, they might mean that it is marginally arable, barely habitable, or incapable of offering much of value to humankind today.

But they might be wrong. Over millennia, something of great value came out of these arid lands, which when combined with other forces, changed the course of human history. The real question might be whether we value this desert in any profound way today.

And so, I have come here on a pilgrimage to seek an answer to that question. I have climbed into the Dhofar highlands, a plateau that sits some two thousand feet above the Arabian Sea. It is home to a scatter of semi-nomadic herding and foraging Jabbali tribes known as the people of the Shahri, the ones who "make mountain talk."

Originally published as chapter 1 in *Gastronomica*, and later included in G. P. Nabhan (2014) *Cumin, Camels and Caravans: A Spice Odyssey* (University of California Press).

There is no kind of talk being heard here right now. All is quiet. There is no wind. I gulp down hot air. My nostrils flare and I pick up a distinctive fragrance in the air, subtle but inviting.

I remember that ancient Greek geographers called this odoriferous country Eudaimôn Arabia or 'Arabia the Blessed.' One of them, Herodotus, noted, "The whole country exhales an odor that is marvelously sweet."[1] After the Greeks, this land came to be known to the wider world as Arabia Felix, a vortex of happiness amid much hardship and struggle. At first, this land offered nothing more than a few fragrant desert plant and animal substances, which were collectively known to the Greeks as aromatikoi. Such aromatic substances have long been perceived by many cultures as having the capacity to generate a sense of happiness, healing, well-being, and harmony with the world.

As I meander up the switchbacks of a goat trail, I wonder how long the "happy" slopes of Jabal Samhan have baked in the torrid sun. My feet kick up dust in the wake of my walking. It has not rained here for weeks.

Heat. Drought. Scientists who call themselves chemical ecologists suggest that aridity has helped rather than hindered the evolution of exceedingly fragrant plants. Over millennia, the Arabian deserts developed into prime habitat for the most powerfully aromatic plants in the world. What these desert plants lacked in productivity, they often made up in fragrance, flavor, and vision-inducing potency.

Perhaps that's because many of them exude aromatic oils from their leaves, which help them resist heat, drought, and damage from herbivores. Such aromatic but highly volatile, fleeting chemicals are concentrated in the floras of arid climes like nowhere else.

Although much of the Dhofar region has low agricultural potential and an uneven distribution of useful wild plants, Arabia Felix could aptly be called the place of emergence for global trade in aromatics. Like Aladdin's magic ring, when properly rubbed, a psychotropic world of incenses, culinary spices, perfumes, and curative herbs can be opened up to delight and refresh the weary.

However sparse its vegetation may be, Arabia Felix is full of highly pungent scents and flavors. It has wild crocuses akin to saffron, barks reminiscent of cinnamon, wild fennel, leeks, garlic and onions, aromatic gums and resins galore. When mixed into a paste with dates and plastered onto pit-roasted mutton and goat meats, an Omani selection of these plants provides the taste portfolio called *khall al-mazza*.[2] When desiring curry-like flavors in savory stews, an even more complex mix of herbs and spices called *bezar a' shuwa* has long been used all across the Arabian Peninsula.

The particular rocky habitat where these herbs grow in the Dhofar region is simply called *nejd* in the ancient Semitic languages of "mountain talkers"—the tribes of al-Kathiri, al-Qara, al-Mahra. The highland cultures of *Jabal Samhan* share a history and preference for landscapes quite different than those of the better-known Bedouins of the Arabian sands. The striking differences in plant composition between these adjacent landscapes is what ecologists refer to as "beta diversity"[3]—a pronounced dissimilarity in the herbs—which a spice collector might find between localized floras as he or she moves from one patch of desert to the next. In general, deserts exhibit high rates of "species turnover" from one arid landscape to another, so that few of the favored food and medicinal plants of one desert mountain range can be found in another just a day's walk away. And so, for as long as we know, they have been traded from one place to another, and savored beyond their place of origin.

Off to the southeast, *Jabal Samhan's* windward slopes dive toward the cooler, breezier, more humid coast of Yemen. To the west, in the domain of the truly nomadic Bedouin, lies the infamous Empty Quarter. It is the austere sea of sand known as the *Rub' al-Khali*. For centuries, it has been the stretch of the Arabian Peninsula least frequented by the hardiest of nomads. Even the Bedu are wary of its paucity of water and the perils of its drifting sands.

Here in the Dhofar highlands, at least there is enough *terra rossa* soil among the limestone to support a scatter of low shrubs, some far-flung patches of wiry grass, resinous bushes of rock-rose, and the withered but bristly stalks of thistles. A few goats and camels, the hardiest of livestock breeds seasonally browse this desert-scrub vegetation. In fact, they sometimes seem to be the only creatures tenacious enough to inhabit the *nejd*, but by no means do they comprise the sum total of all the fauna there.

The small caves I spot along the rocky crest on the western horizon occasionally shelter the stick-gathering hyrax and rock-climbing lizards. My eyes have also spotted larger caves and ledges below cliffs, which serve to protect the meager harvests of spices gathered by al-Qara foragers and herders, for a few of their baskets and bundles are left in their shade.

No one would call the Dhofar highlands a landscape of bounty. On the whole, most of its habitats lack much fertility, fecundity, productivity, and diversity. If its inhabitants do not take advantage of the brief spurts of plant growth that follow occasional rains, they could easily go hungry. The *nejd*, however, is one of Dhofar's intensely arid habitats. Furthermore, it holds a most singular treasure.

Long ago, it was that particular treasure that catapulted some Semitic-speaking nomads out of the desolation of the southern reaches of their peninsula, propelling their descendants toward all corners of the globe. They began to trade their aromatic herbs, incenses, and spices to others in better-watered climes. They exchanged fragrances, flavors, and cures for staple foods and other goods that their arid homeland could not consistently provide. They understood that all habitats are not created equal in terms of the natural resources found within them.

And so, the Semitic tribes were instructed—at least early on in their history—not to remake one place resemble another, but to trade the most unique goods of each to those who lacked them. They made an asset out of one of the inherent weaknesses of their homelands—its inequitable distribution of plant and animal productivity. In doing so, they built an economic model for trade between regions, which initially redistributed both wealth and wonder among peoples.

Later on, that model morphed, for spice trade triggered an economic and ecological revolution that rippled out to every reach of the human-inhabited world. It was the revolution that we now call *globalization*. And yet, it has been difficult for many of us to imagine its origins, for we live and breathe within it as unconsciously as fish do in the sea, as if it has always existed and will continue to exist as it does today.

I hold on to that thought for a moment, for ahead of me I spot my destination—a precious part of those origins—which initially motivated me to travel nine thousand miles from my home to reach this place. I am now far enough up the slope to finally touch—for the first time in my life—the very spark that may have jump-started the engine of globalization.

I reach my hand out and gingerly touch the limber branches of a tree that is about as tall as I am. It has a voluptuous trunk covered in a jacket of ashy-hued bark. I reach farther into its canopy and grasp a thicker branch around its girth, as if I am feeling the bulging biceps of one of my iron-pumping friends. These sinuous branches are laden with small clusters of slightly crumpled but highly aromatic leaflets. I notice that its trunk is indelibly marked with scars—scorings in the bark made by intentional slashes with a knife—and on these scars there are dried-up droplets not of blood, but of a pale white resin that forms perfect tears.

Just beneath the bark are microscopic structures much like tear ducts. These ducts can be stimulated to shed their resin by scoring, the very same means that our primate ancestors obtained acacia gum, gum tragacanth, mastic, or myrrh from other woody plants. Like them, it has long been valued as a medicine, vermifuge, flavorant, spice, and incense.

But that is where the comparisons among gummy incenses stop. For close to four millennia, this particular gum has been regarded as the highest quality incense in the world. It was once the most valuable plant product—and the most widely disseminated—in the entire world. Frankincense. *Food of the Gods.*

I smile as I recall that even the stuffiest of scientists begrudgingly acknowledges the sacredness of this tree every time they recite its scientific name, Boswellia sacra. *I have some familiarity with its distant relatives, the "elephant trees" of the Americas, for I've often collected copal incense off their trunks. And on many winter days, when I suffer from inflammation and pain resulting from an old horseback riding injury, I rub my muscles with the salve of* Boswellia serrata, *the so-called Indian frankincense or "salai."*

I dip beneath the canopy of the gnarly tree, and from a scar on its central trunk, I pull a small but recently crystallized lump of gummy sap. It appears that in the spring prior to my arrival, the bark was scarified in two or three places on its trunk by a Somali migrant harvester. He slashed at the bark with a mingaf—*a short-bladed tool that looks much like a putty knife. He came back a month later and cleaned the wound, and did so a second time at the end of spring as well. The tree's wound then wept and bled for several more weeks.*

The milky sap flowing out of the tree's phloem has already begun to congeal into a semi-solid resinous latex. In fact, the frankincense tappers simply call it "milk"—*luban* in Arabic, *shehaz* in Mountain Talk. But this is the sweetest, whitest, and milkiest of all frankincense—the internationally acclaimed *hojar fusoos*. This quality of frankincense is found nowhere in the world except the *Samhan Nejd* in the Dhofar highlands.

During the height of its use in the Roman Empire, more money was spent on acquiring this superlative form of frankincense than was spent on any other aromatic—incense, spice, or herb—whether traded long distances by land or by sea. In Babylon, those rich enough to afford this incense would bask in its smoke, purifying and imbuing their bodies with its fragrance prior to their bouts of lovemaking.

Once I find a bit of sap that has hardened some, I pinch its gummy substance until it pulls away from the trunk—like taffy. I hold it in my hand and let the sun shine upon the amber globule. It dully shines back at the sun, a cloudy droplet of oleo-resin, almost like a freshly made curd of goat cheese. There is a bluish hue hidden deep in the pearly clouds of these droplets, as if they are fallen pieces of sky, which desire to be sent up to join the rest of the heavens.

Beam it up: That is what people have done over the millennia: they have made a burnt offering of the sacred milk, so that its smoke can rise beyond this world. Smoke from the best frankincense, they say, forms a single white column that flows straight into the sky. If its vapor trail is strong enough to ascend into the heavens, this gift will inevitably reach, nourish, and delight the Creator, the Prophet, or particular saints—whoever is meant to receive these fragrant prayers.

I never thought of incense as a food or a spice until now. Timidly, I place a tiny piece of hojari fusoos in my mouth and gnash it between my teeth, as I might do with any chewing gum. Hints of honey, lime, verbena, and vanilla well up and spread through the juices of my mouth. I smile as I remember that pregnant Bedu women also chew on frankincense gum, hoping that it will encourage the child in the womb to live an intellectually and spiritually elevated life. Both Shahri and Somali harvesters chew on this gum while they "milk" more luban from one tree after another, depositing their harvests into two-handled baskets woven from the fronds of date palms.

I quickly warm to this world of incense, camels, and date palms, for it seems vaguely but deeply familiar to me. I happen to be of a bloodline that traces its origins back to Yemeni and Omani spice traders of the Banu Nebhani tribe. It is plausible that my own ancestors may have wandered these very same hills more than fourteen hundred years ago, before they spread north across the Arabian Peninsula and beyond.

This possibility might suggest why I have felt motivated—even destined—to come to one of the driest and most remote parts of the world—as if to redeem my family origins. But frankly, I am after something far larger than that.

I have come here to dig for the roots of globalization, if the roots of such an ancient and pervasive phenomenon can be ever be traced at all. I wish to track them back to the very first bartering for tiny quantities of aromatic resins like mastic, bdellium, frankincense, and myrrh; for the stoneground seeds of cumin and anise; for the fragrant musk extracted from the glands of deer; for the bite in the leaves of mint or oregano; for the bark of cassia from China and true cinnamon from Sri Lanka; for the sun-dried skins of Kafir limes; for the shavings carved off the kernels of the nutmeg tree; for the withered red stigmas of the saffron flower; for the willowy pods of vanilla, and the pungent ones of chile peppers.

Collectively, these various plant and animal products are ambiguously referred to as "spices" in English just as they were rather coarsely lumped together as *aromatikoi* by the ancient Greeks. Perhaps these languages build upon the ancient Arab concept of *shadhan*—a term used to describe a particularly pungent herb, but one which can collectively refer to strongly fragrant and flavorful substances in general, ones of both plant and animal origin. A related word, *al-shadw*, is used to comment on the intensity of pungency in a pepper, or piece of cinnamon bark, or lump of the *hojari fusoos* grade of frankincense.

A third Arabic word *al-adhfar*, relates to any pungent smell, from musk to human sweat.[4] Indeed, some scholars have suggested that musks, pungent ointments, and rose waters have been routinely used in hot climes in order to mask the odor of human sweat, which would otherwise be the most pervasive smell in desert camps and cities much of the year.

Historian Patricia Crone once offered this litany to circumscribe the many faces and fragrances of aromatics.

"They include incense, or substances that gave off a nice smell on being burned; perfumes, ointments, and other sweet-smelling substances with which one dabbed, smeared, or sprinkled oneself or one's clothes; things that one put into food or drink to improve their taste, prolong their life, or endow them with medicinal or magical properties; and they also included antidotes."[5]

By the early fourteenth century CE, the Italian merchant Francesco di Balduccio Peglolotti documented at least 288 varieties of "spices" arrived into Europe, mostly through Semitic merchants who sometimes referred to their origins in particular Arabian, African, or Asian landscapes. These "spices" ranged from asafetida to zedoary, and included everything from gum Arabic to manna to the madder of Alexandria.[6]

Such spices are the sensuous signposts that may tell us where the trails and rustic roads of globalization first ran; they may remind us of why we have been so engaged with these aromatic products in the first place. And so, a quest to understand the semiotics of globalization must begin with reading spices as signs of deeper desires or diseases that have been embedded in certain segments of humankind for millennia.

For many years now, I have been preoccupied if not altogether consumed with trying to answer a simple question: Why have some individuals, communities, or cultures been content with staying home and savoring what lies immediately before them, while others have an insatiable desire to taste, see, or even possess what comes from afar?

I have wondered why certain peoples culturally and genetically identified as Semitic—Minaeans and Nabateans, Phoenicians and other Canaanites, Quraysh and Karimi Arabs, Radhanite and Sephardic Jews—have played such disproportionately large roles in globalized trade—not merely over the short course of decades or centuries, but over the long haul of many millennia.

As I stand on this dry ridge, panting and sweating my bodily fluids into thin air, I realize why I have decided to begin this journey on this particular ridge in southern Oman, even though it is one that bears a name known only by a handful of tribesmen living in the region of Jabal Samhan. *Incidentally, this ridge happens to cover some hundred hectares of a frankincense reserve being set aside from other uses by the Omani government of* Sultan Qaboos. *In my mind, it looms far larger than a couple hundred hectares.*

It is the perfect launching pad for a spice odyssey, one that will take us to the ancient port of Zaitun on the China Sea, to the Turpan edging the Gobi Desert below the Tien Shan mountains on the border between China and Kazakhstan, to the River Panj separating the Hindu Kush of Pakistan from the Pamirs of Tajikistan, to the coastal ports of Oman, Egypt, Turkey, and Mexico, to the slot canyons of Petra in Jordan and to the sprawling souks, bazaars, and mercados of Syria, Ethiopia, Egypt, Morocco, Portugal, Spain, and Mexico. We will wander down the Incense Trails of the Middle East, the Silk Roads of Asia, the Spice Trails of Africa, and the Camino Real of Central and North America. It will take us back in time, and possibly, it may launch us into considering our future.

But for all of that to occur, we must first go and pay homage to the spindly frankincense tree—even though it is hardly more than a bush in stature—in its primordial *nejd* habitat in the southeastern reaches of the Arabian Peninsula.

How odd it is that its unforgettable fragrance of frankincense comes not from its flowers or fruits but from its wounds, as if it were a saint with stigmata that drip with blood, sweat, and tears! Whether wounded by the whipping of branches during seasonal windstorms, bruised by the browsing of camels or cut open by the crude *mingaf* knives of Omani, Yemeni, and Somali harvesters, this injured bush offers up a few grams of gum that is its only useful product. If it is too badly injured or too frequently milked by greedy tappers, the frankincense bush will succumb to a premature death. These stunted perennials already struggle to survive on sun-scorched scree where rainfall is scant; it does not take very much additional stress to hasten their demise.

For that reason—and because there are few other lucrative products that can be derived from the *nejd* barrens in the Dhofar highlands—it is no wonder that frankincense stands have been traditionally owned, carefully protected, and diligently managed for millennia. As Pliny the Elder wrote of the frankincense groves, which he called "the forests of Arabia Felix" in his great *Naturalis Historia*:

"The forest is divided up into definite portions, and owing to the mutual honesty of the owners, is free from trespassing, and though nobody keeps guard over the trees after an incision has been made, nobody steals from his neighbor."[7]

Outside of Dhofar, I listen to an Omani forest steward explain to me that his job was much like that of a game warden. His task, he says, is to "keep watch over what is precious."

His name is Ali Salem Bait Said. He comes from a family and Jabbali tribe that functioned as traditional owners of a particular frankincense gathering grounds until the late 1960s. That's when the paternal bloodline inheritance of the right to manage and harvest a menzela grove of frankincense finally broke down, centuries after it first evolved. But Ali Salem Bait Said still remembers his family's stories of how to properly care for a productive stand of frankincense:

In the past, [my] people thought of themselves as friends of the tree. They don't scratch down to the bone. They go and cut closer to the bark—not deep—so that they will not hurt the tree. Now [with the suspension of traditional ownership of men-zelas] there is no one to care of the trees. And so there are people who come here that think of them as wild [not managed] and milk them for all they can give, until the trees dry up. [Those migrant harvesters] may not even know the traditional songs for luban, which we sung in celebration of God.

Ali points out the trees that have had branches broken by feral camels, and shows me others, which he believes were milked too frequently. He suggests that at least in his tribe, such occurrences would have been uncommon when centuries-old traditions of menzela-management were still intact.

Later, I have the opportunity to learn about more ancient frankincense gathering and management traditions from a remarkable field scientist and observer of frankincense culture, Mohamud Haji Farah. Although Somali by birth, Dr. Farah has spent several years near Dhofar documenting how indigenous Omani tribal herders and migrant Somali harvesters work with frankincense. Ironically, he focused on Jabal Samhan, the very same area that I was blessed to visit. Of slight build and quiet voice, Farah spoke with discerning authority regarding the indigenous traditions that had evolved around this much-revered spiritual and economic resource.

"Frankincense trees are presumed to possess or house supernatural powers associated with both good and evil spirits ... [And so, it was] a sacred commodity, and its harvesters worked under ritualistic constraints."[8]

I had heard that harvesters were not allowed to sleep with their wives or eat certain foods during the harvest season. Farah does not confirm nor deny this.

Instead, he notes how the chanting of prayers and the burning of incense are still enacted at the beginning of the tapping season. Some harvesters believe that frankincense trees could not survive, thrive, and yield incense in such harsh and desolate arid environments if they did not have sacred powers.[9]

The rituals, Farah surmises, are means of showing respect to the trees and perhaps even pacifying them. He has found that such beliefs were widespread among Arab harvesters—not only in Oman, but Yemen and Saudi Arabia as well. Farah and other scientists who have surveyed the persistence of these traditions guess that such beliefs and rituals promote self-constraint among harvesters. It seems that they discourage would-be trespassers from entering someone else's menzela patch in order to clandestinely milk their trees.

In listening to both Ali and Mohamud, I am struck by just how vulnerable frankincense is on its home ground, and yet how long the harvesting of its incense has persisted—perhaps four thousand years—without widespread decimation of its populations. I wonder whether the ritual constraints and the prayerful gathering of its precious resins have somehow kept frankincense populations from being overexploited, even though this incense has been in transcontinental trade for thousands of years.

Or perhaps, I wonder, do the harvesters in Yemen, Oman, and Saudi Arabia recognize that if they eliminate their most valuable resource, they would have fewer desert plants, animals, or minerals to trade for food? Especially during times of drought or political disruption, the trading of frankincense has been one of the few hands they could play.

For that matter, as one Omani forester explained to me,

"It would not be right to fail to protect this plant, for it is the source of our history."

I begin to think about other desert dwellers I have known, especially herders and hunter-gatherers who have lacked the food crops produced in irrigated oases to fall back on during the worst of times. Having a mythical medicine, spice, or incense to trade was perhaps all that kept them from starvation during those times.

The nomadic Seri Indians, with whom I have lived and worked in Mexico's deserts, offer such an example.[10] As soon as European missionaries arrived on the edge of their traditional territory, they opportunistically engaged these Jesuit priests in unwittingly supporting two of their economic strategies. First, the Seri obtained food by trading incense such as copal, medicines such as jojoba, and spices such as oregano to the priests to send back to Europe. Then, once they knew what the outsiders had in store, they would clandestinely raid their trading partner's pantries for additional food and drink.

As I leave the highlands of Jabal Samhan for the port town of Salalah, I take a handful of frankincense beads along with me to ritually burn that night. They are *modest in size and sit lightly in the palm of my hand. And yet I have heard that they command respectable prices in the souks and tourist shops along the Omani coast of the Persian Gulf and Arabian Sea—perhaps as high as $50 U.S. per kilo—twenty to twenty-five times what a harvester might be paid in the desert for the same quantity. I decide to go into the souks to see if this is true.*

As I later enter the souk, I realize that there is one secret of frankincense commerce that I have already surmised: such a little thing, as diminutive and nearly as weightless as a single grain of wheat, is the perfect commodity to trade over long distances. Of course, its economic as well as mythic value must be made to loom larger than the trade item itself. This, I guess, has been the trade secret shared by most spice traders over the last four millennia:

If you can, carry to the far corners of the earth something as light as a feather that can linger in one's memory forever, but eschew anything as dull and as heavy as lead.

Whenever feasible, trade in potent fragrances and flavors, for they are the tangible corollaries of visions and dreams. They are intermediaries between the physical and spiritual worlds, reminding us that there is more to the world than what we can absorb through the cones and rods of our eyes.

Of course, other desert nomads have simply traded songs from their dreams and visions to farmers who lived in more secure and better-watered places. When I first heard of such trade, I must have smirked, for I thought it was at best a lark and at worst a scam. But now that I have seen the little cloud-like tears of frankincense on the tree, and have inhaled their ephemeral smoke, it all makes sense to me.

These elusive things lodge deeply in our imaginations, far more so than most material stuff. For at least 3,500 years—and perhaps for as long as 5,500 years—incense, spices, and herbs have captured human attention and imagination.[11] They have not only been worth trading for; for some, they have been worth dying for.

Salalah sits on the edge of the coastal plain overlooking the Arabian Sea, sprawling over the site of an ancient trade center, Zhafar. Because it is just a short camel drive of eighteen miles from the highlands to this naturally protected harbor, the ports here have long attracted professions in addition to those of sailors and shippers. They have also harbored incense graders, incense makers, and incense mixers, as well as camel drovers and mule skinners of the kind who have brought aromatic goods from the desert to the sea for upwards of 3,500 years.

Once in the city, it does not take me long to find Salalah's largest souk, where all matter of things sacred and profane can be bought and sold, but where frankincense has long been the featured attraction. How could it not be? Once I approach the dozen or so shops that are constantly sending smoke up toward the heavens, and out toward their prospective customers, I could hardly resist lingering there for a while.

The shops are small, rather gaudy and glitzy, but far more elegant than most spice shops in other Middle Eastern souks. Incense burns while some scratchy recordings of Arabic music play on loudspeakers. I had assumed I could only get frankincense there, but myrrh, sandalwood, and musk are also for sale. In fact, I count dozens of kinds of incense, native perfumes, and aromatic herbs being offered, not merely to tourists but to Omanis as well.

It may be a leap for a Westerner to make, but in the southern reaches of the Arabian Peninsula, incense is regarded as a form of nourishment. There are recipes for over two-dozen incense mixtures and herbal scents included in *Al-Azaf*—the most popular Omani cookbook in shops and marketplaces.[12] Those recipes bring together *oud* oil with black musk, ambergris with sandalwood, saffron with snails, and cloves with rose water, blending them into various divinely fragrant concoctions. But among all of the aromatics sold there, frankincense is the one that shopkeepers let stand alone. A soloist, its olfactory melody is too heavenly for Omanis to ever want it to be overdubbed.

Synesthesia. I begin to feel as if I am stoned, for my senses are bombarded with a mix of images unlike anything they had ever experienced before. This is literally a land of smoke and mirrors. The mirrors are placed to make the shops loom larger, to multiply the colored lights, and to catch the whirls of smoke rising from clay incense burners. Nearly every incense shop is stocked with fashionably shaped aspirators and decanters of perfumes, rustic bags of dried incense, and bowls with glistening samples of both. But add to that the harmonic intensity of loud music, voices speaking a dozen languages, and the memorable profiles of women in brilliantly colored silk gowns, dazzling jewelry, and gorgeous scarves. As the half-dozen kinds of smoke from incense gradually fill my lungs, I begin to feel as if the world is shimmering before me.

An elderly Somali-Omani shopkeeper—her hands and lower arms aflame with intricate patterns inscribed with henna—notices my befuddlement. She smiles, and with a fine British accent, invites me into her little shop. She beckons me to come and sit so that I might learn to distinguish the five grades of luban from one another. She says she will show me how to properly ignite them in a traditional clay incense burner.

She explains that the differences among grades may at first seem too subtle to the uninitiated tourist, but that they are worth recognizing. The top grade, hojari fusoos, commands prices three to four times higher than that of the next level of quality, the nejdi. The trick of the shopkeeper is to quickly discern how much—or really, how little—a visitor actually knows about frankincense.

Feigning alarm—her almond-shaped eyes magnified by the delicate lines of kohl drawn around them—she notes how some of her competitors display low-grade "ore" that is roughly the same color and texture as hojari. *In a whisper, she confides in me that there might be even be some unscrupulous merchants who will try to market their nuggets of nejdi, or even lower-quality shazri, as hojari fusoos.*

"They are out to take the shirt off your back for a few pebbles of frankincense," she frowns. She then swears to me that she has never perpetrated such an impropriety, and that I can place my trust in her henna-colored hands.

I begin to daydream then, not fully hearing the rest of her sales pitch, but instead remembering little fragments of what historians had compiled about frankincense and spices in the ancient economies.

The best frankincense—*hojari* or some comparable grade from the region of Yemen—cost the ancient Romans six denarii per pound. That was roughly the same as ginger; more than black pepper; and twice the price of cardamom. Myrrh was twice the price per volume at that time because it would dehydrate and shrink in size; however, it was never used in the quantities that the Romans transported and consumed frankincense. In late Roman times, the cost of transporting a camel-load of frankincense from the Southern Arabian Peninsula to the Mediterranean was 680 to 1000 denarii, more than five times the cost of living a year in Palestine during the same era. In exchange for frankincense, close to ten million denarii's worth of goods would annually flow back the 1,700 miles from the Mediterranean shores, or from Persia and India.[13]

For a desert region where less than one thousandth of the land's surface could be used to grow crops, it was frankincense that stimulated the flow of goods from better-watered regions to Dhofar and the Hadhramawt. The Semitic tribes of *Arabia Felix* would trade their *al-luban*—which the Romans called *olibanum*—for a range of material goods beyond their capability to produce: silk sashes, muslin sheets, medicinal ointments, dry white wines, emmer wheat, copper vessels, and silver plates. Of course, there were small irrigated oases scattered across Arabia Felix that provided most of the tribes with their dates, cereals, and some other cultivated foods, but trade in Frankincense was what leveraged access to them for the nomads.

Until Arab and Phoenician seafarers gained a certain competence in maritime navigation, transport of frankincense and other goods, over such long distances, could be done only by camel. Dromedary camels appear to have been domesticated in the coastal settlements of eastern Arabia not far from present-day Salalah. They may have been initially managed as a wild resource for the medicinal value of their milk, which fends off microbial infections of the eye—just as frankincense offered its antiseptic *luban* to the Semitic tribes there, long before the era of Abraham. Clay camel figurines made in Yemen close to 3,000 years ago suggest that these creatures soon assumed the status of a keystone species in the Arab economy and an icon of spirituality, for camels provided not only milk, but also wool, meat, flammable dung, medicinal urine, leather, and transportation as well. Because a single adult camel can shoulder as much as 400 pounds of loaded goods and still cover twenty-two miles of desert a day, no other beast of burden could possibly hold its own against it when crossing windswept sands.

It is not surprising that the first appearance of frankincense well beyond its native range—in Egypt between 3,000 and 3,500 years ago—was about the time that camels were tamed and reliably used for long-distance transport. Among the nine hundred and some terms relating to camels in the Arabic language, one can find some wonderful metaphors, which treat them as companions, gifts from Allah, and sailing vessels. Throughout much of their historic range, they were likened to "ships of the desert," capable of navigating vast seas of sand as no other animal could. Camels, spice caravans, and incense trade not only shared a common history, but they launched the Semitic tribes onto a shared economic trajectory. No wonder prints of camel caravans and miniature replicas of dromedaries are scattered throughout the souks of Salalah.

The elderly Somali shopkeeper taps me on the shoulder.

"Excuse me, kind sir. Are you . . . how do you say it, jet-lagged? You looked as though you were falling asleep. . . . Have you traveled far today? Do you want to purchase something from me before you go off to rest?"

I decide purchase a quarter-pound of hojari fusoos and a crudely decorated clay incense burner from her, in part to avoid embarrassing myself any further.

"Please excuse me," I reply. "I have indeed travelled a long way to be here today," I add, as I pay for the dreamy scent of frankincense. "Nine thousand miles from my home . . ."

I have seen how frankincense is found in the wild, its resins collected, and its incense sold in the same landscapes where this has occurred for millennia. It is clear that a little of the harvest could be traded or sold for much more in the outer world, and this fact alone propelled the "Ones Who Made Mountain Talk" to engage in extra-local spice trade, just as others began to do so in other landscapes strewn around the planet. But frankincense trade immediately morphed into something larger and more pervasive than what happened with two hundred other spices. It set up an insatiable desire for "the other," the "extra-local," to propel some people out of the humdrum ordinariness of their daily lives. It stimulated them to imagine something beyond the here and now, something with which they wanted to connect. And that initial stimulus, which led inexorably toward globalization in all its dimensions, began more than 3,000 years ago in remote arid landscapes where Semitic peoples wandered. It made me tired to fathom it all . . .

Weary, I returned to my boarding room, where I began to burn a few tears of hojari fusoos in a simple clay incense burner. As I lay down on the bed, I realized that traveling 9,000 miles through space had not been enough. I must figure out a way to travel back in time. I closed my eyes, and the ethereal smoke of frankincense carried me away.

NOTES

1. Herodotus, in George Rawlinson, *Histories* (London, UK: Wordsworth Classics, 1996). Book One, Chapter 113. Gary Paul Nabhan, *Desert Terroir* (Austin: University of Texas Press, 2011).

2. Lilia Zaouali, *Medieval Cuisine of the Islamic World: A Concise History with 174 Recipes* (Berkeley: University of California Press, 2007), p. 144.

3. Beta diversity is simply described as the rate at which species accumulate as a plant or animal collector moves in a straight line away from any particular point. See Michael L. Rosenzweig, *Species Diversity in Space and Time* (New York, NY: Cambridge University Press, 1995), p. 33.

4. Anya King, *The Musk Trade and the Near East in the Medieval Period* (Bloomington, IN: Indiana University, 2007).

5. Patricia Crone, *Mecca Trade and the Rise of Islam* (Princeton, NJ: Princeton University Press, 1987).

6. Francesco di Balduccio Peglolotti, "The Practice Commerce," translated from Italian, in Robert S. Lopez and Irving W. Raymond, eds. *Medieval Trade in the Mediterranean World: Illustrative Documents* (New York, NY: Columbia University Press, 2001), pp. 109–14.

7. Pliny the Elder (H. Rackham, trans.), *Natural History Volume X* (Cambridge, MA: Harvard University Press, Loeb Classic Library, 1942). Book 43 (12), p. 64.

8. Mohamud Haji Farah, *Non-Timber Forest Product (NTFP) Extraction in Arid Environments: Land-Use Change, Frankincense Production and the Sustainability of* Boswellia sacra *in Dhofar (Oman)* (Tucson, AZ: University of Arizona Dissertation, 2008), p. 45.

9. Mohamud Haji Farah, *Non-Timber Forest Product (NTFP) Extraction in Arid Environments: Land-Use Change, Frankincense Production and the Sustainability of* Boswellia sacra *in Dhofar (Oman)* (Tucson, AZ: University of Arizona Dissertation, 2008), pp. 45–46.

10. Gary Paul Nabhan, *Singing the Turtles to Sea: The Comcáac (Seri) Art and Science of Reptiles* (Berkeley: University of California Press, 2003).

11. William J. Bernstein, *A Splendid Exchange: How Trade Shaped the World* (New York, NY: Atlantic Monthly Press, 2008), p. 53; R. P. Evenshed, P. F. van Bergen, T. M. Peakman, E. C. Leigh-Firbank, M. C. Horton, D. Edwards, M. Biddle, B. Kjølbye-Biddle & P. A. Rowley-Conway, "Archaeological Frankincense," *Nature* 390 (December 1, 1997): 667–68.

12. Lamees Abdullah Al Taie, *Al-Azaf: The Omani Cookbook* (Musquat, Sultanate of Oman: Oman Bookshop, 1995).

13. Caroline Singer, "The incense kingdoms of Yemen: An outline history of the Southern Arabian spice trade," in David Peacock and David Williams, eds., *Food for the Gods: New Light on the Ancient Incense Trade* (Oxford, UK: OXBOW Books, 2007), pp. 20–21; William J. Bernstein, *A Splendid Exchange: How Trade Shaped the World* (New York, NY: Atlantic Monthly Press, 2008), pp. 62–64.

20

THE ETHNOBIOLOGY OF SURVIVAL IN POST-APOCALYPTIC DYSTOPIAS

GARY PAUL NABHAN AND JAMES R. VETETO

E THNOBIOLOGISTS AND ENVIRONMENTAL anthropologists have recently engaged in both critical analysis and applied technical support of emerging expressions of ecotopian and utopian ideals (Lockyer and Veteto 2013). This is an exciting development, as it moves our discipline from being seen as a historical science with purely retrodictive capacity, to a forward-looking science with predictive capacity.

Although these efforts to evaluate and value emerging social movements on the margins of industrialized society are both laudable and ultimately necessary for advancing our species' survival, we must also consider the null hypothesis: Industrialized society may descend into a post-apocalyptic dystopia due to climate change, economic collapse, and/or the proliferation of rogue states and violent social environments (Rabkin et al. 1983; Peluso and Watts 2001; Tuhis-Dubrow 2013). We must consider the possibility that the human species, for one reason or another, will not survive on this planet, even though other life-forms will continue to adapt and evolve here (Weisman 2007).

What then, can ethnobiologists and environmental anthropologists contribute to our consideration of these alternative futures, should the neoliberal technocratic fix fail to resolve the world's currently pressing problems (climate change, population growth, loss of biodiversity, etc.)? To begin with, ethnobiologists conversant with non-Western cultures may be less inclined to accept the logical-positivist assumptions and technological fixes of industrial societies than other scholars. While ethnobiologists have only rarely included dystopian narratives in their previous research, they are likely to be quite accepting and appreciative of anthropologically informed dystopian novels such as those of Alfred L. Kroeber's daughter, Ursula LeGuin (1974), MacArthur Fellow Octavia Butler (1993), and Barbados-based multi-award winner Karen Lord (2013).

Curiously, these fine novelists, among others, appear to value ethnobiologists' lenses into diverse strategies for human survival as significant material to embrace in their own narratives. As Butler's young African American protagonist Lauren Olamina explains to one of her friends in a dystopian version of Metro Los Angeles set in 2025, survivors need to study up and strategize if they are to thrive in the post-apocalyptic era described in *Parable of the Sower*:

"We can get ready. That's what we've got to do now. Get ready for what's going to happen, get ready to survive it, get ready to make life afterward. Get focused on arranging to survive so that we can do more than just get batted around by crazy people, desperate people, thugs, and leaders who don't know what they're doing!" (Butler 1993: p. 55).

When Lauren Olamina's friend becomes dubious that studying what is in the vestiges of libraries might help them survive, Lauren responds by challenging her:

"'Read this.' I handed her one of the plant books. This one was about the California Indians, the plants they used, and how they used them—an interesting and entertaining little book . . . Take notes . . . You'll remember better if you do."

While science fiction such as this was once dismissed as second-class literature by many scholars, Octavia Butler is just one of many "cli-fi" (climate change science fiction) and dystopian drama writers whose artistry and morality cannot be so easily disparaged. The same is true with works such as *Oryx and Crake* by Margaret Atwood (2003); *Back to the Garden* by Clara Hume (2012), *The Road* by Cormac McCarthy (2006), *The Dispossessed* by Ursula Le Guin (1974), *Far North* by Marcel Theroux (2010), and even Barbara Kingsolver's (2012) work of speculative fiction that verges on cli-fi, *Flight Behavior*. While not all of these works are set in a dystopian future, Rebecca Tuhis-Dubrow (2013) correctly identifies their commonality:

"Most of the authors, seek, at least in part, to warn, translating graphs and scientific jargon into experience and emotion. . . . They refashion myths for our age, appropriating time-honored narratives to accord with our knowledge and our fears. Climate change is unprecedented and extraordinary, forcing us to rethink our place in the world."

PARALLEL MOTIONS

Both ethnobiology and science fiction have increasingly focused on climate change. In 2005 Robert Macfarlane lamented the lack of engagement between writers and climate change. Ten years later this is clearly not the case and whole sub-genres such as cli-fi have emerged. The trend has been similar in environmental anthropology and ethnobiology. Ten years ago the literature was scant; today climate change is a central focus of both natural and social sciences (e.g. Wolverton et al. 2014, Veteto and Carlson 2014, Nabhan 2013, Crate 2011, Friese et al. 2011, Crate and Nuttall 2009, Roncoli et al. 2009). For serious minded ethnobiologists—focusing on issues such as cultural preservation and revival, traditional ecological knowledge, seed conservation strategies in the face of climatic catastrophes and war, tribal sovereignty, human adaptation, and a host of other important quandaries—why should an engagement with speculative fiction hold any promise for their work?

Looking over the history of science fiction writing, one cannot cease to be amazed with the enormous predictive power it has shown. In his 1888 novel *Looking Backward*, Edward Bellamy wrote about the use of credit cards sixty-two years before they became reality. AT&T introduced videoconferencing at the 1964 World's Fair in New York, but science fiction writers had been discussing it since Hugo Gernsback's story *Ralph 124c41+*, which was first published in 1911. In *From the Earth to the Moon*, written in 1865, Jules Verne (remarkably) forecasted astronauts launching from Florida in aluminum capsules and fairly accurately calculated the amount of force it would take to propel them out of the earth's atmosphere, over one hundred years before the event actually took place. So many of Aldous Huxley's future imaginings from his 1931 dystopia *Brave New World* have come to pass, at least in part, from antidepressants and genetic engineering, to mass consumerism and sexual promiscuity, that he might be widely considered a seer or prophet if he was born into a different culture. The Internet was foreshadowed by Mark Twain's telelectroscope, which allowed for global communication and social networking in his 1898 short sci-fi short story *From the 'London Times' of 1904.*

Given the remarkable propensity for projecting future events that science fiction writing has shown, cli-fi novels might bear more careful consideration from ethnobiological science, much as we put careful consideration into the oral histories and traditions of our indigenous interlocutors. Cli-fi writers might properly be looked at as myth-builders of our postmodern age.

For example, Kim Stanley Robinson's *Science in the Capital* "hard" cli-fi (science fiction writing characterized by scientific accuracy and technical detail) trilogy shows an astute capacity for predictive power, understanding and integration of contemporary climate science, policy recommendations, and sociocultural change. On the heels of a Hurricane Katrina–like flooding of Washington, DC (published a year before Katrina struck New Orleans; an aspect of the flood was also a fictive 'Tropical Storm Sandy' that bore some resemblance to 2012's devastating Hurricane Sandy), Robinson's protagonists, mostly a group of scientists working for the National Science Foundation, rearrange the entire mission of NSF to study climate change, research mitigation strategies, and employ massive measures to stave off climate disaster for humanity. Along the way they are able to re-start the stalled Gulf Stream and North Atlantic Drift by coordinating a massive international effort to re-salinize the ocean to offset the massive influx of fresh water from melting glaciers, pump rising ocean water into dry lake beds in deserts and drought-stricken regions and back onto melting glaciers at the poles to re-freeze, help elect a U.S. president on a climate change ticket who believes "a scientifically informed government should lead the way in the invention of a culture which is sustained perpetually" (permaculture—mentioned throughout the whole series), present and employ a workable plan for transitioning the United States to sustainable energy sources, and strike a historic, cooperative treaty with China where the United States uses its technical expertise and resources (in exchange for debt relief) to help China immediately transition away from coal and other dirty energy technologies in the face of extreme environmental collapse. Robinson's (2004, 2005, 2007) understanding of climate change is top-notch throughout (relying on careful readings of top climate change scientists, such as the IPCC [2007]) and he captures prominent and more radical environmental social trends such as eco-Buddhism, permaculture, feral foraging, communalism, freeganism, and squatting in his writings. Robinson's central concept of *abrupt climate change* warns that devastating climate change may happen much quicker, with sudden onset, than most scientists are willing to consider.

Other cli-fi writers are similarly suggestive in their observations and prescriptions. Do Atwood's God's Gardeners in *Oryx and Crake* and *Year of the*

Flood (2010), using rooftop gardens as a way to feed themselves and provide defensive positioning against gangs and marauders, a spiritual path, and as resistances against the all-powerful Corporations, suggest a potential model for the future of urban gardening? Does the matriarchal motorcycle gang in 2015's dystopian box-office hit *Mad Max: Fury Road* provide any clues to the roles ecofeminist seed keepers may play in protecting the cultural heritage of garden seeds after a nuclear holocaust? Will marginal, rural, out-of-the-way places like the Siberian tundra in Theroux's *Far North* be more hospitable for humans than lawless cities in a post-collapse, climate change world? These (among many others) are questions that are currently being asked by cli-fi writers, which may be of interest to engaged ethnobiologists as well.

POTENTIAL ENGAGEMENTS

How, then, can ethnobiologists contribute more broadly to helping cultures that still survive on this earth to rethink their places in the world? We can preliminarily provide twelve considerations, which may help survivors of any apocalypse guide their future selection of foods, medicines, and utilitarian plant and animal resources:

1. While there remains some value in reading general references such as Balls (1972)—the interesting and entertaining book on edible California plants likely alluded to in Butler (1993), the more pertinent guides are those that specifically focus on famine foods, such as Minnis' work (1991). Interestingly, Minnis points to the importance of cultural rituals and myths in transmitting knowledge about famine foods between periods of drought, war, or unrest.

2. Secondly, it is important to recognize that climate change, use of toxins, and anthropogenic disturbances to land and water are dramatically affecting the distribution and abundance of historically used edible and medicinal plants, so that some have become locally extirpated or are verging on global extinction.

3. Not only are potentially important wild food plants and animals declining to the point of scarcity, but their pollinators have also become increasingly scarce, leading to possible "food web collapse" (Dobson et al 2009).

4. Chemical, microbial, and thermal contamination of water will likely render some formerly edible fish, shellfish, and aquatic plants inedible, toxic, or hazardous.

5. As Tuhus-Dubrow (2013) aptly emphasized, adequately detailed knowledge of plant and animal usage as foods and medicines is lacking in most written records, so that appropriate dosages or preparation techniques may be unexplained: "It's the accumulated knowledge of millennia that verges on extinction" in many cases, not the wholesale disappearance of the plants and animals themselves.

6. Since 1998, at least twelve herbicide-tolerant weeds have begun to dominate anthropogenic landscapes in North America and elsewhere. Some of these weeds, such as Palmer's amaranth (*Amaranthus palmeri*), common waterhemp (*Amaranthus rudis*), Italian ryegrass (*Lolium multiflorum*), jungle grass (*Echinocloa colona*) and Indian goosegrass (*Eleusine indica*), have long been harvested for food, fuel, or fiber by many cultures around the world. These now ubiquitous agrestals and ruderals are likely to remain prevalent in a post-apocalyptic world.

7. Catastrophic events and ocean rising will likely displace many indigenous (as well as other) cultures, exposing them to unfamiliar habitats and novel ecosystems.

8. There will likely be a greater focus on perennial multipurpose (food and medicinal) plants in the future (Jackson 1980). Fossil fuel and water-intensive monoculture will become increasing vulnerable, and people will revert to using readily available foods and medicines from wild, semi-wild, and managed habitats near their homes or encampments. Perennial plants can survive and reproduce without nearly as much human intervention as annuals. However, human semi-management and incipient domestication has allowed for long-term, fairly intensive production and movement of plant resources that have supported or partially supported complex indigenous societies, such as in the Pacific Northwest of the United States and Canada (Turner et al. 2011, Turner 2005, Peacock and Turner 2000, Turner and Kuhnlein 1983). Alternative agriculture approaches including permaculture (Veteto and Lockyer 2008, Holmgren 2002), natural farming (Fukuoka 2009, 1985), and perennial polyculture (Jackson 2011, 1980) suggest future possibilities and imaginings of interest to ethnobiologists, as models for cli-fi writers, and as survival tools for humankind.

9. The permaculture principle of *Use Edges and Value the Marginal* (Holmgren 2002) will be increasingly instructive, both as model and metaphor. As Turner et al. (2003) have convincingly argued, Indigenous Peoples are drawn to areas having a high incidence of ecological edges (transition zones between two relatively distinct ecosystems that contain higher biodiversity levels) and they actively create and maintain edges; providing themselves with more cultural capital, flexibility, and resilience—all variables of great importance when anticipating potential climate change adaptation. Metaphorically, both ethnobiology

and cli-fi are at the edges of disciplines and genres—ethnobiology a combination of social and natural sciences and cli-fi at the forefront of pushing science fiction into increased interaction with climate science—and the fruitful ground they are exploring can arguably be combined to provide imaginative spaces brimming with more diverse possibilities.

10. Increased teaching of the patterns (family) method of plant identification (e.g. Elpel 2013, Botany Every Day 2015). Rather than learning plant species one at a time, if students of botany and ethnobotany can increasingly be taught both how to identify plant families and their general uses, we may promote a necessary return to the everyday integration of a wide diversity of plants in our lives. For example, if students know that any species in the *lamiaceae* (mint) or *brassicaceae* (mustard) families are safe to use as tea, food, or medicine, it can greatly increase their access and use of plant resources across the world. Likewise, if they know certain plant families, such as rununculaceae, are largely poisonous, they can safely avoid toxic plants.

11. Developing a discipline of *integrative ethnobotany*. Both authors have noticed a trend over the past twenty years or so that a lot of the best ethnobotany is taking place outside of the academies in venues such as Traditional Chinese Medicine schools, Western herbalism schools, primitive skills gatherings, permaculture institutes, and through classes given by roving or place-based, largely self-taught, yet highly knowledgeable ethnobotanists. Along with well-known databases of indigenous uses of plants developed by ethnobiologists (e.g. Moerman 1998), there is now a plethora of non-academic literature from diverse ethnobotany traditions. Knowing how plants are used in Chinese Medicine, Tibetan Medicine, Ayurveda, and Appalachian cultural traditions, for example, gives students and practitioners of ethnobotany a wider range of information to use in an integrative, cosmopolitan approach that can increasingly be utilized in many different locales, due to the migration of plants and peoples that has taken place during the globalization process.

12. We need to widen our palates and pharmacopeias in wider and more uncomfortable realms: edible wild mushrooms, fungi, moss, lichen, and ferns, in addition to insects, snakes, feral animals, and road kill. Done responsibly, this can be accomplished as a form of environmental restoration as well. For example, in Texas and south Arkansas, where wild pigs are destroying whole landscapes and disturbing neighborhoods and farms, a nascent feral pig barbecue tradition is just waiting for participants and local-food entrepreneurs. The Chinese, obviously, are pioneers in incorporating a wide range of living organisms in their

traditional and modern diets. If such practices can be done sustainably, they will release pressure from being dependent on relatively few species for our nourishment, and can help train and prepare us for potential dystopian futures.

To adapt to an uncertain climate change future, it is likely that traditional elders, as well as pragmatically applied ethnobiologists with foraging, fishing, hunting, and farming experience will be more highly valued by society than they are today. Indeed, we absolutely need to continue our work documenting and promoting traditional ecological knowledge (TEK), tangibly working at the grassroots level on ecological restoration to build resilience to dampen or mitigate climate change's impact on communities, as well as testifying in Native (First Nations) land and water rights cases.

However, in addition to maintaining our collaborations with cultural storytellers and wisdom keepers, we also see validity in engaging with cli-fi writers in attempts to coauthor new ethnobiologically oriented speculative fiction ourselves. Today, the term "translation science" refers to novel approaches to innovatively communicating the facts and values of science to diverse constituencies, cultures, professions, and age groups without "dumbing down" or omitting essential details. It may be time for ethnobiologists to invite cli-fi, sci-fi, and other speculative fiction writers and filmmakers into collaborative projects and think tanks. Films such as *Mad Max*, *Maze Runner*, *Hunger Games*, *Legend*, and *The Road* reach far more hearts and minds than ethnobiologists can currently hope to do. Is it not time for ethnobiologists to help renew and reshape the stories and subsistence practices that may be vital to our survival in the future? Our cultures may depend upon it. As the acclaimed environmental scientist Tim Flannery (2010: p. xiv) has asked us to consider,

"What lies on the other side? Where will evolution take us? Intelligent Earth—or *The Road*?"

LITERATURE CITED

Atwood, M. 2003. Oryx and Crake. New York: Random House/Anchor Books.
———. 2010. Year of the Flood. New York: Random House/Anchor Books.
Balls, E. K. 1972. Early Uses of California Plants. Berkeley CA: University of California Press.

Botany Every Day. 2015. Available at: http://www.botanyeveryday.com/

Butler, O. E. 1993. Parable of the Sower. New York: Grand Central Publishing/ Hachette Book Group.

Crate, S. A. 2011. Climate and culture: Anthropology in the era of contemporary climate change. Annual Review of Anthropology 40:175–94.

Crate, S.A., and M. Nuttall. 2009. Anthropology and Climate Change: From Encounters to Actions. Walnut Creek, CA: Left Coast Press.

Dobson, A., S. Allesina, K. Laffety and M. Pascual. 2009. The assembly, collapse and restoration of food webs. Philosophical Transactions of the Royal Society of Biology 364:1803–6.

Elpel, T. J. Botany in a Day: The Patterns Method of Plant Identification. Pony, Montana: HOPS Press LLC.

Flannery, T. 2010. Here on Earth: A Natural History of the Planet. Melbourne, Australia: Text Publishing.

Friese, K. M., K. Kraft, and G. P. Nabhan. 2011. Chasing Chiles: Hot Spots along the Pepper Trail. White River Junction, VT: Chelsea Green Publishing.

Fukuoka, M. 1985. The Natural Way of Farming: The Theory and Practice of Green Philosophy. Japan Productions.

———. 2009. The One-Straw Revolution: An Introduction to Natural Farming. New York: NYRB Classics.

Holmgren, D. 2002. Permaculture: Principles and Pathways Beyond Sustainability. Hepburn, Australia: Holmgren Design Services.

Hume, C. 2012. Back to the Garden. Coquitlam, B.C.: Moon Willow Press.

IPCC (Intergovernmental Panel on Climate Change). 2007. Summary for Policy-makers. In Climate Change 2007: The Physical Science Basis. Contribution of Working Group I to the Fourth Assessment Report of the Intergovernmental Panel on Climate Change. Edited by S. Solomon, D. Qin, M. Manning, Z. Chen, M. Marquis, K. B. Averyt, M.Tignor and H. L. Miller, pages 1–18. Cambridge University Press, Cambridge, UK, and New York, NY.

Jackson, W. 1980. New Roots for Agriculture. Omaha: University of Nebraska Press.

———. 2011. Consulting the Genius of Place: An Ecological Approach to a New Agriculture. Berkeley, CA: Counterpoint.

Kingsolver, B. 2012. Flight Behavior. New York: Harper.

LeGuin, U. K. 1974. The Dispossessed. New York: Harper Perennial.

Lockyer, J. and J. R. Veteto. Environmental Anthropology Engaging Ecotopia: Biore-gionalism, Permaculture, and Ecovillages. New York and London: Berghahn Books.

Lord, K. 2013. The Best of All Possible Worlds. New York: Del Rey/Ballantine Books.

McCarthy, C. 2006. The Road. New York: Random House/Vintage Books.

Minnis, P. 1991. Famine foods of the Northern American borderlands in historical context. Journal of Ethnobiology 11(2): 231–237.

Moerman, D. E. 1998. Native American Ethnobotany. Portland, OR: Timber Press.

Nabhan, Gary Paul. 2013. Growing Food in a Hotter, Drier Land: Lessons From Desert Farmers on Adapting to Climate Uncertainty. White River Junction, VT: Clelsea Green Publishing.

Peacock, S. L. and N. J. Turner. 2000. "'Just like a garden': Traditional resource management and biodiversity conservation on the Interior Plateau of British Columbia." Pp. 133–79. in P. E. Minnis and W. J. Elisens (eds.), Biodiversity and Native America. Norman: University of Oklahoma Press.

Peluso, N. L, and M. Watts, eds. 2001. Violent Environments. Ithaca, NY: Cornell University Press.

Rabkin, E.S., M. H. Greenberg and J. D. Olander.1983. No Place Else: Explorations in Dystopian Fiction. Carbondale, IL: Southern Illinois University Press.

Robinson, Kim Stanley. 2004. Forty Signs of Rain. New York, NY: Bantam Dell.

———. 2005. Fifty Degrees Below. New York, NY: Bantam Dell.

———. 2007. Sixty Days and Counting. New York, NY: Bantam Dell.

Roncoli, C., T. A. Crane, B. Orlove. 2009. "Fielding climate change in cultural anthropology." Pp. 87–115 in S. A. Crate and M. Nutall (eds.), Anthropology and Climate Change: From Encounters to Actions. Walnut Creek, CA: Left Coast Press.

Theroux, M. 2010. Far North. New York: Picador.

Tuhis-Dubrow, R. 2013. Cli-Fi: Birth of a genre. Dissent. www.dissentmagazine .org. Summer edition.

Turner, N. J. 2005. The Earth's Blanket: Traditional Teachings for Sustainable Living. Seattle: University of Washington Press.

Turner N. J. and H. V. Kuhnlein. 1983. Camas (Camassia spp.) and rice root (Fritillaria spp.): Two liliaceous 'root' foods of the Northwest Coast Indians. Ecology of Food and Nutrition 13(4):199–219.

Turner, N.J., I. J. Davidson-Hunt and M. O'Flaherty. 2003. Living on the edge: Ecological and cultural edges as sources of diversity for socio-ecological resilience. Human Ecology 31(3):439–61.

Turner, N. J. L. J. Lukasz, P. Migliorini, A. Pieroni, A. L. Dreon, L. E. Sacchetti, M. G. Paoletti. 2011. Edible and tended wild plants, traditional ecological knowledge, and agroecology. Critical Reviews in Plant Sciences 30(1–2):198–225.

Veteto, J. R. and J. Lockyer. 2008. Environmental anthropology engaging permaculture: Moving theory and practice toward sustainability. Culture and Agriculture 30(1–2):47–58.

Veteto, J. R. and S. B. Carlson. 2014. Climate change and apple diversity: Local perceptions from Appalachian North Carolina. Journal of Ethnobiology 34(3):359–82.

Weisman, Alan. 2007. The World Without Us. New York: St. Martin's/Thomas Dunne Books.

Wolverton, S., K. J. Chambers and J. R. Veteto. 2014. Climate change and ethnobiology. Journal of Ethnobiology 34(3):273–75.

AFTERWORD

Ethnobiology in Metamorphosis

I.

A S YOU WILL HAVE SURMISED by the timbre, tone, and content of the preceding essays, many exciting innovations are emerging in ethnobiology today, but there is still a sense that the work of many ethnobiologists around the world remains undervalued by society at large. That is why my colleagues and I entitled one chapter "Ethnobiology in Crisis." The use of a term as strong as "crisis" is not meant to disparage any researcher's current or past work; instead, it is meant to "raise the heat and rekindle the fire." Ethnobiology matters, but it will only continue to matter to society at large if it takes on new challenges, integrates new and exciting methodologies, and addresses the most pressing problems humanity faces in terms of its cultural relationships with ecological diversity. The following "call to arms" briefly revisits where we have come from, but then lays out a rough road map of where we may want to go. It is not prescriptive as much as it is suggestive, placing a few cairns out along the trails to send us in the appropriate direction.

We can see from these modest innovations and advances that ethnobiology is undergoing a period of blessed unrest. In the first section of this book, we have sketched out hypotheses that may build into a general theory of biocomplexity. In the second section, we demonstrate through case studies how a more nuanced understanding of the links between cultural diversity and ecological diversity may help us solve some of the world's most pressing problems. In the third section, we discuss the ways our communication of ethnobiology must change in timbre and tone to attract and sustain a broad and informed audience.

Classical ethnobiological monographs and museum exhibits will likely hold a special place in the hearts and minds of many readers and observers for many years to come. Nevertheless, our interdiscipline has constantly been redefining itself and its means of communication as the values of its participating cultures become more clearly and vividly expressed.

Moreover, it remains a field dedicated to recognizing and celebrating the knowledge, practices, and values of some of the most distinctive cultures remaining among cultural communities still dwelling deeply in some of the most memorable landscapes on this planet. It is not merely their "ancient" knowledge and values that matter to most of us as it is the living, breathing dynamism of enduring peoples themselves.

Just as Wilson and Kellert (1993) have explored an intangible sense of *biophilia* palpably felt in the wild world that has invigorated the careers of many great naturalists, there are some among us who are attempting to circumscribe, or at least identify, an *ethnobiophilia* that we sense we have had the good fortune to have experienced. It is a luminous sense of the biocultural complexity embedded in the continuity between nature and culture—however we wish to construct those domains—that inspires us as we stand in awe of the many expressions of life on earth. Ethnobiophilia also reshapes our consciousness as we explore what Wade Davis (2002) has called the *ethnosphere*, a domain of cultural facets on earth that includes "all thoughts, dreams, ideas, beliefs, myths, intuitions, and inspirations brought into being by the human imagination since the dawn of consciousness."

Many who call themselves ethnobiologists have had the honor, privilege, and blessing to explore the *ethnobiosphere* through a particular kind of ecotone: the creative tension zone between indigenous sciences and Western science. After entering into a predictable process of initial disorientation that may wreak havoc with our previous assumptions, we humbly find that many of our perceptions of human interactions with the other-than-human world are reoriented; in some cases, perhaps, our thought processes have been rewired as well.

Particularly through cross-cultural dialogues, many of us have not only had to suspend some of our long-held beliefs about how the world works, but have gone through a kind of social metamorphosis that begins to rupture our ethnocentricity. Ironically, such a journey may expose us more to both human suffering and human joy. While all ethnobiological field studies do not necessarily change the world for the better, nearly every ethnobiologist that I know feels deeply changed by her or his exposure to the cusp of the wave where nature and culture surge together, meld, crash, or collide.

And yet, there is no single pathway into the *ethnobiosphere*, nor is there any single entry point into the interdiscipline of ethnobiology. As a field of inquiry that formally took shape a little more than a century ago, ethnobiology is not yet characterized by a stable set of theories, methodologies, field practices, beliefs, and values. At this moment in time, ethnobiology appears to be extremely absorbent and mutable, borrowing ideas from the many other disciplines and social movements with which it interacts. That has been both its blessing and its curse; it has been eclectic and integrative, but at the same time, it has so often borrowed from other fields that it has not yet fully forged its own distinctive identity, unifying theory, or modus operandi.

II.

Of course, such instability is not too surprising, given that it has emerged over barely more than the century of human history; ironically, humanity has perhaps suffered more disruptive demographic, technological, and militaristic change over that one particular century than it has over the entire history of our species. From the very start, it has been immersed in a violent and cathartically changing world, one where both species and cultures have been put at great risk. It is no wonder that such concern for the loss of species, languages, knowledge, skills, human rights, and lives has emerged so poignantly since World War I. We have far too belatedly recognized the immense value of these intangible legacies, which portions of our globally industrialized society still seem to ignore, dismiss, or vilify. Too often ethnobiologists sense that they are living in the damaged domain that ecologist Aldo Leopold (1949) so deftly described. "One of the penalties of an ecological education," he wrote, "is that one lives alone in a world of wounds."

We must concede that both *placed-based* "indigenous" and *displaced* "diaspora" are facing risks and stresses on an unprecedented scale, as are the coastlines, tidewaters, mountain ranges, fertile valleys, farmscapes, fishing villages, and refugee camps they inhabit. So let me be clear: *an ethnobiology for the future cannot function merely as a historic science fraught with nostalgia or romanticism.* It must be forward looking and intent on not merely documenting, but supporting, safeguarding, restoring, or advancing a broad breadth of cultural interactions with the novel ecosystems that will characterize the Anthropocene. Some of these interactions will be found within imperiled, depleted, or dystopian environments, while others will continue to harbor traditional practices that will surely adapt and morph according to their own dynamics in response to the political ecological milieu within which they are embedded.

To work in *better service* to the dynamic peoples, plants, animals, and places to which the interdiscipline has given its attention over the last century or so, some of our colleagues have consciously begun to *deconstruct* our own legacy of being ethnobiologists. That is merely one of many necessary steps we will need to take if we are to *reconstruct* and restore our interdiscipline to its proper place among the arts and sciences. While deconstruction can sometimes seem sense-less, harshly critical, or even painful to some participants in a discipline, it is a necessary descent before our community of scholars, activists, or plain citizens can redirect our trajectory to carry us where we need to go. As environmental writer Bill Kittredge (1996) once wrote, "What we need in our West is another kind of story . . . in which we can find some continuity, taking care in the midst of useful and significant lives."

Some elements of the old story of ethnobiology may now be fading, if not becoming altogether obsolete. So forgive me for a digression as to why that may be true, and what indications there are that the profession of ethnobiologists may unfortunately be declining in influence or relevance, before I attempt to capture elements of our new collective story.

III.

Given the velocity and ferocity of loss all around us, does ethnobiology have much of a future? I often wonder about a paradox that regularly impacts those of us who try to practice the art and science of ethnobiological inquiry, and I would not be surprised if you, too, have recognized that very same paradox. There is a strong feeling among field researchers, scholarly writers, and applied practitioners that ethnobiological research, applications, and teaching in Can-ada, the United States, and Mexico have become more sophisticated, creative, mature, and professional than ever before. And yet the paradox is this: *Such a view is shared by only a small percentage of scholars, biocultural conservation activ-ists, indigenous leaders, and other constituencies within society at large.*

With few notable and laudatory exceptions, our cohorts of ethnobio-logical practitioners have often been marginalized in their own universities and other institutions relative to the recognition given to other comparable interdisciplines. Simply compare ethnobiology's current status with that of bio-technology, conservation biology, political ecology, transformational generative grammar, critical studies, or integrative health sciences, and you will see what I mean. Since the founding of the Society for Ethnobiology in the late 1970s, one can even wonder whether active members of the society have had much substantive impact on the trajectory of the natural and cultural sciences writ large, on the structure of our own scholarly institutions, or on society as a whole.

This, my friends, was not always true for those who were interested in the same questions, issues, and topics that many of us remain interested in today. For decades before the term *ethnobiology* was even coined, well-regarded American scholars of lasting influence—from Bernardino de Sahagún, Hernando Ruiz de Alarcón, Miguel del Barco, Alexander Ross, Thomas Jefferson, John and William Bartram, to Merriweather Lewis and William Clark, Edward Stewart Sturtevant, and Henry David Thoreau—were interested in many of the same relationships among indigenous cultures, plants, and animals as we are today.

These *proto-ethnobiologists*—as well as many indigenous scholars, feminist scholars, and backwoods artisans who practiced the arts and sciences embedded in ethnobiology without being encouraged to publish their work—had wide-spread public appeal and lasting influence in North America. This influence even continued up through the era of ubiquitous "nature study" at the turn from the nineteenth to the twentieth century. These pursuits were not in any way marginalized in scholarly circles nor from the cultural creatives in society at large. Many citizens of all cultures were intensely interested in the cultural knowledges and uses of the natural world around them.

Even after ethnobotany was named by John W. Harshberger in 1896 and ethnobiology was later defined as a sort of synthetic interdiscipline, they held respectable levels of status among the natural and cultural sciences of the Americas. From Liberty Hyde Bailey, Maximino Martinez, and Francisco Paso y Troncoso, to Carl Sauer, Melvin Gilmore, and Edgar Anderson, on to Carobeth Laird, John Harrington, William McGee, Richard Evans Schultes, Claude Levi-Strauss, Paul Sears, Charles Heiser, Scotty MacNeish, and Efrain Hernandez Xolocotzli, ethnobiologists were highly regarded among scientists in other related disciplines.

And yet, something began to happen to the status of ethnobiologists around the very time that the Society of Ethnobiology was founded when some of us gathered in Prescott, Arizona, in 1977. Many of the pioneering interdisciplinary scholars who trained the founders of the Society of Ethnobiology have rightfully become honored members of the National Academy of Sciences or the Royal Academies in their own country: Harold Conklin, Peter Raven, Patty Jo Watson, H. E. Wright, Robert McAdams, Karl Butzer, Kent Flannery, Colin Renfrew, or B. L. Turner, to name a few. Since that time, however, only four esteemed members of our Society who regularly contribute to the ("American") *Journal of Ethnobiology* and attend the Society's conferences—Brent Berlin, Harriet Kuhnlein, Nancy Turner, and Elizabeth Wing—have become members of the U.S. National Academy of Sciences, the Royal Order, or the Royal Society of Canada.

What's more, the great graduate programs in ethnobiology and economic botany that trained field practitioners and scholars over several decades—Harvard, University of Michigan, University of California at Berkeley, Indiana University, University of Arizona, and University of Texas at Austin—hardly offer graduate courses by more than two professors left on campus, and those survivors are quickly aging. Except for the University of Hawai'i, Washington State University, University of California at Davis or Riverside, University of Florida, and Texas A&M University, U.S. land-grant universities have virtually abandoned their legacies in ethnobiology.

It is more likely you'll find vitality in ethnobiology programs at the Native American–oriented colleges such as Haskell Indian Nations University, Kauai Community College, Northwest Indian College, Sitting Bull College, or Kumeyaay Community College, or at experimental liberal arts colleges such as Evergreen College, Prescott College, and Frostburg State University. Elsewhere in the world, Kent in the U.K.; McGill, Simon Fraser, University of British Columbia, and University of Victoria in Canada; Instituto Tecnologico del Valle de Oaxaca, Centro de Investigacion Científica de Yucatán, and UNAM in Mexico have far stronger commitments to ethnobiology than what we see at larger universities in the United States.

That downawrd spiral strikes me as wasteful, if not outright pathetic and perilous. Despite enormously sophisticated and creative interdisciplinary work practices by many long-term participants in the Society for Ethnobiology, we see three prevailing trends:

1. its numbers of members have never reached the thousands,
2. its status among the sciences is not necessarily regarded as highly as we might wish, and
3. its potential impact on science policy and practice has hardly been achieved to the degree that it should have.

The irony of this predicament is that *ethnobiology's many expressions* in general and horticultural as well as medicinal ethnobotany in particular *have never been more widely appreciated in the popular media*. Films such as Mark Plotkin's *Shaman's Apprentice*, Vandana Shiva's *The Giver of Seeds*, Wade Davis's *One River*, Cary Fowler's *Seeds of Time*, and Jared Diamond's *Guns, Germs and Steel* have reached tens of millions of viewers and made celebrities out of these activists, writers, and scholars, despite the fact that they have never engaged with the Society of Ethnobiology.

Today, the best known spokespersons on global issues of natural and cultural diversity hardly ever cite our most innovative practitioners of ethnobiological scholarship. It is as if these "celebrity ethnobiologists" have somehow absorbed the scholarship of our society by astral projection into our meetings rather than by direct, tangible cultural diffusion. While many of them are in fact grateful for the guidance of their more scholarly colleagues and mentors, they do not necessarily offer to promote the Society's work to young and inspired enthusiasts of "folk botany" in the same manner that Bruce Springsteen has honored and promoted the foundational work of Alan Lomax, Woody Guthrie, and Leadbelly in folk music.

We are left with a tragedy as much as an irony: while the lay public in North America and Europe currently have an insatiable appetite for many things ethnobiological, they do not quench their thirst directly through the scholarship that has emerged out of our society. Worse yet, many of these aficionados probably do not realize that the [North American] Society of Ethnobiology and its international and Latin American counterparts even exist. If we are not even on their screen, how do they come to support our endeavors to help our interdiscipline mature, deepen, and grow? How can we more fully engage these enthusiasts with the wonder, excitement, and humility we feel whenever we immerse ourselves in the biocultural complexity of *ethnobiosphere*?

IV.

If we try to reconstruct a more creative, dynamic, resilient, and empowering ethnobiology that is truly in service to cultural and biological diversity, what would it look like? Most of us agree that it would be far more culturally diverse, dynamically critical in its values, ethics, and methodologies, and in greater service to the communities with which it interacts. It would also have a unifying theory or paradigm—perhaps one that weaves together insights from diverse sources to more satisfactorily explain the complex dynamics among biodiversity and cultural diversity, or human cognition and the natural world.

But it would also have to be a theory that seems infectiously inspiring, provocative, and solutions-seeking. Getting a broader range of constituencies that excite us would certainly be in the cards. And should we not advance the names of our U.S., Canadian, and Mexican innovators to their nations' national academies and other positions of honor and innovation internationally? Is it not a blessing to all of us when one of our kind as deserving as Nancy Turner gains recognition for her work from the Slow Foundation for Biodiversity or the Royal Order of Canada? Are we merely about publications and meetings, or are we about promoting an expanded, elevated, and less marginalized role for ethnobiology, its ethics, and its sense of wonder in our society as a whole?

V.

It is time for us to collectively redefine ethnobiology not as a historic ("retrodictive") science with a narrow, quickly aging populace reminiscent of the Shakers, but as a more inclusive, dynamic, ethnically diverse, and inspiring community of activist-scholars, grassroots practitioners involved in predictive science and ethics.

Among the options we need to consider taking to get back on track are the following:

1. Remind *all* scientists that ethnosciences like ethnobiology are "the oldest sciences" extant on earth, and are needed complements to so-called Western science (which has already become multicultural, not just *Western*); in fact, Western science is increasingly "infiltrated" or reshaped by students from all languages, cultures, and continents.

2. Recast ethnobiology as an integrative, dynamic interdiscipline with its own distinctive and distinguished set of theories that link biodiversity and cultural diversity, synthesizing data from other disciplines into something altogether new, compelling, and overarching.

3. Create cross-college programs in ethnobiology at the major state and private universities throughout the Americas and the world in ways that demonstrate it is not a poor stepchild or sub-discipline of any single social science or natural science.

4. Train and promote indigenous scholars to lead interdisciplinary teams to assist their own cultures on how to apply ethnoscientific advances to their own natural resource management, food sovereignty, cultural preservation, language restoration, and public health issues.

5. Decolonize ethnobiology's ideologies, methodologies, forms of expression, ethics, and other values.

6. Demonstrate ethnobiology's relevance as a predictive science in addressing climate change, human rights, language loss, and other pressing societal issues.

7. Request that academies of science, as well as science and conservation foundations recruit, include, and honor leading indigenous and nonnative scholars in ethnobiology to move beyond the paradigm of "Western science."

8. Request that celebrity activists, film stars, and best-selling authors who draw upon ethnobiology as an inspiration and informational source engage in and give something back to the Society of Ethnobiology and the interdiscipline at large.

9. Communicate through the innovations in translational science that better matches media and message with audience, engaging in film, social media, oral storytelling, and festival.

10. Attract the most inquisitive students among every culture we live and work among to experience the thrills and spills of *ethnobiophilia*!

LITERATURE CITED

Davis, W. 2002. *Light at the Edge of the World: A Journey through the Realm of Vanishing Cultures.* Vancouver: Douglas and McIntyre.

Kellert, S. L., and E. O. Wilson, eds. 1993. *The Biophilia Hypothesis.* Washington, DC: Island Press.

Kittredge, W. 1996. *Who Owns the West?* New York: Mercury House.

Leopold, A. 1949. *A Sand County Almanac and Other Writings on Ecology and Conservation.* New York: Oxford University Press.

CONTRIBUTORS

Cecil H. Brown is a linguistic anthropologist with interests in ethnobiology, historical linguistics, and Native American languages. He is the author of numerous books and papers outlining the principles of ethnobiological classification and the use of linguistic data in discerning the origin of domesticated crops.

Kimberlee Chambers, PhD, is the sustainability manager at Organically Grown Company. She works with employees throughout OGC, as well as growers, customers, and industry partners, on projects that advance progress toward OGC's long-term sustainability goals—working toward a healthier, ecologically sound, and socially just food system. Kimberlee's roots in food and agriculture run deep—she grew up on a family farm in Ontario, Canada, and she has conducted multiple applied agricultural research projects with farmers in the United States, Canada, and Mexico while earning her doctorate and master's degress in agroecology and ethnobiology from University of California, Davis, and the University of Victoria, British Columbia.

Geo Coppens d'Eckenbrugge is an economic botanist well-known in Latin America, Europe, and Africa for his studies of the origins and diversity of tropical fruits, including passion fruits.

Paul Gepts's research and teaching program at the University of California, Davis, focuses on crop biodiversity and genetic resources. His many books and scientific articles elucidate the evolutionary processes that shape the diversity of crops and their wild progenitors, with a focus on beans and cowpea, as well as Mesoamerican domesticates. To achieve this goal, he is combining field and laboratory approaches that span the gamut from field explorations in Latin America to marker analyses and genomics. Dr. Gepts is also interested in investigating the consequences of the evolutionary patterns for the breeding of new germ plasm or cultivars.

Rafael de Grenade is an associate research social scientist at the University of Arizona's Udall Center for Studies in Public Policy. She conducts research on agrobiodiversity and food security in the arid Americas. Rafael lives with her family on a small farm and works on local and international food security in her life, teaching, and research.

Robert J. Hijmans is a professor of environmental science and policy at the University of California, Davis. He studies the geography of agricultural development and has a strong interest in the role of agricultural biodiversity in shaping early, current, and future agriculture and human well-being.

Tony Joe is a member of the Dine who has worked as a supervisory anthropologist with the Navajo Nation Historic Preservation Office. He received his graduate degree in anthropology from Northern Arizona University, where he worked for the Center for Sustainable Environments on both field projects and documentation of native-language revival efforts. He is co-author of a chapter on "Assessing Levels of Biocultural Diversity on the Colorado Plateau" in *Safeguarding the Uniqueness of the Colorado Plateau* (Northern Arizona University Press, 2003).

Kraig H. Kraft is an agroecologist and writer based in Managua, Nicaragua, who works for Catholic Relief Services. He completed his PhD on the origins and diversity of wild and domesticated chile peppers at the University of California, Davis. Kraft is the author of a popular blog titled *Chasing Chiles*, and has written for several regional magazines, including *Edible Sacramento*, as well as technical journals. He is currently working on a coffee sustainability project in Central America. He is the author of *Chasing Chiles: Hot Spots along the Pepper Trail*, along with Gary Paul Nabhan and Kurt Michael Friese.

Dana Lepofsky is a professor of archaeology at Simon Fraser University. She is interested in the many dimensions of human-environmental interactions, including traditional systems of ancient resource and environmental management and use by Northwest Coast peoples. Her research collaborations cross communities and disciplines, and focus on the role of culturally valued speices and landscapes.

Eike Luedeling is a senior decision analyst at the World Agroforestry Centre in Nairobi, Kenya, and a senior scientist at the Center for Development Research at the University of Bonn, Germany. He holds a PhD in agricultural sciences from the University of Kassel, Germany. Eike's primary research interests are the application of decision analysis methods in research for development, as well as the projection of climate change impacts on agricultural and horticultural systems.

José de Jesús Luna-Ruiz is a professor at the Universidad Autónoma de Aguascalientes and one of the world's experts on cultivar diversity and biogeography of chile peppers.

Dennis Martinez, of mixed Native American/Swedish/Chicano heritage, has been professionally active for forty-six years as an activist, writer, speaker, and community organizer, in a wide range of environmental and Indigenous cultural activities, both at home and abroad, with particular interest in ecocultural restoration of forest and steppe-grassland ecosystems. He was a recipient of several awards for his long-time pioneering work in ecological restoration, as well as an awardee by Ecotrust for Indigenous Conservation Leadership in Pacific North America. He has recently been intensely involved with national and international Indigenous groups in the effects of climate disruption on Indigenous adaptation, cultural survival, and quality wildlife habitat. Dennis has also been a long-time advocate for the survival of traditional ecological knowledge (TEK) and its potential to work in a complementary way in certain field research arenas with Western science.

Alberto Mellado Moreno is of Comcaac (Seri) ancestry and works on conservation and management of marine and desert species through Mexico's CONANP program in the Sea of Cortés. An oceanographer and aquaculturist by training, he was a founding participant in the para-ecologist program of his tribe in the Sea of Cortés and a founder of Cmiique, A.C., a biocultural nonprofit working among the Comcaac on rights to resources, environmental education, and monitoring.

Paul E. Minnis (PhD, University of Michigan) is a professor emeritus of anthropology at the University of Oklahoma. He conducts research on the pre-Hispanic ethnobotany and archaeology of the U.S. Southwest and northern Mexico. He has co-directed research projects on Casas Grandes/Paquimé in northwest Chihuahua beginning in 1989. He is the author or editor of twelve books and numerous articles. He is a past president of the Society of Ethnobiology, treasurer and press editor for the Society for American Archaeology, and co-founder of the Southwest Symposium.

Laura Monti works as a research associate and cultural ecologist with Prescott College and University of Arizona. She works with students, indigenous and local communities, and organizations on initiatives that strengthen socioecological health and biocultural diversity in the U.S. Southwest and northern Mexico region.

A MacArthur Fellow and recipient of a Lifetime Achievement Award from the Society for Conservation Biology, **Gary Paul Nabhan** is the Kellogg Chair in Southwest Borderlands Food and Water Security at the University of Arizona, where he is also a research social scientist at the Southwest Center. He is the author or editor of more than twenty-six books.

Carolyn O'Meara is an assistant research professor in the Seminario de Lenguas Indígenas at the National Autonomous University of Mexico (UNAM). She is a linguist by training, with a particular interest in anthropological linguistics and semantic typology. She has been working on describing and documenting the Seri language (Cmiique Iitom) of Sonora, Mexico, for the last ten years. She is also a co-founder of N-GEN, a collaboration of social and environmental scientists, indigenous activists, and artists in the Sonoran Desert and Gulf of California region.

Eric Perramond is a human-environment geographer and a political ecologist, and holds a joint appointment in both the Environmental and the Southwest Studies programs at Colorado College. Eric's current research projects focus on the water rights adjudication process in New Mexico and its effects on local, regional, and state water governance, as well as research on Mediterranean terroirs.

Patrick Pynes has been a professional organic beekeeper and gardener in the Southwest since 1989. At present, he serves a president of the Northern Arizona Organic Beekeepers' Assocation, a nonprofit organization that works for the health and well-being of honeybees and beekeepers. Dr. Pynes holds a PhD in American studies from the University of New Mexico. He grew up in Mexico, Honduras, and the Panama Canal Zone.

Thomas E. Sheridan is a research anthropologist at the Southwest Center and professor of anthropology in the School of Anthropology at the University of Arizona (UA). Author and editor of numerous works on the Southwest and northern Mexico, he directs the Hopi History Project, a formal collaboration between the UA and the Hopi Tribe.

David Tecklin is a geographer affiliated with the Universidad Austral in Valdivia, Chile, and the University of Arizona. His PhD project analyzed private and public efforts to regulate the use of forests and coastal areas in southern Chile. His earlier work with World Wildlife Fund included an MA thesis on the mahogany frontier in the Bolivian Amazon.

James R. Veteto is an assistant professor of anthropology at Western Carolina University and a member of the Cherokee studies program. His research focuses on agrobiodiversity conservation, climate change, food and culture, social theory, and alternative political ecologies. He directs the Appalachian Institute for Mountain Studies, a permaculture research institute in southern Appalachia.

DeJa Walker received associate degrees in culinary arts and pastry arts at Johnson and Wales University in Denver, Colorado, and an environment studies bachelor of science degree focused on community, sustainability, and biocultural studies from Northern Arizona University in Flagstaff, Arizona. This love for food and ecology led her to attend the University of Gastronomic Sciences in Bra, Italy, which opened the door to work as a food systems researcher with the Renewing Americas Food Traditions alliance and other nonprofits. She then returned to Denver, landing a job teaching baking and pastry arts back at

Johnson and Wales University, and now, after exploring some entrepreneurial opportunities, she is currently monitoring populations of the threatened desert tortoise in the Mojave Desert.

Benjamin T. Wilder has recently joined the faculty of the University of Arizona, where he coordinates U.S.-Mexico research collaborations, including the N-GEN collaborative, which he co-founded. His PhD dissertation, "Historical Biogeography of the Midriff Islands of the Gulf of California, Mexico," was done through the Department of Botany and Plant Sciences, University of California, Riverside. It resulted in a book co-authored with Seri Indian naturalist Humbert Morales and with botanist Richard Felger on the flora of Tiburon Island. He has studied with the preeminent ecologists of western Mexico Exequiel Escurra and Rudolfo Dirzo.

Felice Wyndham, PhD, is an ecological anthropologist, human ecologist, and ethnobiologist currently working with the Ethno-ornithology World Archive project at the University of Oxford. Her ethnographic and landscape education has occurred primarily in Rarámuri and Ayoreo communities in the Sierra Tarahumara of northern Mexico and in the Paraguayan Chaco, respectively.

INDEX

acacia, 233, 236–37

activism, 4–5, 70–71, 73–74, 160

adaptive radiation, 48, 50

agrobiodiversity: best practices for, 194–96; climate change and, 188–89, 192, 194; cravings and, 189; culture and, 189; endangered species and, 192–93; food safety and, 194; food sovereignty and, 194; food supply and, 187; GMOs and, 194; health and, 189; importance of, 186–89; industrial agriculture and, 184–85; issues for, 193–94; livestock and, 192–93; loss of, 186–91; orchards and, 190–92; outsourcing and, 191; patenting and, 194; pollinators and, 194; poultry and, 192–93; restoration of, 184–90, 194–96; seeds and, 189–90, 195

al-adhfar, 267

al-Kathiri, 263

allelochemicals, 54–58

All Taxa Biodiversity Inventory (ATBI), 27, 29

al-shadw, 267

Amazon Conservation Team (formerly Ethnobiology and Conservation Team), 31–32

American Association for the Advancement in Science, 15

American Bison Society, 173

American Chestnut Foundation, 177

American chestnuts (Castanea dentata), 177–80

American Livestock Conservancy, 161, 192–93, 195

ancestral diets: adaptive radiation and, 48; cravings and, 51; critique of, 53–56; dietary variations of, 46, 51, 54–55, 57; farming and, 46; foraging patterns and, 46; human diversity and, 51–52; human evolution and, 50–51; parameters of, 45–46, 53–54; secondary compounds and, 54–58

Anchorage Declaration, 70

Appalachian Regional Reforestation Initiative, 177

Aquaculture Institute (Sonora, Mexico), 171

Arabia Felix, 262–63, 268, 273

archaeology, 20–21, 200–202, 206–7, 223–24

Argumendo, Alejandro, 243, 245

Arizona-Sonora Desert Museum, 146–47, 153

Automated Similarity Judgement Program (ASJP), 200

Barlow, Connie, 237–38

Basso, Keith, 152, 223–24

beardtongue (*Penstemon barbatus* (Cav.) Roth), 89

Berry, Wendell, 19, 170

Berry's Rule, 170

beta diversity, 263

Biocultural Network in Mexico, 32

Biocultural Network of Sonora, 32

biodiversity: endangered species and, 47, 86, 184; habitat restoration, 24–25, 31–32, 88, 162, 167; human diversity and, 51–52, 199–200; linguistic diversity and, 13; loss of, 13, 23, 27, 78, 215–20; of oases, 98; overharvesting and, 157–58; restoration of, 29, 73–74, 84–89, 185–86, 215–20, 281–82; traditional ecological knowledge and, 84–92, 283–84

biscuit-roots (*Lomatium* spp.), 171–72

bison (*Bison bison=Bos bison*) 172–76

Blanco, Guadalupe Lopez, 225–32

boarding schools, 39, 150–51

Buffalo Bird Woman, 67–69, 71

Buffalo Commons, 173

Bureau of Indian Affairs, 88

Bureau of Land Management, 76

caguamas, 226

California condor (*Gymnogyps californianus*), 88, 215–20

California Rare Fruit Explorers, 191

camas (*Camassia camas*), 171–72

Campbell, SueEllen, 23, 259

Center for Sustainable Environments (of NAU), 85, 160–62, 171, 245

chaparral, 218–19

Chelonia mydas, 29

children, 144–45, 153–54

chile pepper (*Capsicum annuum*): archaeology and, 200–202, 206–7; associated plants of, 204; climate and, 204; consensus modeling for, 201, 206–7; dating of, 199, 204–5; distribution of, 205–7; domestication of, 206–7; genetics of, 200–201, 206–7; macroremains of, 199; maize and, 199; microremains of, 208; origins of, 197–98, 207–10; paleobiolinguistics (PBL) and, 205–7; species distribution modeling (SDM) and, 199, 207–10; squash and, 199; varieties of, 198, 206

chinquapin (*Chrysolepis chrysophylla*), 177

cli-fi, 278–84

climate change: agrobiodiversity and, 192, 194, 199; biodiversity loss and, 4; catastrophic events and, 277, 281–82; consequences of, 24, 30–31, 70; dystopian novels and, 280–81; food diversity and, 186, 281–82; food safety and, 281–82; science fiction and, 279; traditional ecological knowledge and, 41, 69, 247; tree crops and, 192; water safety and, 281–82

Cmaam Quiscama Quib Iti Hascama Ihiip, 230–31
Cmiique Iitom, 28, 226
Cochimi-Yuman, 98
Colorado Plateau: biodiversity of, 75, 84–92; cultural diversity of, 75, 80–83, 89; Native Americans and, 84–86; restoration of, 160
Commission for Natural Protected Areas (CONANP), 31–32, 138
Conservation International, 31–32
coprolites, 234, 236, 238
Cousteau Society, 31–32, 171
Crosby, H.W., 99, 104, 216–17
Cultural Conservancy, 161, 172

dah yiitihidaa tsoh, 89
dah yiitihidaa'ts'ooz, 89
Darwin, Charles, 47, 50
datura flowers (*kotadopi*), 252–55
Desemboque, 33
desert tortoises, 69, 151, 227
Dhofar highlands, 261–62, 265, 268

Eaton, Boyd, 43, 45
ecological determinism, 90
ecological imperialism, 99
ecological restoration: of American chestnut, 177–80; of bison, 172–76; of camas, 171–72; consumption and, 157–58; food security and, 157; heritage foods and, 158–60, 163–65, 178–79; hunting and gathering and, 158; methodology for, 157–58, 162–67; overharvesting and, 157–58; overhunting and, 172–73; of oysters, 170–71; Renewing America's Food Traditions and, 160–62; salmon and,

159–60; of scallops, 170–71; of sea turtles, 225–32; traditional ecological knowledge and, 170–72
Empty Quarter, 263
epazote (*Dysphania ambrosiodes*), 56
ethnobiology: advantages of, 16, 20–21; as an agent of change, 4–6, 70–71, 73–74, 160, 289–92; dystopian novels and, 278–81; as ecological science, 20; ethnoecology and, 20; future of, 288–96; goals of, 5–9, 289–92, 295–96; graduate students and, 3–4, 16, 88; history of, 36, 291–92; importance of, 3–4, 289–90; improvements of, 11, 13–16; indigenous, 28; as interdisciplinary, 5, 12, 24, 290, 292–94; poetry and, 249–54, 257; as a predictive science, 220, 281–83; self-reflexivity of, 36–37, 289; traditional ecological knowledge and, 7–9, 283–84, 292–93
ethnobiophilia, 289
ethnobiosphere, 289–90
ethnography, 20, 223

Farah, Mohamud Haji, 269–70
Farque, Tony, 171–72
fire suppression, 157, 218–19
First Nations Aquaculture Program, 171
flotation, 236
Flower World, 256
food diversity: ancestral diets and, 46, 51, 54–55, 57–58; dietary variations of, 283–84; heritage foods and, 173, 184–87, 243–48
food security, 157, 184, 247–48
foodsheds, 159–60, 167–70, 176
food sovereignty, 160, 247–48

frankincense (*Boswellia sacra*): care of, 269; grades of, 264–65, 273; importance of, 264, 268–69, 275; *luban* of, 265; offerings of, 266, 269–70; *shehaz* of, 265; trading of, 266–68, 271–75; transportation of, 273–74; vulnerability of, 270–71

gene flow, 201
genetic drift, 50, 58
geographic determinism, 90
global climate models (GCMs), 199
globalization, 264, 267
Grand Canyon National Park, 76, 78, 216, 238
Grand Canyon Trust, 85
Grand Canyon Wildlands Council, 85
Grande Ronde, 171–72
Grierson, Bruce, 55–56
Grupo Tortuguero Comcaac, 171, 229
Guanacaste Conservation Area of Costa Rica, 27

hallucinogens, 251, 254–55
hawkmoths (*Manduca* spp.), 251–55
heritage foods, 96, 158–62, 185
Hia C-eḍ O'odham, 39, 152
Hill, Jane, 147, 256
historic determinism, 90
hojari fusoos, 264–65, 267, 273
Home Orchard Society, 191
Homo erectus, 46–48, 57
Homo sapiens, 48, 57
honey mesquite, 234–35
Hopi, 80, 86, 88–89, 216
Hopi Cultural Preservation Office, 245
huerta, 103–4
human genetics, 52–53, 57–58

Human Genome Project, 52
hunter-gatherer(s), 28, 45, 145, 150–51, 156–57, 217, 225, 236
Hurricane Katrina, 280

incense, 269–72
Indian paintbrush (*Castilleja lanata* A. Gray), 89
in situ conservation, 97–98, 137–38, 243–48
Institute for Culture and Ecology, 172
Institute for Tribal Environmental Professionals, 89
integrative ethnobotany, 283
International Potato Center (CIP), 245
International Union for Conservation of Nature (IUCN), 215
Intertribal Bison Council, 173, 176

Jabal Samhan, 261–62, 269
Jabbali, 261–62
Java Man, 44–47, 51, 57
Jerusalem artichokes (*Helianthus tuberosus*), 173
Joint Fire Science Agency, 219
Jordan, William R., III, 156–59, 180

Klamath River, 217
kotadopi ñe'e (datura song), 251
kwaatoka, 88

land managers, 15, 86, 217
landscape ecology, 19–20
Le Guin, Ursula, 257, 278
Leueconostoc, 64
lexicons, 38–41, 146
linguistic diversity: biodiversity and, 13; loss of, 13, 23–25, 41, 146–54;

Nahuatl and, 205; Navajo and, 80; Otomanguean languages and, 197; paleobiolinguistics (PBL) and, 201, 205–6; proto languages and, 197, 205; retention of, 25, 31, 88–89; study of, 147–48; Ute-Aztecan languages and, 28, 80, 256

The Log of the Sea of Cortez, 228

luban, 265, 273

luqui, 247

macronutrients, 54–57

mammoths, 236, 238

Mapí-ócë-mídi, 67

Martin, Paul, 233–42

Martinez, Dennis, 172, 218–19

MaxEnt, 199, 204

Maxidiwiac, 67–68

Mazatecan-Zapotecan, 206

McGee, Harold, 65, 231–32

megafauna, 47, 233–42

Mesa Verde National Park, 76

mesquite, 233–42

Mexican National Commission for the Knowledge and Use of Biodiversity (CONABIO), 27

microbial diversity, 63–65

Midwestern Fruit Explorers, 191

missionaries, 96, 98–99

MOFGA, 191

monoculturalism, 39–41

Moosni Oofija, 29

mosnipol, 227

multiculturalism, 39–41

multilingualism, 39–41

Nabhan, Gary Paul, 30, 149–50, 172

National Bison Association, 173, 176

National Endowment for the Arts, 257–59

National Geographic Society, 31–32, 171

National Institute of Biodiversity Conservation, 65

National Park Service, 76, 86, 91, 219

National Science Foundation, 280

Native Seeds/SEARCH, 161, 245

natural selection, 47, 50, 58

The Nature Conservancy (TNC), 78, 86, 88

NatureServe, 166

Navajo sedge (*Carex specuicola* J.T. Howell), 86

nejd, 263–64

Next Generation Sonoran Desert Researchers, 31–32

oases: biodiversity of, 98; characteristics of, 100; climates of, 98–99, 103; crops of, 99, 105–6, 122–23, 127, 135–36; cultural diversity and, 133–35; dating of, 135–36; farming techniques of, 99–100, 103, 129–32; heritage foods and, 96, 137–38; historical documentation of, 103–4; importance of, 97, 99; maps of, 105–6; missionaries and, 96, 98–99; oral histories of, 105–6; political ecology of, 132–33; in situ conservation and, 97–98, 137–38; soil types of, 122; species-area power curve of, 122–23, 127; species distribution models of, 127, 129, 135–37; study of, 97, 100, 103–7; surveys of, 104–5, 107–21

Ocean Revolution, 171

O'odham, 39, 146–47, 151

oral history, 37, 70, 88, 216

orchards, 190–91

Orientalism, 36–37
oysters (*Cassostrea corteziensis*), 170–71

paleobiolinguistics (PBL), 199–201
para-ecologists, 29, 31–32, 69, 88–89, 228
parataxonomists, 27–28
Parque de la Papa, 243–48
petroglyphs, 216–17
pihol ñe'e (peyote button songs), 251
Pima Jimsonweed Song, 250–51
poetry: ethnobiology and, 249–54, 257–59; Flower World and, 256; of healing, 255–56; *kotadopi ñe'e* (datura song), 251; of O'odham origin, 249–50; *pihol ñe'e* (peyote button songs), 251; of Prairie Falcon Flying, 252–54, 259–60; science and, 257–59; traditional, 151–52; traditional ecological knowledge and, 250–54; translations of, 250–54; Wilderness World and, 256
political ecology, 18–21, 132–33
pollination ecologists, 252, 256
potatoes, 243–48
Prairie Falcon Flying's song, 252–54, 259
public awareness, 14–15, 288–89
Punta Chueca, 33

reducción, 98
Renewing America's Food Traditions, 160–62, 166, 172–73, 245
Ricketts, Edward, 228, 257
Rosenberg, J., 147, 149, 152
Rub' al-Khali, 263

Sachromyces, 64
Sacred Datura-Hawkmoth Song, 253–54
Sacred Sites and Gathering Grounds Initiative, 153–54

Said, Edward, 36–37
salmon, 160
Salmon Nation, 159
Samhan Nejd, 265
scallops (*Atrina maura* and *A. tuberculosa*), 170–71
science fiction: climate change and, 279; dystopias and, 278–80, 284; as predictive, 279–80, 282–84
Sea of Cortes, 69, 170–71, 217, 225, 231
sea turtles, 69, 225–32
secondary compounds, 54–58
Seed Savers Exchange, 161, 187, 190, 245
Seenel Iitxo, 29
Sense of Place Project, 146
Seri: cultural diversity and, 28–32, 39; ecological restoration by, 170–71; ecological restoration byC, 216, 225; traditional ecological knowledge of, 69, 146, 149, 152–53, 225
Shahri, 261–62
shehaz, 265
Sheridan, Thomas E., 18–19
Slow Food Ark of Taste, 180, 190, 192–93, 196
Slow Food International, 31–32, 180
Slow Food USA, 161, 193
Society for Conservation Biology, 259
Society for Ecological Restoration International, 160
Society of Ethnobiology, 216, 292–94
Sonoran Desert, 28–29, 160, 234–35
species-area (power) curve, 122–23, 127
species distribution modeling (SDM), 199–201
spices: globalization and, 264, 267; grades of, 267, 273; harvesting of,

263; trading of, 264, 266–68, 271–75; transportation of, 273–74; uses of, 267, 269–70
stories, 151–52, 230–31
Streptococcus, 64
Striplen, Chuck, 218–19
subsistence skills, 150–52
sunflowers, 67–68, 88
Syngenta, 189
Szent-Györgyi, Albert, 258

Tarahumara (Rarámuri), 39
taxonomies: of heritage foods, 167–70; regional, 24–30, 38, 146–48, 227, 246; universal principles of, 27
"Terralingua: Partnerships for Linguistic and Biological Diversity," 85
The Ghosts of Evolution, 237–38
Tiburón Island, 30, 217, 231–32. *See also* Isla Tiburón
Tohono O'odham, 39, 145
Tohono O'odham Community Action, 146–48, 153–54
Tosni Iti Ihiiquet, 30
TNC. *See* The Nature Conservancy
traditional ecological knowledge, 88; biodiversity and, 84–92, 283–84; climate change and, 247; endangered species and, 215–20, 228–32; Ethnobiology 5 and, 15; ethnobiology and, 283–84; loss of, 91, 146–54; medicinal, 30–31, 247, 256, 270; retention of, 31, 153–54; songs and, 250–54; value of, 24, 87–88, 91, 281–82; Western education and, 88
Tropical Storm Sandy, 280

Twilights of the Mammoths: Ice Age Extinctions and the Rewilding of America, 242

U.N. Food and Agriculture's International Undertaking on Plant Genetic Resources, 246
United Nations Declaration on the Rights of Indigenous Peoples, 32
U.S. Bureau of Land Management, 219
U.S. Fish and Wildlife Service, 76
U.S. Forest Service, 76, 172

velvet mesquite (*Prosopis velutina*), 234–35
Veteto, James R., 37, 224
vultures, 217–19

Wallace, Alfred, 47–48, 50
Wallace's Line, 49
wapato (*Sagittaria* spp.), 171–72
Where Our Food Comes From, 186–87
wild chile pepper (*C. annuum* var. *glabriusculum*), 204
Wilderness World, 256
Wildlife Conservation Society, 173
Willamette Resource and Education Network, 172
Willamette Valley, 171–72

Yoruk, 217
Yoruk Tribe Condor Program, 217
yucca, 151, 235

Zepeda, Ofelia, 147
zica cmotomanoj (leatherback sea turtle), 227
Zuni, 80, 88–89

The Southwest Center Series

JOSEPH C. WILDER, EDITOR

Ignaz Pfefferkorn, *Sonora: A Description of the Province*

Carl Lumholtz, *New Trails in Mexico*

Buford Pickens, *The Missions of Northern Sonora: A 1935 Field Documentation*

Gary Paul Nabhan, editor, *Counting Sheep: Twenty Ways of Seeing Desert Bighorn*

Eileen Oktavec, *Answered Prayers: Miracles and Milagros along the Border*

Curtis M. Hinsley and David R. Wilcox, editors, *Frank Hamilton Cushing and the Hemenway Southwestern Archaeological Expedition, 1886–1889*, volume 1: *The Southwest in the American Imagination: The Writings of Sylvester Baxter, 1881–1899*

Lawrence J. Taylor and Maeve Hickey, *The Road to Mexico*

Donna J. Guy and Thomas E. Sheridan, editors, *Contested Ground: Comparative Frontiers on the Northern and Southern Edges of the Spanish Empire*

Julian D. Hayden, *The Sierra Pinacate*

Paul S. Martin, David Yetman, Mark Fishbein, Phil Jenkins, Thomas R. Van Devender, and Rebecca K. Wilson, editors, *Gentry's Rio Mayo Plants: The Tropical Deciduous Forest and Environs of Northwest Mexico*

W. J. McGee, *Trails to Tiburón: The 1894 and 1895 Field Diaries of W J McGee*, transcribed by Hazel McFeely Fontana, annotated and with an introduction by Bernard L. Fontana

Richard Stephen Felger, *Flora of the Gran Desierto and Río Colorado of Northwestern Mexico*

Donald Bahr, editor, *O'odham Creation and Related Events: As Told to Ruth Benedict in 1927 in Prose, Oratory, and Song by the Pimas William Blackwater, Thomas Vanyiko, Clara Ahiel, William Stevens, Oliver Wellington, and Kisto*

Dan L. Fischer, *Early Southwest Ornithologists, 1528–1900*

Thomas Bowen, editor, *Backcountry Pilot: Flying Adventures with Ike Russell*

Federico José María Ronstadt, *Borderman: Memoirs of Federico José María Ronstadt*, edited by Edward F. Ronstadt

Southwest Center Series *(continued)*

Curtis M. Hinsley and David R. Wilcox, editors, *Frank Hamilton Cushing and the Hemenway Southwestern Archaeological Expedition, 1886–1889*, volume 2: *The Lost Itinerary of Frank Hamilton Cushing*

Neil Goodwin, *Like a Brother: Grenville Goodwin's Apache Years, 1928–1939*

Katherine G. Morrissey and Kirsten Jensen, editors, *Picturing Arizona: The Photographic Record of the 1930s*

Bill Broyles and Michael Berman, *Sunshot: Peril and Wonder in the Gran Desierto*

David W. Lazaroff, Philip C. Rosen, and Charles H. Lowe, Jr., *Amphibians, Reptiles, and Their Habitats at Sabino Canyon*

David Yetman, *The Organ Pipe Cactus*

Gloria Fraser Giffords, *Sanctuaries of Earth, Stone, and Light: The Churches of Northern New Spain, 1530–1821*

David Yetman, *The Great Cacti: Ethnobotany and Biogeography*

John Messina, *Álamos, Sonora: Architecture and Urbanism in the Dry Tropics*

Laura L. Cummings, *Pachucas and Pachucos in Tucson: Situated Border Lives*

Bernard L. Fontana and Edward McCain, *A Gift of Angels: The Art of Mission San Xavier del Bac*

David A. Yetman, *The Ópatas: In Search of a Sonoran People*

Julian D. Hayden, *Field Man: The Life of a Desert Archaeologist*, edited by Bill Broyles and Diane Boyer

Bill Broyles, Gayle Harrison Hartmann, Thomas E. Sheridan, Gary Paul Nabhan, and Mary Charlotte Thurtle, *Last Water on the Devil's Highway: A Cultural and Natural History of Tinajas Altas*

Thomas E. Sheridan, *Arizona: A History, Revised Edition*

Richard S. Felger and Benjamin Theodore Wilder, *Plant Life of a Desert Archipelago: Flora of the Sonoran Islands in the Gulf of California*

David Burckhalter, *Baja California Missions: In the Footsteps of the Padres*

Guillermo Núñez Noriega, *Just Between Us: An Ethnography of Male Identity and Intimacy in Rural Communities of Northern Mexico*

Cathy Moser Marlett, *Shells on a Desert Shore: Mollusks in the Seri World*

Rebecca A. Carte, *Capturing the Landscape of New Spain: Baltasar Obregón and the 1564 Ibarra Expedition*

Gary Paul Nabhan, editor, *Ethnobiology for the Future: Linking Cultural and Ecological Diversity*